KĬNG
YELLOWMAN

SERIES EDITOR

Sonjah Stanley Niaah

ADVISORY BOARD

Carolyn Cooper
Julian Henriques
David Katz
Deborah Thomas
Jo-Anne Tull

Word, sound and power. This is the definition of the musical vibrations of Jamaican music. The music of Jamaica influences and has been influenced by countless other music forms throughout the Caribbean and worldwide. At the intersection of creation, production, consumption and globalization of Jamaican music, and from an interdisciplinary perspective, Sound Culture begins a long overdue focus on the history and evolution of sounds, tracing the movement from mento to ska and on to rocksteady, reggae, dub, nyabinghi, dancehall and the various styles of reggae fusion. The series covers all Caribbean music that intersects with Jamaican sounds, and artists in the region who work within the musical genres from Jamaica. It examines those who have blended their national musical forms with Jamaica's and acknowledges that, in addition to shaping culture, social relations, economics and politics, Jamaican music has influenced popular cultural production internationally. In particular, reggae has resonated with the disenfranchised and marginalized all over the world, its rhythm and melody appealing to soul rebels from Japan to South Africa, and Croatia to New Zealand. Sound Culture is intended as a record of the colossal impact that Jamaica has had on the planet through its musical vibrations.

KING YELLOWMAN

Meaningful Bodies in Jamaican Dancehall Culture

BRENT HAGERMAN

The University of the West Indies Press
Jamaica • Barbados • Trinidad and Tobago

The University of the West Indies Press
7A Gibraltar Hall Road, Mona
Kingston 7, Jamaica
www.uwipress.com

ISBN: 978-976-640-851-0 (print)
978-976-640-852-7 (mobi)
978-976-640-853-4 (ePub)

Cover image: Yellowman backstage at the Opera House, Toronto, 2008.
Photo by Andrew Atkinson.
Cover and book design by Robert Harris
Set in Minion Pro 11/14.5 x 24

Printed in the United States of America

For Kate, who worked harder, parented longer, and kept the accounts out of the red so that I could turn this idea into a reality.

Contents

Part 2. Meaningful Bodies in Jamaican Dancehall Culture

Preface

STANDING BACKSTAGE AT A NEGRIL BEACH CONCERT IN February 2013 with the moon illuminating the Caribbean Sea was where I experienced peak reggae moment. I stood beside Jamaican deejay King Yellowman, whom I had been researching for several years by this point and had even received a PhD based on a dissertation I wrote on him. Earlier that night I sat in a black Toyota HiAce driven by stoic Sagittarius keyboardist Simeon Stewart. I was in the third row of seats, behind 1980s dancehall star Johnny P and the van's disc jockey in charge of the CD player. The king himself was enthroned in the front passenger seat. I thoroughly enjoyed these long drives from Kingston to various venues around the island, often in the middle of the night. They were part of my field research on Yellowman, and I always relished the enroute entertainment provided by him. Give him an audience – even a few of us in a minivan – and the king would hold court. This usually included a rich array of off-colour jokes, ridiculous boasts and lively sparring with clever jibes and playful insults. He thinks of himself as a comedian, so it is natural that he enjoys cracking up an audience as much as he enjoys dominating a music stage.

During that drive I asked Yellowman whom he was sharing the night's bill with (because these tourist shows generally boasted two or three well-known artists and this would often be my only chance to see them). To my immense surprise, Toots Hibbert was going to close the show. My holy reggae trinity is Toots and the Maytals, Bob Marley, and Yellowman. The first two (Marley, of course, with the Wailers trio) represent the four dominant subgenres of Jamaican popular music in the 1960s and 1970s: ska, rocksteady, early reggae, and roots reggae. Yellowman represents the subgenre that started producing hits around the early 1970s and blossomed in the 1980s: dancehall. But no sooner had Yellowman told me that Toots was on the bill, than he lamented we could not stay for it because he needed to get back to Kingston for an early flight. Needless to say, I was disappointed.

He and Johnny P "killed" their sets that night, but what happened after, I think, tells you more about Yellowman than what he does on stage. Knowing I wanted to meet Toots, he pretty much commanded the promotor (Yellowman is the king, after all) to hurry Toots over to the venue so I could meet him, which I did. Knowing that I was also a massive fan of the Wailers, he pointed out a figure a few metres away while we were waiting and asked, "Do you know who that is?" Then he took me over and introduced me to Bunny Wailer. So here I was with the three pillars of reggae: a Wailer, a Maytal and the King of Dancehall. But it struck me that while the first two had been part of what reggae historians construct as the golden era of Jamaican music, Yellowman was on the ground floor of the music that has dominated Jamaica ever since. The Wailers and the Maytals had two decades of hits and innovation; dancehall is currently beginning its fifth and Yellowman was its first global star.

As I will show in this book, many of those historians completely misunderstood his significance. Yellowman almost single-handedly popularized dancehall reggae outside of Jamaica in the early 1980s. At a crucial moment in music history, when Bob Marley's 1981 death seemed to leave a vacuum in reggae music for many in the international community, Yellowman stepped in with a new sound and gave reggae a much-needed shot in the arm. But it was not the kind of shot many reggae lovers were counting on. His hedonistic lyrics praising sex were wildly popular with his fans but condemned widely around the reggae-listening world and by moral gatekeepers back home. I say the international community because Bob Marley's death, while felt greatly in Jamaica, was not the death knell for reggae music that foreign journalists prophesied. Jamaica's music industry in the early 1980s was prolific beyond belief and, arguably, far more competitive than its larger counterparts in the United Kingdom and United States.

The thing about Yellowman's popularity outside of Jamaica is that his very celebrity status in Jamaica was misunderstood. What was often missed by his international fans was that Yellowman should never have become a star in the first place because, as a "dundus", or black person with albinism, he should have stayed out of the spotlight, out of the music business and wallowed away in a home for the unfortunate, as demanded by the entrenched Jamaican codes of race and masculinity. But Yellowman did not. His desire to deejay dancehall reggae was just too great.

The research I had conducted on Yellowman leading up to my first interviews with him in 2005 left me with one impression: there was a dearth of material on one of reggae's most prolific and controversial superstars. Trying to pin down a simple discography was a herculean task. Yellowman recorded for several Jamaican producers, each of whom was free to release tracks as singles or albums, license them to offshore record labels to be compiled as "greatest hits" compilations, or license entire albums to still other labels that might market them under a different name and with alternative artwork in a separate country. Because of this, it is difficult to accurately track when singles and LPs were released in which markets. Even the basic facts of his life – including his birth year and hometown – were often inaccurate, and the usual places one would go for this information at the time, such as Allmusic .com and *The Rough Guide to Reggae*, did little more than spin the same well-worn one-dimensional story about Yellowman. And don't get me started on Spotify, which does not know the difference between an album of new Yellowman material or a collection of previously released tracks and lists albums by the date of the reissue rather than the original release.

In fact, the more sources I dug up, the more I was disappointed that there seemed to be only one angle, one side, one "riff" about Yellowman. It was as if every journalist had either asked him the same questions or simply copied the biographical sketch offered by their peers when writing about the man they billed as the King of Dancehall or the King of Slack. What was this one riff? Popular depictions of Yellowman portray him solely as a slackness deejay. Even my preliminary research hinted that Yellowman was a far more complex character than these glosses allowed and that he routinely overlapped the culture and slack categories. I came to understand in the course of my research for this book that while his representation in many Jamaican sources allowed for this complexity, the narrative picked up by much of the foreign press ignored it. Suffice it to say, my preliminary research on Yellowman left me longing for more context to his music and life. This book is my attempt to provide that context.

From a historical and sociological perspective, it is easy to see why Yellowman would be a worthy candidate for scholarly research. But what really made him a compelling subject to write about was the interpersonal interactions between us. Over the course of my research I felt like Yellowman watched out for me as much as I watched and listened to him. As a music journalist in a previous career, I had had the opportunity to interview dozens of musicians, many of them people I deeply respected, but I never assumed that our relationship was anything but professional. My experience with Yellowman was unlike any other, and part of this is due to his generous spirit. For instance, there were several times when he made sure that either he accompanied me to rough parts of the ghetto, or enlisted a friend to do so, so that I felt safe. He routinely took me on private reggae fieldtrips around Kingston to meet historic reggae figures and seemed to sincerely enjoy my awestruck enthusiasm. I once asked if he could help me organize a dancehall panel at an academic conference and he immediately got on the phone and told several artists that their participation was required. Then he held court at the university – even though I was supposed to moderate the panel – bantering with me like old friends, which ensured the capacity crowd was entertained and that the event was a success.

I have thought a lot about these experiences, and tried to figure out where the brand-savvy entertainer who desires a favourable representation in the literature ends, and where the good-natured deejay begins. I wrestle a bit with these lines in this book and try never to completely ignore or downplay them. Still, unlike with other interviewees in the music business, I have never sensed that any of these acts came with the understanding that I would reciprocate in kind. Nor did Yellowman's kindness ever come off as artificial.

After fifteen years of assessing Yellowman and what he means to Jamaican and, indeed, global popular music history, I feel more strongly than ever that a biography of such an important figure is long overdue, as is an in-depth scholarly analysis of his career and representation. It is my hope that by combining these two I can offer new insight into Yellowman's life, career and use of slackness. I feel that the best way for readers to know him is to combine the two, and for this reason I have tried to present not only the man who led the charge to take dancehall from the slums of Kingston to the four corners of the earth, but also the man who risked missing his plane in Kingston so that I could stand among the holy trinity of reggae.

Acknowledgements

THE NUMBER OF PEOPLE WHO HAVE HELPED ME is about as long as the list of boasts in a Yellowman song. I am grateful to each of them for their support and assistance.

Carol Duncan was the "Top Ranking" mentor who helped bring the dissertation this book is based on to fruition. As a scholar and dancehall fan, she motivated me to produce research that merged academic scholarship with reggae-fan readability. The resulting manuscript (spoiler alert: it's two books in one!) flummoxed some early reviewers but stayed true to that vision.

Siobhan McMenemy, who helped literally write the book on how to turn a dissertation into a publishable book, went above and beyond in assisting me to do just that.

The fact that you are reading a book at all is largely due to the efforts of Erin MacLeod, who gave me encouragement over the years, championed the manuscript with the University of the West Indies Press, and helped refine its framing.

The dancehall scholarship of Sonjah Stanley Niaah is one of the building blocks supporting this work, and she has also kindly offered a home for this study within the Sound Culture series, for which I am delighted.

Shivaun Hearne's patience and skill made the editing process much less painful than it could have been, and the finished product more readable.

My Jamaican fieldwork was aided in innumerable ways by scholars, musicians and friends. Accomplishing this research without the help of Simeon Stewart, Yellowman's manager and founding member of Sagittarius band, would be nearly inconceivable. His knowledge of the Jamaican music industry and reggae history provided me a portal through which to view Yellowman's career. He opened many doors for me and provided the necessary connections to make my fieldwork much smoother and far more enjoyable than it would have been otherwise. In addition, he housed and fed me and drove from Negril to Kingston in the middle of the night to make sure I caught a flight home on time. I am also grateful to the rest of the Sagittarius 2008 line-up (Desmond "Desi" Gaynor, Zemroy "Zimma" Lewis, Duwayne "Shotta Yut" Hoilette) for sharing their stories and allowing me to get in the way of their work.

Thank you to everyone who assisted my research in Jamaica, some by granting interviews, others by providing intangible supports: Abijah, Philip "Fatis" Burrell, Charlie Chaplin, Captain Barkley, Alan "Skill" Cole, Sly Dunbar, Yumiko Gabe, Sophia Graham, Lisbeth Haddad, the Jah Love crew (Culture Dan, Pampi Judah, Rashorni, Natty Field Marshall, Dainion "Dr Brains" Geohagen), Maurice "Black Scorpio" Johnson, Sister Bernadette Little of Alpha Boys School, Mellow, George Phang, Ingrid Robinson of St Michael's Theological College, Owen "Willa" Robinson, Anthony "Red" Rose, Jah Rubel, Josey Wales, Tel's Studio, and, of course, Ted, for driving me all over Kingston and sometimes beyond.

Many others offered their help during my fieldwork, and I thank them: Jah Ben Rittenhouse, for his enthusiasm about the project and his assistance in organizing my research trip to the United States, filming concert and interview footage, and being willing to spend a few weeks on the road attending reggae concerts and sleeping in a Boler camping trailer; Josh Chamberlain, for introducing me to the importance of sound system culture, filming the Jamaican interview footage, and being an excellent reggae resource; and Andrew Atkinson and David Popplow, for shooting the Toronto show.

I am grateful for the scholars who have offered feedback, answered questions, given advice and provided forums for me to present my work: Carolyn Cooper, Donna Hope, Sonjah Stanley-Niaah (and all the organizers of the International Reggae Conference at the University of the West Indies). Kathryn Shields-Brodber, Barbara Lalla, Pam Mordecai and Peter Patrick provided valuable insight while I was researching the art of tracing. Natasha Pravaz, Sarah King, Kay Koppedrayer and Richard Walker provided helpful feedback on early drafts. Michel Desjardins, Ron Grimes, Jenna Hennebry, Andrew Herman, Scott Kline, Wayne Marshall, Janet McLellen, Jason Neelis, Barry Stevenson and Chris Ross offered advice along the way.

Thanks also to the industry professionals, reggae journalists, friends and fans who went above and beyond expectation in providing me with interviews, archival material, contacts, advice and encouragement: Chris Brito,

David "Magixx" Cunningham, David Dacks, Nicky Dread, Kent Hayward, Ray Hurford, Joakim Kalcidis, David Katz, David Kingston, Adam Kirk, Brad Klein, Heather Lamm, Beth Lesser, Packy Malley, Steve Martin, Roger Steffens, Howard Thompson, Scott Wicken and Terry Wilkinson (Yellowman's number one fan).

Yellowman has been abundantly generous throughout this project, allowing me extensive access to his life. For that, I am grateful. When I first sat down with him to ask for his involvement in this project, I wasn't sure how he would respond. I had planned on a series of interviews in Jamaica, spread out over a few years, and to observe him at work, both on stage and in the studio. This was a lot to ask a reggae legend who spends up to six months on the road each year. Yellowman's initial response was to tell me that a project of this scope would be very time consuming. I thought he was excusing himself due to his schedule constraints. Quite the opposite, he was warning me about the necessary time and effort this project would require of me to do it justice and he wanted to make sure I was committed. Since that day, Yellowman has opened his house and his history to me as I probed the meaning of slackness and culture in his music. He introduced me to musicians and producers who granted me interviews I never could have arranged myself. Philip "Fatis" Burrell, for instance, told me he never grants interviews. But when Yellowman explained the nature of my project and asked him to speak with me, he agreed. Others were only too happy to oblige, out of their respect for the King of Dancehall. The "all-access pass" Yellowman granted me enabled me to undertake valuable research into dancehall culture, and also amounted to a reggae fan's dream come true.

Finally, thanks to Avalon, who had to wake up on more than one birthday without a dad because he was on a plane to Jamaica to research this book. And you gotta admit, a book is a far better gift than a lousy a T-shirt.

Introduction

YELLOWMAN IS A MOST UNLIKELY REGGAE STAR. In a genre that gains authenticity through racial and ethnic identifiers such as blackness and dreadlocks, both of which associate Jamaicanness with Africanness, Yellowman appears to be lacking in every category. Yet by 1982 Yellowman was the world's foremost Jamaican music star and dancehall's first global phenomenon. Over the next three years he would reach unprecedented success, becoming the first dancehall artist to release a record on a major label (*King Yellowman* [1984]), the first reggae artist to collaborate with hip-hop artists (with Run-DMC on "Roots, Rap, Reggae" in 1985 and with Afrika Bambaataa on "Zouk Your Body" in 1988), the first deejay to be nominated for a Grammy Award (1985), and he influenced the professionalizing of the dancehall industry through his use of, among other things, a live touring band instead of pre-recorded backing tracks. Then, by mid-1985, he risked losing it all to cancer when he was given just a few years to live after doctors discovered a tumour growing on his jaw. Several successful battles with cancer later, Yellowman is still touring the world and is received by fans globally as one of reggae's most beloved ambassadors and a sort of second Bob Marley.

Yellowman's journey to becoming the world's biggest dancehall star was fraught with hardship and controversy. The meanings ascribed to the "dundus"[1] body in Kingston in 1957, the year of his birth, led to his abandonment by his parents. Born Winston Foster, he was left in the gutter on Kingston's Chisholm Avenue in his first week of life. He told me that abandoning children with albinism was a routine practice in Jamaica at the time and this is how he ended up in orphanages and government institutions until the age of twenty-three. The dundus body is racially questionable because its yellow skin does not easily fit the colonial-derived categories of white, mulatto and black. The dundus's place in society was tucked away from public view and the scorn that came with it. Merely walking down the street would invite

1

castigation – calls of "dundus bwoy" or "yellow man" – to remind him of his physical difference. At the orphanages and in school, he was often on his own and suffered regular beatings at the hands of the other residents. This physical abuse would continue as a teenager when many of Kingston's producers had the aspiring deejay violently removed from their studios when he attempted to audition for them.

In this real-life rags-to-riches story, Winston Foster overcame severe adversity because of this cultural displacement which saw him orphaned, impoverished, humiliated and abused – all because of his skin colour – to become Jamaica's top star. That he did this by revalorizing the dundus as a desirable sexual symbol is almost beyond belief, first performing under the name Ranking Dundus and then, ultimately, Yellowman.

Yellowman made it his mission to prove his detractors wrong when they told him he was worthless. Materially, his worthlessness would be alleviated by 1982 when he found himself in the enviable position of being the second musician on the island able to afford a BMW. The first was Bob Marley. But his self-worth was never in question, despite being shown almost no love his entire childhood. Hatred forged resilience, neglect fostered ambition and the indomitable drive to succeed bore a creativity that would be measured not just in wealth and radio hits but in constant controversy, international success, two Grammy nominations (1985, 1998), a loyal global fan base and a musical legacy as one of Jamaica's most significant reggae legends – no easy feat in a land that has no lack of reggae legends.

DANCEHALL, SLACKNESS AND CULTURE: A PRIMER

Dancehall is a multivalent term whose meaning can change depending on the context. Dancehall often refers to a subgenre of reggae music from the 1980s until the present that has roots, dating back to the late 1960s, in deejays and singers performing over vinyl records played by sound systems around the island. It is an extension of earlier forms of Jamaican popular music, but unique in that it is tightly woven into, and is a response to, the economic, cultural, political and social realities of late twentieth-century Jamaica (Hope 2006). The physical space where sound system dances occur is also the dancehall, as historically the term "dancehalls" referred to music venues. There need not be a "hall" per se, as many of these dances happen outdoors. Dancehall is also what happens in that music – musically, lyrically, ideologically – and in that space – fashion, dancing, community, culture, ideology. It is a "state of mind, a spontaneous happening that occurs when hundreds of people get together in a building or yard or field or parking lot and tap into thousands of watts of raw reggae power" (Jahn and Weber 1998, 9). And just as hip-hop has come to refer to both a music genre and a culture,[2] dancehall is also a subculture and social movement that sustains and is sustained by music, artists, fans, community, sound systems, dance and fashion. Importantly, this cultural system was created by Jamaican underclasses and scholars have highlighted its subversive character, particularly in the ways it offers resources for self-representation to disenfranchised youth and a counterculture to the elite economies, culture and values of the Jamaican upperclasses (Cooper 1995, 2004; Hope 2006; Stanley-Niaah 2010). In fact, Hope's (2006, 25) definition of dancehall revolves around the term "dis/place", meant to highlight the revolutionary and transformative character of the culture "effectively creating its own symbols and ideologies and negating, shifting, removing and replacing those functioning in the traditional sociopolitical spaces".

Whereas I use the term "dancehall" in this book to refer on the surface to the subgenre and subculture, the above meanings are inherent and will be teased out, particularly in terms of how Yellowman's lived reality occurs within dancehall (in that he is both a creator of and product of dancehall) and his performance of dancehall includes self-representation, subversion and critique, and allowed him to move from a position of social displacement to global superstar.

This book is concerned with two concepts that in dancehall – and reggae culture broadly – are often thought of as binary categories, and even opposite subgenres: slackness and culture. Mention these terms to longtime reggae fans and they can easily categorize reggae artists using them. But for readers less familiar with reggae culture, an orientation to these constitutive tropes is in order.

In reggae parlance, "slackness" generally refers to performances and lyrics that are overtly sexual in nature. In Yellowman's case, his slackness is centred on masculine heterosexual potency, sexist objectification of women and graphic sexual narratives. Yellowman's reputation as a live deejay was built on his crude and explicit lyrics and this slackness won him legions of fans who appreciated the bawdy nature of his lyrics and performances, rocketing him to the top of the reggae industry. But his slackness also earned him vocal critics who portrayed him in opposition to artists like Bob Marley, who made music known as "roots", "conscious" or "culture" reggae.

Defined by its very opposition to slack reggae, the word culture here refers to reggae concerned with political and religious matters, and issues of social justice and black history. More specifically, it depicts music that is lyrically and thematically concerned with Afrocentric biblical exegesis, Ethiopianism, Ital Livity, Jahworks, a view of Haile Selassie as God and/or the second coming of Christ, repatriation to Zion/Ethiopia, celebrations and promotion of African culture and history, songs calling for the fall of Babylon, theocratic political critiques of Babylon's machinations, black nationalism, and a concern for the "sufferahs", or underclasses.

The dichotomy between culture and slackness is, of course, a social construct, but one that has had considerable traction in the reggae industry and has helped shape how fans, journalists and scholars understand artists. Yellowman has largely been ignored by serious studies of pre-dancehall reggae and African diasporic popular culture precisely because he is constructed as a slack artist. It was assumed that his sexual songs offered only debased entertainment, not the kind of reasoned social, political, or cultural critique found in the music of cultural artists like the Wailers, Burning Spear, Dennis Brown, Gregory Isaacs, Israel Vibration, Culture, Jacob Miller, Sugar Minott, the Itals, and Black Uhuru.

Like a few other scholars before me, particularly Sonjah Stanley-Niaah, Carolyn Cooper and Donna Hope, I am attempting to free Yellowman's slackness from reductive understandings like the one above. Slackness has been utilized by Yellowman both consciously and unconsciously for various ends, none of which fall into the neat master narrative of slackness as opposing culture reggae. This book's purpose is not to revalorize Yellowman or redress his reputation at the hands of music critics and scholars, though it may do that. Its main purpose is to systematically decode the politics of slackness in Yellowman's life and songs, providing new ways to theorize slackness and contextualize a misunderstood Caribbean musician and tradition.

NOTES ON ORGANIZATION AND METHODOLOGY

This book is divided into two parts. Part 1 tells the life story of Yellowman and also provides a contemporary snapshot of him as I engaged with him during my fieldwork, which included interviews, studio sessions, tours and concerts, and trips to significant Kingston locations in his life. Part 2 comprises five chapters of scholarly analysis that probe the dominant issues I see Yellowman's life and music presenting for academic study.

Yellowman's birth name is Winston Foster but he thinks of himself as Yellowman. Unlike a stage persona that is turned on and off, the name Yellowman is central to his identity, connected as it is to his physical body and his body of work. As such, I have used both names selectively, not interchangeably, in part 1. I use Yellowman to identify the deejay only after he officially adopts this nom de plume and Winston to differentiate when I am speaking about his life up until that point. I feel this approach better represents how he views his own life and identity.

I have sought to better understand Yellowman by not only engaging with the scholarly and popular literature on Jamaican music and through a close examination of his vast discography, but also via theoretical lenses that allowed me to view Yellowman through scholarly discussions of moral regulation and religious values, constructions of masculinity, beauty, and race, and discourses of slackness and culture. Absent from the literature was Yellowman's own understandings of himself and his music, and this, I felt, was integral to understanding how he used slackness both intentionally and unintentionally.

In order to access these views, I undertook ethnographic fieldwork. Over a period of several years I spent considerable time observing and interviewing him, starting with my initial interview at the Montreal International Reggae Festival in July 2005. I sat opposite him in his kitchen overlooking Kingston, sharing chicken patties and coconut water; I watched him performing in concerts and recording in Kingston studios; I accompanied him for one week while he was on tour in the United States and Canada, talking to him and his band in green rooms and hotels and hanging out with him in my tiny 1980 Boler travel trailer; I drove to gigs with him in the middle of the night to Negril, Ocho Rios and Port Antonio; I walked with him through the streets of Trench Town and Franklin Town, visiting important sites from his past; I accompanied him to Maxfield Park Children's Home and Alpha Boys' School, where he spent much of his youth education; we visited old record shops and studios, some of which are now crumbling from disrepair; I stood beside him at a neighbourhood sound system party in Concrete Jungle. Some of these interactions were connected to culturally and historically significant locations. Some of them, like grocery shopping or going out for ice cream, were mundane. But in each instance, we continued a long discussion about his life and dancehall culture. Some of these interviews were formal and structured, but others were casual conversations. I also followed up with telephone calls between 2007 and 2020 to fact-check and make further inquiries when needed, and in 2015 facilitated a panel discussion with Yellowman, Josey Wales and Johnny P at the International Reggae Conference at the University of the West Indies in Kingston. Unless otherwise indicated, all quotes from Yellowman are taken from personal interviews with the author during these periods.

Because Yellowman is so well respected in the Jamaican music industry, his blessing allowed me access to many other helpful sources that enabled me to better understand Yellowman's life and career. These included members of his contemporary circle such as his family and band, and also many key music industry professionals (artists, promoters, producers, managers, entertainers, soundmen, record label heads, former employees). Over and above these formal interviews, I have gained understanding into the meaning of his celebrity through ad hoc conversations with reggae fans both in and outside of Jamaica – such as the secretary of a University of the West Indies–associated Catholic residence where I stayed, who assured me she was never a fan of his kind of music but, of course, she attended his concerts in the early 1980s, because he was the top deejay – and reading comments fans had left on social media sites like YouTube.

I first broached the idea of an academic research project and critical biography with/on him in 2006 in the green room of Peabody's Concert Club in Cleveland before his set. He listened to my pitch and agreed to the long process, and he has been immensely patient and generous with his time. Despite all this, the book is not an authorized biography of Yellowman. Our understanding was that he could read what I wrote and correct facts, but that the framing and analysis was mine alone. It is also not a fan biography that seeks to simply celebrate and promote an artist's accomplishments while providing a historical sketch of their career. Nor is it an exposé intent on muckraking and furnishing its audience with tales of debauchery, sex, drugs and lawlessness. It is also not a hagiography, though I do admit to a sympathetic yet critical representation.

By critical biography I mean a biography that is enriched by critical analysis. It seeks to go beyond what many commemorative music biographies promise: a life story put in the context of the subject's cultural and, at times, political milieu. It does this by evaluating Yellowman through interdisciplinary scholarly lenses, but not in the sense of evaluating the merit of Yellowman's artistic output. Instead, it presents arguments supported by theoretical perspectives drawn from cultural studies, which is alert to the power struggle over hegemonic values that are negotiated in popular culture.

I have tried to keep personal opinions about Yellowman and his music to a minimum. I am indeed a fan of his music and my appreciation of his talent has only increased since beginning this research, but I am not without a strong critical view of many of his albums and even some of his values. However, this project is not an exercise in evaluating Yellowman's music on an aesthetic basis and, therefore, I have been careful to refrain from such indulgences in the text.

Instead, contained within the biographic narrative is a focus on the antecedents to, and the development of, Yellowman's views on sexuality, race, religion and masculinity – all of which are geared towards seeking a new understanding of an artist who has been gravely misunderstood by journalists and scholars alike. My intent, then, is to provide a critical biography – a critical interpretation of Yellowman's life, his role in Jamaican music culture and the ideologies both in and behind his repertoire – that seeks not to sensationalize the controversial deejay (indeed, he has done a good job of that himself), but instead to unpack how he was understood by his critics and fans and how he understood/understands his own repertoire and legacy.

This critical examination is sympathetic to the subject's opinions and intentions. When I presented Yellowman my idea for writing a critical biography that was focused around the themes of slackness and culture, he agreed, I believe, largely because the way I chose to frame his life and career was different from how he is normally written about. I saw him as an artist who employed slackness as social activism but was not defined by his role as a slackness deejay. Rather than wanting Yellowman to dictate a sort of authorized biography to me, I was interested in his point of view and description of life events in order to get a deeper understanding of his views on slackness and moral values and to take seriously his own interpretations/ intended meanings of his songs. In Talal Asad's (1993, 276) essay on *Satanic Verses*, he defends his use of Salman Rushdie's own thoughts on his novel because, he says, an author's intended meanings should not "be fenced off as being irrelevant to the novel". He cites Rushdie, not because he believes him to be "the best authority on his work, but because glosses by Rushdie the embattled author are a crucial part of the book's context and therefore of its meaning".

Music journalists and scholars can rightfully read their own meanings into musical works and life stories and that method could work here. However, in reading the scholarly literature and public discourse about Yellowman, I discovered that much of it fails to consider how Yellowman's songs are understood by the local Jamaican dancehall audience, and often I have found glaring discrepancies between a music journalist's interpretation of a song and Yellowman's intended message. By knowing something of the background of why the songs were written, checking my transcriptions of his Patwa with the author himself, and being able to contextualize them in his life and Jamaican dancehall culture, I have been able to take into account multiple ways that meanings are produced and interpreted. These differing meanings are at the heart of how Yellowman, slackness and dancehall have been constructed in reggae histories.[3]

In addition, for most of his career Yellowman has been an embattled artist. Besides being the scapegoat for the entire slackness movement, he has been the subject of several newspaper articles maligning his use of sexuality in his songs at home and abroad, and scholars and historians have often failed to contextualize him in his social milieu. Further to this, many of his personal opinions – outside of his song lyrics – are not published anywhere outside the popular press, and those articles often tend to be little more than promotional glosses. These opinions are a valuable part of the meaning of his work and so I have sought to include them here.

As such, the life story presented here is predominantly based on how Yellowman remembers his life and events, sees his fame, and understands his milieu, though the analyses of his life and career are entirely my own. There are, of course, problems inherent in this: people see themselves very differently than those around them do. Memory can be selective and subjects and informants can filter events and stories, tailoring them to ensure a positive representation. I sought where possible to corroborate these events with other sources. I have balanced this autobiographical view with other interviews and published material and, in instances where I found discrepancies, I have left both accounts in the text to present multiple truths.

There is another reason I include Yellowman's voice here. As a critical biography, this book is influenced in method and theory by scholarly eth-nographies. Following scholars like Brown (2001) and Goulet (1998), this project includes the voice of my research subject as a way of displacing any singular authority on my part. As the writer, I wield a very real authority over this text and the people represented in it; many readers will only know Yellowman through what I choose to write (or omit, either intentionally or unintentionally). Being mindful of these issues, this book presents Yellow-man's voice both implicitly and explicitly. He is not an avid storyteller in the confines of an interview but he is a highly praised griot on stage and on record. His voice is the basis for this project as I am using the "text" of his songs and interviews to interpret his use of slackness.

One of the difficulties in writing this book has been representing song lyrics and interviews in a way that is accessible to international readers but faithful to the Jamaican language, Patwa. The first challenge has to do with spelling. As an oral tradition, there is no single standard way to represent the language orthographically, and spellings of common words change from source to source. Even the name of the language, presented in this book as Patwa, is often spelled patois in direct quotations included in the book. To make matters more confusing, reggae's material culture – record labels, liner notes, magazines – do not always use the same spellings employed by linguists. Even two Yellowman albums might represent the word "me" using standard English or Patwa ("mi") and revolve between Patwa spellings, as in the case of "fe" or "fi", which translates variously as "to", "for", the verb "must, should", or as part of a possessive pronoun ("fe dem" means "theirs"). Yellowman might also switch between standard English and Patwa, as he often does for "the" and "de", "cause" and "kaa" or "down" and "dung", and his pronunciation does not always match the spelling on an album's cover, as in the case when he says "Dem a mad over me" on the album *Them A Mad over Me* (1982g). For this reason, in their *Dictionary of Jamaican English,* Cassidy and Le Page (2002) often list several spelling variants in their entries.

The second challenge has to do with translation. Yellowman is a Patwa speaker and, where I translate his voice into standard English, I risk blurring his intended meanings. I am mindful here of paying attention to what Brathwaite (1984) has theorized as "nation language". I have treated his lyrics as published texts and have tried to represent them in Patwa in order to maintain as much of his original intent as possible. My interviews with Yellowman that are transcribed in the book come across differently, though. The interviews sought to increase my knowledge of Yellowman's life and music by soliciting his perspective and seeking clarification and explanation where needed. Yellowman's responses to my questions were meant to be instructive, and he was cognizant of communicating his meaning to a non-native Patwa speaker, an activity he is familiar with, given the number of international press interviews he has granted. With this in mind, Yellowman tended towards standard English in the interviews, though he usually abides by Patwa grammar.

Where possible, I privilege reggae sources from the period the book discusses for representing the Patwa spellings of song titles and lyrics, and Cassidy and Le Page (2002) for all other spellings and grammar. For words not covered by these sources, I have attempted to choose the most common spelling I can find in the interest of consistency. For clarity, I have chosen not to represent Patwa pronunciation of many standard English terms (so "born" instead of "bawn") except where this is an already well-established practice in reggae culture, such as: the/di, make/mek, because/kaa, no/nuh, you/yuh, upon/pon, in/inna, out/outta. I have also included translations of Patwa, based where possible on Cassidy and Le Page (2002), in endnotes. My approach is imperfect, but hopefully useful for a wide readership.

Finally, this book is also part reggae travelogue. Biographies tend to be nostalgic; they privilege and/or construct a golden era in their subject's life. I was privileged to be able to indulge in a sort of reggae tourism during my research by spending time with Yellowman on tour, in the studio and visiting historically significant music personalities and places in Kingston with him. Through Yellowman I was able to meet and interview several reggae musicians and producers. It is these accounts that balance any nostalgia in the text; this discursive technique allows me to present a contemporary portrait of Yellowman at the same time as I attempt to reconstruct the historical subject.

In addition, I came away from my experiences with Yellowman with a sense that he is genuinely appreciative of the support of his fans over the years. I wanted a book about Yellowman to be accessible to his fans and fans of reggae generally. The addition of on-the-ground interviews with Yellowman will help it to do just that, and by splitting the book into two parts – the life story and the academic analysis – I hope to make it easier for readers interested in one or the other to readily find their place.

MEANINGFUL BODIES: THEMATIC AND THEORETICAL ROADMAP

This book is about bodies – human, artistic, and intellectual – and how the meanings they represent have been constructed, contested and altered. On the surface, its scope appears to be singular. It is about Jamaican dancehall's first superstar, Yellowman, a dundus whose sobriquet celebrates his skin tone. But it uses Yellowman both as a case study and a jumping-off point to explore critical issues in the cultural studies of the African diaspora concerning sexuality, gender, race, class, subjectivity and representation. It evaluates the meaning-making practices of both reggae and reggae historians. It also offers a new perspective on how religious symbols associated with Rastafari are appropriated by reggae artists. Underneath this surface, then, its location is broader. It is about reggae and dancehall culture at large, audiences both Jamaican and international, and historians, journalists and scholars around the world who have had a hand in contributing to the body of knowledge on dancehall – or, more importantly, the way we understand that body of knowledge. On one hand, then, this book is an examination of Yellowman's body of work, considering the meanings ascribed to his albino body. On the other hand, there are other bodies under the microscope as well.

Chapters 1 through 10 comprise part 1 and chronicle the life and times of Yellowman. The biography charts his early life, rise to fame, dominance of dancehall, and considers his legacy. It also includes initial analyses into his use of slackness and foregrounds the main thematic elements of the book, addressed in part 2.

Part 2 is devoted to a scholarly analysis of Yellowman's career and includes chapters 11 through 15. It begins with an introduction that foregrounds the book's central thesis that Yellowman's use of slackness was far more complex than his critics allowed. Ultimately, slackness functioned in his music to allow him to contest his racialized and essentialized representation as a worthless dundus. Each chapter unpacks the nuance and multiple uses of slackness in Yellowman's music.

Chapter 11 begins by unpacking the meanings attributed to the albino body in Jamaican cultural history to show the extent of cultural displacement Yellowman had to overcome. I contextualize albinism in Jamaica's colonial legacy, including ways that African and Western ideologies of race mapped meanings onto the albino body. I show how Yellowman's dundus body was interpreted in Jamaica, based on sexualized and racialized meanings. As a person with albinism, Yellowman stood outside normative Jamaican understandings of race, masculinity, and sexuality so that he was thought to be without race, emasculated and sterile. I argue that Yellowman's repertoire or body of slackness served to revalorize his dundus body in the Jamaican imagination. He first embraced his albinism – inherent in this stage name Yellowman. Using slack lyrics, he then cunningly subverted embedded Jamaican cultural notions of sexuality, gender, race, nationality, and beauty. I show how Yellowman inverted society's representation of him by turning albinism into a site of super-sexuality where the yellow body is refashioned as the "modern body". He both drew on and repurposed sexualized and racialized understandings of both albinism and blackness in his songs. In addition, I am interested in the way Rastafari has been appropriated by Yellowman to help alter his representation in dancehall. Yellowman mobilized Rastafarian symbols in the interest of convincing his audience of his blackness and, therefore, inclusion in the Jamaican nation. Yellowman's deployment of Rastafarian symbols (such as Haile Selassie, ganja, the Ethiopian flag and the African continent) helped him adopt a black African identity and further allowed him to alter his outsider status.

Chapter 12 is a cultural history of a body of knowledge: reggae histories. It examines the assumptions of reggae historians – both popular and scholarly – and their selectively written narratives. It interrogates their moral and aesthetic biases that constructed reggae history based on a simplistic categorization that fails to consider how artists and their target audiences understand the subgenres of reggae. I show how reggae histories have viewed Bob Marley's career as a golden age of reggae both musically and culturally, and established Yellowman as the music's nadir, ushering reggae into an era of musical de-evolution and moral disintegration called dancehall. These histories at times reproduced orientalist tropes that positioned reggae as exotic and Bob Marley as mystical, presented over and against "normal" Western music. Even though Marley's reggae was composed and produced in part to appeal to American and British fans of rock and rhythm and blues (R&B), it was established as authentic reggae, often by white music journalists representing reggae to other white fans. Further, dancehall, because of its lack of Western moral and aesthetic qualities, has been represented as having less musical value, which fails to acknowledge that dancehall's musical aesthetics are rooted in non-Western traditions and should not be judged by Western aesthetics alone.

This politics of nostalgia ignores the fact that the tastes of Jamaican audiences have evolved in the years since Marley. Histories of reggae that seek to view it as a discrete time capsule that was closed along with Marley's casket have done reggae a tremendous disservice by ignoring the music's natural evolution and artists who spearheaded it. And this is the complex legacy of Yellowman: controversial because of his skin colour, his bawdy performances, his overtly sexual lyrics and his place in history as the man who severed roots reggae's domination, yet also the man who helped move reggae forward as a genre by ensuring that dancehall transcended its regional appeal and pushed it onto the world stage at a time when the music press in England and the United States had all but written off post-Marley reggae.

Caught up in the imaginary construct of reggae history is the notion that Bob Marley's music was chiefly concerned with valuable political or social critique, whereas the slack music of Yellowman is essentially about baser concerns – sex and partying – and therefore of little cultural value. One of the points this argument hinges on is Marley's links with and usage of Rastafari as a religious world view of resistance and liberation. This chapter also interrogates the linkages (constructed and real) between Rastafari and reggae to a greater extent than other studies and problematizes the established narrative that Yellowman and dancehall led to the "de-Rastafarianization of the youth culture" (Burton 1997, 138).

Chapter 13 focuses on Yellowman's body of slack music and its uses in social criticism. Slackness has been employed by Yellowman for several reasons – from entertainment to social, political and religious critique. To be sure, the main reason Yellowman deejayed slack lyrics was that they were popular and allowed him to build a fan base. Yet Yellowman's slackness functioned and was used in several cogent ways in his material, sometimes consciously, often not. Whereas chapter 12 demonstrates that reggae histories have assumed slack music offers no valuable political or social critique, here I present a counterargument using some of Yellowman's slack songs. My thinking is informed by Cooper's work on slackness as a "metaphorical revolt against law and order; an undermining of consensual standards of decency" (Cooper 1995, 141). I also consider Obika Gray's (2004) theory that the Jamaican underclasses in the late 1970s and early 1980s employed slackness as a deliberate tactic to contest the moral sway of mainstream society and apply it to Yellowman, who was at the forefront of the slackness movement at the time. By offering an alternative value system that upheld the mores of the lower classes, Yellowman contested mainstream society's attempt to define authentic Jamaicanness and disrupted the Christian, colonial, and upper-class agenda of policing the sexuality of the black poor.

Chapter 14 is based on a body of moral values that themselves are concerned with sexualized bodies. I focus on the histories and ideologies of sexuality that influence the creolized sexuality of Afro-Jamaicans. I show how Yellowman's sexual ethics are in keeping with a narrowly defined sexual respectability (LaFont 2001) and argue that one way slackness functions in his songs is for the purposes of moral regulation. His album *Galong Galong Galong* (1985a), for instance, contains several sexually explicit lyrics, yet does so to promote a specific kind of sexual morality. In the title track, Yellowman tells us in sometimes graphic detail that prostitution, homosexuality, oral sex, and pornography are acts that are against Rastafari and "Jah law". So, while sex is used only for entertainment in some songs, he also uses slack lyrics to regulate morality in others. Further, Yellowman often uses licentious lyrics to trace moral shortcomings for his audience with the purpose of espousing correct sexual behaviour according to his ethical perspective. Using his popular song "Galong Galong Galong", I unpack his use of the Jamaican discursive tactic known as "tracing" as he employs it alongside slackness to call out immoral behaviour, humiliate those who engage in it and bolster his own moral superiority.

In chapter 15, I argue that Yellowman's ability to rupture the traditional Western dualistic split of flesh and spirit by continually mixing slackness and culture in his songs is not only derived from a West African non-dualistic framework, but also has a parallel in the Rastafarian Babylon/Zion polarity. Under the Rastafarian rubric, the body is not anathema to the spirit as long as it maintains purity. By focusing on the lyric "you can't go to Zion with a carnal mind", I demonstrate that for Yellowman the body, sexuality and slackness are not degraded and sinful, as in Western Christian traditions. Yellowman's morality and sexual ethics are rooted in an African-based ideology that was sex-positive, life affirming and stood apart from the platonic dualism of Eurocentric thought that divided the world into the elevated spiritual realm and the denigrated physical realm. Instead, respectable sexuality and a natural body are morally upstanding attributes and perfectly acceptable in Zion.

PART I.

THE LIFE AND TIMES OF YELLOWMAN

CHAPTER 1

Abandoned

The Early Life of Winston "Yellowman" Foster, 1957–1971

Me a go tell you me life story
Said when me did born me mother disown me
Me mother said, "Lord, what a ugly baby"
Well one time, God, me never have no money
Me wear one pants that patchy patchy
Said Squidly, lord, and Welton Irie[1]
Me walk down de street dem a laugh after me
Some a walk some a talk some a dem a scorn me
And some a dem a talk 'bout fly a follow me
And some of dem a say, "Him smell funny, eee"
But now me turn a man and turn a emcee
De girl dem a rush me
A weh me say no bodda love me fe me deejay money[2]
    —Yellowman, "Life Story" (1982b)

MAXFIELD PARK HOME, FEBRUARY 2008

When Yellowman returned to Maxfield Park Children's Home in February 2008, it was unclear to me if he was welcomed or scorned yet again. Yellowman was taking me on a trip through Kingston, a sort of walk down memory lane of places where he grew up, and while the reception he met was almost always positive at the stops we made in Trench Town, Chisholm Avenue, Channel One Studio and Sonic Sounds Studio, our initial welcome at the Maxfield Avenue orphanage was cold. Usually I witnessed people in inner-city Kingston see Yellowman step out of a car in front of one of these locations and do what I imagine impoverished people the world over instinctively do when a celebrity is in their midst – they ask for money. Yellowman often obliges, even borrowing a few hundred Jamaican dollars from his driver to offer as hand-outs because he rarely carries cash himself. He was once quoted in a 1983 press article saying that his ambition was to become a millionaire so that he could help out the poor and he has told me that he has given large sums of money to the Maxfield orphanage (Saunders 1983). During the time I spent with him, I witnessed what I felt to be a genuine concern for the impoverished "sufferahs" of the ghetto. This concern has increasingly been the subject of Yellowman's songs since 1985, when he survived his first brush with mortality in the form of a cancerous tumour in his jaw. It is also this concern that his many detractors ignore when they construct essentialized caricatures of him based on his slack material. In their defence, Yellowman has created for himself a hypersexual identity, a sort of cross between a Jamaican Casanova whom women across the island desire and pornographic autobiographer detailing his fantastical sexual escapades in language that is vulgar and offensive to mainstream moral sensibilities, at the same time inviting the listener to take the position of voyeur. In reggae discourse, this is known as slackness and because of Yellowman's sexually charged performances and lyrics, the media dubbed him the King of Slack.

It was this King of Slack persona that was on my mind as we walked around Maxfield Park Home searching for an employee named Miss Stowe, a worker at the orphanage whom Yellowman remembered fondly. The first worker we approached stood behind a security gate at one of the children's residences and sucked her teeth when she saw Yellowman approach. The children in her charge knew who the famous visitor was and, as I had seen children do all over Kingston that day, they flocked to him. The woman at the orphanage avoided eye contact when Yellowman asked her if Miss Stowe was around. When she finally did look him in the eye, it was to say spitefully, "It's not just you that special", and then coldly instructed us that we could find Miss Stowe at the Jelly House, where infants and toddlers are kept.

Later, as we were leaving the orphanage, I asked Yellowman about this woman's demeanor. Did she treat him this way because she disproved of his slackness? At the time I was intimidated by her and somewhat taken aback by her conduct, so decided not to ask her myself. It turns out, however, there is potentially another layer to this incident. It was Yellowman's opinion that this lady had incorrectly assumed that he had quickly forgotten his roots as he climbed out of the ghetto and gained fame and fortune. According to him, this is not so. In 1984, as Yellowman's international fame was peaking, he says he played a sold-out show at the Felt Forum inside Madison Square Gardens and donated a large sum of money from it to the Maxfield Park Children's Home. But in what I would learn was typical Yellowman fashion, he gave the money to his manager and never bothered to see if the donation made it to the orphanage. Poor management and a hands-off approach to his finances would eventually cause turmoil for him as he would blame an old manager for losing two of his houses and getting him in the middle of a financial disagreement with the Salvation Army of Zimbabwe over a large advance payment for a concert he never played. Money slipped easily through Yellowman's hands – if he made US$20,000 on a short tour of the United States during the 1980s, he might spend most of that on jewellery for his wife and a leather suit for himself. He made good money in those days, and he spent a lot of it. Regardless, as we walked around Kingston that day, Yellowman vocalized his insistence that he had not forgotten his roots and that, unlike many reggae artists, he still stayed connected to the ghettos that forged him.

BLUEBERRY HILL

Yellowman remembers Maxfield Park Children's Home as a place where he was often teased by the other kids, suffered racial slurs and spent a lot of time by himself in the large mango tree outside the Jelly House. As he became older, he used to sing to the younger children, his love of music an obvious source of enjoyment in an otherwise grossly underprivileged childhood. Miss Stowe was one of the few workers at the orphanage Yellowman remembers taking an interest in him. Upon finding her at the Jelly House, I had a difficult time getting her to talk to me about his childhood. She seemed happy to see him, apprehensive to see me, a foreign researcher with a digital recorder and a camera. Again I thought of Yellowman's controversial career and I wondered if Miss Stowe was disappointed that the vulnerable child she helped raise and sent to a nearby Methodist church on Sundays for Christian instruction became the country's most infamous and lustfully obscene poet.

I had heard stories that the nuns at Alpha Boys' School, where Yellowman spent much of his teen years, abhorred his career choice and refused to let him back on the property. Yellowman himself downplays this and defends his career choices by saying that while the church and government were always against him, the "people dem", meaning the general population, love him. After much research, I am inclined to think that this is true, at least so far as the "people dem" are confined to reggae fans. There is a large contingent in Jamaica who argue that artists such as Yellowman produce music that is unacceptable in polite society or, worse, that dancehall has led to the general depravity of youth culture on the island which is now only concerned with sex, violence and material possessions. Editorials and letters in the Jamaican papers are only one place to find this openly expressed. Yellowman, on the other hand, sees nothing wrong with talking about sex, be it graphic, humorous or vulgar, in public. One of his often-repeated arguments is "We all come from sex so how can it be wrong?"

Dancehall itself has a stigma among older Jamaicans. It is the music that invades their homes at night through the enormous speaker towers of mobile discotheques called "sound systems" or, simply, "sounds", offering open air dances in neighbourhoods across the country on a nightly basis. Sound systems are mobile deejay businesses that play records for dances, sometimes called "lawns", but have the added live element of a singer or talk-over artist, or what in Jamaica is called a deejay.

It is also dancehall that has embraced and propagated slackness on the island in a way far greater than any previous generation's popular music. I wondered if this is what Miss Stowe meant when, in response to a question about whether she likes Yellowman's music, told me, "I only like 'Blueberry Hill'. I'm a western fan so I don't really go for the reggae." Yellowman's cover of "Blueberry Hill" (1987a) was a reggae anomaly and a chart topper,[3] partly because of the ludic audacity of a deejay singing Fats Domino's R&B hit, and the latent sexual subtext that was magnified by the very fact the King of Slack was performing it. The popularity of the song ballooned when Fats Domino himself was invited to Jamaica for a series of concerts alongside Yellowman. The two artists shared a duet on the song and Yellowman proudly remembers that Domino paid him the enormous compliment of calling his version his personal favourite. The song also came to represent a triumphant comeback for Yellowman after struggling to overcome the second of his many bouts with cancer and is instructive for understanding the love and loyalty fans have for Yellowman. His ability to overcome extreme adversity – first a horrendous childhood and then several life-threatening cancers – has triggered the highest admiration from people around the world. Yellowman's whole life has been about proving that he is not only up to the task at hand, but that he can surpass expectations. The culture and society that he was born into labelled him worthless based on class and colour, and his rise to fame was accomplished by demonstrating his worth time and time again. Jamaicans of all stripes, even many of his detractors, began to appreciate and respect him for this.

Another important aspect of "Blueberry Hill" (1987a) when looking at the life of Yellowman is the fact that he chose to sing it, not deejay the song in his trademark talk-over style. This was a direct attempt to prove to fans that he was well after he underwent major cancer surgery in 1985 and part of his jaw and neck muscles were removed. He had to miss out on Sunsplash 1985 due to his recuperation but introduced the song as a sort of comeback at Sunsplash 1986. But even moreso, the song was a salvo to critics to signal that he had the ability to perform several styles of music very successfully. In an industry where artists are often lumped into general categories such as deejay or singer, or even confined to a tighter deejay typology such as "bad-man deejay" (songs about criminal activity), "slackness deejay" (songs that are sexually explicit), "girls dem deejay" (songs that focus on women and are particularly concerned with their sexuality) or "Rastafari deejay" (songs that espouse a Rastafarian world view), Yellowman has attempted throughout his career to prove that he is an "all-rounder" (Hope 2006).[4] An all-rounder is a deejay who does not confine his or her material to one of the above categories but performs thematically diverse material. That he can deejay either slackness or culture is the subject of several Yellowman songs. The fact that he is most often characterized as simply a slackness deejay means that these attempts have gone largely unnoticed by many outside of his immediate fan base. Within that fan base, however, Yellowman is known as a diverse musician whose music can be slack or cultural, and when he tours in North America or Europe, he is often thought of more as a roots reggae performer than a slackness dancehall deejay. One of the themes of this book, then, is how Yellowman sees himself as a second Bob Marley, first because both musicians enjoyed comparable celebrity status at home and abroad, second because both musicians were responsible for globalizing their respective subgenres of reggae, and third because Yellowman understands his essential message to be analogous to Marley's cultural repertoire of positivity and empowerment.

LORD, WHAT AN UGLY BABY

Yellowman only remembers seeing his mother once as a child. He recollects seeing a woman come to the Maxfield Park Home and the staff telling him later that it was his mother. He believes she told them his birthday and his father's name, but she never took the time to visit her son. Why Pearl Golding and Ivan Foster decided not to raise their infant boy is a matter of speculation because no first-hand accounts of Yellowman's parents exist. But it is accepted as fact by all who relay the story, including Yellowman himself, that he was orphaned because he was born a dundus, a person with albinism. There were other children with albinism at the Maxfield Park Home, as it was a common occurrence to abandon them at that time in Jamaica.[5] A birth certificate exists, as Yellowman found out when he applied for his first passport as an adult, so perhaps they took the trouble to register his birth with the authorities. It is possible, however, that it was the orphanage, going on information from Pearl Golding, who registered the birth.

Winston Foster was born 15 January 1957 at 54 Chisholm Avenue, in the Maxfield Park area of Kingston.[6] It would be almost twenty years until Maxfield Park's Channel One Studio would find itself at the epicentre of a new style of reggae that would take Jamaica by storm. Yellowman would be one of the deejays responsible. In 1957, Pearl Golding lived at 54 Chisholm Avenue and gave birth at home to the child she would name Winston. This address and name are on his birth certificate. While Winston was born into a home in the familial sense of the word, that security would be fleeting. He was found soon after his birth in a shopping bag, tucked into a garbage dumpster. This may not be as heartless and inhumane as it first appears; Yellowman figures his mother put him in a place she knew someone would find him. Perhaps Pearl and Ivan were still unsure in those early post-natal days if they would brave public contempt and keep him? Truly, if his parents wanted the infant dead there are far more perilous places in Kingston they could have left him. But find him someone did, after which he was taken to his new home, the orphanage on Maxfield Avenue at which he would spend the first ten years of his life.

Since Yellowman has become famous, inevitably he has become the target for people claiming to be related to him. In Jamaica and even England, he has had people approach him telling him they are family members:

Author: You don't know any relatives?

Yellowman: No, don't know grandparents.

Author: Have you had anybody that's come forward?

Yellowman: Ya, people come to me but, because I grow already, I just say "Ya ya ya." Even people come from England and say I'm your auntie. I just say "Ya ya ya."

Author: So no family?

Yellowman: No family but mine.

Author: Do you just assume that you were abandoned because of your colour?

Yellowman: Ya, man, I definitely know it was that. Because you have other people like me [and] they get abandoned also.

Yellowman told *Flair Magazine* in 1987 that his parents attempted to re-establish a relationship with him in 1981. "I never knew my parents. . . . It's after I get big that I know parents. In 1981 they came and claimed me, which they should have done earlier. They tried to explain, but I didn't listen to them. They said they were poor so they had to leave me" ("Yellowman: 'In 1981 My Parents Came to Claim Me But . . .'", *Flair Magazine*, 6 January 1987). When I asked him about this, he said it was not his parents who came to claim him, but more distant relatives like an aunt and reiterated that he never met his mother or father. He explained to the *Sunday Gleaner* in 2002 that he was not sure who his family was and did not trust anyone claiming to be family after he became successful ("Yellowman's Family Second Only to God", *Sunday Gleaner*, 17 February 2002).

THE KING OF KINGSTON

When me take up de mic and started to chat
But tell you Yellowman him are de king of de crop
Well anytime me chat me say de crowd haffi rock
—Yellowman, "King of the Crop" (1984e)

The house where Winston took his first breath is gone and the new building in its place is now home to the Jamaica Council Church of God Seventh Day. Yellowman took me to this church though neither of us realized at the time that we had chosen their Sabbath, a Saturday, for the journey. As our driver pulled the car into the lot, we could hear singing through the open windows and saw some parishioners starting for their cars. As we stepped out of the Honda taxi, a small group of female churchgoers recognized Yellowman and started towards us. I was nervous about this encounter; here was Yellowman, a deejay who built his career largely on songs of a sexual nature, about to speak to what I assumed were socially conservative Christians. Would they, offended by his presence, drive us off the property? But unlike at the orphanage, there were no leering eyes and sucking of teeth. Instead, the ladies were overjoyed to see the celebrity.

They were proud that he was one of them – from the same streets – and no matter what his songs contained, he was welcomed and treated as a star. A man leaving the church parking lot stuck his head out the car window and, as he passed, he greeted Yellowman with one of the salutations I had come to expect everywhere I travelled with him in Kingston: "Yes, King", or "King Yellow!" or simply "King!" I learned an important lesson that day that validated Yellowman's claim that the "people dem" loved him. Here was a constituent I was sure would be offended by the King of Slack, yet they were proud that the King of Dancehall remembered his roots and returned to the streets where he was born. As a sign of the reciprocal respect between entertainer and his public, Yellowman is now welcomed as a king in a neighbourhood where he was once, literally, refuse.

At the Maxfield Park Home, young Winston would be cared for by the state. No prospective parents were found for the boy with albinism and friends were few and far between. Yellowman tells stories of near adoptions and hopes for a normal life: an attendant at the home wanted to adopt him but her other children said no; a doctor from Canada, Dr Box, talked of adopting the child but nothing ever came of it. He was used to being let down, overlooked, disappointed.

When he was old enough, he attended nearby Russell Primary School where a Mr Daley used to organize a band with the school children. In class, Winston would sit on the back bench, alone. "Nobody want to sit with me, no other children. And when I go to the canteen, no other children want to sit with me", he remembers. At school, a pattern began that would not be broken until much later in life: he was physically abused for being different. In the canteen, other kids made fun of him and took away his meal; when school let out for the holidays he was beat up because he had no one to protect him. Winston did not fight back, most likely seeing the futility in it. He started to exhibit violent behaviour in his teenage years, and he credits music for helping to turn him away from what might have spiraled into a life of crime. By and large, even his lyrics, with notable exceptions, have largely steered clear of the type of gun violence that dancehall became inundated with in the late 1980s and 1990s.[7] The experience made him tough, physically and spiritually. He endured what he calls "getting my ass kicked" and spat invectives to his attackers defiantly.

SWIFT-PURCELL

For Winston Foster, who had grown up in an orphanage in an area bordering inner-city Kingston and had seen his fellow orphans adopted while he remained ignored, life was about to go in a new direction. In 1967, at age ten, he would exchange the simmering congestion and heat of Kingston for life in the country as he would be moved from Maxfield Park Home to the Swift-Purcell Industrial School and Home for Boys in Belfield, in the parish of St Mary.

As an adolescent in St Mary, Winston was protected from Kingston's ghetto life, but he remained at the mercy of the state. The new school offered new opportunities. He would go on long field trips with the school to Port Royal, Negril and the Jamaica Broadcasting Corporation (JBC) television station back in Kingston. But he would also suffer from sun exposure on regular trips to the beach at Robin's Bay or Annotto Bay. He liked going to the ocean to swim but had to cover his skin the best he could to avoid onlookers making fun of him, choosing to wear clothes in the water instead of a bathing suit. When he did expose his skin to the sun, he would suffer burns because "in those times we never had no lotion". When we discussed this in his kitchen in 2009, he pulled up his sleeves to show me the difference in the skin between his lower arms and his upper arms. The upper skin was clear and smooth but the lower arms were rough and had some sores.

Now, five decades later, Yellowman feels no need to hide his skin in public. Years of singing about his own desirability have convinced him of his own physical beauty. When I accompanied him in the streets of Kingston, he routinely wore short pants – themselves a rarity among Jamaican men – and short-sleeved shirts, and on stage he often dons sleeveless basketball shirts. People who are not aware of who he is stare, some children still giggle. Yellowman ignores oglers and refuses to cover up in public. He now wears his yellow skin as a badge of honour. In part, it is what helped him gain recognition.

Despite enjoyable field trips, Winston's life did not improve at Swift-Purcell. He was now subjected to pranks at the hands of his adolescent classmates on top of constant verbal abuse. The first signs of his violent behaviour started to show.

> We used to go to the bushes to do work, like clean up, like at a farm. Swift-Purcell had a banana farm and a cane farm. I remember one time all the boys got together and said, "Let us go to the Banana Walk." And then a group of guys – I thought they were friends – tied me up to a coconut tree and leave me there. I was there overnight and the next day when they do a head count, and they said, "Where is Winston, where's white man?" Some other guys must have pointed out the group of guys I was with, so they start flog them and they say I in the Coconut Bush. When they go there, I was still tied to the tree.

When Winston was freed from the tree he was livid. He sought out the boys and wanted to kill them. He hit one of them with a piece of wood, knocking him out, but the rest of the group ran to the headmaster. This incident crushed him; he realized that the friends he thought he had finally gained were no different than the other boys he had known at Maxfield. He was alone in a crowded school and the rest of the boys refused to go anywhere, or do anything, with him. The teachers, who had not realized the extent of his ostracism until the coconut tree incident, acted accordingly and stopped sending him to do chores with the other boys. He recalls, "The teachers start to watch out for me more because of this incident and go out to the board of the school. The headmaster gave orders to watch and he tell them never let this get outta hand. They felt like I was going to get very violent." But it was too much for the pre-teen to take. Almost a week after this humiliation, he ran away from Swift-Purcell with just the clothes on his back; he had no other belongings. He spent between three and five days on the road alone, surviving off bananas, soursop, chocolate (fruit from the cacao tree) and other food he could find growing freely. His only mode of transportation was walking and he stayed off the main roads during the day because he would be instantly recognizable to anyone searching for a runaway boy with albinism. He slept under trees, hidden from view, and when people did see him they would call out derisions like "Hey, look at the dundus bwoy" or "Hey, backra master, weh you doing so? Weh you come from?"[8] Keeping to himself, Winston ignored the taunts and kept walking, through Highgate and Robin's Bay, all the way to Annotto Bay on the north coast.

The teachers at Swift-Purcell had alerted the authorities when he was discovered missing, and even though he was cautious, Winston's time on the lam would be short. "When I was in Annotto Bay, I saw a police car pull up and they grab me and take me back to Swift-Purcell. And then I get punished."

Winston remained at Swift-Purcell for a total of four years and then was again transferred to another institution for unwanted children. This time it was to Alpha Boys' School back in Kingston. The year was 1971.[9]

CHAPTER 2

From Alpha to Eventide
The Teenage Years, 1971–1976

ALPHA BOYS' SCHOOL'S RECORDS SAY THAT UPON ENTERING the school, a children's officer examined Winston Foster and described him as boy with albinism who had "defective eyes and unhealthy skin". The report states that Winston had a difficult time adjusting to the school and suggests it may have been because he had albinism. His lack of family support and connections were noticed by the school. Former Alpha principal Sister Bernadette Little (email to author, 28 July 2009) had this to say about the school's records on Winston Foster when I spoke with her: "There is a section in the children's officer's report that stated that during the first three years that he was at the school at Alpha, no relative had come to see him, which leads one to suspect that he may not have had any worthwhile relationship with any family member." She added that this may have accounted for his alienation from the other children.

What is usually listed simply as Alpha Boys' School in reggae histories (and is now called Alpha Institute), is actually part of a series of institutions: Alpha Business College (1925–2000), Convent of Mercy Academy – a high school (1894 until present), Alpha Primary School (1892 until present), the Jessie Ripoll Primary (1980 until present), Alpha Infant School (1892 until present), a preparatory school (1894–1984) and a boarding school for girls (1894–1969). Founding mother Jessie (Justina) Ripoll, a Jamaican of Portuguese descent, was a member of Holy Trinity Cathedral Catholic Church and an active member of the Ladies of Charity. She was moved by the plight of the poor in the years after the abolition of slavery and was particularly troubled by the homeless children in Kingston. In 1880, she pooled her money with two friends, Josephine Ximenes and Louise Dugiol, and purchased a forty-three-acre property on South Camp Road. The trio established a girls' orphanage and began to admit boys four years later. By 1890, Ripoll and her companions were joined by the Sisters of Mercy from Bermondsey in London, England, and by the spring of 1891, the three founders joined the Order of Mercy. Ripoll took as her religious name Sister Mary Peter Claver. The two schools, known as industrial schools, taught scholastics but also trained their students in practical skills – laundering, sewing, cooking, cosmetology and lace-making for the girls, and printing and bookbinding, gardening, music, tailoring, carpentry, and tile and block making for the boys – in order to allow them to be self-sufficient upon leaving. By 1935, Maxfield Park Children's Home began sending boys to Alpha and by 1937 there were four hundred boys enrolled in the school (Hyatt 2011; Sister Bernadette Little, email to author, 28 July 2009).

Alpha Boys' School enjoys a reputation in reggae history as a sort of musician factory. Its earliest band was a drum and fife corps, which began in 1893, and a boys' choir was started in 1917. The music programme there turned out several of Kingston's top musicians in the early 1960s, including Skatalites members Johnny "Dizzy" Moore, Lester Sterling, Tommy McCook and Don Drummond. The fact is, though, that the nuns who ran Alpha did so because of the second part of the school name: School for Abandoned Children.

When Winston moved to Alpha, he was still considered an abandoned child by the state. His transferal to Alpha would prolong his exposure to taunts and verbal jabs, as well as physical beatings at the hands of his classmates, but it would also shield Winston from the alternatives available to him, a life spent on the streets hiding from public view with little or no employment prospects or, worse, a life of crime. And Alpha would provide Winston a valuable intangible asset: friends.

Just as when Yellowman returned to Maxfield with me and faced the scorn of one of the workers, Alpha Boys' School is not as proud of its most famous student as it is of the other musicians whom it graduated. In an institution run by strict Catholic nuns under the leadership of Sister Ignatius, Yellowman's career was not looked on favourably due to his penchant for sex talk. He returned there later in life with an offer to do a free concert to help raise funds for the school but was denied entrance to the grounds. School head Sister Ignatius would not accept the offer from Yellowman because she did not approve of his slack lyrics.

> I knew that Sister Ignatius did not accept the offer made by Yellowman to do a benefit for Alpha Boys' School since she disapproved of the content of some of his lyrics, but the actual details of what took place between them is anyone's guess, since Sister Ignatius alone would have been able to shed further light. Furthermore, I must add that Sister Ignatius was one who said nothing to disparage anyone, she is one of the most charitable persons we know and rather than speak ill of another, she would maintain silence. She spoke ill of noone and that is no exaggeration. (Sister Bernadette Little, email to author, 26 June 2009)

Indeed, when Sister Ignatius was interviewed by the *Gleaner* about former students on two occasions, she even mentioned Yellowman and only had positive things to say. Yellowman, she remembered, was a good gymnast and a skilled cabinet maker ("Sister Ignatius of Alpha", *Gleaner*, 16 March 1999; "Tribute to Sister Mary Ignatius: A Musical Inspiration", *Gleaner*, 14 February 2003).

Most of the school literature detailing the famous musical alumni does not mention Yellowman. He is listed, however, on the Alpha Old Boys' Association website under the achievements and alumni honours section for Excellence in Personal Achievements in Popular Performing Arts alongside luminaries such as Don Drummond, Johnny "Dizzy" Moore, Lester Sterling, Tommy McCook, Cedric "Im" Brooks, Leroy Wallace, Vin Gordon, and Leroy Smart (Hyatt 2011). And Sister Bernadette Little noted that she was encouraged by an article in the *Sunday Gleaner* (13 November 1983, 4A) that featured Yellowman as a family man, "which showed his willingness to transcend the past and to give his family the love and devotion he did not receive from his own family" (email to author, 28 July 2009).

At Alpha, Winston would receive Catholic instruction. He went to mass, took communion, knelt at the cross and listened to sermons. He learned by heart the Lord's Prayer, Psalm 23 and the Hail Mary, and had to do rosary beads, the Stations of the Cross and go to confession. These rituals and meditations became meaningful to him and made him feel closer to God. But he would later harbour resentment against the Catholic Church for the sexual abuse of children, and he cites that as one of the main reasons he has not continued with Catholic observances.

Alpha represented a new era for the teenager; at Alpha, Winston would, for the first time, be part of a team with other boys. His school record shows that Winston was good at gymnastics but took little interest in his studies (Sister Bernadette Little, email to author, 26 June 2009). He played on the Alpha Boys' football (soccer) team, wearing the number 10 on his jersey and playing centre forward. The sport became an escape for him, away from the hassles of life as an outcast. He became quite a good player by his own measure and this endeared him to other boys, so that for the first time in his life he had friends. He eventually made captain and finally, at least within the confines of the school, enjoyed some measure of respect.

Besides football, he competed in acrobatics at Alpha and with area schools. Students would take turns doing tricks; Winston's repertoire included walking on his hands, backwards somersaults, somersaults over a rope, a back flip and crab walking. A budding entertainer, Winston enjoyed pleasing a crowd and was even rewarded with the top prize on a few occasions. Although he never incorporated these acrobatic maneuvers into his stage performances later in life, his ability to sustain the attention of the crowd was minted during this time. By the 1990s, his usual performance style – walking slowly or standing in one spot while deejaying – underwent a change as he started to draw on the physical entertainment of his acrobatic days. Contemporary Yellowman concerts see him running, leaping, jumping and stretching constantly. He rarely stands still, his energy boundless. He trains daily to stay healthy and remain in shape for his physically draining performances, jogging in the Kingston hills where he lives. The reason that he does this is simple: he is an entertainer, and the decisions he makes about what his performance will look like (costume included) and what his lyrics entail are more often than not based on pleasing his audience. He says, "I do that because I found that people love movement on stage. They like to see an artist move with the music. Because those days I used to just walk around . . . but now I'm running. Because that bring more entertainment for the people. If you notice, sometimes when I start jump they scream."

The acceptance that he first found at Alpha was addictive and he has been craving it ever since. This yearning for public approval helps explain Yellowman's use of slackness – it was extremely popular. One of the common reasons given by reggae artists when asked why they do slackness is that they are simply giving the people what they want. Yellowman's star shone the brightest in dancehall because he was the most adept at interpreting and delivering what the dancehall audience wanted to hear.

EARLY MUSICAL INFLUENCES

Winston really started paying attention to music at Alpha, where he was introduced first-hand to the sound system deejaying culture that he would go on to dominate, but he began his love of music at Swift-Purcell, where he remembers always singing. Jamaican music fans in the late 1960s had home-grown sounds and they were fed a steady diet of pop music from England, America and the rest of the Caribbean. The songs and styles he heard during his youth in the 1960s and 1970s helped shape his later approach to dancehall.

FOLK MUSIC

Jamaican popular music revolves around the polarities of innovation and tradition. New reggae songs are often created by adapting older "riddims", themes, lyrics and melodies. The resulting songs are new creations, but they also pay tribute to the musical traditions of the past. One of the obvious ways we see this in Yellowman's music is through the versioning practice discussed elsewhere in this book. But the maintenance of tradition is also conspicuous in the way he adapted the lyrics of popular folk songs he would have heard in his youth. "Donkey Want Water", released on the *For Your Eyes Only* LP (1982a), reworks the mento song of the same name (also called "Hold 'im Joe"). He breaks into a chorus of "Day-O" during his set heard on *Live at Reggae Sunsplash* (1983b). "Hill and Gully Rider" was covered on *Nobody Move* (1983c) in a roots reggae style. And he recorded a cover of the Folkes Brothers's "Oh Carolina" on the *Prayer* album (1994b).

NOVELTY SONGS

One of Yellowman's talents is his ability to draw on a wide array of musical traditions, both Jamaican and international, often in the same song. Besides inserting mento lyrics in contemporary songs, he might also, for instance, rework a nursery rhyme like "This Old Man" or a novelty song like "Army

Life". These were popular additions to his set lists in the early 1980s where he would build improvised lyrics around them. Then there is his popular "I'm Getting Married" (1982g)[1] that is a cover of *My Fair Lady*'s "Get Me to the Church on Time" with the inclusion of lyrics from Sam Cooke ("Bring It on Home"), Rod Stewart ("If You Think I'm Sexy") and, of course, Yellowman himself.

RADIO

These diverse tastes were not the result of early Jamaican radio. Radio Jamaica, the first local station, began in 1939 (under the name ZQI), and in 1959 the island got its second station, JBC. But these stations offered very little excitement to teenagers in the 1960s. Mostly, Jamaican radio was programmed to please the island's elite, who preferred jazz, classical and light pop. If local artists were featured at all, they tended to be of the commercial variety, such as Millie Small's runaway hit "My Boy Lollipop", not the sounds of Kingston's musical revolutionaries. Jamaicans who wanted more diverse music were often able to pick up radio stations from Cuba, Trinidad, Panama and the United States. American stations provided music fans hours of country, rock and R&B. Yellowman would occasionally record Spanish Caribbean songs like "Guantanamera", break into a lyric from a country song such as John Denver's "Leaving on Jet Plane" and "Country Roads" (though the latter follows more the Toots and the Maytals' version than John Denver's), and rock (heard primarily in lead guitar sounds on songs like the version of "Lost Mi Love" on *Live in Paris* (1994a), but his love of R&B features heavily in his repertoire. Examples include his covers of Barbara Lynn's "You'll Lose a Good Thing" and Betty Wright's "Girls Can't Do What the Guys Do", both found on *King Yellowman* (1984a), Sam Cooke's "Another Saturday Night" from *Just Cool* (1982b), and Fats Domino's "Blueberry Hill" (1987a).

SOUND SYSTEMS

Besides American radio, the other place that Jamaicans heard R&B was on the sound systems. Sound systems were formed in the ghetto to provide much-needed entertainment in communities where few people could afford to buy records and in a time when the radio was not catering to their tastes.

Sound systems were the only place to hear these records, first R&B and later ska, rocksteady and reggae. "When a sound was hooked up and turned on, the entire neighbourhood could hardly help but hear it play. People would drift over as the evening wore on, enjoy a bottle of beer, have a dance, a little food and take in the latest recording" (Lesser 2008, 4). This is how Clement Dodd and Duke Reid started; both men had early sound systems that were merely radios or turntables connected to a speaker and set outside their respective liqueur stores to draw in customers (Hutton 2007b, 85).

Winston did not attend sound system shows until much later, but these loud dances held in outdoor spaces broadcast music for anyone within ear-shot to hear. Other American songs that he would adapt from this period include "Girl Watcher", a cover of the 1960 hit by American pop band the O'Kaysons, found on his album *Tiger Meets Yellowman* (1986c), and Frankie Ford's "Sea Cruise" on *King Yellowman* (1984a).

GOSPEL

Winston spent time in Methodist and Catholic churches growing up, and also absorbed the gospel tradition of Jamaica. Later in life, he would pepper set lists with hymns. At one point on *Live in London* (1983a), he leads a sing-along through choruses of "He's Got the Whole World in His Hands", "And the Lord Said", "Something in My Heart Like a Stream Running Down" and "Amen", one after the other. He even released "He's Got the Whole World in His Hands" on *Them A Mad over Me* (1982g) and "I Shall Not Remove" on *Reggae on Top* (1993c).

ROCKSTEADY

In 1967, as Winston was moving from Maxfield Park to Swift-Purcell, Jamaican music was undergoing a transition from rocksteady to reggae. The yearly independence festival, inaugurated with the island's 1962's independence from Great Britain, launched an annual song competition in 1966. Toots and the Maytals took first prize that year with "Bam Bam", a song Yellowman would cover early in his career (Yellowman and Fathead 1982d). Vocal trio the Jamaicans won the following year with "Ba Ba Boom", a celebration of both the festival and rocksteady. Studio One had ruled the ska era, with the

Skatalites as the studio band, and Treasure Isle studio ruled the rocksteady period, with Tommy McCook and the Supersonics as the house band (itself derived from ex-Skatalites members), but now a Chinese Jamaican business owner named Leslie Kong became a driving force in the industry as it turned into what is, in retrospect, called early reggae. Working out of his combination ice cream parlour, restaurant and record shop at 135a Orange Street, Kong's Beverley's label produced some of the greatest tracks of the early reggae period.

Toots Hibbert, the gospel-influenced leader of ska sensations Toots and the Maytals, had served a prison sentence for ganja possession (Barrow and Dalton 2004, 107), missed most of the rocksteady era and was back out on the street and in the charts. His first song for Kong was "54-46", a narrative about his incarceration – the song's title was his assigned prison number. Toots also released "Do the Reggay" and coined the term for the new musical craze. The song "54-46" has since become one of reggae's all-time classic songs and Yellowman's cover of it, known as "Nobody Move" (1983c), is still a staple in his live shows and is featured on the reggae radio station Blue Ark on the video game *Grand Theft Auto V.*

As a Maytals fan, Yellowman enjoyed ska and early reggae, but in some ways it is rocksteady – the music that the Maytals missed out on – that forms the most important musical building block of his career. Rocksteady had itself supplanted the faster jazz-influenced ska music of the early 1960s. Rocksteady had a slower groove, downplayed the role of the horn section, relegating it to a supporting role, whereas previously it had often provided the melody in ska. And rocksteady's dominant innovation would alter the sound of Jamaican music permanently and eventually form the basis of what Yellowman and his contemporaries called dancehall. Specifically, this had to do with the role of the bass and drums: reggae's heart and soul. Ska bassists, influenced by American R&B and jazz, played walking bass lines, often on stand-up basses; rocksteady bassists, such as Jackie Jackson, preferred electric instruments and shifted the role of the bass away from counter-melody to dominant melody. Bass lines became repetitive and took a lead role in songs, so much so that long after a rocksteady hit faded from the limelight, its bass line might find new life in a series of newer hits for years to come. This practice of writing new songs on old bass lines or complete rhythms would become known as "versioning" and the bass lines themselves would take the name "riddims". For instance, Yellowman's cover of "Bam Bam" was voiced on Sly and Robbie's instrumental riddim "Taxi". Yellowman's version was the first vocal version to be released, and the riddim has since become one of dancehall's all-time favourites, finding a new international audience in 2006 with Buju Banton's hit "Driver A".

This musical innovation is important to note here because it is integral to understanding the music of dancehall and, subsequently, Yellowman as an artist. Deejays are said to "ride the riddim" when they match lyrics along to the cadence and structure of the song. Riddims are the foundation of modern reggae and a deejay's ability to ride or perform on top of a riddim is central to their popularity. As such, when Yellowman was making the transition from urban Maxfield Avenue to Swift-Purcell in the country, the shifts in the music industry that would pave the way for his brand of dancehall were already underway.

CALYPSO

While ska, rocksteady and early reggae are remembered in the history books as the sound of Jamaica in the 1960s, as a youth Winston was also enthralled by another style of music at this time, one that was not even Jamaican – Trinidadian calypso. As the decade waned, Winston's musical tastes still included American black music alongside Jamaican popular hits but, like youths all over the Caribbean, one of his favourite singers was Slinger Francisco, better known as the Mighty Sparrow. Calypso, like Jamaica's mento, was still popular in Jamaica; Winston would have grown up hearing calypso and mento, but by the early 1960s it was no longer the music of the youth. By the 1970s, calypso and mento both would begin to be relegated to tourist centres on the north coast, though both maintained staunch fans, especially among older music listeners. Many of the men who would later become reggae's greatest contributors, such as Wailers bassist Aston "Familyman" Barrett, would spend time playing calypso for tourists in hotels or even on cruise ships to pay the bills.

But for Winston, in the mid-1960s calypso was anything but tourist music. For him, Sparrow, the king of calypso, was a breath of fresh air away from the trials of life as an orphan with albinism. Sparrow's use of double entendre, humour and veiled sexuality had a significant impact on Winston as he slowly developed into a songwriter himself. Sparrow's wordplay was second to none, his timing impeccable, his subject material varied and timely, his humour universal, his popularity massive and his creativity boundless – all skills that were already valued in Jamaican music and would increase in cultural currency with the shift to dancehall in the 1970s.

In the mid-1960s, Sparrow was the undisputed top calypsonian and had been so since the mid-1950s. Sparrow was everything Winston desired to be: popular, skilled, respected, rich, independent. While it seemed unlikely at the time, a decade later he would go on to achieve just that. Yellowman eventually adopted Sparrow's love of language, particularly slackness, and covered Sparrow songs such as "Big Bamboo" (1991a) and shared stages with him including a show at Madison Square Garden's Felt Forum in November 1983. His love of calypso can also be heard on "Happy for the Rest of Your Life", off *Reggae on the Move* (1992), a cover of Jimmy Soul's 1964 hit that was itself a rewrite of "Ugly Woman" by Trinidadian calypsonian Roaring Lion in 1933.

He also experimented with calypso-reggae fusion, first on his major label cross-over album *King Yellowman* (1984a) with the song "Reggae Calypso", and then on a clash album with General Trees called *A Reggae Calypso Encounter* (1987). That album was mostly pure dancehall, though the tracks "Trees in de Place" and "Trees and Yellow in de Place" indeed fuse the two styles.

REGGAE

Once at Alpha, being back in Kingston also meant Yellowman being closer to the music industry and the early 1970s was a time of intense excitement in reggae. Michael Manley's socialist-leaning People's National Party (PNP) defeated the conservative Jamaica Labour Party (JLP) in 1972 and fundamentally altered the mood of the country in short order. "Afrocentricity, black consciousness, Rastafarian theology and militant anti-imperialist solidarity all informed a new national zeitgeist" (Chang and Chen 1998, 53). This is relevant here because these themes were central to many cultural reggae songs of the era.

Deejay culture was starting to come into its own with deejays becoming as well-known as Kingston's brightest singers. U-Roy, Big Youth, Lone Ranger,

Michigan and Smiley, Trinity, Dillinger, Jah Woosh, Dennis Alcapone, and Doctor Alimantado were among the top deejays of the decade. It was at Alpha that Winston's love of deejay music would develop, and it was in those halls that he first tried his hand at deejaying and singing in front of others.

He was also drawn to the roots reggae often sung by Rastafarian artists, but he would get flogged with a cane by Sister Aloysius or Sister Ignatius for singing them.[2] He recalls, "'Cause they used to say those songs was disturbing. Back in those days, those songs were discriminated against by society, especially the political society, because those songs used to open eyes. And then them used to consider those songs non-message – they didn't carry any message." His favourites included "Marcus Garvey", Burning Spear's heartfelt tribute to the pan-Africanist organizer turned prophetic figure in Rastafari mythology, and "Stir It Up", a song written by Bob Marley that Yellowman often cites as an example of Marley's slack lyrics. He singles out the lyric "I'll push the wood / I'll blaze your fire / I'll satisfy your heart desire" (Wailers 1973a) to demonstrate the double meaning of the song: "wood" is Caribbean slang for penis and "blaze your fire" and "satisfy" here could allude to intercourse. Under this reading, the chorus, "We could stir it up", becomes a suggestion for sex with the line "I'll stir it every minute / All you got to do, baby, is keep it in it", furthering the metaphor.

He began making up his own lyrics and dreaming the dream that many ghetto youths shared: breaking out of poverty through a career in music. Before he ever attended a sound system or saw a live deejay at a stage show, Winston started entertaining his new friends by making up lyrics, while another beat out a rhythm on a can: "I deejay to people at school, but not on a mic. You did have some guy use the paint pan [pail] and make music with it to make riddim. I deejay over it."

SISTER IGNATIUS'S SOUND SYSTEM

By the mid-1970s, sound systems were the dominant way for Kingston's ghetto dwellers to hear new music. Winston did not have the opportunity to attend sound system dances outside of the school but he would be able to absorb a version of sound system culture within the walls of Alpha. Head nun Sister Mary Ignatius Davies was known for having her own sound system for playing dances at the school for students and alumni. Called the Mutt and Jeff Sound System, it was named after the two Alpha employees she had purchased the equipment from. There were no deejays, but Yellowman well remembers hanging around the sound when it was playing rocksteady and reggae hits and even some deejay tracks by U-Roy and Big Youth.

The music programme at Alpha gained prestige in the reggae world when some of the students went on to create the Skatalites, and founded a music genre known as ska. The role Alpha played in preparing the architects of Jamaica's indigenous music is repeated in many histories on reggae, with Sister Ignatius specifically singled out for her work with the Alpha Boys' School music programme.

Yellowman never attempted to enrol in the music programme or the Alpha Boys' Band, not playing an instrument himself. But the music culture at Alpha influenced him nevertheless, and he is proud of his association with other musical luminaries on the island who attended the school.

Music and friendship were the two gifts Alpha bestowed on him. He would break curfew to stay up late in the dormitory with his friends listening to the radio and singing. Punishments included floggings, but the risk was worth it. "The guys used to like me 'cause I was a comedian. They used to come around me because when you're around me you're never bored." Despite his hard life, he developed a natural demeanour that made people like him. As I witnessed in the time I spent with him, he is always cracking jokes, many of them off-colour, and when he is the centre of attention on his own terms, he enjoys it immensely.

Breaking curfew was not the only thing Winston was punished for at Alpha. His acerbic tongue that later became one of his trademarks in the dance often got him in trouble with the sisters. He says, "To tell you the truth, I was very rude in school. Not violent, though, but rude. I would back answer; if you talk to me and you say something I don't like I would say something back." The standard mode of punishment was a slim cane but, due to his sensitive skin, a doctor had told the sisters to beat Winston on the bottom of his feet where his skin was tougher so that it would mask any welts and marks. Winston was considered a troublesome boy and, according to his memory, spent weeks locked up – not allowed to go outside and play or eat with the other boys. Still, he says the relationship between him and the nuns was good, although it is difficult to ascertain exactly what that relationship was. Sister Ignatius has since passed away. She frowned on the career that

Winston went on to forge because of his slack lyrics but, as Sister Bernadette has suggested, even if Sister Ignatius were alive it is doubtful that she would disparage Yellowman.

THE EVENTIDE YEARS

> Gun man, say tell me weh you get yuh gun from?
> You must a get it from the foreign land
> You want come shoot dung your own black man
> Gunshot a it nuh respect no one
> It kill soldier man, it kill policeman
> It kill policeman, also badman
> It kill badman, also civilian
> It kill civilian, also Christian
> It kill animal, also human
> —Yellowman, "Gun Man" (1982g)

Just as Swift-Purcell and Maxfield Park could not find a suitable permanent home for Winston, Alpha failed to adopt him out. But after completing high school there, he was not allowed to live independently. Another government institution was found for him to live in: Eventide Home for the Unfortunate. According to Alpha's records, he was discharged on 1 June 1974, which would make him seventeen years old.

Eventide was built on Slipe Pen Road in Kingston 5 in 1870 to house elderly women. The area is now known as Torrington Park. By the late 1970s, it had opened its doors to other unfortunates such as the destitute, infirm, elderly men, and children.

> Yellowman: After Alpha, they think my life don't have any direction. Nobody want to adopt me, want me to live with them, because Alpha contact a lot of people and they say no, they always turned down. Because I was growing up I had to leave, so they found Eventide Home for me; that's the only place that would accept me at that time. . . . Eventide is a place for neglected people, people who they think life don't have any direction. Finished. That's the reason why they call it Eventide – is like the evening of people's life.
>
> Author: Would you have been free to leave Eventide if you wanted?

Yellowman: They wouldn't allow that.

Author: So, if you didn't become an artist and get famous what would have happened to you?

Yellowman: I don't know. Still at Eventide-type place or maybe I wouldn't be here.

Winston now was faced with the daunting task of creating a life for himself and finding a place in society where the double stigma of "unfortunate" and "dundus" would not plague him. By his late teens, Winston was eager to get on with his life. He knew his opportunities were few and that, with his colour, his pariah status and his institutional background, the odds were stacked against him to make it out of the ghetto. But Winston had ambition and he was determined to better his lot in life. He answered an ad in the newspaper and got a job at the Hope Gardens Zoo on Hope Road, but he made sure to keep this a secret. Outside employment was not allowed at Eventide, and if the authorities there knew about his job, they would expel him. The secrecy had to go both ways, though, and he did not tell his employer or fellow workers that he was living in the poor house, as that would add to his discrimination at work. At the zoo, Winston was responsible for cleaning out the pens and feeding the animals. He would rise early and walk the almost ten kilometres to work. He enjoyed the work and being with the animals and appreciated the opportunity to finally have some autonomy in his life. A pay cheque and a job were tremendous achievements after years of institutional living.

Despite the positive effect of having meaningful work, there were also nefarious forces threatening to lead him in dangerous directions. Yellowman likens his time spent at Eventide to incarceration in a prison. He felt as an inmate, because he was not granted permission to leave permanently. His frustration at his physical and social imprisonment started to manifest in his actions. He began to fight with others at Eventide and on the street. He gravitated towards the Kingston underworld of gangs, dons and political thugs. It was during this time, and due to the influence of these new friends, that Winston started carrying a gun, a .38 pistol.

His increased frustration and violent behaviour mimicked what was going on in the city at large in the mid- to late 1970s. The political awakening of black youth culture in the African diaspora in the wake of independence of many African countries from their colonial regimes manifested in several ways on Kingston's streets. In America, a new sense of militancy and political agency led to "questioning the legitimacy of establishment democracy and encouraging an active opposition to the corrupt inequalities of American life" (White 1982, 41). In Jamaica, black youth became disenchanted with a system that many felt offered no hope or future for them. Some, like the Wailers, turned to music and created beautifully crafted cries for justice. Others turned towards violence: "Many of them became *rude*. 'Rude boy' (bwoy) applied to anyone against the system. It described the anarchic and revolutionary youth of the poorer classes and the young political 'goons' (mercenaries of the two political parties), as well as the Rasta-inspired 'cultural' rude boys (like the Wailers) who rejected white standards. Some of the youths became predatory, harassing the very poor" (41). This criminal element was immortalized in many songs of the ska and rocksteady era, notably by Alton Ellis, Prince Buster, the Wailers and Derrick Morgan. But by 1966–67, the level of violence on the streets of Kingston was elevated from the petty crime and drug peddling of the rude boys into what was to become a culture of politically supported gang violence (Stolzoff 2000).

During the time Winston was at Eventide, political violence in Kingston was rampant. The two-party system that had emerged in the wake of the first general election in the 1940s polarized the community under either the ruling party, Michael Manley's socialist-leaning PNP, or Edward Seaga's right-of-centre opposition party, the JLP. Based on an entrenched system of distribution of benefits to party supporters, or what Gray calls the "discriminatory use of state largesse" (Gray 2004, 26), political support in Jamaica is marked by aggressive partisan loyalties that have led to a culture of political violence, particularly in Kingston, St Andrew and St Catherine (Hope 2006). In these parishes can be found what is known as garrison constituencies: political strongholds controlled by one of the political parties and associated with "positional gun warfare and the illegal gun trade" (Figueroa and Sives 2003, 75). They are communities that live beyond the law but with political support; they are safe havens for lawbreakers as long as the criminal activity is directed externally: "the tight integration between local party structures and criminal gang organizations [ensures] a fair measure of political protection from police action" (Harriott 2000, 16). According to Figueroa, a garrison community is "one in which the dominant party can, under normal circumstances, control the voting process" (Figueroa 1994, 6).

Outbreaks of violence during election campaigns were commonplace as political thugs used violence to intimidate rival supporters. Michael Manley (1982) estimates over eight hundred people died during the 1980 campaign and Hope (2006) suggests that number may be closer to one thousand.

This tumultuous mix of violence and politics was part of everyday life for residents of downtown Kingston. Eventide was in a PNP-controlled garrison. Winston witnessed PNP gunmen coming on the grounds to intimidate the residents and to ensure their support. Many of his friends at this time were PNP supporters, and some of them enforcers, and Winston followed suit. Soon, normal life included guns and political intimidation. He took his gun to political rallies and even shot it in the air on occasion, but, in his words, "I never shoot anybody. I shoot after people in political rivalry but nobody never get hurt. It was like a rivalry, like tribal war, you know, tribalism. . . . I never consider myself as a PNP." Perhaps carrying a gun, hanging around gangsters and fighting were ways for a dundus outcast to exercise some means of agency, to be in control of his present and future. Ghetto youths had little idea of what life was like outside the ghetto. His job at the zoo afforded him some measure of autonomy, but it was doubtful a custodial vocation would allow him to escape ghetto life and Eventide. With very few opportunities present, Winston's ambition found an outlet on the streets, where the excitement of violence and criminal power dulled the sting of poverty. And it may have sunk him into a life of crime if music had not saved him.

It was at Eventide that Winston started getting in trouble with the law. Most of the Eventide staff did not like him or trust him, probably because of his criminal associations, and they blamed him when things went wrong at the home. Once, he was detained at the police station by investigators when two gunmen killed a police officer on Eventide's grounds. He was eventually let go due to lack of evidence. Yellowman recalls, "Me and the police never have good relations because I used to move around [with] a lot of rough guys like George Phang, Umpi, Starkey, Mardo, Linky Roy, Tunda. . . . The police kill all those guys. Out of all those guys only George is there." These "rough guys" not only introduced Winston to the seedier side of Kingston, but the ones who survived, like George Phang, would prove to be a blessing to the albino deejay in the years to come, when having intimidating friends helped him break into a music scene that was dead set against having him be part of it.

CHAPTER 3

Ranking Dundus

Breaking into the Music Business, 1977–1978

KINGSTON HAD NO SHORTAGE OF DESTITUTE GHETTOS AND in the mid-1970s they were filled with youths striving to win over record producers with their lyrics, their style and their stage appeal. The ambition that drove these youths was inherited from Jamaican leaders such as Marcus Garvey, who espoused black nationalism, pride of self and Afrocentricity. Yellowman's many years of suffering humiliation and floggings at Maxfield, Swift-Purcell and Alpha forced him to love himself, since no one else would. It was this confidence and ambition that pushed Winston to hit the hot pavement and knock on the doors of all the studios in Kingston knowing that a music career would be a surefire ticket out of poverty.

It was a tradition among Jamaica's music producers that auditions were held, usually on a weekly basis, to find new talent. Kingston's cut-throat music industry survived on fresh sounds – the next best thing – and any youth who promised to give one producer an edge over the others was destined for an audition. The level of competition among studios was heated. Besides being on the look-out for new vocal talent, studios also encouraged new sounds from their musicians. This is how Sly Dunbar, for instance, came up with the popular "rockers" drumbeat in the mid-1970s to help Channel One compete against Bunny Lee's "flying cymbal" sound (Sly Dunbar, interview by author, 4 September 2006).

By this time, Winston had deejayed and sung in front of friends enough that he felt he could audition at one of these studios. Knowing that this was how the industry worked, Winston went in search of producers.

Before I start deejaying in dance and stage show and doing recording, I used to go to every studio back in the late 1970s coming into the 1980s. All those studio, I go to all of dem: Harry J, I go to Channel One, Joe Gibbs, Music Works. I go to Dynamic Sound, Sonic Sound, Aquarius. I go to a lot of studio and they turn me away. Some even beat me, whoop me ass, man, ya. Like they say, what me a doing there? [They] come out and kick [me].

Studios employed muscle to keep out the riff-raff. They would reject Winston and use racial slurs that emphasized his lack of blackness like "white man", "dundus", "Molotov", "red bwoy", "red dog" and "yellow dog". "Those days racism was in the sky high", he remembers. "They think that a person like me wouldn't sell [records] or wouldn't make it." Studios told him that a dundus could never have the talent needed to sing on record, implying that he was worthless to them and society: "I would go to Joe Gibbs and I would say, 'I am a artist and my name is Yellowman¹ and I would like to do a song for you.' And him say, 'Who you? Man like you can't do song.' And then the other artists would jump on me and kick me out. Not Joe Gibbs himself, but he's the one who instigate it." Despite this rejection wherever he went, Winston's resolve remained firm: "Maybe because I'm strong, maybe because I have a strong mind and a will power, you know? There's something that God give me, you know? 'Cause I never give up on anything if I set out for that." The beatings would take their toll, though. Today his face is disfigured, mainly due to operations to remove cancerous tumours in his neck, head and jaw, but he feels that the many beatings he took to his head and face have also contributed to it. "I got a lot of beat up", he says, "I got hit in my face and my head." But "I never considered it serious [at the time]", and so never went to a doctor or hospital for treatment. Instead, it was all part of growing up scorned in the ghetto.

SOUND SYSTEM CULTURE

Winston could hear sound systems and radios playing reggae music made by other youths who also had the odds stacked against them. Kingston was filled with sound systems, each drawing dancers and music lovers to both indoor and outdoor venues that were more affordable than live music concerts.

Thousands of dance goers would turn out weekly, especially from Friday evening to Sunday morning to dancehalls and lawns and other ritualised dance spaces across Jamaica. From an iconic venue such as Forrester's Hall at Love Lane and North Street, Kingston, to the ubiquitous zinc or bamboo, or coconut frond (or any combination of these) enclosed space with or without a roof annexed to a rum bar or by itself, dancehalls sprang up in large numbers across Jamaica, signalling the making of a cultural revolution that was to have a profound ontological impact on Jamaica and the world. (Hutton 2007a, 18)

The deejay style started with emcees in the 1950s filling the gap between record changeovers – sound systems had only one turntable in those days – and lulls in a song by jive talking announcements like American radio deejays, introducing songs and improvising banter. Count Machuki (aka Winston Cooper) was the first person to talk over records, or "toast" or "chat" as it is known in Jamaica, on 26 December 1950 at a dance run by renowned sound system operator Tom the Great Sebastian. "Machuki began the tradition of Jamaican deejaying adding his own vocal inflections to cover any dips in a record's energy" (Salewicz and Boot 2001, 16). The practice became an art form in its own right as other aspiring deejays picked up on Machuki's new trend. By the 1960s, King Stitt would be the first deejay to release a record and by the end of the decade U-Roy would revolutionize the art form and set the template for dancehall reggae and, ultimately, Yellowman. U-Roy had worked for Coxsone's Downbeat sound system as a secondary deejay but it was with King Tubby's Home-Town Hi-Fi that he enjoyed the most success. Tubby was a gifted producer and innovative technician. The studio experiments of Tubby and a few others of dropping out the vocals and re-mixing the instruments became known as dub. It was Tubby who first added echo and reverb to a deejay's voice – something that quickly became a mainstay in the dance – and part of U-Roy's mystique was the sound of his words echoing. U-Roy started recording with Lee Perry and Keith Hudson, but went on to chart with records cut at Duke Reid's Treasure Isle studio. In 1969, he had three records in the top spots on the radio charts: "Wear You to the Ball", "Wake the Town" and "Rule the Nation".

As Yellowman started trying to gain access to the sound system culture in the late 1970s, one of the biggest stars of the deejay scene was Studio One's Lone Ranger (b. Anthony Waldron). Lone Ranger is something of a template for Yellowman. Not only was Yellowman heavily influenced by his style and lyrics, Lone Ranger was one of the first deejays to make a splash on the international stage, a stage Yellowman would one day dominate.

Lone Ranger was part of Clement "Coxsone" Dodd's last great surge of talent in the late 1970s, before he moved his operations to New York. Dodd, who had been one of the top producers from ska's advent into the early 1970s, was losing ground to other studios, particularly Channel One, which churned out hit after hit in the deejay and dancehall styles. Dodd fought back with a clutch of records in the burgeoning dancehall style by artists like Michigan and Smiley (*Rub a Dub Style*) and Lone Ranger (*On the Other Side of Dub*).

Lone Ranger was the resident deejay on Virgo Hi-Fi. His humorous lyrics and penchant for injecting scat-like noises such as *rybit, oink* or *bim* would be picked up by others, especially Eek-A-Mouse, Yellowman and Fathead. Lone Ranger and General Echo did more than any other deejay previous to Yellowman to shift the focus of reggae away from "the cultural chants of the mid-1970s, as exemplified by Big Youth, to pure 1980s dancehall chat" (Barrow and Dalton 2004, 255). Bradley (2001) suggests that Lone Ranger's new style was adopted from his British upbringing where he would have witnessed deejays such as Clint Eastwood and General Saint, Papa Levi, Peter King, and Tippa Irie on sound systems like Front Line International and Saxon. The British deejay style put more emphasis on entertaining a crowd and altered the delivery of the lyrics by speeding them up. The widespread influence of this new style reflected the "liberating atmosphere of 1980s dancehall [where] it was remembered that the primary purpose of going out was to enjoy yourself" (Bradley 2001, 506). This was a purpose that Yellowman would embody as much as anyone else.

Lone Ranger's work with Studio One produced dancehall's biggest hits in 1979, such as "Never Let Go" and "The Answer", and he went on to reach #1 on the British reggae charts with the song "Barnabas Collins", inspired by a vampire character on the American television show *Dark Shadows*. While his album *Barnabas in Collins Wood* was recorded by Alvin Ranglin, Lone Ranger returned to Dodd's studio for hits with "Love Bump", "Natty Chalwa" and "Tribute to Marley" and his subsequent work for Channel One, such as "M16", remain classics in the dancehall. Lone Ranger's dominance in dancehall in those few years would wane as new artists like Yellowman, Welton Irie, Eek-A-Mouse and Josey Wales would take his place at the top.

Lone Ranger opened the door to a new era of music that celebrated good times and proved that there was an international audience ready and willing to get behind the new music genre called dancehall. Yellowman is considered the deejay who popularized dancehall globally, but Lone Ranger had made important international strides before this. Yellowman would learn from Lone Ranger, even adopting much of the deejay's stylistic and thematic oeuvre, and open up dancehall to legions of fans around the globe.

When deejays first started, they were seen by musicians as gimmicky street-level performers who were not serious, but by the late 1970s deejays were starting to overtake singers as the most popular entertainers on the island. And the sound system was the reason for this – sound systems were the domain of the deejay, not the singer.

Sound systems played the same role that radio historically played in North America and the United Kingdom – they gave new artists exposure and had the potential to launch careers. American music journalist Lester Bangs, writing in 1976, was surprised at the state of Jamaican radio when he visited the island to interview Bob Marley: "Jamaican AM radio almost never plays reggae. After a week of very little beyond Helen Reddy and Neil Diamond, I would be anxious to get the hell out of this place and back home just so I could hear some Toots and the Maytals" (2004, 52–53).

Yellowman credits the sound systems for giving him his break. They drew their audience by playing popular songs or exclusive dubplates recorded by singers specifically for that sound, having good quality equipment and boasting the best deejays who would perform live.[2] A popular sound would not only have a recognized deejay, it would also receive pre-release copies of newly recorded material from the island's top producers. This way, the new songs gained exposure and feedback in the dance, and the sound could attract patrons who knew they would hear fresh material on any given night – songs that were not yet available in the record shops.

Typically, the sound's selector would spin a record of a popular song by a singer or vocal group, such as Dennis Brown, Alton Ellis, Bob Marley, the Mighty Diamonds, the Heptones or Sugar Minott, and then, after it finished, they would play an instrumental version of the song (called riddim, dub or simply version). Deejays would then chat lyrics over the instrumental. Riddim tracks were geared towards deejays who could improvise lyrics on the spot and they kept a running competition to one-up each other with the best lyrics. While sound systems were the venue of the live deejay, some sounds did carry a resident singer as well. Deejays were selling records by this time but the excitement of seeing them improvise in the dance added to the dancehall experience. The deejays might not know what riddim was coming next or might have an unknown sparring partner on stage to interact with. This established a culture of spontaneous creativity where an artist could potentially present a different performance every night.

Initially sound systems in those days would only have one resident deejay, but sometimes that deejay might bring an apprentice on stage. A dance could start as early as seven in the evening and not finish until the sun came up the next day. And a deejay would be expected to entertain for the entire night, pausing while the singer's version of a song played on the turntable – or interjecting lyrics between the phrases if the mood seemed right – and only given breaks when aspiring local talent would fill in. Deejays had to be versatile to keep an audience interested, both in musical style and content. As deejay Burro Banton put it: "Sometime you have fe go like a preacher, and next time you have fe go for the girls" (Burro Banton quoted in Stolzoff 2000, 99).

The sound systems also acted as an audition ground for record producers. If a producer came to a dance and liked what a deejay was doing, he would offer to take them into the studio and put it on record. Yellowman remembers that "all the producers used to come, like Sly and Robbie and people like Gussie Clark, Junjo, Black Scorpio, Jammy's, Tubby. All a dem used to come, all the producers used to come in de dance" (interview by Joshua Chamberlain, 17 January 2007). For a deejay like Yellowman, the sound systems were also a venue to practise new lyrics in front of a discerning crowd. Many of his early songs were worked out live in front of an audience long before they were committed to record. But in 1977 Winston Foster had not yet performed for anyone outside of his circle of friends. All that was about to change.

LITTLE MAFIA

Since it was Winston's body and not his voice that was his impediment, his next plan of action would prove to be ingenious. The studios did not want him because their eyes told them he was probably worthless before they even got a chance to hear him deejay. What he needed were critics who could vote with their ears. He found those critics at the nightly sound systems. Sound system operators were interested in any artist who could keep the fickle crowds entertained. Unlike at the studios, a would-be deejay had a chance to show the sound's operator right away if he or she could please the public. In order to break a song, producers would have to pay for studio time (including in many cases a band, an engineer and tape), pay to manufacture a record, then use their sound system connections to get the new disc heard on a popular sound just to see if the public liked it. Many producers owned studios and/or sound systems but there was still an element of risk involved in the outlay of money to an engineer, band and record manufacturer. They had to invest considerably more time and money in an unestablished artist than did the independent sound system operator who could try out budding artists for free and decide only after he heard the crowd's response if the new artist had staying power. For Winston, there was an added bonus: sound systems operated in the dark at night, so artists who got a chance on the microphone were not in the public eye. In fact, deejays in those days rarely interacted with the crowd and many faced the selector, not the audience. Beth Lesser, a Canadian photographer, journalist and author who covered dancehall for *Reggae Quarterly*, confirms this:

> People weren't watching the deejays. If you go back before everybody started going on stage shows and making videos and doing everything for the camera, back before that, it was just dark. It's actually such an interesting experience to be at one of those old dances because it is just so totally foreign. It's not like anything you've ever seen in Canada or the United States. It's dark and you just feel the music. You dance or stand there and just listen. It's totally an aural experience. (Interview by author, 21 January 2009)

So, to give a dundus a chance at the microphone was less costly financially and socially than to give him a chance in the studio. Thanks to a connection, one sound system let Winston try his hand at the microphone.

Winston started his deejay career in 1977 at age twenty on a small local sound called Little Mafia that used to operate in the Barbican neighbourhood of Kingston.[3] He began deejaying simply under the name Winston. Yellowman insists he had never been to a sound system dance previously, aside from the one at Alpha. The first time he attended a real Kingston sound system was with the intention of performing on it. He had a friend who lived in Franklin Town, and whose daughter's babyfather was Tony Mafia, owner of Little Mafia. This was the connection Winston needed to get on the microphone in front of people. The problem was, even though Tony Mafia agreed to let Winston deejay as a favour to his babymother, he made sure it was after the crowd had left for the night. Yellowman recalls, "I used to only get the mic when the dance was over, when everybody leave, like when them packing up, like two minutes before them pack up when there was no crowd there. They don't put me on until everybody leave. That's way in the morning in daylight, when they packing up. [But] I keep on going there."

Hoping for a break, Winston returned again and again to Little Mafia but Tony only let him take the microphone after the main deejays were done and the crowd had thinned. Little Mafia was not a big sound; it was what is known as a house set with only small speakers, not the type of sound that could shake the neighbourhood with rumbling bass. But this is where Winston found a sympathetic soundman and this is where he would begin to win over the dancehall audience.

Now that he was actively trying to break into the dancehall scene, Winston started visiting other sound systems and checking out other dances. He remembers seeing his first deejay clash between Jah Love sound system with Brigadier Jerry and Stereophonic sound system with General Echo at Half Way Tree (Yellowman, interview by Joshua Chamberlain, Kingston, 17 January 2007).

Winston returned to Little Mafia five or six times and the same thing occurred; the main deejay would perform while the crowd was present and a few minutes before packing up Tony would let Winston take a turn. Deejaying to an almost nonexistent audience would not last long, however. After several attempts to get Tony Mafia to put him on earlier in the night, it was the tiny crowd's reaction that convinced the soundman to try Winston out in front of a larger audience. He says, "The people who used to stay used to talk in the streets, so it start getting to everybody ears. They hear because they used to tape cassettes. One night the guy who deejay right through the night – they said no, they want to hear me, they don't want to hear him anymore. That's when I get my big chance. I do that for a couple of years." The way Yellowman tells it, his initial rise in dancehall was organic and based on word of mouth and bootlegged cassette tapes that floated around Kingston in the days after a dance. A few people who heard him at the end of each night told their friends until enough people wanted to hear him during the main part of the entertainment. When he was able to show off for a crowd, he was a hit.

The exact chain of events here is murky. The liner notes to *Live at Reggae Sunsplash* (1983b) say that the first time Yellowman deejayed in front of people, the crowd pointed fingers at him and laughed, shouting "dundus come off". Yellowman himself has offered two versions of this story, and both deny that this happened in this way. He has said that the first time he took hold of the microphone he expected boos, "but they don't start pointing finger, you know?" The second agrees that there were fingers pointing at him but offers a different explanation as to why: "That's when everybody start pointing finger at we, you know? Like they say that guy going to be something".

Perhaps this story has been confused with another instance that occurred not long after Winston's first stint at Little Mafia. As the popularity of his weekly deejaying at Little Mafia grew, so did his opportunities. One night after the show he was approached by the owner of a club called Spanish Jar on Orange Street. Soon Winston was booked to play his first stage show or club gig. At sound systems, the deejay talks over records and often there is no stage to speak of, just a little standing room near the selector. At a stage show, Yellowman would have to perform with a live band for the first time on a stage. When he walked onto the stage at Spanish Jar, he started deejaying about bad-boy General Starkey and then broke into one of his signature tunes: "I'm Getting Married", a deejay version of the "Take Me to the Church on Time". Usually this went over well with the Little Mafia crowd, but there was a problem this time; people starting booing. While it is possible that the booing was racially motivated because of Yellowman's skin colour, Yellowman insists that this was a political act. The song mentions church bells ("Ding dong the bells are going to chime") and as the bell is the symbol of the JLP,[4] the crowd assumed he was singing a political song. Political parties were in the habit of taking popular reggae songs and putting their own lyrics to them, just as some artists outrightly supported one or the other party in their songs. This was a dangerous occupation in Kingston, and there were producers and artists who had to leave the island because their songs got used that way (Beth Lesser, interview by author, 21 January 2009).

It is possible that these versions of events are meant to show Yellowman in a better light by proving that his talent was recognizable immediately.

It is certainly plausible, given the way he was treated as a dundus growing up, though, that early crowds did indeed laugh at him and call him off the stage, just as studio owners kicked him out of their auditions.

There are other layers to the story as well. Yellowman is adamant that the crowd at Little Mafia liked him immediately and showed no prejudice against him. There is a good reason to believe this is true – the crowd at a dance would not have been able to see what he looked like. Small sound systems had no stages for a deejay to stand on. Deejays would often face the selector, not the audience, or even remain completely behind the sound console blocked from view. The implication of this cannot be overstated – the Little Mafia crowd only heard Winston's voice and, because they could not see him, their evaluations of his deejay skills were not negatively affected by any prejudices they may have harboured against his appearance.

> Author: So, at this point at Barbican, [the audience] couldn't see you, is this right?
>
> Yellowman: Right, they couldn't see me.
>
> Author: So, they didn't know what you looked like. Is this partly why you became popular, do you think?
>
> Yellowman: Ya man, the voice, the voice was very good on the mic. It sound good.
>
> Author: I would think as a studio owner it would be the same thing.
>
> Yellowman: Ya, it's the same thing but because they think that a person like me wouldn't sell or wouldn't make it.
>
> Author: So they were prejudiced because of that?
>
> Yellowman: Right, and remember, those days racism was in the sky, high.
>
> Author: So, then the sound guys could try you out on the mic to see if you were any good.
>
> Yellowman: Right. Ya, ya.

Later Yellowman would be among the pioneers who treated the dancehall space like a stage show, aware that his visual presence in front of an audience could carry a dramatic effect. Drummer Sly Dunbar and Owen "Willa" Robinson, a "box man"[5] for Aces International sound system, corroborate this (Sly Dunbar, interview by author, 23 February 2009; Owen "Willa" Robinson, interview by author, 21 February 2009). Both have said that Yellowman was the first deejay they saw to turn and face the audience. Deejays like Brigadier

Jerry, even though he was one of Jamaica's most popular deejays at the time, used to face the selector and have his back to the crowd. Eventually Yellowman turned the dancehall deejay role into a visual performance by dressing up for it and deejaying to the audience just as a singer would direct their performance at the listeners. The element of "performance" shifted from just a vocal performance to a full-body aural and visual performance. Yellowman saw that his role as a deejay was no different from that of a singer – he was there to entertain the audience. He craved the positive attention that comes with being adored onstage and probably thought it odd that the other deejays hid from the audience. He would later tell a journalist that he preferred doing stage shows over sound systems because he liked people to be able to see him – this was a far cry from where he began (Saunders 1983). For now, it is not hard to imagine that the young person with albinism was only interested in proving he could deejay and was thankful that he could do it in the dark.

FULL UP A LYRICS

> A ram Yellow come a fe ram it
> Kaa Yellowman him no chat it with 'prentice[6]
> Kaa Yellowman him full up a lyrics
> —Yellowman, "Who Can Make the Dance Ram?" (1983e)

Yellowman insists that he never rehearsed lyrics before arriving at a sound system and at times he told me that his first attempt to make up lyrics was actually on stage at Little Mafia. In a culture where credibility is gained by a deejay's ability to improvise and remember their lyrics without ever writing them down, Yellowman's talent has become legendary. Producers I have spoken to agree that he often recorded an entire album in one session without prepared lyrics. Paul Wexler (2001), in the liner notes of the VP compilation *Look How Me Sexy*, states that "Yellowman's ability to freestyle, or compose and perform songs off of the top of his head, remains the stuff of reggae legend to this day". He quotes producer Lloyd Campbell as an example: "Yellowman went into Tuff Gong Studios and voiced 30 songs straight. . . . Yellowman didn't repeat one line twice in any song, he wasn't checking for anything on paper; it was all just coming out of his head like a computer."

Yellowman tells the story of recording two tracks for the *King Yellowman* (1984a) album, "Disco Reggae" and "Strong Me Strong", in New York for producer Bill Laswell. Laswell brought Herbie Hancock into the studio for the session and both watched Yellowman as a riddim tape was cued up for him to deejay over. The way Yellow tells it, both men were amazed that he could cut the tracks in one take each, without ever hearing the riddim before. This may seem far-fetched to the uninitiated, but in dancehall this is the norm. Songs like "Zungguzungguguzungguzeng", "I'm Getting Married", and "Body Move" were all recorded in one take. He might arrive at the studio with an idea for a story, but the lyrics "just flow" once the riddim starts rolling.

This narrative does not take into account, however, that often the songs recorded in the studio had already been worked out live in the dance. In an interview with Beth Lesser, Yellowman boasted about his skill at improvising lyrics: "If you love it, it's easy! You only want to have lyrics and long remembrance. If you good, you know, you have lyrics come straight to you in the dance" (Yellowman 1982, 8). He told another interviewer in 1986, "I don't really write songs – I collect phrases. I always have a different idea in music, so it's never too difficult to come up with new things. From coming up in the sound systems I have that idea, to pick out a little lyric by Gladys Knight or Teddy Pendergrass or Sam Cooke and put it into reggae, so people can be familiar with it" ("Overcomes Affliction: Yellowman Rippin' 'n' Rappin' Again", *Los Angeles Times*, 15 October 1986). This skill applies to live performance and the studio equally: "Most of the lyrics I do on record, is in the studio I make them up. Like 'I'm Getting Married'. Junjo just call me and say I must do an album and I just listen to the rhythms and the lyrics come to me" (Yellowman 1982, 8).

He told me, however, that he used to deejay "I'm Getting Married" live before this. This discrepancy is like the finger pointing incident above. It may be a case of misremembering, or it could be an example of boasting that is part of deejay culture. Many of Yellowman's lyrics are filled with self-praise and braggadocio. His stories about his own life follow suit. The exact song in this scenario is not as important to him as making the point that he possesses special skills.

Going along with not rehearsing or composing, Yellowman says he has never written down a lyric, either before a performance or even after in the interest of remembering it. When he records or performs, he says his lyrics come to him "on the spot: even up 'til now I don't write song. I just build a story and that's it." In my experience, his memory for lyrics is incredible. On numerous occasions I have asked him to clarify a particular lyric from a song recorded in the early 1980s. Typically he may say that he never performed that song after voicing it in the studio, or "I do a lot of songs that I don't even hear after", and ask me to play him a bit of it so he can remember what it sounds like. I then play him a clip of the song on my laptop and after hearing the first line Yellowman can deejay the entire song, word for word.

Whether the lyrics were made up earlier and mentally rehearsed is not really debated. What matters is that the deejay can arrive at the mic, without paper and pen, and appear to extemporize for the entertainment of the audience. A deejay must also be ready to chat lyrics at a moment's notice. Ninjaman's manager insisted her client could be woken out of a deep slumber and be ready to deejay masterfully in an instant (Stolzoff 2000). This skill is one of the deejay's ultimate weapons to stay on top and Yellowman's insistence that he had this ability the first time he walked onto a stage should be read in this context.

I had a confusing conversation about this very thing with Yellowman during the winter of 2009 when I tried to determine when he started making up lyrics. When we got on the subject of that first Little Mafia appearance, I assumed that he must have had lyrics ready for the occasion and that, like any musician, he had practised his "set" at home before arriving at the dance. Here is the conversation we had, a discussion that in retrospect shows my own ignorance about the deejay trade and just how stuck I was in non-dancehall forms of thinking about performance and music:

Author: When did you start making up lyrics?

Yellowman: Dance.

[My notes from my transcription journal are informative here: "Yellowman says this with an 'obviously stupid – where did you think I started?' tone."]

Author: In the dance? You didn't make up any lyrics before you went to a dance?

Yellowman: No, right there in the dance. I was so, I am so versatile that I can look at a bag and deejay about it.

Author: But you must have been practising this at home?

Yellowman: No, never. That's the reason why I can do two album in one day.

Author: You didn't have to practise your trade before going in public?

Yellowman: No, that's different. That's the reason why I'm so great. Bekaa none of these songs I do – they're my songs but I don't write, put pen to paper. I just go to a studio and they play de riddim and I make up a lyrics.

Author: But back at Eventide were you singing and deejaying to people?

Yellowman: Ya, but it was my lyrics.

Author: That's what I'm trying to figure out. You were deejaying lyrics, making up lyrics, before you went to Little Mafia?

Yellowman: Ya, right. But the lyrics I deejay at Likkle [Little] Mafia, it weren't the lyrics I sing before.

Author: So you didn't practise [specific] lyrics?

Yellowman: No.

At this point I asked Yellowman when he started making up lyrics. He answered that this probably occurred at Alpha Boys' School in the early 1970s where he would deejay as a friend would beat out a rhythm on a makeshift drum.

Author: So, you would have been practising your style at Alpha?

Yellowman: Not really practising, you know, just deejaying. Like a guy would come to me and say, "Yellow, sing a song fe me", and me just deejay a song.

Author: Sing and deejay or just deejay?

Yellowman: Sometimes sing a Sam Cooke or a Fats Domino, or a Dennis Brown, or a Bob Marley, or a Burning Spear song or a Jimmy Cliff, you know?

Author: So, when you go to Little Mafia you don't have any lyrics in your head?

Yellowman: No.

Author: And is that the first time you're actually on a microphone?

Yellowman: Ya, first time.

Author: What did you deejay about? Can you remember?

Yellowman: No, can't remember because the riddim played and I just deejay.

The above conversation eventually reveals that Yellowman had been "writing" lyrics since he was at school but that he is careful to distinguish between his ability to mentally compose and ever putting words on paper, and never uses the term "practice", whether it refers to lyrical content or style. Practice in this context would insinuate that his talent is not innate, that it has to be developed. Authenticity in dancehall, like hip-hop, is garnered in the ability to demonstrate innate skill manifested in one's freestyling prowess. Deejays have to be ready for battle at any moment and their credibility increases if their talent is seen as a natural part of their character, as opposed to a rehearsed act that is performed at a specific time and place.

Stolzoff's (2000) revealing ethnography of the deejay and sound system culture in Kingston in the 1990s provides a further example of this. Aspiring deejays and singers attempt to break into the market by hanging outside studios and hustling soundmen and producers for an audition to buy their latest song. Every day the entertainers need to convince studios, soundmen, producers, and famous deejays of their talent in order to get a chance to go from street corner hustler to, potentially, dancehall superstar. Two of the tools budding entertainers use to draw attention to themselves and distinguish themselves from the fray are profiling and flexing. Profiling is "the practice of showing off through conspicuous display" or "acting the part of the dancehall entertainer" (134) whereas "flexing requires that one be able to seize the moment. For example, when a soundman drives up, these entertainers need to be ready in an instant to convince him to record their songs" (137). Entertainers need to always project confidence and be ready to perform in an instant in an industry where a chance to audition may be fleeting. Like Ninjaman, Yellowman is ready – and perhaps more importantly, needs to appear ready – at any time to shift from sleep to deejay mode, or to open his mouth and extemporize a lyric in the studio or on stage.

After listening to countless hours of Yellowman deejaying, both live and on record, I have come to understand that when he says he had no complete lyrics prepared in advance before that first show, he meant it. However, like a jazz musician improvising a solo over a well-known chord progression, Yellowman has several lyrics and thematic riffs that he often returns to. We do not know the content of that first night's songs but, judging by live dancehall tapes in those early years, he probably had already started to develop his arsenal of lyrical riffs that he could pull out extemporaneously and mix in with any subject he chose to deejay about – be it a paper bag or some character in the dance. Lyrical riffs that are repeated in several of his songs include "Love girl fat a me no love dem slim / When dem fat they run your body hot / When dem slim they give you everything", "Lie down pon a riddim like a lizard pon limb", and "Natty sat upon the rock and watch the wicked dem drop." There are dozens more phrases that Yellowman employs in several songs, and he often subtly alters the wording and meaning of the phrase to fit each new song and circumstance.

In some artistic contexts, Yellowman's bragging would be seen as pretentious. In dancehall, though, it is part of the culture of competition, which in itself is an exercise in exaggerated masculinity. There is a tradition among dancehall artists similar to woofing (boasting) and signifying (insulting) in American rap, where a deejay brags about their own skill (whether it be on the microphone, in the bedroom, or earning money) at the expense of their rivals. Yellowman's songs often position himself as the most popular deejay with the most girlfriends, the power to earn the most money, and the most highly skilled, whereas his rivals come off as underlings. This theme plays out in songs like "Society Party" (1984e), "Who Can Make the Dance Ram?" (1983e), and "Zungguzungguguzungguzeng" (the latter with the hilarious lyric "Tell yuh Yellow voice it sound like FM / The other rest of voice sound like AM" [1983e]).

Braggadocio is as central to Yellowman's music as it is to his life. One of the recurring themes of this book is that Yellowman had to convince his audience of his worth as a person and a deejay. One of the ways this occurs is through convincing his listeners that he is a not only a good deejay, but the king of deejays due to his natural talent. He had started to do that on Little Mafia in 1977, but in order to truly succeed, he also needed to win over the music industry.

FROM WINSTON FOSTER TO RANKING DUNDUS TO YELLOWMAN

Hi, my name is Yellowman
And down in Jamaica they call me Mr Sexy
—Yellowman, "Mad over Me" (1982g)

Winston deejayed at Little Mafia on weekends, at first under his own name, Winston Foster, and made sure he kept the fact that he was living at Eventide a secret so that the stigma would not plague him. He eventually branched out from Little Mafia and made the rounds to several sound systems, such as Gemini and Virgo, attempting to get his name out. As he began to gain a reputation on the sound systems, it was inevitable that the audience would notice his unique complexion.

> Author: What happened when people started to see you?
>
> Yellowman: That's when the people surprised and the colour thing became, like they want to see who is this man. Because in those days I sound like a big, big man because I have a big voice but I have a little body.
>
> Author: But you were tall.
>
> Yellowman: Ya, but the body, you know. And they was fascinated by that and surprised, you know? And then my type of people never used to come out, they always hiding. But after me come out you have albino doctors, police, lawyers, entertainers.

Soon, after people realized the deejay they were listening to had albinism, they started calling him Ranking Dundus, an ironic pairing of terms since ranking in Jamaica means "top rank" and dundus connotes worthlessness or bottom rank.

The name Ranking Dundus would not last long. As a defiant symbol of self-pride in his deejay abilities and his skin colour, Winston started wearing all-yellow outfits and wholeheartedly accepted yellow as a symbol of strength: "I start walking in the street wearing yellow tings, yellow clothes, eat yellow things." As Winston became known in the dancehall people in the neighbourhood around Eventide began to recognize him in the street and started calling him "yellow man". "And I say, 'Ya, that's a good name. Yellow submarine, Yellowman, ya.' So it would be a popular name, you know?" The name stuck and Yellowman soon embodied the new persona, often wearing a yellow derby hat seen on the front of albums like *Live at Aces* (1982b). A few years later, when producer Junjo Lawes gave him his first car, a BMW, he even had it painted yellow.

Jamaican music has a long history of noms de plume but dancehall artists have embraced the practice to a much greater extent than their mento, ska, rocksteady and reggae forebears. While many would continue the male Jamaican youth culture's love of Hollywood westerns (Josey Wales, Clint Eastwood, Lone Ranger) or choose stage names that either suggested their microphone dominating status (Super Black, Ranking Toyan, Admiral Bailey, Major Worries, Brigadier Jerry, Dr Alimantado, Lieutenant Stitchie, Prince Jazzbo, Shabba Ranks, Cutty Ranks) or their allegiance to Rastafari (Jah Thomas, Jah Stitch, Jah Rubel, Prince Far I), Yellowman's name was as unique as it was appealing in a self-depreciating sort of way. No other entertainers with albinism had been welcomed on sound system stages and now here was this one banking on his albinism to create hype for his stage act. Soon other deejays with albinism would follow suit, such as King Mellow Yellow and Purpleman. Unlike calypsonians, whose sobriquets were designed to show grandeur (Mighty Sparrow, Lord Kitchener, Atilla the Hun), there was a tradition among reggae artists to progress from a humbler name, say Prince Jammy, to a regal name – King Jammy – only when the title was deserved. Yellowman underwent a similar progression. In 1982, he released an album *Mister Yellowman* (1982d), but 1984 brought *King Yellowman* (1984a), a name he has used since the Jamaican press dubbed him King of the Dancehall in the wake of an historic performance at Reggae Sunsplash 1982.[7]

THE DEEJAY TRADE

> Who can make the dance ram? Who can make the dance ram?
> Who can make it cork? Who can make it cork?
> No other deejay in dis island, ongle [only] Yellowman can, Yellowman can
> Who can make the dub play? Who can make the dub play?
> Night and day, night and day
> No other sound in dis island ongle my sound can, de champion
> —Yellowman, "Who Can Make the Dance Ram?" (1983e)

As he gained experience and absorbed influences from other deejays, Yellowman's repertoire of lyrics, vocal styles, jokes and antics quickly grew. One reason Yellowman was able to rise to the top and remain a popular deejay for so long was that he had a versatility rarely seen at that point. While other deejays stuck to one or two styles, Yellowman was able to mimic the slower "rootsier" style of older deejays like Big Youth but also chat faster like British deejays. Whereas pioneers like U-Roy excelled at interjecting short lyrical bursts in between vocal lines, General Echo and Lone Ranger added narrative to deejay lyrics, telling full-blown stories and developing narrative arcs over several songs. Yellowman learned from this and became adept at the practice. His "I'm Getting Married" (1982g) or "Mister Chin" (1982d) drew on cultural tropes that every Jamaican knew and understood and he weaved them into humorous stories. It is no wonder these songs have remained two of his most loved. Yellowman also peppered his sets with alternative vocal styles. He claims to be the first deejay to introduce a sung chorus into a deejay track. He built up a repertoire of American R&B, soul, and country and western songs that he would extemporaneously break into amidst a deejay set. Yellowman's song "Love Struck" (1982f), for instance, is built on the melody and lyrics of Ray Charles's "Hallelujah, I Love Her So". And crowds went wild when he sang Sam Cook's "Bring it on Home", which he broke into on several of his recorded tracks.

He could also dip into the "rock-stone", gravelly voice, turn around and chat in a sweet lighter voice or interject Lone Ranger–style scats like "bim", "bong" or "brrrrrring". Yellowman was conscious, too, of not being contained within one genre. Many deejays, for instance, only chatted Rasta-centric material, just as many singers only sang love songs. Yellowman crafted his talent in such a way as to foster versatility and his repertoire shows this. His live shows and albums routinely feature a mix of culture and slack songs, love songs and political songs, humorous songs and serious songs, covers and originals, roots reggae and dancehall. The guiding agenda behind this was simple: Yellowman wanted to please everyone. He desperately wanted fans and admirers, and he wanted to belong. Growing up shunned and scorned had a profound effect on him psychologically. He longed to be the centre of attention and would do anything to achieve that.

YELLOWMAN ON RACE

Yellowman's use of humour went a long way to endearing him to the public and using the stage name Yellowman was probably an extension of this humour. That sense of humour was also one of the main reasons a deejay with albinism could get away with (a) performing on stage at all, and (b) performing slackness. There was always a sense that Yellowman was in on the joke that here was a deejay with albinism fashioning himself as a sex symbol when everyone knew this is a ridiculous thing. He played off people's fascination with the spectacle of freakishness he presented to them onstage and gradually convinced them that a dundus was not a freak, through sheer exposure, humour and the ability to bridge racial difference.

Called the "floating signifier" by Stuart Hall (1997), the idea of race is problematic, to be sure, especially in this context. A social construct though it is, race in the Jamaican context has been defined in European terms by focusing on physical differences of hair, skin, and body. This is to say nothing of the role that race has historically played in identity. In reggae discourse, as in other cultural arenas, race is often reduced to skin colour: black or white, and their accepted amalgams which have, historically, included categories such as mulatto. One of the problems of social acceptance for the dundus is that yellow skin is not included in the colonial-derived categories of "white" and "black" as racial signifiers.

Yellowman's thoughts on race are notable for their selective framing. In many of our conversations, and indeed in published interviews and songs, he clearly presents the narrative of being discriminated against due to his albinism. When he talks of being subjected to racism, he is defining race based on skin colour, which is yellow. Yet in many of our discussions he spoke about his colour as "high colour". This is a term that designates light skin in Jamaica, though as demonstrated in the conversation below, the term also connotes upper class. It is doubtful that during his youth anyone would have associated him with upper-class privilege normally attributed to lighter-skinned Jamaicans. When I asked Yellowman about the reaction of early crowds to his slack lyrics, he responded, "Because of my colour it was very fascinating to the people, like a man like me, high colour, doing that type of lyrics. . . . They say a guy like me with such a high colour would be doing society lyrics, like clean lyrics for the uptown people. But I doing it like a street, for the street. Dancehall is street, just like rap, because rap comes from dancehall."

The reaction of the crowds was clearly fascination and for Yellowman this fascination had to do with crossing class boundaries – an uptown deejay chatting rude songs. Others I interviewed suggest, though, that this fascination had more to do with the fact that it was socially unacceptable for a dundus to be performing at all, not a high-coloured deejay performing street lyrics. I asked Desmond Gaynor, Yellowman's drummer in Sagittarius since 1982, about this backstage at the B.B. King Blues Club in 2008:

Desmond Gaynor: It was the first time in Jamaica we had an albino [in public]. Albino was like a reject, unacceptable in human society because of his difference. Any albino was seen as different. He don't look the same. And part of his success at the beginning was because of his uniqueness – that he was an albino. And everybody wanted to see who this albino was. When he started out in the dancehall, everybody went ahead of him when the hosting of the deejay thing was going on. And he was the last to hold onto the mic because nobody wanted to use the mic after him.

Author: Was the audience the same way or did they treat him better?

DG: Even audience had prejudice.

Author: Did you go to those shows?

DG: I went to one or two. Nobody would give him the mic and he was there up front trying to hold onto the mic and he was shoved aside. And when the time came and he started doing his lyrics everybody started listening. But he was still cast aside 'cause he didn't fit into the scheme of things. They call him Ranking Dundus.

Author: Did he win over an audience?

DG: Yes, he won them over because his lyrical content was different.

Author: How?

DG: It was entertaining, it was funny. He would use any simple situation and make it hilarious. And because it was funny people started listening.

Author: Did he poke fun at himself? Was in on the joke?

DG: Yes, because he didn't have a problem with it. Because fun has been poked at him since he was a child, and he accepted that 'cause he can't change it.

Author: Would people see Yellowman as a black man or not?

DG: People have mixed feelings about that. They can't identify Yellowman as a particular race, he's just an albino. (Interview by author, 12 August 2008)

Race and colour were social constructs that were constantly reified throughout Yellowman's life. Names like "whiteman", "yellowman", "redboy" reinforced that he stood outside of mainstream blackness. In part 2, I return to this discussion of race and show how Yellowman plays with the concept to suggest at times that he is white (or high-colour), black, yellow, or some combination of all three. Further, his deconstruction of simply black/

white racial binaries allowed him to dismantle the otherness associated with albinism and problematize any insinuation that he was without race. Even today, he often does not identify as a specific racial category, preferring to trump categories based on colour with humanity: "I consider myself both [black and white]. Most of my audience is white and black and Hispanic. I wouldn't look at a white man and say 'I'm white' or a black man and say, 'I'm black.' I'm a man, I'm for the people, I love the people."

WHY THEM A FIGHT I SO?

> Why dem a fight I so?
> A true me yellow and dem a negro
>   —Yellowman, "Why Them a Fight?" (1982a)

> If me try fe reach de top dem wan' see Yellowman drop
> And if Yellow don't try at all whole a dem say dat me a slip and a fall
> Kaa Yellowman chat it after all by Saint Peter, by Saint Paul
>   —Yellowman, "King of the Crop" (1984e)

By 1978, Yellowman was starting to get somewhere. He had a new name, sound systems were letting him perform, audiences were appreciative, and fans hailed him on the street. But other deejays where he would perform were not so kind. They would make fun of him in their lyrics, refuse to hand the microphone to him and, worse, publicly shun him by acting as though it needed sanitizing after he used it.

On a trip to Trench Town in February 2008, Yellowman and I met up with Mellow, who used to be the selector at a sound system called Black Art. Mellow remembers when Yellowman still had to prove himself on stage every night alongside vindictive rival deejays. "In them days, most man never want give Yellowman the mic. Them scorn him" (interview by author, 16 February 2008). Yellowman adds to the story, "The other deejays were jealous and used to scorn me. When I finish deejay on mic, I pass the mic to them, they use a kerchief, a rag or a towel to cover it up."

Yellowman interpreted this contempt as jealousy as much as prejudice because of what he saw as his natural superior talent. But unlike the crowd, he was not having luck in winning over the deejays. Depending on whom you talk to, many people suggest it was they who first offered Yellowman the mic, leading Beth Lesser to jokingly quip to me, "It's amazing how many people in Jamaica were the first people who ever gave Yellowman the mic" (interview by author, 21 January 2009). In a 2007 interview, Yellowman said that sound systems afforded him an opportunity to get known but that it was fellow deejay Eek-A-Mouse who was instrumental in helping him become an established deejay and welcoming him onstage:

> Yellowman: I couldn't get no opportunity to hold the mic because dey would [not] give me da mic. Here comes Eek-A-Mouse, him take the mic and give it to me and people start sey yeah, great . . . the other entertainer them vex, like them mad. But being as Eek is so tall and big dey used to scared of him, you know? So dey didn't say anyting but I notice that they mad 'cause they leave and they talk and they go away you know . . . but Eek was alright. (Yellowman, interview by Joshua Chamberlain, Kingston, 17 January 2007)

He confirmed this in interviews with me, and spoke further about the experience, pointing out the role played by George Phang, Philip "Fatis" Burrell, Jim Brown and General Starkey, who strong-armed anyone who tried to keep him from performing.

> Yellowman: Eek-A-Mouse used to rough up guys to give me the mic because Eek-A-Mouse used to like me. And George Phang used to rough up guys and say, "Give him the mic." "Only Yellowman we want to hear alone" – Starkey used to say that. And Jim Brown used to do the same thing – he's another don from the other party, [from] Tivoli Garden.
>
> Author: How long did this go on for? As soon as a selector would hear you would he be won over or did George Phang and his crew have to use their muscle for quite a while?
>
> Yellowman: It go on for a few months.
>
> Author: Until you built your name?
>
> Yellowman: Ya, until after I do Tastee's now, then that's it.

In the winter of 2009, I accompanied Yellowman to meet two of these enforcers, men who are legendary both on the streets of Kingston and in the music business. Like Yellowman, Philip "Fatis" Burrell and George Phang had grown up in the ghetto around Eventide Home and, like Yellowman, they had harvested fame and riches in the music industry. Both became noted producers. Well-connected and intimidating, Fatis and Phang were integral to Yellowman's rise. It is doubtful that Yellowman could have gained a foothold in the industry in those early days without the help of men like them to act as protectors.

In the early 1980s, Phang was a small-time hustler with his hand in many businesses, including music. In Beth Lesser's book of photography and essays on dancehall in the 1980s, there is a picture of Phang, probably in his late teens, looking baby-faced and rotund, with a hat cocked to one side. Already a major player at that point, he would go on to rule dancehall for a few short years after Volcano's Henry "Junjo" Lawes left Jamaica. But for now, his biggest contribution to reggae would be making sure Yellowman's career was on the rise.

We found Phang perched on a chair alongside a wall at the garage he owned in Kingston. He was conducting business on his mobile phone while eating his lunch on his lap from a Styrofoam take-away container. Beside him an employee washed and shined his massive black Cadillac Escalade as it sat parked under a shade tent. Phang was pleased to see Yellowman and was happy to talk about his life in the music business and role in Yellowman's career.

When I asked Phang how long he had known Yellowman, he responded, "Me and Yellowman almost come from the same den you know. Seen? From Yellowman a bwoy and me a bwoy deh inna de town we run up and dung" (interview by author, 17 February 2009). He used the Hollywood character Rambo as a metaphor for describing Yellowman's life of discrimination in the 1970s: "Him grow up rough still, you know, seen? Him grow up like real Rambo – he had to have LP named *Rambo* (1986b), seen? But he lift himself above the water and lift himself [above] people who were like prejudice with him and mek himself a career. Me really proud of him." Phang downplayed the part he played in lifting Yellowman above that water.

Phang's career trajectory is unique, to say the least. An intimidator turned producer – he would eventually produce three Yellowman records for his Power House label, all released in 1985 (*Walking Jewellery Store*, *Galong Galong Galong* and *Yellow Man Meets Charlie Chaplin*) – Phang's era in dancehall was short lived. He became the manager of the Arnett

Gardens Football Club. The man whom the *Jamaica Observer* referred to as a "prominent Arnett Gardens political activist" has attempted to shake the stigma that he is a gangster, going so far as to successfully sue a tabloid that referred to him as a don. A don, in the Jamaican context, "is oriented around indigenous symbols of the ghetto gunman who may sometimes have political or narco-political linkages. Political dons are affiliated to one of the two major political parties in Jamaica . . . and generally oversee the running of garrison communities" (Hope 2006, 92). When I inquired about this, he laughed away any insinuation that he left the music business to concentrate on full time gangsterism, preferring to see his work as supporting his community.

> George Phang: Well, I no say really stop [music], but hear what happen: you see the community that I come from – Arnett Garden[s] in Trench Town, is a political stronghold. We have a football team named Arnett Garden[s] Football Club, and the club really kinda go down. Now as a product from inna the ghetto and ting me say me going to put back some energy inna de club fe bring back the club together. So me pause the music thing and get into the club full time and get it together. Right now Charlie Chaplin is de manager down there. That's what really slow me up inna de music ting.
>
> Author: People say that you got into a life of gangsterism. Tell me about that.
>
> GP: [*laughing*] What I'm staying still, why people say that is because of the community I come from. People say Bob Marley come from a gangster thing too. A de community weh we come from. If you ever say that Yellowman come from a gangster business too, a de community he come from. Now, you come from a community where it is a tribal community, where politics fight a lot in those community. Growing up there, people will say we pon area deso him inna de gangster thing. Not really a gangster thing but where you come from people put a block pon your way. I'm glad to say you just have to live with it and show them, say [that] we not a gangster. We're a real hardcore Jamaican man. (Interview by author, 17 February 2009)

The physical scars of his past are hard to miss. He has been shot on three different occasions, with a total of twenty-four bullets. The most serious was in a drive-by shooting in March 2003. He showed me where the bullets tore through his arms, now blotched with scar tissue. Phang told me a bit about that fateful day when I interviewed him:

Author: I heard you were shot.

George Phang: Nineteen bullet me get.

Author: At the same time?

GP: Ya man.

Author: What kind of gun was that?

GP: Rifle, AK and 9 millimetre.

Author: How do you live after that?

GP: Well, God know best and he just preserve my life.

Author: What happened?

GP: Me just play domino one night and a car just drive up and fire pure shot. Them call it drive by shooting. (Interview by author, 17 February 2009).

The *Jamaica Observer* published Phang's account of the shooting, which reads like the westerns so loved by reggae culture: "When I dropped on the ground, I had to use my foot and turn over the domino table so that the gunmen couldn't get a direct aim on me. I managed to reach my firearm and started to fire at them with my weaker hand, the left hand, but when the thing ended I got 19 bullets – six in my belly and the rest in my arm, leg, foot and shoulder" ("Phang: 'I Never Ordered a Hit on Omar'", *Jamaica Observer*, 21 October 2012).

A few days later I accompanied Yellowman to the home studio of another intimidator on those early sound systems who turned into a famed dancehall producer: Philip "Fatis" Burrell, aka the Xterminator. Adorned in pastel colours and rimmed with hibiscus hedges, Fatis's house was tucked along a winding lane in Red Hills, far up in the mountains above the fray of Kingston. The contents of the producer's driveway, not to mention his address, are enough to prove that he has had tremendous success in the music business.

Fatis produced two albums for Yellowman, *Yellow like Cheese* (1997c) and *New York* (2003), but his greatest success came on his Xterminator label in the 1990s when he had hits with Capleton, Ninjaman, Ini Kamoze, Luciano and Sizzla, among others. Katz ("Philip 'Fatis' Burrell Obituary", *Guardian*, 6 December 2011) calls him "one of the most important Jamaican record producers of the digital dancehall era" and says that Fatis was instrumental in spearheading the Rasta renaissance in the mid-1990s that transformed computer-based reggae by returning to the use of real instruments in a hybrid form and bringing Rastafarian artists like Capleton and Sizzla back to the fore.

Fatis notoriously hated interviews and photos, allegedly even smashing a camera at an airport when a fan attempted to snap a quick shot. Fortunately, because I was there with Yellowman, he consented to speaking with me. While we talked, we stood outside the studio in his garage filled with boxes of 45s that he has produced.

Fatis first met Yellowman in the Slipe Pen neighbourhood near Eventide. He was part of the group Yellowman gravitated to in his late teens and helped "promote" Yellowman to the community. Along with Phang and others, he would silence the rival deejays who would try and make fun of the yellow-skinned deejay on stage. Those rivals, he insists, called Yellowman names out of jealousy. Like Phang, the scars of the ghetto upbringing were visible on the producer, who had lost the use of one his arms, which hung limp at his side, apparently due to a knife wound.

Fatis proudly listed off memories of Yellowman – his triumph at the Tastee Talent competition in 1979; a show in New York where he watched as Yellowman, consumed with his own performance, actually fell off stage, landed in the crowd and was levered by them back to his feet; the church people who "lick out" or criticized Yellowman because of his slackness, standing in the crowds to watch him perform. Yellowman, he agrees, was certainly outspoken and lewd – "Yellowman just raw", he says of his lyrics – but Fatis complained that critics did not realize his humorous side, and his kindheartedness. The press constantly popularized Yellowman's slack-ness, while ignoring his cultural lyrics and social commentary (interview by author, 23 February 2009). One of the hits of the Fatis-produced album *Yellow like Cheese* (1987c), for instance, was the socially engaged "Budget" where Yellowman takes issue with the high cost of living.

The interview with Fatis was brief and more rose-coloured than informative about those early sound system shows where he helped Yellowman have a chance on the microphone. But being at the producer's house and studio was a chance to see how reggae artists create their songs. When I met him at his house in Kingston in February 2009, I was there with Yellowman to hear new riddims that would provide the foundation for the deejay's next record. We were driven there by reggae singer Abijah, Yellowman's much younger brother-in-law, whose song "Heavy Load" appeared on Sly and Robbie's 2006 Grammy-nominated *Rhythm Doubles*. Abijah, whose father was a member of the Mystic Revelation of Rastafari, was also recording his new album with Fatis (*Fatis Presents Abijah*, 2009).

Fatis had the riddims prepared for the artists and while I was there Yellowman auditioned them, listening for ones he liked. When Yellowman would connect with a riddim, he would try deejaying over it, quickly finding a rhythm and matching lyrics to it. This was Yellowman in improv-studio mode. We were there the month after Obama had been inaugurated as the first American black president and Yellowman was riding the wave of Obama fever, trying out tribute lyrics.

Sadly, Fatis passed away of a stroke in 2011 and that album remains unfinished. But his role in Yellowman's rise is not forgotten by the deejay. As Yellowman's popularity grew in 1977 and 1978, the help of Phang, Fatis and Eek-A-Mouse was paying off. More people heard and liked Yellowman, and the crowds began to boo any deejay who dared withhold the microphone from him. As the soundmen saw the crowd standing up for the dundus on stage, the power of the rival deejays diminished. Yellowman explains, "The reason why they couldn't kick me out [is] the sound owners they love me because I was pulling the crowd so they couldn't do anything like studio, you know." His popularity with dancehall crowds was just starting, but in 1979 he would enter a national music competition that would change his life and lead to Jamaica becoming "mad" over Yellowman in more ways than one.

CHAPTER 4

Mad over Me

Tastee Talent Competition to Aces International, 1979–1981

BY 1979 THE DEEJAY TRADE WAS BEGINNING TO make international inroads. Trinity's *Shanty Town Determination* and *Three-Piece Suit* helped spread the talk-over gospel beyond Jamaica's shoreline and Michigan and Smiley's *Rub a Dub Style* laid the foundation for the two-deejay combination that would work so well for Yellowman and Fathead a few years later. Yellowman's star was on the rise, but he was still living in a poor house in a politically volatile area of Kingston. What he needed was an opportunity to break free.

Yellowman's big break came in 1979 at age twenty-two at the newly established Tastee Talent Contest. Initiated by the Tastee Patty Company, the talent search was the island's leading talent competition from 1979 to 2013, with semi-final events every two months and a grand finale once a year. There was a cash prize and twelve dozen patties for the winner, but besides the food and money it was the prestige that came with winning that helped make his name.

When Yellowman entered the semi-finals held at Cross Roads, it was only the second stage show he had been on. Dressed in all yellow clothes that had become his trademark, he did well because, he says, he had name recognition in the dancehall community by that time. He had been building a reputation in Barbican and other sound systems. By his own memory, he slaughtered the competition during the semi-finals singing the song "Me Kill Barnie" (also called "Barnabas Killing"): "That was the theme song that mash up the place." The song was an answer to Lone Ranger's "Barnabas Collins". When Philip "Fatis" Burrell recalled watching the Tastee's semi-finals in Cross Roads, he remembered that Yellowman, dressed in a yellow track suit, had the crowd frozen in place in awe of his talent.

Owen Robinson, aka Willa, would later become Yellowman's driver. In 1979, however, he had never met the deejay but had seen him walking along Slipe Road dressed in his yellow hat and suit and heard people calling to him – some with favourable greetings and others with derision. The first time Willa saw him perform was at the free Cross Roads event for Tastee's. "It was awesome, it sound very good, and everybody cheer and everybody seem to love him. His voice was very powerful and his lyrics was good. I said to myself this guy is going to go places" (Owen "Willa" Robinson, interview by author, 21 February 2009). During the finals held in July at Half Way Tree, Yellowman was beat out by nine-year-old Nadine Sutherland, Paul Blake and Claudette Richardson.[1] The added publicity, however, would soon pay off. Yellowman was mentioned in a September 1979 *Daily Gleaner* ("Music Round-a-Bout", *Daily Gleaner,* 8 September 1979) in the wake of this show as Winston Foster, but by 1980 the paper was using the name "Yellow Man" when reviewing a May Day deejay competition won by Richard McKenzie. In the article, Yellowman, who received J$500 (US$280) for placing second, is described as "another popular contestant" who "delighted the audience" ("Montegonian Beats 37 in Dee Jay Contest", *Daily Gleaner,* 28 May 1980).

Even though he did not come first at Tastee's in 1979, many people remember this show as his breakthrough. George Phang's reaction was "me know him a superstar that. Trust me, everybody just take onto him" (interview by author, 17 February 2009). Yellowman himself has never forgotten it: "'King Yellowman' . . . has never forgotten where he gained his first opportunity to show off his talent. Each year Yellowman still attends the Tastee contest, where he performs for free to the thousands of Tastee fans" ("Tastee Showdown Contest", *Daily Gleaner,* 22 March 1989). In 1985, Tastee even decided to change the name of the top trophy to the Tastee Winston Foster Trophy. At the tenth anniversary of the talent show in 1989, Yellowman would again perform alongside his original competition, only this time he was the star of the show. He "crowned the night's festivities" and "set not only the entire Cross Roads on fire, but had all guests of honour in fits of laughter. He put to most effective use, the famous 'King Yellow Poise and Pose' while he deejayed 'Science Again' and 'Everyday a Walk an' a Talk'" ("'Stylistic' Ivor Wows 'em", *Daily Gleaner,* 6 December 1989).

All this time, Yellowman had kept it a secret that he lived at Eventide, but he would not have to keep that secret much longer. In the audience at the Tastee competition was the man who would transport Yellowman from playing small neighbourhood sounds or one-off nights on larger sounds like Gemini or Virgo, or alongside General Echo at Stereophonic, to travelling all around the island with a formidable hi-fi called Black Scorpio.

BLACK SCORPIO

At 6 feet 7 inches, Maurice Johnson, known as Jack Scorpio or Black Scorpio, is tall and imposing, but his sense of humour and ludic play make it easy to see why he and Yellowman get along so well. In February 2009, Yellowman took me to Johnson's Black Scorpio studio where we talked to the producer about his history with Yellowman. Scorpio had a talent for business even as a youth. His father was a higgler selling pumpkin, yam, sugar cane and banana around town, and, eager to teach his son the trade, he purchased a bundle of cane for the boy for twelve shillings when he was twelve years old. "I turn around and sell it for fifteen shilling", remembers Scorpio (interview by author, 19 February 2009). He got his start in the music industry in 1968 when he took money he made from working on a road crew and bought a small turntable and speaker, called a Dulcimina.[2] "That was my sound system, what me start from. And me buy my first two LP, which was 'Feel Good All Over' with Delroy Wilson and 'Heptones on Top', two Studio One LP. Delroy was a youth who inspire me, you know. Get this music in my brain when I hear him sing 'I Am Not a King' and 'Feel Good All Over'." Scorpio calls this turntable his first sound system. He would set the stereo on the windowsill of his father's house, connect it to a car battery because his parents did not have electricity, and host parties with his two records. In 1969, the budding entrepreneur built a shop in front of the house and set up a fish fry. People would come and buy a meal and sit down and listen to the Dulcimina.

> I have the music a play and man come by and I use to sell fry fish and dumpling every Friday night, and it develop into a thing with man play domino and gamble. . . . In 1969 me go buy an amplifier downtown from a guy named Bigga. Me have a tube amplifier now and two likkle box [speakers]. I build up fast because the vibes . . . me buy a likkle bicycle and buy flour and thing for Friday.

When he purchased the amplifier, Scorpio christened his sound Special I, "because it was so special to I". The tense political climate would dictate a name change, however, as the JLP was at that time using the slogan "High Up" (commonly pronounced "I Up" in Jamaica) and Scorpio felt it dangerous to appear to be affiliated with a political party. In 1970, using his astrological sign and signifying the influence of the Black Power movement, he changed the name to Black Scorpio. His own nickname, "Jack", came from the name of a horse he bet on at the track – he's also dubbed the "Horseman". Because so many of Jack's crew used to be into horse racing, his sound even has its own nickname: the Horseman Sound.

The first two deejays on Black Scorpio were Lord Sassafrass and General Trees. Throughout the 1970s Black Scorpio's popularity grew, aided by the fact that Jack toured it all over the island. Many towns he played in did not have a Delco (generator) nor electricity, so he had to make sure that the promoter provided a generator to run his ever-larger amplification system.

Like many sound operators, Scorpio wanted to get into the recording business. His chance came when there was a pink-eye outbreak on the island and Sassafrass came up with a song called "Pink Eye", convincing Scorpio to record it while it was timely. Scorpio decided to take Sassafrass to King Tubby, a well-known studio owner and producer, but upon reflection felt that this might backfire. Tubby would determine whether to release Sassafrass's song or not, so chances were it might collect dust on a shelf in his studio and never see the light of day. Instead, Scorpio took the producer role himself, paying for the session and releasing the song on his newly minted Horseman label. After "Pink Eye", Scorpio and Sassafrass recorded "Pocomania Jump" in 1985 at Harry J's and the song became Scorpio's first number one hit.

In the late 1970s and 1980s, the established sound systems all had their regular deejays. Lone Ranger was on Soul to Soul; Josey Wales and Charlie Chaplin were on U-Roy's sound, Stur-Gav; Brigadier Jerry deejayed on Jah Love; Welton Irie chatted on Virgo; Bobby Culture was on Jack Ruby; Papa Ritchie was on Studio 54; Admiral Bailey and Chaka Demus were on King Jammy's; General Trees and Sassafrass were on Black Scorpio; Supercat and Ninjaman were on Killamanjaro; Ringo was on Gemini; Tiger was on Black Star (Yellowman, interview by Joshua Chamberlain, Kingston, 17 January 2007). This gave deejays steady work and, as their popularity grew, their affiliated sound's fortunes grew with them. At this point in his life,

Yellowman was still bouncing from sound to sound, trying to gain exposure and impress the owners of the sounds enough to give him a full-time gig.

After the Tastee Talent competition exposure, Yellowman went to see Jack Scorpio and asked him for a chance to deejay on Black Scorpio.[3] Scorpio, impressed with the youth's win at Tastee, agreed. When Yellowman started deejaying on Black Scorpio alongside Sassafrass and General Trees, Black Scorpio was a big sound. Scorpio remembers Yellowman's ambition in those early days: "When he come to me he still looking fe bust. I personally start the real career of that youth. I buy him first yellow suit he ever wear in him life."[4]

Yellowman still had to deal with dissatisfaction from his peers who were none too pleased that a newcomer was getting most of the attention. "Yellowman was a star from day I see him, you know", remembers Scorpio, who admits that Sassafrass and General Trees were jealous of this. Worse still, deejays from competing sounds would lash out at Yellowman for his colour during sound clashes. Ironically, for a man whose colour kept him out of the music industry originally, it was now being seen by some as simply a gimmick that Yellowman used to further his career.

One of the most famous incidents of fellow deejays both attacking Yellowman for his albinism and suggesting that it was his colour, not his talent, that was the cause of his fame, was at a dance held at Skateland between Black Scorpio and Jack Ruby's Hi-Fi. Scorpio estimates that this was one of the largest dances he had, with between five thousand and six thousand people present. It was here that top deejay Nicodemus attacked Yellowman, calling him a dundus bwoy. The term "bwoy" is used in a pejorative sense and signifies someone who is subservient. There is also the connotation of the word's use by elites during the slavery period to deflate black masculinity. In an attempt to gain favour with the crowd, Nicodemus sought to belittle and embarrass Yellowman by suggesting that the only reason Yellowman was famous was because of his unique colour, not his talent. People only came to see him because his colour made him a spectacle. He also insinuated that Yellowman's masculinity was questionable. Yellowman, used to such taunts and well equipped to wield his own insults during deejay competitions, turned the tables on Nicodemus. He fought back using a strategy that would find its way onto several of his future albums; he would attack Nicodemus's sexuality by insinuating that since he was from Ocho Rios, a resort town with a reputation for the homosexual activity of tourists, he must also be gay. Not only that, he would do it with humour, causing, as Scorpio puts it, "Nuff forward inna de dance."

> Jack Scorpio: One of the biggest dance I keep at Skateland, I never forget when [Yellowman] killed Nicodemus. That's how me know say that youth coming strong like me, you know . . . that's how him mek him name. One of the biggest dance weh him really now take over the big time. . . . [It was] the biggest discrimination inna at Skateland where actually at least about five or six thousand people in dat, rammed. Black Scorpio and the sound dem call name Jack Ruby. Never forget, Nicodemus upon Jack Ruby and Yellowman and Sassafrass upon Scorpio.

> Author: Who was discriminating against Yellowman?

> JS: Nicodemus.

> Author: What did he say?

> JS: Dundus bwoy and one ray ray ray.[5] . . . I never forget how he, Yellowman, just sit down upon me sound. I say to Yellowman, "Yellowman you me brother, you wait likkle one." . . . When my time come and Yellowman time come, Yellowman took up the mic you know and say, "Yes me a dundus you know. But me no come from Ochi [laughs]. Let me tell you dat – when Yellowman talk, nuff forward inna dance, don. Kill Nicodemus, the great Nicodemus from deso. For Nicodemus was the hardest deejay in Jamaica at that time.

> Author: So he was the biggest deejay?

> J: The biggest deejay. (Interview by author, 19 February 2009)

Yellowman remembers the clash well.

> Author: When Nicodemus was making fun of you, calling you dundus bwoy, was it just for fun?

> Yellowman: No, he took it serious. But I turn it into fun.

> Author: What did you say that night?

> Yellowman: I say, "I'm a dundus bwoy but me no go a Ochi where there a whole heap a batty men and them ting there", you know?

Yellowman would not have to deal with rival deejays taking cheap shots at his colour much longer. His star was on the rise and it was becoming clear that dancehall fans were quickly electing Yellowman as king of the dancehall.

THEM A MAD OVER ME

> Over me, dem a mad over me
> Over me, girls are mad over me
> A inna Jamaica, also Miami
> Over me, dem a mad over me
> —Yellowman, "Mad over Me" (1982g)

The Skateland clash made Yellowman a star. Scorpio was on the road every weekend touring to every corner of Jamaica with Yellowman, Sassafrass and General Trees in tow and the crowds were getting larger and larger. Fame had finally hit for Yellowman and everybody wanted to see him and hear him. When Yellowman was due to play at a dance, crowds would gather outside the gates waiting for his arrival, not wanting to be fooled by an unscrupulous promoter trying to draw crowds by falsely advertising a celebrity's name. The car or van containing the star would pull up slowly to the gates and drive past the crowd. When I interviewed Spanish Town deejay Captain Barkey in 2009, he remembered that when the fans saw Yellowman at a venue, they would rush the gates at once, sometimes breaking them. On one particular night, Black Scorpio's crew arrived at the venue and the street was thick with fans, who proceeded to surround the van Scorpio was driving. Everybody wanted a glimpse of Yellowman. The throng of people was so powerful, though, that the sheer force of bodies pressing against the vehicle turned the van over on its side, pinning the artists and soundmen inside, unable to open the doors. The van had to be righted before the musicians could exit. Soon, Scorpio would have to enlist bodyguards to protect Yellowman when he arrived at a concert.

By this time, Yellowman could literally stop traffic in downtown Kingston. Producer Philip "Fatis" Burrell told me that Yellowman could park his BMW at Cross Roads in Kingston and the whole place stood still. "No one else could do that, not even now" (interview by author, 23 February 2009). When I met Josey Wales, one of Yellowman's good friends and a fellow chart-topping deejay, in his Waterhouse neighbourhood, he explained to me just how popular Yellowman was at this time:

> I don't think Bob [Marley] had that great respect in those budding years like Yellow had when he stepped to the music. . . . Deejay reggae was just busting

out. [It was] something exciting and new, so here comes this guy who looks different, and talk that get out of order. The people appreciated him then as the king, he always reflects on his background and where he comes from. People think, "Oh God, if a guy can bring it from rags to riches, this is a good pattern to follow." And Jamaican people like to follow good patterns. [They] respected him for overcoming all his struggles in his life. To become so successful that people run and bawl and crave and grab and photograph – the paparazzi was all over him, and so was the kids in the ghetto. Everywhere he walks people would follow him all over, kids, whatever. People bun up them dinner 'cause Yellow outside – "let me see him, Lord, let me touch him" – he fascinates the people's minds and their musical taste buds. At that time, Jamaica and the world was ready for this. And I don't think you'll see another one like him. Shabba came this close – make it bigger in terms of Grammy and all that, but the dent Yellow [made] and the footprint sank deep into the minds of reggae fans. Yellow did that. (Josey Wales, interview by author, 25 February 2009)

Yellowman's fame meant that Scorpio had to construct a stage for him to stand on so the crowd could watch him. One night, Yellowman told the crowd that he wanted all the young aspiring deejays to join him on stage; so many answered the call that the stage collapsed. A new sturdier version had to be constructed. No longer could the deejays simply stand beside the selector, they were now raised above the crowd, making the dance become more like a stage show and further bridging the gaps between the dancehall space and the live music concert. As Yellowman's popularity grew, he was innovative in finding ways to make dancehall – as a music genre, a culture and a space – more like live band culture.

Scorpio's relationship with Yellowman goes above and beyond the other producer/artist partnerships Yellowman has had over the years. Yellowman's 1980s material can almost be cleanly divided into three groups: Jo Jo Hookim recorded his first three LPs at Channel One, Junjo Lawes largely dominated Yellowman's 1983–84 material with the exception of *King Yellowman* (1984a), and George Phang released three albums with him in 1985. Each of these producers worked with Yellowman intensely for a short period of time. But Scorpio, who did not produce a record for Yellowman until 1988's *Don't Burn It Down*, has continued to intermittently release Yellowman albums ever since. More amazing is the fact that he and Yellowman have continued working together after Yellowman was stolen away from Black Scorpio on two separate occasions by businessmen who would be able to offer Yellow-man more money and greater exposure. The second occasion was after a sound system clash between Black Scorpio and Jack Ruby Hi-Fi at Skateland. Budding dancehall producer Henry "Junjo" Lawes had already established himself with Barrington Levy and it was Levy who introduced Yellowman to Lawes, thereby effectively robbing Scorpio of the opportunity to bolster his own producing career. Before this was to take place, however, Scorpio would suffer an even greater blow, one that would relegate his sound system temporarily to the background.

ACES INTERNATIONAL

One night in 1980, Scorpio travelled with his Black Scorpio crew to a dance east of Kingston in the parish of St Thomas, unaware that this night would go down in dancehall history. A dance outside of the island's few urban centres was sure to eclipse any other entertainment options and, sure enough, this Black Scorpio dance was the biggest show in town with everybody anticipating the arrival of Yellowman. The dance was a rousing success with so many patrons rushing the gates to hear and see Yellowman that the police had to "lock it off", or shut it down, around midnight. Scorpio jokes that this was probably the biggest event ever to happen in St Thomas: "Police and soldier curfew a dance, they lock we off, lock off our sound." This was considered the country and, unlike Kingston's sound clashes, there would only be one sound playing, and then only on the weekends. Yellowman's reasoning on why the dance was shut down was because of the range of patrons: "You see, [in] that area, one of the reason why they curfew the dance, they know say everybody going come – badman, everybody", so to stop trouble before it started, the police sent the revellers home. When word got around that the show was shut down because of the audience capacity, a big change was afoot.

Owen "Willa" Robinson worked for Aces International as a box man (roadie) at the time. He remembers the events of that night well:

> Willa Robinson: I was with the sound Aces, working with them. And the Saturday night, Black Scorpio was at a dance in St Thomas and we were playing in Port Morant. And that night, our dance was flopping because everybody gone down to Black Scorpio because they heard Yellowman is down there mashing up the place.

Author: So you didn't go?

WR: No. And then I heard that the police mash up the dance, one, two o'clock, and search up everybody and raid it and everybody have to leave, lock it off. In the morning, the news is going around so our boss, Jimmy Wynter, ask us to go down and check with him [Yellowman] because we were having a session at his place the Sunday night. So we go down there and talk to him and he come with us. So we take him to a club, the boss give him a room, food everything. And in the night, when the session start, a lot of people mash down, a lot of people come in to listen to this Yellowman. The dance ram. A lot of money make. A lot of money.

Author: And how much did Jimmy Wynter offer to pay Yellowman?

WR: Jimmy ask him how much him charge and Yellowman say $1,000 so Jimmy give him $1,500. [Yellowman remembers this figure as J$2,000.]

Author: And that was a lot of money back then for a deejay?

WR: Ya man, '80, '81, a lot of money. At the time, I was making $20, pulling box and helping around the sound. (Interview by author, 21 February 2009)[6]

Aces at that time had no resident deejay so it was a coup for Wynter not only to hire a deejay with a draw, but to snatch one of the island's top deejays away from a big Kingston hi-fi. Wynter owned a bar called Luz Night Club and his sound system, Aces, played there every Sunday night. At the time, Scorpio was paying Yellowman J$800 a night, which he says "a whole heap a money that". At J$800 a night, Yellowman was making good money, but the J$1,500 or J$2,000 that Wynter would pay him was phenomenal. For the man who had to prove himself before he could ever sing a syllable into a microphone, Yellowman's talents and reputation had finally secured him an enviable position in the industry that should have been out of his reach as a person with albinism.

Scorpio was understandably angry that Wynter had stolen his star but he understood what was at stake. Scorpio could not match Wynter's offer and knew Yellowman had to go where the money was. Not keen on burning bridges, Yellowman made sure to clear the move with Scorpio before defecting: "Yellowman come to me and say, 'Bwoy Scorpio, Jimmy waan me fe come chat his sound.'" Scorpio had lost his crowd puller but Yellowman's deal with Wynter was not exclusive so Jack would still benefit from Yellowman's presence on his sound occasionally. However angry he was back then, today Jack sees the event in perspective: "Yellowman need a break too, you know. I had Sassafrass, General Trees, they had a name too. I had two deejay already and Aces did never have none." The fact that Yellowman and Scorpio would reunite several times to make albums together over the next few decades shows that the feelings between them could not have been too antagonistic.

Willa Robinson, like countless youths who followed sounds around, was a low-level gopher doing whatever Jimmy Wynter or Aces' two selectors, Shaggy and Stereo, needed done. Besides setting up equipment and running the wires, Willa sometimes got the chance to play records when Stereo or Shaggy needed a break: "Sometimes [Stereo] met a lady and wanted to dance, he'd allow me to take the selection. He'd pick them out for me. So, I just play, I just put them on the turntable and me and Shaggy might tune it up, you know?" But with Yellowman now taking a lead role at the sound, Willa's job description would change and he would spend the 1980s at the side of the world's top deejay.

Yellowman had no car or licence, partly due to the fact that his eyesight has always been poor, a condition associated with albinism. Today, Yellowman has to squint to read and when one of his three cellular phones rings he has to hold it close to his eyes to read the screen. Bright lights frustrate this condition and make driving, particularly at night after a show, impossible. Yet a car-less musician in Kingston, a city with a range of options for public and private transportation, is not a rarity: when Sly Dunbar was a busy session drummer in the mid-1970s he was known for taking a taxi everywhere he went (Sly Dunbar, interview by author, 4 September 2006). People joked about it so much he named his subsequent record label Taxi. For Yellowman, buses and route taxis had too many prying eyes. To avoid uncomfortable jeering, he used to walk everywhere. "A lot of people never like me, you know, so I try to keep out of them way, keep out of public."

But as Yellowman's musical stature grew, being out in public became not only bearable but fun: "After Spanish Jar, Tastee's, Little Mafia, that's when the public thing come in. [I] start get used to public. [It's] because of the music, [that's] why people like and respect me." And a star needed private transportation. As such, Willa's job description was augmented to include driver, eventually taking over the job from Stereo. He first used Wynter's Datsun 510 or Triumph, and later rental cars, before Yellowman owned his yellow BMW, which adorns the cover of the album *Just Cool* (1982b). Willa was in charge of getting Yellowman to and from each show, and his first order of duty was to take him home to Kingston after he performed that first show on Aces. With so much travelling, it was not always possible to get Yellowman back to Kingston after each show. In these cases, Yellowman would be put up in a hotel and Willa and the others would sleep on the speaker boxes in the car. For Yellowman, having Willa drive him to Kingston would prove tricky as he did not want Aces – or anyone, for that matter – to know that he lived in the poorhouse.

> The first Sunday he worked for us we took him back to Kingston. We said, "Where do you live?" He said, "Just leave me at the stop light by the bakery, right by Tropical Tatta." We were going to play the following Friday so him said, "Come back here and pick me up here about 2 o'clock." He was living at Eventide, poorhouse, but he didn't want to tell us that. (Owen "Willa" Robinson, interview by author, 21 February 2009)

Willa knew where Yellowman lived, but he kept the secret. He used to work on Slipe Pen Road and was used to seeing Yellowman walking around the area in his yellow tracksuit. When he saw him walking out of the parking lot of Eventide one day, he figured out where Yellowman lived. A few weeks after Yellowman started chatting for Aces, he would move out of Eventide and live with friends in Franklin Town. Breaking out of the poorhouse was something he had desperately wanted to do, but it would come on the heels of a terrible tragedy at the home.

YELLOWMAN AND FATHEAD

With Yellowman at the helm, Aces International was quickly transformed into the number one sound on the island with people flocking to hear the deejay with albinism. This was quite a feat for a country sound. Previous to this, aspiring deejays and singers would take turns on the mic at an Aces dance. The singer who was most often with them was Jah Rubel, and he continued as Yellowman travelled all over the island with Aces.

At one show in St Catherine parish, Yellowman met Vernon Rainford, an aspiring deejay who went by the name Fathead. Fathead's trademark was punctuating the lines of other deejays with scat words like "bim" or animal sounds such as "ribbit" or "oink", picked up from Lone Ranger's deejay arsenal. Yellowman recalls,

> I met him at a dance at a place named Above Rock, near Stony Hill, in the country, in St Catherine. He live up there. It was an Aces dance, when Aces travelled around local deejays would get up on Aces. I did like how Fathead sound cause he used to back me with the "right" and "ribbit", you know? So, I tell him he can follow me to next dance, because we did have a series of dance in the St Catherine area. [That] was probably 1980.

Yellowman and Fathead became sparring partners on stage, offering a deejay combination where Fathead supported Yellowman. They went on to release several albums together in the early 1980s but would have a falling out, some sources say due to Fathead feeling that he was not being paid enough for his contributions. Fathead would drift out of the industry and his involvement with drugs would ultimately lead to his death from a gunshot wound in Miami in 1988.

EVENTIDE IS BURNING DOWN

> Why do de wicked man a pressure de poor man?
> Eventide what a fire
> Eventide what a fire
> Eventide fire it a murder
> Me couldn't stand de pressure
> Lord me haffi jump and holler
>
> The fire start burn from quarter to one
> Fire Brigade never come til twenty passed one
> Tank God fe de fire station
> Say Jah Jah bless all de fire man
> Eventide is burning down, burning down, burning down
>   —Yellowman, "Eventide Fire" (1980)

The fire that occurred at Eventide on the morning of 20 May 1980 was tragic; 153 women lost their lives, making this the worst loss of life in a fire at that point in Jamaican history. At the time of the fire, there were seven hundred residents. The master of the home, David E. Dunkley (2011), complained that the institution was plagued with financial problems resulting in underpaid staff who often lacked sufficient training, resulting in poor living conditions for the residents. But worse than this was the political climate in Jamaica in the spring of 1980 leading to the general election that would prove to be Jamaica's bloodiest up till then. Eventide had already been the victim of politically motivated violence and some felt that the fire was just the latest in these events. JLP supporters were blamed for the arson in what was an ever-increasing civil war between the parties:

> One opinion on the cause of the fire argued that it was the result of political maneuvering during the final months leading up to the most violent general elections in Jamaica's recent history. There were in fact a number of reports to the police from persons living at the home that gunmen had entered the premises more than once, claiming they had come to kill the staff and inmates for reasons connected with their alleged political affiliations. Moreover, gunmen besieged the premises of the Home just six months after the fire and this time injured two persons. One of them, Mr Harold Tefler, a meal van driver for the Home, was stabbed and then beaten while unloading the meal van. The other victim of this recent attack on the Home was a 63-year-old female resident, Miss Vera Wynter. Miss Wynter was sitting on the veranda "taking in a little fresh air" she said, when the gunmen opened fire on the premises hitting her several times. (Dunkley 2011)

Yellowman remembers gunmen descending on Eventide and gangsters showing up with guns tucked in their belts in order to intimidate the residents. The area was a PNP stronghold and JLP supporters would be scared into voting for the PNP. Perhaps recognizing the role political violence played in the fire, Prime Minister Michael Manley proclaimed the day the women were laid to rest in a mass grave inside National Heroes Park, 26 May 1980, a day of national mourning.

The fire broke out in the women's ward and was contained there, so Yellowman was not physically harmed. He did witness the fire, however, and was somewhat traumatized by seeing the women die. During the 1970s and 1980s, Kingston in an election year was a bloody place to be and so the teenager was already used to seeing death. "I see people killed, shoot down back in 1980s when the politics was on a rampage . . . by police and bad boys." It affected him to the point that sometimes he stayed off the streets.

De biggest ward pon de compound
Dem burn it dung straight dung to de ground
153 lost their lives
If you think say a joke look inna me eye
Kaa when dem die me say de whole world cry
All who still alive pray to Jesus Christ and gwaan a church
Some of dem sick, dem couldn't move quick
Some of dem blind, dem never have no time
Some of them dumb, but de whole of dem bun
Eventide fire, what a fire
(Yellowman, "Eventide Fire" [1980])

The Eventide fire was a blessing in disguise for Winston as it finally allowed him to throw off the shackles of institutional living. "I don't even know if they looked for me", he says today, "since they hated me so much. [They were] just glad to get rid of me." Today he says of the fire, somewhat jokingly, "That's how I break out."

He moved in with friends in Franklin Town temporarily, and his anger at the senselessness of the tragedy was captured on vinyl. Under the name Yellowman, he made his first record, "Eventide Fire", only one month after the calamity.[7] The opportunity to record arose when independent producer Leon Synmoie, from Winston's old neighbourhood of Chisholm Avenue, heard him singing at Eventide. Leon used to visit Eventide to see his baby-mother, and on one of these trips he heard Winston singing with some friends. Leon worked with Alvin Ranglin's GG Records but produced artists independently as well. Leon attended dances and hung around sound systems, always with an eye out for new talent. As Yellowman's reputation was growing, Leon took the chance to record, renting studio time at Byron Lee's Dynamic Sounds, and arranged to use Lloyd Campbell's riddim "Let Me Tell You Boy" for the deejay to voice over. Yellowman had been turned away from this studio before, but since Leon was renting it, the owner had no decision over who used it. It was Yellowman's first time in the studio and he became frustrated trying to adapt to the new surroundings. Used to making up lyrics on the spot in the heat of a dancehall show, the sterility of the studio, with no audience or other artists to feed off, took its toll.

"I was nervous", he says of the session. "Now I do a song in ten minutes, but that song I take like an hour to finish." The fact that he was ashamed of his prolonged performance on "Eventide Fire" suggests that an hour was considered a long time by Jamaican studio standards. To anyone used to recording studios, an hour to voice one song is still a quick recording pace. But Jamaican artists at that time, especially ones with the constraints of money and studio time, became used to recording live off the floor using only a few takes.

"Eventide Fire" was released on the Thrillseekers label in 1980.[8] Synmoie also recorded a track called "1980"[9] and issued "Lover's Corner" on GG Records in 1981. "Eventide Fire" failed to register as a hit for Yellowman either on the radio or in the dancehalls but it served two functions. First, it allowed Yellowman to make the transition from sound system deejay to recording artist. Distributed by Byron Lee's brother, Neville Lee, through his company Sonic Sound, the single probably received no airplay but it did manage to help further instantiate the name Yellowman on Kingston's dancehall scene. Second, the man who would become known for lyrics about pleasure, partying and sex started his recording career with an undeniable reality song. By this time, Yellowman says he was doing "pure slackness" in the dancehalls yet his lyrics on this song speak to the atrocity of loss of life, offering searing social commentary and presenting salient critiques of a system where the poor are left to burn. Cultural songs in reggae can come in many forms, such as religious, Afrocentric, and social commentary. Social commentary includes reality lyrics, lyrics that may not directly call for social justice and equality but do so implicitly through their use of ghetto narratives that show the sharp divide between black and white or rich and poor. "Eventide Fire" (1980) was a reality lyric because it described a very real event. It also critiqued Jamaica's classist society. At first, he asks in the song, "Why do the wicked man a pressure the poor man?", a thinly veiled attack on the political thugs whom both parties employed to do their bidding. The song then dispels any rumour that the tragedy was accidental: "Eventide fire it a murder."

Interestingly, there is also an allusion to Jah in Yellowman's first song: "Jah Jah bless all the fireman." The lexicon of Rastafari filtered into Jamaican popular music starting in the 1960s. By 1980, it was normal to hear Rasta terms in songs by artists who would not be identified as Rastafarians themselves. Later chapters will examine Yellowman's use of Rasta symbols, particularly as he moved towards using more Jah language. His trademark vitriol for Christianity, found later in songs such as "Fools Go to Church on Sunday" (1982c), is also present here. After lamenting that 153 people lost their lives in the fire, he says, "All who still alive pray to Jesus Christ and gwaan [go] a church", making sure to use a guttural mocking tone on "gwaan" to enforce the pointlessness of the church. Like much of his later material, the line between seriousness and humour is shaky at best. It is hard to tell if he is being serious or laughing at the expense of the infirm when he rhymes the verse: "Some of dem sick dem couldn't move quick / Some of dem blind dem never have no time / Some of dem dumb but the whole of dem bun [burn]."

Musically the song also signifies an important step for both dancehall and Yellowman. He voices the chorus using the melody of "London Bridge" ("Eventide is burning down, burning down, burning down"). Paul Gilroy (1987) has criticized Yellowman for using nursery rhymes, saying that this has led to the de-evolution of reggae. Yet other singers, such as Max Romeo and Jacob Miller, had already used nursery rhymes and children's songs to great effect ("Three Blind Mice" and "The Ants Come Marching" respectively) but Yellowman was quickly establishing a style that was heretofore rare for deejays. He was alternating between singing a chorus and chatting a verse. Deejays and singers up to this point were usually separate entities, so for Yellowman to take on both roles was significant because it would point the direction that he would move dancehall in the coming years.

LIFE IN THE GHETTO

> Cause living in de ghetto ain't easy
> Kaa man life in de ghetto ain't easy
> Sometime you got to go to bed hungry
> —Yellowman, "Life in the Ghetto" (1982a)

Now that Yellowman was out of Eventide, he still was not really on his own. He moved in with friends in the PNP garrison of Franklin Town for a period of about six months. Today, walking around Franklin Town, you get the sense that this is a close-knit community. Unlike in Concrete Jungle, there are no concrete high-rises, only small wooden or stone houses with corrugated zinc fences and roofs. The streets are narrow – one car width – and the pavement is littered with trash and potholes. It seems as though the government forgets these areas. Utility poles have nests of wires stretching from them to nearby houses; those who cannot afford electricity simply take it. Gullies run like veins throughout Kingston – depositories for rainwater, sewage water, plastic bags, old refrigerators and numerous other trash items. The gully in Franklin Town was small but it still stank, the smell of grey water trickling down the crack between the sidewalk and the road. Here Yellowman lived in a small house at 4 York Road with several other people. They shared a yard with a house behind where the deejay Ringo lived. He was also known as a slackness deejay who released a popular song called "Two Lesbian Hitch" and he can be found on *Superstar Yellowman Has Arrived with Toyan* (1982f) covering Yellowman's hit "I'm Getting Married".

Yellowman took me back to Franklin Town to see the house he lived in and meet his old neighbours. He also had other reasons for going back. One Friday evening in 2009, I pushed a cart around a grocery store in Kingston as Yellowman loaded it up with food to take to his former neighbours. We drove to Franklin Town to visit and attend a fish fry. When we got out of the car, we were immediately greeted by several youths Yellowman knew. We entered a dark yard and knocked on a door. The door was partly open but the doorway was covered by a bed sheet acting as a curtain. When the man who opened the door saw Yellowman, he smiled. Once inside, Yellowman distributed the grocery bags and directed one of the youths to take other bags to a few different houses. It was like Christmas, with Yellowman playing Santa Claus. But the people did not seem to be overly surprised, leading me to believe that this was a normal thing. For the rest of the evening, we visited other neighbours and hung out at the sound system party going on a few streets away. All the while Yellowman greeted people as old friends. Again and again I was told by the folks there how much Yellowman meant to them. The owner of a bar recounted how Yellowman would deejay at a sound system he ran in the old days. He finished the conversation by making sure I knew that anyone in the neighbourhood would do anything for Yellowman. If anyone accosted Yellowman, they would protect him, and his guests, he told me, could expect to enjoy the same level of protection.

This evening was most likely designed to demonstrate to me that Yellowman had not forgotten his ghetto roots. Staying in touch with the ghetto is an important part of the reciprocal relationship reggae stars have with their Jamaican fan base. Reggae is essentially ghetto music; it was born of the ghetto and is overwhelmingly thematically linked to the ghetto. An artist's credibility with dancehall fans depends on their ability to stay connected with the fans' concerns. Reggae is traditionally the music of the underclass, the ghetto dwellers, the sufferahs and, as such, an artist is rewarded for remembering their own roots in the ghetto with fan loyalty.

Yellowman is mindful of this and actively facilitates his relationship with the ghetto by visiting old friends and neighbours in his former neighbourhood of Maxfield Park, attending a fish fry and delivering groceries to former neighbours in Franklin Town, or showing up on a Tuesday night at Bebo's corner in Concrete Jungle to deejay on the mic alongside old sparring partner Squidly. He is also accessible to his fan base while out in public or after a show. I had witnessed Yellowman going back to these places and being treated like a king. He obviously enjoyed the attention and I suspected that part of the reason for going there was to bask in that attention. While he made a point of showing me that he had not forgotten his roots, this was also about maintaining credibility with his fans.

Alleyne's (2005) work on race and ethnicity in the Caribbean suggests that not keeping ties to the ghetto could result in a successful person being viewed as "letting down the race" or "playing white". Instead, "the greatest praise given to successful blacks (especially sportsmen and entertainers) is that they remain loyal to the humble communities from which they sprang" (238). For Yellowman, it is imperative that in order to be taken seriously as a black man, as opposed to a dundus or a white man, he must keep those ghetto connections. In a society where race and ethnicity are powerful categories for identity construction and representation, Yellowman's lack of physical blackness is compensated for by his adoption of symbols of blackness such as Dreadtalk (Jah or I and I), the Ethiopian-Rasta colours of red, gold and green, or the Afrocentrism found in his lyrics. His ongoing maintenance of ghetto ties also facilitates his representation in society as a black man.

But there is a further reason to remain connected to the ghetto. Artists like Yellowman are not respected uptown. They live uptown but high society disdains them. Yellowman told me that several of his uptown neighbours are prejudiced against him – he may surmise this is because of his colour but it most likely also has to do with his reputation for slackness and his connections to the underclasses. It is in the ghettos that reggae artists get the most respect and it is this respect that keeps them going back there. When

Yellowman brings a few bags of groceries to the ghetto, he proves to the inhabitants that he is worthy of their respect. It is a two-way, give-and-take relationship. They can boast about their ties to a superstar and Yellowman can boast about his ties to the ghetto, thereby claiming authenticity and gaining credibility.

In short, Yellowman returns to the ghetto for three reasons. First, to command general respect among his fans; if you want to present yourself as authentic you need to maintain that link. Second, the ghetto is a site where Yellowman can prove his blackness and dispel any doubts that he is "playing white". Third, he loves the spotlight; uptown people sometimes rebuke him but the downtown people crowd around him and treat him like a king. He goes there to feel like a star and be respected for his accomplishments. He still craves the attention and admiration of fans and wants to project a genuine love for the people, a love that he accurately believes has been reflected back to him over the course of his career. As one of reggae's most recognized international stars, Yellowman is mindful of staying connected to his Jamaican fans. This is why, he told me, he chooses to live in Jamaica instead of in New York with his wife and children; he needs to stay close to the Kingston music industry, as that is the geographic heart of reggae. So, for Yellowman, travelling through downtown Kingston to tour me around orphanages, studios and neighbourhoods was as much about publicly instantiating his continued ghetto credibility as it was facilitating my research on his life.

CHAPTER 5

Ram Jam Master, 1981

Me are de ram jam master
Me are de bad super duper
Yellowman him are de teacher
One thing Yellowman can't understand
Weh every music me do it go number one
　　—Yellowman "Ram Jam Master" (1984c)

YELLOWMAN WAS AMONG THE ISLAND'S TOP DEEJAYS IN 1981, sure to make any dance ram. In August, he won the Festival '81 National Deejay Contest held at Ranny Williams Entertainment Centre on Hope Road in Kingston, beating out Welton Irie, Nicodemus, Johnny Ringo and Toyan. This contest grew out of the annual Festival Song competition as it became clear that the popularity of deejays was equal to that of reggae singers. Lesser (2008, 102) has said that Yellowman's success had to do with timing; he was a remarkable deejay at a time when the art of the deejay was exploding:

> When Winston Foster arrived on the scene, dancehall broke loose; this albino deejay appeared out of nowhere and took Jamaica by storm. He succeeded because he represented everything dancehall culture stood for and also embodied every current musical trend. He was a deejay at the height of deejay dominance. He was both topical and slack, his irreverence thrilled a population who craved excitement. Yellowman was a deejay mischief-maker; he entertained people, outraged them, made them laugh. He became Jamaica's second reggae ambassador, after Bob Marley, and he was able to take dancehall to places reggae had never been before.

No longer were deejays considered to be beneath singers, nor were they now simply live entertainers on sound systems. The late 1970s saw several deejays begin successful recording careers, which led to demand for a similar product. Enter Yellowman. Within one year – by Sunsplash 1982 – there would be no doubt who was the top entertainer in Jamaica. In the wake of that historical concert, Yellowman would be dubbed the King of Dancehall by the Jamaican media. Leading up to this event, however, was a whirlwind year which began with a controversial single, and a true story, about police brutality.

SOLDIER TAKE OVER

The soldier take over
Take over de whole of Jamaica
Dem a mogel [model] inna jeep and tanker
Me say look out, look out de soldier a come
Dem a look fe de badman weh de fire dem gun
And if you no run deh goin' shoot you to de ground
—Yellowman, "Soldier Take Over" (1981)

Despite his success and fame as a live deejay, Yellowman knew that the sound system gigs could carry him only so far. They paid well, but the top deejays on the island were the ones like U-Roy, Big Youth, Michigan and Smiley, Trinity, Lone Ranger, Clint Eastwood and General Saint, who had records and international audiences. Up until this point the studio culture remained closed to Yellowman, outside of his limited work with Leon Synmoie, who recorded "Eventide Fire" (1980). Now, as the ace-in-the-hole for Aces, he was finally able to crack into the record industry. Jimmy Wynter had no interest in the recording business at the time, however, because between Aces, the night club and an alleged ganja business, he had other sources of money. Rarely did artists book studio time themselves, so it took another producer to usher Yellowman into the studio culture.

With a producer named Lowell "Tanka" Hill, Yellowman scored his first hit on the sound systems with a song called "Soldier Take Over" (1981).[1] The song was recorded back in his Maxfield Park neighbourhood at Jo Jo Hookim's Channel One studio. Home to Jamaica's most in-demand rhythm section, Sly and Robbie, Channel One spent the late 1970s building a respectable reputation as one of the island's top studios, especially for dancehall. While

Hookim had turned Yellowman away once, he now allowed the celebrity dundus deejay studio time.

The song's title comes from the 1966 rocksteady song "Soldiers Take Over" by the Rio Grandes. Reggae constantly reinvents itself by drawing on its past for present inspiration. Like most deejays and singers, Yellowman's thematic palette would often be inspired by previous artist's work, just as his rhythm tracks were always part of the vast storehouse of old and newly created riddims. The riddim for "Soldier Take Over", for instance, was called "Mad Mad". It was originally a Studio One riddim made famous by the Alton Ellis song of the same name and Michigan and Smiley used the riddim on their 1981 hit "Diseases". The riddim would give Yellowman one of his biggest hits in 1983 as "Zungguzungguguzungguzeng" (1983e), but, in the meantime, "Soldier Take Over" was enough to help him further his campaign to dominate reggae.

Whereas the Rio Grandes song was about soldiers controlling rudies or gangsters, the subject of several rocksteady-era songs, Yellowman's lyrics were a broad-based attack on what he saw as a military state endangering innocent civilians. The song is based on an incident between Yellowman and the army; he was stopped during a curfew and made to walk on his knees.

Yellowman: One night I was coming from Slipe Pen Road going to Eventide Home. I was walking through a road named Ivory Road and I bumped into soldiers. They were like, "Come here, red bwoy . . . you do the song named 'Radication'[2] and all them thing? You always deejay about soldier. So, we going make you march pon your knee." Him say, "You march from yaso [here] pon your knee to deso [over there]." So, they make me march pon my knee on the asphalt for maybe 'bout half hour to a hour. When I get up all my knee sore, the skin peeling off my knee. That's when I wrote that song, because I was jeering them in the song.

Author: So you didn't talk back?

Yellowman: No, I couldn't talk back [they had guns] and we were at a place where nobody else could see. There was around six of them.

Author: Did you start singing that song right after that?

Yellowman: Ya man.

Author: How long after that until you recorded it?

Yellowman: Like about four or five months after. Because that was a hit music inna de dance when me deejay.[3]

In revenge, Yellowman pokes fun at the military using toilet humour ("Some wear helmet / When they can't find a toilet they doo-doo inna it") and belittles the lack of agency soldiers have over their own lives ("Government boots are not your own" [1981]). But just as "Eventide Fire" subtly mixed humour and social concern, "Soldier Take Over" is a bold statement on the island's police state from the point of view of ordinary Jamaicans caught in the crossfire.

The song is a concise political statement and shows Yellowman as a defiant citizen and musician determined to shame the soldiers who humiliated him, but also willing to risk further suffering and even sanction in order to speak his mind. He takes them to task for racial slurs, misuse of authority, unprovoked violent behaviour and their lack of intelligence:

Say on my way to Up Park Camp[4]
Me bruk [meet] a jeep load, it full a soldier man
Dem say, "Come here bwoy, you favour [look like] gun man"
You a idiot bwoy, me name a Yellowman
He said, "Shut your mouth before you feel me Remington"
Him kick away me foot and he box me inna me face
He box me inna me face and him kick away me foot
He said, "Red bwoy I don't love how you look."

Reggae has a proud history of critiquing authority, but Yellowman's song is particularly important here insofar as he has been criticized for being non-political and non-cultural. At a time when Yellowman was chatting almost pure slackness every night on Aces sound, his second record, "Soldier Take Over", was tame by comparison and, most importantly, was another example of social commentary. His mix of slackness and social commentary would fuse more and more over his recording career.

Public reaction to "Soldier Take Over" was positive; people were frustrated by the behaviour of soldiers and police and Yellowman's song gave voice to this anger. The song made Yellowman a hit island-wide: "Everybody, especially the youth boy dem, like that music", he says today. The song was too political to play on the radio, but Yellowman says it was a hit in the dance. But by hit, he does not mean the song was played by sound systems, only that his performances of it were wildly popular – at that time sound systems only spun records of singers, not deejays. Deejaying was still considered a live entertainment form and the reason people went to the dance was to hear and see live deejays, not recorded versions of them. As such, Yellowman's songs got very little play on sound systems other than his own performed versions.

> People never played deejay records on sound systems in the 1980s. They only played singers, deejays were live. There might be a soul sound system that didn't have deejays and they maybe played them, because they mix it up. The soul sounds a lot of times mix it up and play a little calypso, American soul, etc. They might play a few deejay records. But the real downtown sound systems only played vocals.[5] (Beth Lesser, interview by author, 21 January 2009)

Sagittarius keyboardist Simeon Stewart offers a different take on this, saying that sound systems would often play deejay records early in the night, before the deejays arrived.

Yellowman turned an earlier run-in with the law into another hit in the form of "Operation Radication" (1982e) the following year. Several versions of this song already existed when Yellowman tackled it, and he had been chatting it in the dance before recording it. His former Franklin Town neighbour Ringo had released a song called "Radication Operation" in 1980 and Eek-A-Mouse released "Operation Radication" in 1981, but these tracks bear little similarity to Yellowman's other than the titles. Yellowman's version seems to have come from Fathead, who sang "Eradication Operation" on *Live at Aces* (1982b), and indeed, Fathead deejays along with Yellowman on "Operation Radication".

Yellowman's version is based on a true story indicative of the rising instances of police brutality in the wake of the 1978 Green Bay killings, where five JLP supporters were shot, allegedly by soldiers, at the military range in Green Bay, St Catherine. Jamaican police have, from time to time, set up special squads to fight crime or quell violence. Cooke ("Story of the Song: 'Operation Ardent' Reveals Buju's First Brush with the Law", *Gleaner*, 3 July 2011) lists thirteen such squads formed between 1976 and 1999 including Echo Squad (June 1976), Ranger Squad (March 1980) and Eradication Squad (February 1981). "Operation Radication" tells the story of Yellowman's run in with the Eradication Squad at a roadblock:

They had this police squad called the Eradication Squad. I had a confrontation with them, they fight me. I was driving through New Kingston on Oxford Road going towards the old embassy building. I said to the cops, "Is it Gregory Isaacs you looking for?" 'cause I was playing joke. And one of the guy come over and start punching me and kicking me. They start cursing bad word so I start cursing bad word back to them and they say I don't have any manners and they start fight. They drew their guns at me and say if I lift my hand what and what they gonna do.

When another radio car arrived, the police officers who arrived broke up the fight and gave Yellowman the names of the officers who had beaten him up. He took them to court, resulting in two of them being suspended.

Yellowman recorded the song for Lloyd Campbell using the Itals' "Inna Dis Ya Time" riddim. A singer named Butler, who was a selector on Aces, sang chorus on Yellowman's version. "Operation Radication", when it was released as a single, was banned from the radio. The song, as can be expected, was a hit in the dance, though.

The fact that "Soldier Take Over" and "Operation Radication" were censored from radio was nothing new. Jamaica had strict guidelines on the types of songs that were deemed fit for airplay and Yellowman's material would routinely fail the censorship guidelines. Yellowman considers any song of his that failed to get airplay a song that was banned: "You still have a record jury where they play music and just throw it off the air if it don't sound properly or fit for airplay." In reality, though, very few deejays were getting airplay in those days, so it may be an over-reaction to equate this with systematic censorship. Still, in the years to come, several of his songs would be either refused airplay from radio stations or were removed from the radio after complaints were made about their content. His outright slack tunes never had a chance on the airwaves but, in Jamaica's political climate, any song that could be misconstrued as supporting one of the two political parties was also subject to censorship.

Of course, Yellowman was also subjected to censorship over his slackness. When he first started deejaying, his lyrics were tame compared to the full-on slackness style of later years. "I would say a little. Not much when I start with the sound systems." But as his songs became slacker, he became the target of not only radio programmers, but moral gatekeepers as well.

SLACKNESS IN THE DANCEHALL TRADITION

In 1989, American hip-hop act the 2 Live Crew caused widespread controversy with their album *As Nasty as They Wanna Be*, with the song "Me so Horny" (2 Live Crew 1989) being singled out for particularly harsh criticism by social conservatives such as the American Family Association. The MTV generation had already been subjected to the black and white Parental Advisory stickers on albums deemed to contain explicit content since 1985 after the Recording Industry Association of America succumbed to pressure from the Parents Music Resource Center. But in Jamaica, thanks to artists such as General Echo, Shabba Ranks and Yellowman, "Me so Horny" was at least a decade late on the slackness trend. The fact that the song talked openly and graphically about sex was not in any way novel to the Jamaican dancehall audience. General Echo's *The Slackest LP* (1979)[6] and *12" of Pleasure* (1980) albums, with songs such as "Bathroom Sex", "Lift up Your Dress Fat Gal", "Me Know Everything about She Pum Pum", "This Are the Cockie Tribulation", and "She Have a Pair of Headlamp Breasts", set the slackness standard, a standard Yellowman would meet and eventually surpass. General Echo provided Yellowman with his most direct lyrical mentor. Yellowman was a cultural sponge, able to absorb musical trends both local and global and refract them back through his unique lens as an insider/outsider, hero/anti-hero. In the late 1970s and early 1980s, slackness happened to be the trend that he was most successful at refracting and it was the trend that carried deejays to the top of the dancehall culture.

During that period, many of the main popular deejays, including General Echo, Rankin Joe, Trinity, Clint Eastwood and Welton Irie, indulged in slackness to varying degrees. The deejay trade previous to this was set in the mould laid out by U-Roy's more cultural-minded raps ("Dread inna Babylon") and Big Youth's Rasta themed tracks such as "I Pray Thee". Trinity was the first major deejay to anticipate the shift away from the Rastafarian-centric lyrics of his mentor, Big Youth, towards "the more material/carnal concerns of the next decade" (Barrow and Dalton 2004, 255). Of particular note is his "Three Piece Suit" (Trinity 1975), which included suggestive lyrics like:

> Man you should a see me and the big fat ting
> Tell you when I scrub her in a Constant Spring
> Tell you when me dub her in a Constant Spring

Tell you when me love her in a Constant Spring
Tell you when me dub her pon the big bed spring
Inna me three-piece suit and ting

"Three Piece Suit", however, was tame in comparison to what would come next.

Far from being an anomaly at dancehalls in the late 1970s, slackness was big business and the largest crowds gravitated to the sound systems that had slack deejays. But deejay culture was in its infancy as far as the recording industry was concerned, still eclipsed by singers, so it was in the dancehall that slackness remained. There were, however, sound systems such as Jah Love Music that frowned on slackness and only played cultural songs, but the majority of sound systems recognized that having a slack deejay was good for business. Even U-Roy's more culture-minded Stereograph sound system had Ranking Joe, a U-Roy protégé with songs like "Cocks Man", "Fuck in a Dance", "Lift up Your Frock" and "Sex Maniac". Dancehall journalist Beth Lesser explains, "That was just the style back then; you could not do anything else. Ranking Joe was [slack] and Charlie Chaplin was when he started. About Ranking Joe in the late 1970s, I don't think you could get anybody to go to a dance if there wasn't slackness there. It wasn't slackness the whole night, it was just part of the dance" (interview by author, 21 January 2009).

Dancehall has been blamed for the rise of slackness, and Yellowman himself for its genesis. The "Dean of American Rock Critics" Robert Christgau, for instance, called him "the man who invented slackness, for better and mostly worse" ("Music", *Village Voice*, 16 April 2002). But Jamaican dancehall culture did not invent slackness. Slackness is not unique to dancehall nor, in fact, to Jamaica. Dancehall shares its slack heritage not only with its immediate Jamaican forebears – reggae, ska, mento – but also with other music of the Caribbean, such as Antiguan benna and Trinidadian calypso.

Slackness is an instantiated, if not controversial, institution throughout the Caribbean and can be traced back to songs from the slavery era (Warner 1985), American hokum blues and the sea shanties brought to the Caribbean by British sailors and Irish indentured workers (Nye 2007). Lusty double entendre and licentiousness were no strangers to the British of antiquity. Shakespeare, for many the epitome of high British culture, was a very slack playwright by Jamaican standards. Shakespeare's work was filled with vulgar puns on all manner of sexual topics such as genitalia, sodomy, venereal disease, masturbation, semen, same sex copulation and prostitution. The very term "vulgarity" today connotes crass sexual language, but in Elizabethan England it referred to the common, or low-class, folk. Shakespeare, then, wrote in the language of the common people and his audience would have understood these puns, even though contemporary audiences are largely in the dark regarding their original meaning. More than this, the bard's popularity was in part due to his slackness; even in sixteenth-century England, sex sold. And in a society where brothels were licensed by the bishop of Winchester and stood in the same district as the theatres, plays spoke openly about sex. Shakespeare and his contemporaries gave their characters lines about "fucking, pricks, cunts, ejaculation and buggery" (Kiernan 2007, 16, 26).

The case of calypso is instrumental in understanding Yellowman's slackness for, like dancehall, it was targeted by critics for its playful sexual openness. Given the popularity and high regard of Shakespeare in British literature, calypsonian Attila the Hun found it strange that kaiso or calypso was censored for bawdy content at the same time that European playwrights and authors were heralded as high culture, even though their content was often smutty. He made this point in a 1938 recording called "The Banning of Records", a song that itself was banned:

> To say these songs are sacrilegious, obscene or profane
> Is nothing but a lie and a burning shame
> If kaiso is indecent then I must insist
> That so is Shakespeare's "Venus and Adonis"
> Boccaccio's tales and Voltaire's *Candide*
> *The Martyrdom of Man* by Winwood Reade
> But o'er these authors they make no fuss
> But want to take advantage of us. (Quoted in *Eldridge 2005*)

Attila the Hun's song speaks volumes about the Eurocentric attitudes towards African diasporic culture, where salaciousness was equated with African immorality and animalistic tendencies. Victorian mores and puritan austerity dominated the managing of sexuality in the colonies, but those authorities turned a blind eye to examples of slackness from Europe's own past. Attila the Hun would probably have smiled when, several years later, Jamaican dancehall fans criticized the same inconsistency regarding socially sanctioned displays of carnality at the annual calypso and soca carnival while slackness in dancehall was routinely demeaned.

Until reggae's popularity rose in the 1970s, calypso was the most popular music form in the English-speaking Caribbean. While the Caribbean is marked by diversity in language, geography and ethnicity, there is a basic set of sociomusical attributes shared by the region. These include "the presence of an Afro-Caribbean cultural common denominator; a history of musical syncretization; the strength of oral traditions; the emergence of the lower-class, African-influenced work songs, religious musics, [and] Carnival traditions" and songs that "display an uninhibited delight in sexuality" (Manuel, Bilby and Largey 1995, 233, 237). Typically, these inhibitions have been expressed using double entendre and humorous puns meant to share their meaning with their audience semi-covertly, in a manner appearing on the surface inoffensive to mainstream society so as to limit sanctions against the artists. The intended audience shares in the joke, as well as appreciates the use of the linguistic devices and the overall high jinks of the act. The public reacts approvingly to a dirty calypso because it feels it is "a piece of smut cleverly put over" (Warner 1985, 128). Caribbean song is oral tradition and Caribbean wordsmiths and their audiences highly value language and performance. The use of colloquialisms, puns, heckling, insults and double entendre in calypsos reflects this love of language, a love routinely on display in Yellowman's lyrical escapades.

As the top calypso singer, the Mighty Sparrow's repertoire included many songs filled with double entendre, thinly veiled narratives about sexual exploits, wanton women, and male prowess. Calypsonians were adept at making slack themes sound innocuous and, as a result, calypso and mento enjoyed a certain respectability in Jamaican society that reggae and dancehall lacked. Yellowman calls calypso uptown music, whereas the music he performed was street music. In articulating the reasons for this difference, he once told me, "[Sparrow] wasn't gross like me, because I was very gross. If Sparrow say 'sex', I say 'fuck'. And if Sparrow say 'pussy', I say 'vagina'. I was very blunt." You get a sense in this quote that Yellowman relished his notoriety, even though he protests the double standard in Jamaica that favoured calypso despite its racy themes. Sparrow's use of the term pussy was indirect, disguising pussy cat for female genitalia as in the song "Sell the Pussy". Yellowman employed double entendre as well, but was also known for wiping away all pretence and talking about sex as sex. This shocked polite society, of course, but also broke a cultural tradition of not using plain talk in the interest of maintaining privacy (Sobo 1993). This could be one reason why Yellowman was effective as an agitator in dancehall; he was one of the first who broke through the unwritten code that sexuality must be hidden beneath double entendre.

Yellowman remembers suggestive calypso on the radio, even though its subject matter was at times vulgar. Everybody knew it was slack, but since it used masked language it was deemed acceptable. As a youth, Yellowman loved the way Sparrow disguised sex in metaphor and found the titillating subject material humorous. When calypsonians wanted to sing about the male phallus, they used euphemisms such as "golden sword", "wood", "coil", "bamboo", "ram", "banana", "water hose", "stick", "pogo stick", "rod of correction", "drum stick", "key" or "blade". A vagina could be referred to as a "garden", "saltfish", "pussy", "pum pum", or invoked with numerous automobile images such as "gearbox". Popular actions for a male enacting sex upon a female included "flooding", "wetting" or "eating" (Warner 1985, 108). In "Congo Man" (1964a), for instance, the Mighty Sparrow's humour and food metaphors allow him to cross into forbidden territory of race and sexuality. Borrowing white Western society's racist trope of the African cannibal, Sparrow cooks up a white female intruder but insists he "never eat a white meat yet".

The calypso master's true meaning is never far from the surface of his songs. While Sparrow may appear to be talking about seafood, the song "Salt Fish" (1976) speaks of the pleasures of a woman's vagina. In the "Village Ram" (1964b), it is not livestock that is the song's subject but the calypsonian's claims that he has the power to sexually satisfy any woman. Likewise, the "Big Bamboo" (1965) is not about forestry products but rather a boastful calypso about the size and strength of the singer's penis. And in "Sell the Pussy" (1969), the song's narrator insists that his girlfriend's cat should be sold to put food on the table in a humorous, if not problematic, tale of pimping one's lover for money.

This is not to say that mainstream society did not know what the songs were about, or were unaffected by them. The wordplay is often transparent so that, for instance, a general audience knows what Lord Kitchener (1967) is referring to when he says "climbing Mount Olga", what Baldhead Growler

(1967) means when he speaks of his big sausage, or what Mighty Sparrow (1996) is talking about in "Ah Fraid Pussy Bite Me". Other examples include Sparrow's "Sparrow Water de Garden", "Bendwood Dick", "Jook for Jook", "Meh No. is 69" and "Leggo Me Stick". In Lord Kitchener's "Little Drummer Boy" (1977), drumming is a euphemism for sex, and Kitchener recounts how many ladies are impressed with his skill at drumming. He adds a laugh after the word to relate to the listener the double meaning of the song. "Little Drummer Boy" was also used as the basis for slack Jamaican songs by both Prince Buster and Lee Perry.

It is helpful to remember that the Trinidadian middle class frequently complained about vulgar calypsos and did not tolerate excessive slackness or gratuitous performances with suggestive body movements (Warner 1985). In fact, many of the criteria used to discredit Yellowman's slack dancehall against Bob Marley's cultural reggae were used by calypso moralists as well. In an essay on the calypso as Caribbean literature, Hill (1974) contends that a "great calypso" must be both timely and timeless and must have moral merit, with the composer possessing insight into understanding or improving the human condition. It is clear from his comments that most of the sexual-themed calypsos lack this, and therefore lack merit: "Calypsos have a moral quality . . . when they are genuinely conceived rather than the product of some rhymester alien to the milieu who composes salacious ditties for the pop record market" (Hill 1974, 296). All of Hill's examples of great calypsos omit slackness: "Death is Compulsory" by Lord Kitchener, "The Human Race" by Lord Pretender, "Federation" by the Mighty Sparrow, and "Black Is Beautiful" by the Mighty Duke.

As with later dancehall, the calypsonian was alternatively lauded and denounced in Trinidad for their irreverence in song and hedonistic lifestyle (Manuel, Bilby and Largey 1995). Censorship, too, was used by moral gatekeepers to try and contain the perceived threat to normative values of both. Yellowman complains that many of his songs were banned in the 1980s, but calypsonians had endured the same as many as five decades before. "Any song criticizing the state or dealing with Afro-Trinidadian culture or religion was subject, however unpredictably, to banning. Calypsonians were required to submit their lyrics to censorship offices before singing them, and policemen were posted in tents to monitor performances. Tents hosting objectionable songs could be shut down and singers' licenses revoked.

Shipments of allegedly subversive records pressed in New York were dumped in the sea" (190). Songs with a sexual subtext were also censored and banned by radio, and Calypsonians were regarded by many Christians as singing the devil's music. For years, radio would not play any calypsos during the period of Lent (Warner 1985). Yet Mighty Sparrow, who is the most popular and successful calypso performer since the 1950s and whom Rohlehr calls "the calypso laureate of the West Indies" (Rohlehr 1970, 89), had several risqué songs and remained at the top of the genre. "The way around outright vulgarity or open embarrassment is the use of double entendre, stretched to the very furthest ends of the calypsonian's fertile imagination. In its milder form, this device allows the calypso to escape the self-imposed censorship of the radio stations; in its more vicious form, it parallels the very vulgarity or eroticism it is seeking to mask" (Warner 1985, 129).

Warner's (1985) typology of calypso divides the genre into three categories: (1) political and social commentary, (2) anecdotes, and (3) sexually oriented material that establishes male machismo at the expense of the feminine. All three types link their genealogy to the satirical social commentary of slave-era songs. Enslaved Africans used songs to ridicule each other and their masters. These early songs, like later calypsos and dancehall tracks, were improvised, and they foreshadowed the political commentary of calypso and reggae by employing flattery and satire. And by couching their criticisms of the elite class in double entendre, wordplay and creolized language (originally French Creole and later English Creole in Trinidad), only select members of their audience – fellow slaves – understood their meaning. "The calypsonian uses a certain range of images that the public immediately recognizes as capable of conveying the double meaning" (129). Operating in a privileged liminal space between insider and outsider allowed the enslaved Africans to critique oppressive societal structures in what Gilroy (1993) called "double consciousness". The use of double language acted as a strategy to veil criticism of the elites and protected the singers from serious repercussions for contesting the established hegemonic rule.

The early sexually charged calypsos of the slavery era allowed slaves to please their master and peers at the same time ("The Beat, Sound and Soul of Calypso", *People* [Trinidad], January 1978). According to Rohlehr, this technique is derived from the African custom of permissive criticism of one's leader during a set aside time and context through a song or story (Rohlehr

1990). In modern times, this strategy is still in effect, found in music styles around the Caribbean.

We can see the links between Yellowman's slackness and risqué calypso in several of the themes both take up: boasting about sexual prowess and physical endowments; espousing a breeding farm approach to male-female relationships; instantiating male ego through boasting about the number of sexual partners; songs about paternity, either boasting about it or denying it; songs about a sexual appetite so ravenous that the singer would be satisfied having sex with any woman; liberal use of phallic symbols; and, of course, double entendre.

Today Yellowman finds the differing attitudes towards sexuality in calypso and in dancehall to be unfair. Both are slack, he argues, yet dancehall has been continually demonized while calypso gets away with blatant sexuality. Noted dancehall producers George Phang and Philip "Fatis" Burrell both made this point to me in interviews. The Jamaican middle class is against dancehall's open sexuality yet they excuse the erotic gyrating called "wining" that accompanies calypso. As Boxill points out, "the higher classes determine what is acceptable and what is not" (in Stolzoff 2000, 244). The same can be said for erotic lyrics. When a deejay sings about sex in dancehall, it is called slackness; when a calypsonian artist sings about sex, it is considered bawdy.

Besides calypso, mento was another influential music form in Yellowman's life, and one that also had a suggestive side. In 1951, Stanley Motta became the first producer in Jamaica when he opened a studio and started recording mento artists. The music had a tremendous impact on Jamaican popular music and many subsequent Jamaican artists employed themes, lyrics, melodies, and rhythms from the mento era in their songs.

Before the 1950s, mento was the closest thing Jamaica had to an indigenous popular music. It is derived chiefly from rural digging songs or ring-play songs, and when mento moved into the studio arena in the 1950s, an urbanized form of the genre evolved out of the club culture of Kingston (Manuel, Bilby and Largey 1995). It was this new urban mento that had an increased emphasis on suggestive lyrics, an innovation to accompany the wining (winding or thrusting the hips) dance movements of mento's dancers, which had become more pronounced and erotic. "On Saturday nights in Kingston, popular dance bands would play music that positively encouraged quite lascivious dancing that was far removed from the restrained, traditional rural music"

(Barrow and Coote 2004). It seems that for mento the erotic element was focused on the dance performances that accompanied the music and less on the lyrics. The dance was viewed as "vulgar and indecent, with its pelvic movement and intimate body contact (called 'rent-a-tile')" (Senior 2003, 315). A typical foreign description of mento at the time is found in a 1950 *Dictionary of Folklore*: "An erotic Jamaican dance. . . . Its music is slower and more voluptuous than that of the rumba. The woman tantalizes her partner into a frenzy with seductive rolling of the haunches and belly and works herself into a state of autointoxication" (quoted in Senior 2003, 315).[7]

Just as I am linking the erotic lyrical content of Yellowman to the bawdy nature of many mento and calypso songs, some have suggested that the erotic "dry grind" or "dub" found in contemporary dancehall dancing have antecedents in the "winey" or "winding" style of mento dance (Ryman 1980). Founder of the National Dance Theatre of Jamaica Rex Nettleford (1994, 7) has linked the erotic movements of dancehall to mento: "The movements in dancehall are nothing new; in my own youth I witnessed and participated in mento sessions which forced from executants the kind of axial movements which concentrated on the pelvic region." As can be expected, mento, like its cousin calypso, was preoccupied with risqué accounts of intimate acts, and "most mento songs were often wryly humorous accounts of everyday life among the Jamaican poor, with plenty of references to the perennial topic of sex". In general, though, mento's risqué lyrics were less suggestive than Trinidadian calypso tradition.

This is not to say mento was devoid of slackness; sexual activity was a favourite topic of Jamaica's mento singers. Trinidian calypso songs like "The Big Bamboo" and "Don't Touch Me Tomato" ("All you do is you feel up, feel up / All you do is you squeeze up, squeeze up") received mento treatment by Jamaican artists such as the Wrigglers (2010). Continuing the produce market theme was Tony Johnson's "Give Her Banana" (n.d.) ("Give her banana in the day / Give her banana in the night / If you do she'll treat you right"). Lord Power had his share of slackness and made little attempt to disguise it. His "Strip Tease" is self-explanatory, while his "Let's Do It" revisits the bedroom activities of famous lovers in history: Adam/Eve, Marc Antony/ Cleopatra. The Adam and Eve theme was popular, and was also employed in a polite form by Lord Flea's "It All Began with Adam and Eve". General Echo updated it on his *Slackest LP* and Yellowman used this version for his own remake in 1982. Both dancehall deejays, as can be expected, were far more blatant than their mento cousins.

Lord Lebby and His Jamaican Calypsonians' song "Dr Kinsey Report" (1955) was a popular mento song based on the sexual behaviour of men and women, choosing Kinsey's *Sexual Behavior in the Human Male* (1948) and *Sexual Behavior in the Human Female* (1953) as its frame. In the song, Lebby says Kinsey's report is "all about my favourite indoor sport" and goes on to complain that the sexual behaviour – read infrequency – of women is inadequate: "My own experience of a human dish is they're not always everything a fellow wish." "Dr Kinsey Report" not only foreshadows the kinds of topics Yellowman would populate his songs with, but also his tendency to mix the risqué with the righteous. On the B-side of the record was a popular back to Africa song called "Etheopia".[8] Lebby stands as an excellent example of a Jamaican artist who, two decades before Yellowman, sang slack and cultural themes back to back.[9] Garnice (2011) presumes that judging by the availability of this record today, compared to any other mento 78 rpm record, it must have been a popular record. This is at a time when mento was declining in national popularity and its salacious material was confined to sound systems, live concerts and private homes (White 1982).

Mento still had some popularity in the 1970s. Stanley Beckford, for instance, had his biggest hit in the early 1970s with the Starlites singing "Soldering" (1975), a euphemism for sex. The fact that "Soldering" got airplay even surprised its author, though it was eventually banned from Jamaica radio stations (Forgie 1993). It did, however, inspire response songs by some of dancehall's early deejays like U-Roy.

The influence of mento and calypso on Yellowman and dancehall was tremendous. His ability to improvise and ride a riddim have direct antecedents in the tradition of both musical styles and his body of work, which often focuses on the body itself, has many lyrical and musical quotes or tributes to these earlier styles. He based some of his material directly on mento songs, such as the aforementioned "Adam and Eve", but, apart from borrowing themes and lyrics, he wholeheartedly adopted the sexually liberal nature of risqué mentos and calypsos. Calypsonians have composed a substantial number of songs about their insatiable sexual appetite and it is accompanied by the suggestion that the singer's prowess in the bedroom "causes innumerable females either to cry in ecstasy, beg for more, or groan in agony if they cannot cope with their too-ardent lovers" (Warner 1985, 115). Yellowman has several songs that exhibit the same theme. Yellowman reinvented himself as a super sexual dundus where his yellow "modern body" becomes an aphrodisiac for all women and is the source of his grandiose carnal powers.

Calypso, mento and dancehall artists enjoy boasting about sexual conquests and talents. Each tries to impress the audience with the extent of their insatiable sexual appetite. They take a breeding farm approach to relationships and intimacy, seeking out successive coital partners, often for the sake of impregnating them. Offspring feature for several reasons in these songs, often as proof of manhood, but also as a foil to contest the paternity of a lover's child. Yellowman's songs often mention that his girlfriends either have given birth to yellow babies – proof of paternity – or the babies are not yellow, so he does not have to support them. Of course, generous physical endowments are also a favourite theme, such as in Yellowman's "Sit under You".

Yellowman also found a template for slackness in the styles of music that dominated after calypso and mento. Ska, rocksteady and early reggae often employed thinly veiled language and metaphorical imagery when they talked about the bedroom – songs such as "Rough Rider" (Lloydie and the Lowbites), Jacki Opel ("Push Wood" and "Grinding") and "Action Wood" (Dermot Lynch) used Patwa and double entendre to sing about sex – but some acts like Cock and Pussy, Melinda Slack and Lee Perry, and the Sexy Girls took suggestion (mostly) out of the equation. Prince Buster released several slack songs including "Wreck a Pum Pum" (1969) ("Tonight I want to wreck a pum pum / A fat, fat girl to wreck a pum pum"), a song about rough sex. Prince Buster had an impact with his slackness. Lord Creator covered the song and the Rude Girls recorded a response to his track called "Wreck a Buddy" (buddy being a euphemism for penis). Yellowman later borrowed this title for his own song (also called "Ram Jam Master" (1984c)), though other than the title, Yellowman's graphic description of his courtship with several women, a hint of a similar bass line ("Ram Jam Master" uses Jackie Mittoo's "Evening Time" as its riddim), the songs are completely different.

Unlike Yellowman, Prince Buster's slack songs did not define him. His musical achievements both behind and in front of the mixing board were broad, from Beatles covers, rudeboy rocksteady, and ska, to Rastafarian-themed material. For his audience, "Buster's appearance on sex records represented only one aspect of his multifaceted persona" (Walker 2005, 239).

His slack songs were banned from radio but through the sound systems, jukeboxes and uptown parties they gained an underground audience. Buster had serious culture credibility too: he was the producer who brought Rastafarian drummers Count Ossie into the studio for "Oh Carolina", commonly thought to be the first recorded connection between Jamaican popular music and Rastafari, the first instance of Rastas recording on popular music and the first instance of Rastafarian music (drumming) being used in a popular song (Bradley 2001). Buster's credibility as a culture artist was further instantiated with his conversion to the Nation of Islam and its association with the Black Power movement. Further to this, Buster's own sound system, Voice of the People, boasted a cultural name.

While Prince Buster was one of the dominant artists making slack records in the 1960s, early reggae enjoyed many sex-themed hits among fans. Lee Perry produced several of these, such as "Doctor Dick" and "Rub and Squeeze", both of which, incidentally, featured Bob Marley's wife, Rita. Max Romeo's 1969 hit "Wet Dream" even managed to enter the British charts, reaching the top 10, yet was banned by BBC (Walker 2005, 239). Romeo would later become better known with songs of Rastafarian and cultural import such as "War in a Babylon", "Rasta Bandwagon" and "Macabee Version". Even cultural group the Heptones had their "Fatty Fatty" banned by the radio because of perceived rudeness, Walker points out. Another cultural group who sang slackness was none other than the Wailers. The Wailers, held up as the epitome of roots and culture by the foreign music press, indulged in slackness in songs such as "Making Love", "Do It Twice", "Guava Jelly", and "Kinky Reggae", among others. The album cover for their *Soul Rebels* album even went so far as having a woman holding a machine gun with her shirt open to expose almost the entirety of her breasts. To be fair, though, this was issued against their wishes.

General Echo was the first to simply drop the double entendre and make slack lyrics explicit in the late 1970s. He took the popularity of slackness in the sound systems to a new height. But it was Yellowman, whose slackness seemingly knew no boundaries, who took it from the relative confines of the dancehall space into the public eyes and ears. When contained in the dancehall, the mainstream public were safely buffered from it, but when Yellowman became more popular than any previous deejay, and especially any slack performer, the mainstream had to notice it. First issued on live tapes of dancehall performances that were played in buses and taxis around the island, and then marketed as live sessions on vinyl, by the turn of the decade, blatant slackness had progressed from the live arena of dancehall and entered the studio, where it thrived. Clint Eastwood's *Sex Education* (1980), Ranking Joe's *Saturday Night Jamdown Style* (1980) and Welton Irie's *Army Life* (1982) complimented the bawdy material Yellowman was deejaying at the time.

Yellowman performed slackness in the dancehall for one reason – it was popular. As such, for Yellowman, slackness was just entertainment – a strategy used to build his name and reputation, win fans and sell records. Desmond Gaynor, Yellowman's drummer since 1982 and founding member of the Sagittarius Band, remembers what it was like in those early days when Yellowman began chatting slackness in the dance

> Desmond Gaynor: The church was considered the moral compass, you know? So the culture back then would not approve of you saying things, or allow things to be said within earshot of your elders.
>
> Author: So Yellowman was going against the moral compass of society?
>
> DG: A little bit. He was really targeting his lyrics, like cutting across the grain. It was his experience . . . he was just being Yellow, it was entertainment 'cause he wanted to be different.
>
> Author: He wanted to be different/he was different – are you saying he used that as his hook?
>
> DG: He used that as his hook, yes. (Interview by author, 12 August 2008)

While slackness was used as a hook to win him favour with the audience, Yellowman insists that since sex is natural, singing about it should not be controversial. Slackness to him is simply an example of reality lyrics, a catch-all phrase that artists use to legitimate anything from rude lyrics to gun violence. Reality lyrics usually connote culture or consciousness but, used in this way, they can blur the lines between slack and culture. For Yellowman, reality in this context means "every day". It is a way to express an aspect of the culture he lives in, and this aspect – open sexuality – is contested by the upper classes: "Sexual lyrics was reality and entertainment at the same time. But maybe the way how I put it sound gross to the people, some people. But it was entertainment, so it didn't bother me."

Yellowman's success was aided by the fact that he had a sharp wit to dress up slackness using humour. He singles out his sense of humour as one of the keys to entertaining an audience:

> Yellowman: The people did love me and the way I do it [slackness], [and] the voice, because I used to put it in a kinda laughable way, entertainment way. Like I would say, "you look pon her head it, don't have no hair, between her leg it have a nine inch tear / back one sign says be good beware / of 'gina" [from "Dry Head Adassa" (1988a)].
>
> Author: So it was always funny?
>
> Yellowman: Ya. It was always funny to the people. Them laugh.

Josey Wales agrees that Yellowman's use of humour went a long way to endearing him to the public and making his slackness acceptable to the many, but in his opinion Yellowman began to take slackness to an extreme past the normal humour of his early material and of General Echo. "Echo had more humour to his slackness, Yellow was like the Lady Saw of today. Yellow sing about sex more raw than Echo. Echo would sing like 'Bathroom sex it carry the swing'. Yellow sing, 'Call me yellow, the yellow baby, put the yellow something in the Yello B'" (Josey Wales, interview by author, 25 February 2009).

Yellowman's popularity grew as he focused more on slackness, particularly among female fans. More women started going to the dances he was chatting at and that, of course, brought extra male patrons. He says, "When I start [on a new] sound system, girls start like that sound because I talking about sex. And the girls dem would love when I talk about sex. So, my fans was a lot of girls and the guys used to come because of the girls."

That songs about female body parts, casual sex with several partners and bedroom boasting appealed to anyone other than adolescent males may seem surprising to some readers. I doubted this sentiment when he first broached it. Surely lyrics such as "give me vagina"[10] or "want a virgin" (1988a) do nothing but objectify women, reducing them to sexually submissive conquests, and ignore that they are thinking human beings with agency over their thoughts and bodies. Certainly, Yellowman's slackness oppresses women by portraying them as sexual objects, who, robot-like, desire sex all the time, particularly with him. To be sure, this is a valid critique of a man whose repertoire includes lyrics such as "Watch how she fat she just a bubble pon top / Inna dat me rock inna dat" (from "Love Fat Thing" [Yellow-

man and Fathead 1982d]).[11] My initial analysis of his songs about having
sex with hundreds of women were that they were nothing more than the
male ego gone wild, pseudo pornographic episodes meant to entertain the
testosterone-rich crowds.

But as I read the scholarly literature on dancehall and slackness, I found
corroboration for his claims that women did, indeed, love his slackness,
and I came to understand that there are other ways to view this material.
The women who loved his performance in the dancehall were by no means
submissive or somehow lacking clear choices and agency. I also came to
realize that my initial assumptions were based on a second wave feminist
critique that equated the sexualization of women by a male artist and male
dominated industry as inherently sexist, as it catered to the male gaze and
reproduced traditional gender roles that reduced women to sexual objects
and reaffirmed male power over women. Many practitioners and scholars
of dancehall were more in line with third wave and intersectional feminist
approaches that dismissed the idea that sex is a dirty word not to be uttered
by feminists. I'm paraphrasing here, but this is the gist of Camille Paglia's
(1992) classic treatment of Madonna and feminism: the second wave saw
any sexualized performance by a woman as upholding inequality, whereas
Paglia argued that in music videos like "Justify My Love", Madonna critiqued
the very basis of sexism in the music industry by undermining patriarchal
control over how women should be represented.

The point here is that starting with third wave feminism, performances
of female sexuality can be empowering for women. Similarly, particularly
in the dancehall space, male performances that celebrate female sexuality
are often appreciated by women. I am reminded of Cooper's (2004) point
that dancehall can overturn the repressive gender hierarchy and have a
liberating effect on women. Some dancehall songs sung by both men and
women "celebrate the economic and sexual independence of women, thus
challenging the conservative gender ideology that is at the heart of both
pornographic and fundamentalist conceptions of woman as commodity,
virgin and whore" (Cooper 1995, 142–43).[12]

Yellowman's female fans are not turned off by songs that appear to objectify
them, nor, as far as I can tell, do they see these songs as one-dimensional. Yellowman became the King of Dancehall because he had the largest audience,
and it was his slack material that was the most popular, even when (or perhaps

because) it was banned by Jamaican radio. Yellowman drew on the heritage of slackness in Caribbean music and amplified it louder than any previous artist. He did so to please his audience and expand his notoriety, but he used slackness in several ways. It helped him overcome his ostracization due to his skin colour, and convince his audience of his worthiness and credibility as a dancehall deejay. The fact that a dundus was deejaying sex lyrics both played into his popularity among dancehall patrons and made him highly controversial among the higher classes. He ruptured socially constructed codes of race, sexuality and masculinity by promoting the male dundus as a hypersexual object of female desire and rode a wave of popular support among music fans that ultimately saw dancehall replace the roots reggae of the Marley era as Jamaica's primary popular sound culture. What is more, he did this with extremely coarse lyrics and an explicit performance style that stripped away much of the double entendre of dancehall's forebears, such as reggae, rocksteady, calypso and mento.

CULTURE AND SLACK ON THE SOUND SYSTEMS

> Favourite colour man it yellow and black
> Sometime me culture sometime me slack
> Know 'bout me Bible know me scripture
> Know 'bout me roots also me culture
> Deejay fe baldhead and Rasta
> —Yellowman, "Under Mi Fat Ting" (1985a)

Each deejay who was steady on a sound system would work with that sound every night they had a show. For a busy sound system like Aces, that meant Yellowman worked six out of seven nights a week. Josey Wales remembers that "only Tuesday our day off. Sound system play from Monday to Monday. Rest on Tuesday, record and recuperate" (interview by author, 25 February 2009). If a sound did not have a show during the week, though, many deejays took the opportunity to go hear their peers at rival sounds. The relationships between artists like Charlie Chaplin, Josey Wales, Brigadier Jerry and Yellowman was fraternal and, besides helping to promote their own career, these visits allowed the deejays to have fun sparring with each other and to pick up new lyrics.

But there were rules, particularly around slackness. With Yellowman at its helm, you could expect an Aces dance to have a lot of slackness. Later, when Henry Junjo Lawes's Volcano sound system was one of the island's most popular, the same was true. But there were a few sounds that were known as strict cultural sounds and frowned on slack lyrics. Two of these, Stereograph (aka Stur-Gav) and Jah Love, were Rasta-run sounds. When Yellowman came to guest with them, he would be told by either U-Roy at Stur-Gav or Brigadier Jerry at Jah Love to "keep it clean". Similarly, promoter Worrell King remembers taking Yellowman on his first tour of the Cayman Islands in 1983 where he had to keep "reminding him to keep it clean. Cayman then – it is a bit more relaxed now – one dirty word and you were off the stage" ("Worrell King: The Principled Promoter", *Gleaner*, 23 June 2002). The Cayman tour was such a success that Yellowman was back there again soon after. Switching up his style for different audiences never bothered Yellowman, a strong proponent of the "give the people what they want" philosophy of entertaining.

> I could show you tapes from twenty-five, twenty-seven years ago where he comes to Junjo's sound, Volcano, and we worked the mic together. And could play you tapes when he come to Stereograph in Spanish Town in 1983 and he tone it down. 'Cause there's a respect for U-Roy and a certain type of crowd. 'Cause Stur-Gav was playing for a mostly Rastafarian crowd 'cause we were changing the thing to a strictly culture. Most people could not get away with what he run away with – both culture and slack. (Josey Wales, interview by author, 25 February 2009)

During a conversation with some of Jah Love's contemporary deejays in February 2010 at the Twelve Tribes of Israel headquarters, I asked them about the politics and optics of a slackness deejay chatting on a culture sound. Was it odd that the King of Slack deejayed on Jah Love? These deejays – Culture Dan, Pampi Judah, Rashorni and Natty Field Marshall – presented three arguments. First, slackness and songs about sex are not bad in and of themselves. Second, they contain adult content and as such there is an appropriate time and place for their performance. The Jah Love sound system prides itself on being a family-oriented sound system and so deejays should not chat slackness when they are guests of Jah Love. Third, artists must make a living. Slackness sells and, therefore, if an artist chooses to chat slackness to make themselves financially successful, they should not be looked down upon. Taken together, slackness from this point of view is not bad; there is simply a time and place where it is appropriate and Yellowman had no problem complying with this.

VERSIONING AND THE REMIX AESTHETIC

> Some deejay na no lyrics
> They come inna de dance and pirate de lyrics
> Open them ears and listen to it
> Tape on cassette a weh deh tape it
> And go a dem yard and practise it
> Go a foreign dem de do it
> And a fool up de crowd 'bout a dem mek it
> And come back a Yard 'bout big and broad
> I want hit de whole a dem with a microphone cord
> —Yellowman, "Na No Lyrics" (1987c)

Yellowman was prolific and his lyrics were clever, but he has been criticized for robbing many of these lyrics from his rivals. For instance, "Society Party" (1984e) was previously done by Brigadier Jerry and Sassafrass, Josey Wales was deejaying lyrics that ended up in Yellowman's "Herbman Smuggling" and several people had versions of "Too Greedy" including Brigadier Jerry, Lone Ranger, Josey Wales, Supercat and George Nooks before Yellowman released his. Add to this every deejay's insistence that they are an "original" or that their song was "the original" of a particular theme or style and it can be hard to keep the lineage of a song straight. Often lost in this conversation, though, is the fact that deejay rivalries in the late 1970s and early 1980s were often ritualized for dramatic effect rather than being hostile, and the creation of reggae songs generally happens within a participatory model that is in keeping with remix culture.

> Josey Wales: There wasn't any copyright; we weren't even looking for that. I have sung songs that other people own them but it is my song. They record word for word . . . they couldn't [do] that in your country but this is Jamaica. I don't mind if you sing my song, 'cause I feel good, even if I'm not recognized. You know, I know, and the public know.

Author: Abroad we don't recognize where those lyrics come from – we don't have the context the fans here do.

JW: Ya, within that time, reggae didn't have a broad base . . . didn't matter . . . when Yellow start touring everybody start recognizing this song is a Shabba, this is a whatever, so some find its rightful place now and then. . . . There was a lot of robbery, Yellowman get a whole heap a rob from all a we at that time, but thanks to God for all of that robbery 'cause we are inheriting from it now. So those was good robbery. (Josey Wales, interview by author, 25 Feburary 2009)

Yellowman is widely known to have borrowed several of his lyrics from other deejays, as Josey Wales explains in the above quotation, but the idea of borrowing or stealing lyrics has a particular cultural context. Several musicians I talked to admitted that this was a rampant practice but insisted that in those times it was acceptable. Live tape sessions sped up the transmission of lyrics between deejays, as a favourite lyric could get passed around to several entertainers. "Lyrics travelled from one end of Jamaica to the other in 24 hours or less. Lyrics that were flashed in the dance in Kingston on a Saturday could be heard in Ochie on a Sunday" (Lesser 2008, 147). Lesser gives several examples of lyrics that were freely transmitted between deejays: Tappa Zukie's "People Are You Ready" was originally Welton Irie's, General Echo's "Arlene" began with Johnny Ringo, and Sassafrass claims that Yellowman songs such as "Society Party" (1984e) and "Poopin' Contest" were his. "Yellowman did about a hundred of my songs", he told Lesser (Lesser 2008, 147).

Not only were contemporary popular lyrics fair game, a deejay might reach back to previous eras of reggae, ska and even mento to find phrases, ideas, story arcs and complete lyrics. Yellowman uses mento lyrics in songs such as "Hill and Gully Rider" and has also borrowed catchphrases from one of Jamaica's first talk-over artists, King Stitt. Stitt's lyrics

No matter what the people say
these sounds lead the way
it's the order of the day from your boss deejay
I King Stitt
up it from the top to the very last drop
(quoted in Davis and Simon 1982, 112)

find their way into various Yellowman songs such as "Lost Mi Love" (1982d) ("No matter what the people of the world may say / Before me go a bed me say me know me haffi pray / She gone with the boss deejay").

Yellowman says that lyrics were passed around much more back then, but insists that it was a more collegial atmosphere where deejays respected each other. In a newspaper article from 1983, for instance, he talks about his great respect for many of the deejays who influenced him, and whom he subsequently borrowed from (Saunders 1983). He admitted in 1984 that the idea of spelling out lyrics in song (such as "L.O.V.E. love you" in "Lost Mi Love") came from Peter Metro and that he and Metro shared ideas: "Sometimes Metro get a lickle idea from me and I get a lickle idea from him" ("Yellowman Takes Over", *Cool Runnings: Reggae Roots Magazine*, 1984, 5). He says,

> Those days it wasn't competition. Those days we idolize each other. Those days we use each other's lyrics. If you come to Virgo you hear Welton Irie singing General Echo or Ringo lyrics. Go to Stereophonic or Gemini you hear Ringo doing Echo lyrics or Echo doing Ringo lyrics or you hear Brigadier doing Echo lyrics in a clean way. At that time, Brigadier was the clean deejay.

Of course, the lyrical borrowings worked both ways, with deejays using Yellowman's lyrics as well. He also speaks to the fact in "Na no Lyrics" that some deejays would tape live sounds just so they could steal the lyrics of another artist.

Yellowman was a cultural sponge, soaking up musical and lyrical influences both from Jamaica and abroad. He essentially curated the best lyrical ideas around at the time and reworked many of them for his own songs. In a review of a September 1983 show in Toronto, Liam Lacey ("Yellowman Is Proof Positive That Jamaican Music Thrives", *Globe and Mail*, 26 September 1983) was impressed with the broad musical and lyrical palette of Yellowman's songs but noted that "there is nothing truly original about what he does – the precedents for each of his singing styles are well-established in Jamaican music – but his fluid synthesis of different kinds of patter and his stage dramatics are great fun". Lesser puts Yellowman's borrowing into perspective, pointing out that since he was a popular recording deejay, he was in a privileged position to be the first to put many ideas on record, thereby canonizing them and laying claim to them:

Everybody did that, yes, everybody borrowed. He just happened to record a lot so he, it was kind of like a race. Somebody would come up with a lyric and whoever was recording at the time would get to put it on record and, you know, that's the way it goes. There're some deejays like poor old Jah Mikey walking around and he had his lyrics, "dance haffi cork, liqueur sell off" and, you know, they're probably his lyrics and he never ever got to record them I think. Other people recorded them instead. (Interview by author, 21 January 2009)

Sometimes Yellowman tells his audience where a lyric came from. At a concert at Rissmiller's Country Club in Reseda, California, in September 1982, Yellowman announced the song "Pain" (1982c) with the words "This done by mi bredren called Brigadier Jerry. The ting called, the great sounds called the 'Pain'. Originate by mi bredren called the Brigadier the General." Similarly, "Bad Boy Skanking" (1982d) begins with the spoken introduction: "This originate by a man called Junie, and this one come to make you feel irie, done by Fathead and me."

As Josey Wales stated, sometimes an audience would know who the originator of the lyric was. When Yellowman sang "Me Kill Barnie", it was obvious to the crowd gathered at Tastee's that he was using a popular lyric in the dance and putting his own stamp of originality on it. The song "Barnabas Collins" had been an earlier hit for Lone Ranger, and Yellowman was seen as a clever lyricist to work that into his own song. Often this cultural genealogy would be lessened or lost as the music first left Jamaica, and then filtrated out from the dancehall communities in other countries. A Jamaican audience would see Yellowman in his milieu and understand, first, many of his local cultural references and, second, to what extent he put his own stamp on cultural borrowings. International audiences, especially those with no Jamaican connections or dancehall affiliations, came to see Yellowman in a very different light. For them, as the first and biggest dancehall star of the decade, he was the virtual creator of many trends. For instance, there are several Yellowman lyrics that are reworkings of earlier songs by other artists, and can be viewed as responses or "counteractions" to them. His "Shorties" (1984b) for instance, works in lyrics from Michigan and Smiley's "Diseases". Whereas "Diseases" admonished girls for wearing pants and thereby breaching traditional codes of femininity, "Shorties" skilfully (and slackly) praises short skirts; "Want Vagina" (2016) was a part of the "Punanny" craze started by Admiral Bailey, "Under Mi Fat Thing" (1985a) was one of the hundreds of songs inspired by Wayne Smith's "Sleng Teng", and "Body Move" (1983c) liberally lifts Barrington Levy's lyrics from "Money Move" and "Dances Are Changing".

In reggae culture, these are not considered either cover versions or rip-offs of an earlier artist's work. Instead, they are respected as unique iterations of earlier themes, lyrics, melodies, or rhythms. Speaking of "Under Mi Fat Thing", Yellowman told me how his version differed from the myriad other versions out there at the time: his was recorded with a live band. To get the full significance of this you have to understand that the original "Sleng Teng" song was built on a digital riddim created by Wayne Smith on a Casio keyboard. When King Jammy recorded and produced the song, he did so with the Casio keyboard providing bass and built in drum machine, thereby instigating what many commentators consider the most important shift in reggae in the 1980s: digital instrumentation. For Yellowman to buck this trend is significant indeed. Of course, Sly and Robbie, the duo who recorded the live band version of "Sleng Teng" that Yellowman deejays over on "Under Mi Fat Thing", are responsible for this. Of course, Yellowman also recorded over a digital "Sleng Teng" riddim on "Reggae Ambassador" on the King Jammy–produced *Yellow Fever* (1999) album.

Like all Jamaican popular music, new dancehall artists draw on the roots of the tradition in order to create something new. "Versioning", as it is called, is one of the vital lifelines of Jamaican music, ensuring that new artists engage with tradition but also challenging them to constantly deconstruct that tradition in an attempt to rebuild old sounds and lyrics as something new. Hebdige (1987) suggests that versioning is at the heart of "all Afro-American and Caribbean musics: jazz, blues, rap, R&B, reggae, calypso, soca, salsa, Afro-Cuban and so on" (12). In calypso, for instance, several different song lyrics can be composed on one tune, and many blues songs traditionally shared similar lyrics, melodies and rhythmic accompaniment. Robert Johnson's "Sweet Home Chicago" was an adaption of a Kokomo Arnold tune "Old Original Kokomo Blues" and his "I Believe I'll Dust My Broom" cops the melody from Leroy Carr's "I Believe I'll Make a Change" (Wald 2004).

These are all forms of versioning. Versioning in itself is an example of remix culture which was central to African American genres like hip-hop and disco. DJ Kool Herc, a Jamaican who moved to the Bronx, laid the foundation for hip-hop when he began using two turntables to extend the drum breaks in songs, deconstructing an existing piece of music to fashion a new artistic creation. These "breakbeats" eventually inspired later rap artists such as Public Enemy, Marley Marl and Run-DMC to create their backing tracks from the sampled works of other artists. One of the best-worn samples of this period of rap was Clyde Stubblefield's drumbeat known as the "Funky Drummer", performed in the James Brown song of the same name.

Disco also shares the remix aesthetic. Early remixers such as Tom Moulton manipulated existing songs by adding extended drum-breaks, and ultimately introduced the remix craze to mainstream pop music through the 12-inch remix albums in the 1970s.

Reggae's credentials as a remix originator predate both disco and hip-hop. Early versioning occurred in ska and rocksteady, but when deejays like U-Roy began chatting over existing rocksteady songs, first on sound systems in the 1960s and then on record, this took versioning to a whole new level. Instrumental B-sides, simply labelled "version", became the foundation for aspiring deejays to chat over in the dance. Soon, dub recording pioneers like Lee Perry, Herman Chin-Loy and King Tubby were experimenting with studio remixing techniques in the early 1970s, innovating a brand new approach to versioning that influenced the world of dance remixes in the 1970s and 1980s.

Small (1998) explains that genres of music created by musicians in the African diaspora share a uniquely African musical value system based in expressiveness, improvisation, rhythm, adaptability and participation. Whereas in European art, music the focus is a music object (sheet music, a performance), in the African context the focus of music was experience. For Small (1998), this is demonstrated in the different ways that music took root in the Americas among Europeans and Africans. Europeans brought a repertoire of songs with them, and privileged practice and performance methods that attempted to recreate the songs faithfully each time in the interest of preservation and transmission. This applies to both a classical musician playing from a Mozart score, and an Appalachian balladeer singing an Irish murder ballad.

Africans did not have the privilege of bringing physical culture, such as instruments or sheet music, on the treacherous Middle Passage. Instead, they brought with them musical practices that could be described using the theory of a remix aesthetic. Africans in the diaspora learned European music forms but routinely manipulated them, merging European approaches to chord progressions, melody and harmony into new genres like jazz. Instead of preservation and transmission, the remix aesthetic emphasized the adaptability of music and allowed for continual innovation. The idea of authorship, too, differs. The remix aesthetic is geared towards collaboration and participation, whereas European art music conventions privilege individual composition.

The notion that music is a static object, a product, is based on twentieth-century modes of production and consumption, when the term "music" started to refer to the media used to listen to songs: a vinyl record or a compact disc, for example. Before this, as Turino (2008) says, for much of the world, music was an activity, as in "to make music". Remix culture merges these two ideas: the act of making music can occur with a music product. An existing song can be remixed into a new composition; an existing riddim can provide the foundation for a new song; existing lyrics can be repurposed in a new context; an existing record can be looped to form a breakbeat for an MC to rap over.

Versioning not only allows for an artist to create a new work out of existing material, it also has the benefit of educating modern listeners on the ongoing history of the genre and culture. As a dancehall deejay, Yellowman created songs that often have musical, lyrical and thematic antecedents in the songs of his contemporaries, but also in reggae, ska, mento and calypso. A good example of this is his song "Zungguzungguguzungguzeng" (1983e). The lyric is mostly his own, but Yellowman borrowed the melody from a deejay at a political rally for PNP presidential candidate Michael Manley in the early 1980s, turning the line "You shouldn't trouble Mr Manley, boy" into "Jump fe happiness and jump fe joy, you no fe call Yellowman no boy". The backing riddim for "Zungguzungguguzungguzeng" is also an example of how the Jamaican music industry continually reinvents itself, feeding off the old to create the new. Known as "Mad Mad", "Diseases", "Dutty Rub" or "Johnny Dollar", the rhythm track was originally recorded by Studio One and first used on the Alton Ellis song "Mad Mad" in 1967. Riddimbase.org lists 189 different versions of this riddim. When Yellowman does a version of "Mad Mad", it is not considered a cover. Instead, it is seen as something unique because the artist has not tried to recreate a previous song as much as built on it (or several versions of it) in their own style, adding a stamp of originality in the process. Yellowman's versioning practice in "Zungguzungguguzungguzeng" also set in motion further innovations by other artists. As Marshall ("Follow Me Now: The Zigzagging Zunguzung Meme", Wayne and Wax, 2007, http://wayneandwax.com/?p=137) shows, the melodic meme of the chorus has been used in at least sixty versions between 1982 and 2019 – that is, sixty different artists who borrowed Yellowman's melody for their own songs, either as a pastiche, to cite or quote him, or just as a melodic hook for their own work.[13]

In an interview that Yellowman did with Chamberlain (2010), he explains how deejays build thematically, lyrically and rhythmically on other works. First, at a dance the selector will play a record with the vocal mix – usually a popular song by a singer. Next, they will play the riddim, dub or version, meaning the instrumental backing tracks. This is designed to allow the "deejay to extemporize on the same riddim, which came to be known as 'part two'" (22). Deejays often worked off the same themes in the song and their lyrics were seen as a "counteraction" to the sung version.

> Yellowman: What I used to do, I used to deejay the lyrics to match the vocal version. Like, Dennis Brown would sing a song, [Brown would] say, "Hold on to what you got, hold on to what you got." So I have to find something quick. Meanwhile that the vocal version playing I thinking up something, you know. That's when the part two come. I would say, "Hold up pon de woman weh you got, hold up pon de woman weh you got, whether she white or whether she black, whether she in her pants or frock, hold up pon de woman weh you got." You know . . . that's how I used to do it. (Chamberlain 2010, 23)

This is how deejays would construct lyrics on the spot in the dance. The selector would play a John Holt, Alton Ellis, Sugar Minott, Barrington Levy, or Barry Brown song and, after each track, play the instrumental version for a deejay to respond to. Yellowman often began his responses by saying something like "Now here come another counteraction for satisfaction / Dem a selection a juk[14] you like a medicine injection / I Yellowman come to rock de nation and tell everyone" (introduction to "Can't Hide from Jah" [1983e]).

It is possible that Yellowman's "Can't Hide from Jah" evolved at a dance after the selector played the Heptones' 1979 song of the same name. The song's title is also inspired by Ken Parker's "I Can't Hide" (1970) and Yellowman uses the "I Can't Hide" riddim on his own "Natty Sat upon the Rock" (1982d), a song that is based on Lone Ranger's "Sat upon a Rock" and also borrows from Yellowman's own "Can't Hide from Jah" lyrics. The themes, lyrics and riddims of each song, then, are networked with several other in the reggae canon.

We could theorize that reggae songs are composed with the collective voice – new artists engaging with the creations of their forebears so that the final product has contributions from and homages to a long lineage of musicians, singers and deejays. As Hebdige (1987, 11) puts it, "African, Afro-American and Caribbean music is based on quite different principles from the European classical tradition. The collective voice is given precedence over the individual voice of the artist or the composer." The whole idea of originality in reggae culture is vastly different from that in mainstream music. Jamaican artists often boast that they are "originals" or that they originated some trend, when in fact it is easy to see that the trend existed long before them. In Yellowman's song "The Ark" (1984), for instance, he begins the track by announcing "This one originate by I, Yellowman, and promote by a man call Leon. Dis one is a different counteraction called Noah and the Ark." Yet the song is actually based on Lone Ranger's 1977 song, "Noah in the Ark". When a journalist once asked Yellowman if deejays like Lone Ranger influenced him, he responded, "Yeah, yeah, those DJs did influence me but I come in my own style y'know, original" (Saunders 1983, 15). Beth Lesser clarified the meaning of the term "original" in reggae culture for me:

> You have to understand they have a really different concept of what "new" or "original" means in Jamaica. Because I've heard people say things like, you know the big song "Army Life" [by Welton Irie]? Someone will come and say, "I'm original, I did 'Navy Life'." And I'm completely new and original but it has exactly the same tune and lyrics and they just changed the word navy or something. So, you get a lot of that. It's just a different interpretation. People will tell you they've written something original because they changed one word in the song and they really really see it that way: it's original. (Interview by author, 21 January 2009)

Lesser shows how the same interpretation is used regarding riddims:

> It's very very tricky because when you use the word original you may mean that it is the very original – the first time it was put down on record. Or you mean it is original, meaning you got people to come into the studio and copy the first one but nobody else has actually used that particular version of it. There's

nothing cut and dried in any of this, and this is what's so lovely about it, it is completely fluid. (Interview by author, 21 January 2009)

This same interpretation of original can be applied to innovations deejays claim for themselves and the culture of braggadocio that is so intrinsic to the music and its practitioners. I have argued above that the underlying motivation throughout Yellowman's entire career has been a quest to prove his worth over and over, and this has not stopped now that he is in his sixties. In interviews with the press or with me, Yellowman is always ready to list off his accomplishments, a continuing attempt it seems to legitimate his King of Dancehall status.

> I am the first one who ever been on a major label as a dancehall artist. I am the first one who hit the Billboard chart as a dancehall artist with a single called "Strong Me Strong". And I'm the first dancehall artist who ever collaborated with rap artist. I'm the first dancehall artist who in the *Guinness Book of Records*, and the only dancehall artist. I am the first dancehall artist who nominated for a Grammy. That's the reason why they call me the King of Dancehall all over the world.

Yellowman claims he popularized the use of a sung chorus and narrative in deejay music: "I bring chorus into dancehall. I bring story to dancehall. Because back in the days deejays only talk straight. They never have any chorus like you would sing." The pride in his accomplishments extends to more material achievements in dancehall culture, such as dress code:

> Deejays used to dress up in sequins, then I start bring in t-shirt, cap, gold chains and jeans in the dancehall. And I bring camouflage in the dancehall too. When I first start dress like soldier, people used to laugh at me and nowadays it became a big fashion. I am the one who wear the tracksuit and then everybody start. Remember in the 1980s every rapper wear tracksuit? [That's] because of me.

It does not really matter that Big Youth, for instance, sang choruses in the 1970s, or Aston "Familyman" Barrett wore combat gear in early Wailers promotional photos and onstage. What matters for Yellowman and his fans is that he offered an interpretation of these trends and was therefore an original. Yellowman's music, like all Jamaican reggae, is steeped in tradition, and while Yellowman certainly brought originality in style, performance and lyrics, he did so within the existing creative tradition of Jamaican music.

CHAPTER 6

Jamaica Proud of Me, 1982

Proud of me, Jamaica proud of me
Kaa everyting me talk 'bout is about me country
Me talk 'bout Super Don and the man Barry G
You have Yellowman, don't you 'get Nancy[1]
You have Yellowman, you have Louie Lepkie
But nothing in this world impossible fe me
Me sleep on dry land and walk pon sea
Me coming like Jesus from Galilee
Say twenty dollar come in like nothing to me
　　—Yellowman, "Jamaica Proud of Me" (1983b)

IF THERE IS ONE YEAR THAT CAN BE called Yellowman's it was 1982. That is the year he shook the reggae industry to its foundations and fundamentally changed the game. Yellowman placed several records in the top ten of the *Daily Gleaner*'s Hit Parade, which was based on sales from local record stores. The paper called "I'm Getting Married" "one of the fastest rising records to hit the No. 1 slot" ("Yellowman Still Reigns", *Daily Gleaner,* 18 March 1982). By 12 June, "Mister Chin" would reach the coveted top spot, despite the radio's refusal to play it.

Yellowman's dominance in the dancehall not only gained him favourable press at home and abroad and legions of fans, but even other deejays started to comment on just how big Yellowman became. Lovindeer, for instance, released a tribute to Yellowman in 1982 called "Yellow Fellow (Straight to Yellowman)":

I want to know tell me who is Yellow fellow?
Everywhere you go all you hear is Yellowman . . .
For the sweetest girls anywhere
The man you protect is Lovindeer
But if you have a session and you want it fe ram
The one you fe check for is Yellowman
Yes yes Yellow fellow are de best

This meteoric rise saw Yellowman move from sound system celebrity to studio star, undertake his first international tours, and be crowned the King of Dancehall at Sunsplash 1982.

DANCEHALL'S CASSETTE CULTURE

Taping of live dancehall sessions was common in the late 1970s and early 1980s and was encouraged by sound men because it freely advertised their sound throughout the island and abroad. The tapes circulated freely among fans and were heard on buses and taxis, often the very day after the live session. Live session tapes helped to spread the hype about an artist and allowed a greater demographic to hear their songs. And for artists like Brigadier Jerry, live tapes meant that he could garner the reputation of being one of the most popular deejays on the island without ever stepping into a studio to record a track. In fact, Lesser (2008) surmises that one reason for the increase in live session tapes in the early 1980s was due to the demand for Brigadier material, since none was available on record. The motivation behind the tapes was never profit; no one sold them, and collecting them became a major pastime for fans.

Yellowman's sets at Aces, Black Scorpio, Gemini and Virgo were taped by fans and would then make their way around the island and be played loudly from buses and taxis – important mediums for the spread of dancehall culture and its proliferation into the mainstream public sphere. On a New York tour stop in 2008, Zimma, Sagittarius's bassist at the time, told me about hearing these tapes while he was in high school. His family was Christian, however, and frowned on dancehall. His parents and grandparents discouraged him from listening to it, saying reggae was evil.

Zimma: But they can't shelter from what is played on the bus [when] you used to go to school. That is where we would get all this stuff. The driver would just put in a tape of last night's show at the dancehall and everybody would be quiet. That half hour to forty-five min ride to school, that's where a church boy would get his dancehall experience, education.

Author: What was your first impression of Yellowman?

Zimma: I thought, "whoa" he just said that thing? I said to the next child next to me – did you hear that? He said the "P" word, 'cause of course you can't even say. I think that's what popularized the arena of the dancehall in Jamaica. Because you could play whatever you couldn't play on radio. There was no censorship, just raw culture. You want the real thing, go to the dancehall. (Zemroy "Zimma" Lewis, interview by author, 12 August 2008)

Sound system tapes were transnational products, moving to England, Canada and the United States long before social media. Fans of dancehall in these countries got to hear Yellowman from these session tapes before he released any studio albums.

SOUND SYSTEM LPS

It was only a matter of time until record companies would take what was going on in the dancehall scene seriously. In 1982, Heartbeat Records released the first live dancehall session on LP, called *A Dee-Jay Explosion inna Dancehall Style*. It was recorded at popular dancehall venue Skateland on 20 January 1982 and featured Gemini Discotheque. The deejays recorded that night included Yellowman, Eek-A-Mouse, Welton Irie, Brigadier Jerry, Ranking Toyan, Sister Nancy, Michigan and Smiley, Sassafrass, Trinity, and Johnny Ringo. The album marked the first time that a live dancehall session was officially released, not merely bootlegged. Not long after, on 10 February 1982, Lloyd Campbell and Jimmy Wynter recorded a live Aces dance and released it as *Live at Aces* (1982b). While the majority of the record is Yellowman, or the deejay in combination with Fathead, Aces singer Jah Rubel contributes two tracks and Little Harry one. Yellowman insists, however, that Campbell did not secure permission to release the recording: "Lloyd Campbell, he pirate that album. He come to the dance first and ask me and my manager if he can do a live LP. So we say we will charge him a certain amount of money.

But he don't want to pay so we say 'no, it can't go on then'. So, he come and he get somebody to tape it through the amps" (Yellowman 1982).

Live at Aces (1982b) is a vastly different album from Yellowman's studio records of the time. Both in the studio and on the sound system, Yellowman deejayed over pre-recorded backing tracks. But unlike his studio material of the era, Yellowman does not hold back his slackness; instead he is raw, rude and fully irreverent. He boasts about his sexual desirability and special sexual abilities, describing sexual exploits and counting the number of girl-friends he has. His sexual appetite is so large, he tells us, that he is not picky about whom he sleeps with, at one point telling the female subject of the song "Under You", "I woulda sex off your mother and your sister too, true."

Sex is used to get easy laughs from the crowd and he uses slackness to combat prejudice and racism directed at his albinism. Whether it is saying that his "yellow body" is a desirable commodity that women seek ("Watch how me sexy / You want me yellow body? / Run come get it", from "She Boom" [1982d]) or using his uniquely coloured sexual organs as part of the joke ("Look under me and tell me what you see / It's one pair a balls on me yellow body", from "Under Me" [1982d]), Yellowman's lyrics can be seen as successful attempts to nullify the Jamaican cultural associations of the dundus with freakishness.

In addition, slackness is used here to minimize or disparage another's sexuality and therefore their personhood. The song "Fathead Sweet" depicts a common scenario from calypso to dancehall: two artists comparing their sexual appeal. After telling Fathead that Yellowman has 120 girlfriends, Yellowman surmises that if he stole Fathead's girlfriend, Fathead would have no choice but turn *maama-man*, or gay. This is a good-natured jibing towards his sparring partner, but the broader implications of questioning an opponent's sexuality, calling into question their sexual respectability, and using non-heteronormative sexualities as the brunt of a joke are numerous and will be analysed in part 2 of this book.

For a comparison of Yellowman's slackness on record and his slackness live in the dancehall, the song "Funky Reggae Party" is instructive. Listed on the album as "Mighty Diamonds Selection" (because the riddim used by the song is "Party Time" by the Mighty Diamonds), a much cleaner studio version of the song also appears on *One Yellowman* (1982c). Here are the lyrics from the *Live at Aces* (1982b) version:

Watch the one inna de shorts
Watch how the girl a wind up her ass
I don't know if she wear her baggy [panties] or drawers
Watch the one inna de pants
Dat deh one she come from Portland
Dat deh one me knows a Indian
Dat deh one must love Yellowman
A weh me done deejay she going give me romance
Watch the one inna de frock
Dat deh girl rush me cock
Watch the one inna de white
Dat deh one is a damn sodomite [lesbian]
I hear say she can't boil a pot a rice
Every day she get up it's a fuss and fight
The girl dis a use the acid and knife
Watch de one inna de red
She feel up me two seed like four leg
Watch the one inna de red
Eh, pon the bed and open your leg
Eh, pon the bed and open your leg
I tell you likkle girl I going push in me peg

In the studio, most, if not all, of the sexual references are removed. In fact, the entire focus of the song is altered. In the live version, the song is meant to name different girls present at the dance who either want to be with Yellowman or have already been with him and blatantly turns each woman into a sexual object that leering male eyes consume. Alternatively, the studio version on *One Yellowman* (1982c) is about the dancehall space. The chorus "This a de funky reggae party dedicated to people over forty" is added and Yellowman establishes himself as the responsible host trying to improve the dance experience for his patrons:

Come offa de road mek de dance overload
Come offa de street mek de dance well sweet
Your boss deejay at de mic emcee
You don't know what me name is Mr Sexy

He does indulge in his trademark self-referential boasting, as in "Watch the one inna de pants / Lord she love Yellowman", but unlike the live version, slackness is missing. Even the title of the song is a pseudo-cultural reggae reference: it is a nod to the Bob Marley/Lee Perry collaboration "Punky Reggae Party", a song about punk and reggae genres sharing space in British clubs.

That the live version is slacker by far is telling: the dancehall audience wanted and received Yellowman's rawest material. But records went beyond the dancehall, not only to Jamaican media but abroad to fans in North America and the United Kingdom and the rest of Europe. Yellowman tailored his material carefully for each audience and still does this today. Because of this, Yellowman is a different artist to different groups. Locally, and globally there are two separate Yellowmans. Before the internet age, his local and international audiences would only be familiar with material directed towards them. Songs and albums were licensed to various local and international recording companies, and were released under various names in each country, or released only selectively. For instance, many foreign fans would not have known songs like "Fools Go to Church" because it was never released as a single and can only be found on an LP that came out on a Jamaican label, Hit Bound. The song "Nobody Move, Nobody Get Hurt" however, was not popular in Jamaica but is one of the mainstays of his international concerts.

This is not to say Yellowman's records were not very slack – increasingly he released ruder material during the early 1980s. But even today, there is a difference between what Yellowman does in the dancehall and what he does on record, and this is indicative of the difference in the Jamaican and global audience. At Yellowman's concerts outside of Jamaica, he downplays his slackest material. His set lists from his 2008 North American tour generally included these songs: "Oh Carolina", "Freedom Walk", "2 to 6 Supermix", "Operation Radication", "Lost Mi Love", "Blueberry Hill", "Yellow like Cheese", "Letter to Rosie", "Duppy or Gunman", "Sea Cruise", "Nobody Move, Nobody Get Hurt", "One Yellowman", "Mister Chin", "I'm Getting Married", "Bam Bam", "Mad over Me", "Still Be a Lady", "The Good, the Bad and the Ugly", "Zungguzungguguzungguzeng", "Jamaica Nice/Country Roads" and "Ooh We/Sea Cruise". At his concerts I attended in Jamaican resort towns between 2008 and 2015 – which were largely for tourist audiences – he mixed his more conscious material and added in slacker tunes such as "Use Your Rubber Rubber", which, although it is about safe sex, becomes slack when Yellowman uses the microphone as a penis in order to demonstrate for the audience how to put a condom on.

I heard Yellowman chat at a sound in Kingston's Arnett Gardens – a hometown crowd with no tourists in sight – alongside Squidly to a small local audience in winter 2009. Here he did the song "Dry Head Adassa" (1988a), a slack song about a girl who shaves her pubic hair. When I asked him about it later, he told me that he does not sing that while on tour outside of Jamaica because it is the kind of song Jamaicans alone appreciate. Concert tapes of Yellowman's shows abroad in the 1980s document an artist at the height of his popularity revolving between crude slackness and cultural material. Today his international shows include some slackness, but it is toned down. His Kingston shows, however, still give the audience a shot of the raw King of Slack. The Kingston audience also has no problem with Yellowman chatting culture and slack side by side: "To them it was entertainment, they understand. They know that is my style, I can switch from one to the other."

There are other differences between Yellowman's local and international concerts as well. When I have seen Yellowman perform in Canada or the United States, he is either a headliner at a club or theatre gig, or billed alongside several reggae artists at a festival. The first time I saw him in 2006, he headlined the Montreal Reggae Festival. Depending on the venue his sets range from forty-five minutes to a few hours.

In Jamaica, he might be one entertainer in a list of twenty and, unless the show is for the tourist market in resort towns like Negril or Ocho Rios, the headline spot would most likely be given to a younger and current hit maker. Rarely would he play longer than thirty minutes. When I went with him to Ocho Rios in February 2008, the bill included several other artists from the 1980s: General Trees, Flourgon, Pinchers, Josey Wales, Leroy Gibbons, Sanchez, Peter Metro, and even a sound clash between Scorpio and Jammy's. At a Negril show in 2009, he shared the bill with Frankie Paul, Charlie Chaplin and Admiral Bailey. A 2010 Negril show included Jah Rubel and Echo Minott. A 2013 Negril show saw Yellowman open for Toots and the Maytals. A 2015 show in Port Antonio was shared with Abijah. These shows were in tourist resort towns and so had a mix of local and foreigners in the audience. Yellowman's set at these shows was structured differently from his foreign concerts. Rarely performing with Sagittarius in Jamaica, Yellowman either sings to prerecorded backing tracks or to a generic backing band. Expecting that resort goers enjoyed a little hedonism, his songs display more overt slackness. Knowing their love of Bob Marley, he also includes a Marley medley. He runs through his own hits, but never sings a song through entirely and often walks off stage in mid song – a highly effective performance device that gets the crowd excited and they call him back again onstage for more.

FROM SOUND SYSTEMS TO STUDIOS

Yellowman's popularity at this point meant that producers were scrambling to get him into the studio, so much so that his sheer volume of recorded output over the next few years was astonishing. In 1981, Yellowman released many singles into the local market using several different producers and labels. Yellowman's first full-length albums did not come out until 1982 and were usually compilations of singles already released. Time and again Yellowman would run into producers who had turned him away a few years earlier only to welcome him into their studio now that he was a financially viable investment. Of these producers, Joe Gibbs and Coxsone Dodd were the only ones against whom Yellowman harboured an ongoing grudge for the especially harsh treatment he suffered at their studios.

Unlike the music industry in America and England, reggae artists rarely signed a traditional record deal in Jamaica. Instead, they would work with a single producer or studio for a period of time, often until they could get a better deal elsewhere, and then move on. Some, like Yellowman, would record for several producers simultaneously. Freelance producers looking for a hit with the deejay of the moment called upon Yellowman to voice lyrics over riddims they either built (meaning they paid a studio band to record) or bought from other studios and producers. As such, Yellowman's output in Jamaica was massive for the first few years of the 1980s. There were hundreds of singles issued, many of which never made it to a full-length album and were never released outside of the island. Tracking these releases is fraught with difficulty. The Roots Knotty Roots online discography of Jamaican music contains a disclaimer stating that a release date given on the site "should be read as plus/minus one year" due to the challenges of determining when a song was released after it was recorded (www.reggaefever.ch/rkr/guide).

The year 1982 would prove to be Yellowman's most prolific one, with at least fifteen album releases. To put that in perspective, in the 1950s and early 1960s many artists, like the Beach Boys and Beatles, for instance, routinely released up to three albums per year, but by the 1970s and 1980s artists generally released one album a year, if that. A comparable American artist would be Run-DMC, who released one record each year between their 1984 debut and 1986. In their entire career, they released just seven albums. Bob Marley averaged one album per year in the 1970s (though had two in 1973 and none in 1975). His total career count of studio albums: thirteen. This goes up to sixteen if you take into account live albums and the *African Herbsman* compilation. Michael Jackson had a four-year gap between 1982's *Thriller* and 1987's *Bad*, and only released ten solo studio albums during his life.

It is difficult to determine Yellowman's exact discography because his albums were often released by more than one company using different names, and albums were often collections of previously released singles. Producers licensed records to companies in several markets, so an album like *Mister Yellowman* (1982d) was also released as *Duppy or Gunman*. Some record companies changed the name and cover image of an album for a re-release so that *Jack Sprat* (1982a), originally released in 1982 on GG's, came out as *Hotter Reggae* on Jam Rock with a slightly different track listing, and then was issued as *Life in the Ghetto* on Tassa Records in 1990. This practice has routinely confused journalists, who have vastly inflated the number of albums Yellowman has released, and possibly led to the rumour that he landed in the *Guinness Book of World Records* for the most albums released in one year. In fact, Yellowman told the *Gleaner*, "Nuff people nuh know seh me innah the *Guinness Book of Records* too, for the most albums released in a year" ("King Yellowman from Rags to Records", *Gleaner*, 25 December 2005). However, when I contacted Guinness World Records to corroborate this, Jamie Panas, US press and marketing assistant, told me he was unable to locate a record of Yellowman in their database.

By my estimation, Yellowman released seven studio albums in 1982, each with separate material (*Them A Mad over Me*; *One Yellowman*; *Mister Yellowman* (aka *Duppy or Gunman*); *Jack Sprat* (aka *Life in the Ghetto* or *Hotter Reggae*); *Super Mix* (aka *Bad Boy Skanking*); *Just Cool*; *For Your Eyes Only* (aka *Divorced*),[2] four combination or clash studio records (*The Yellow, the Purple and the Nancy*; *Yellowman, Fathead and the One Peter Metro*; *King Mellow Yellow Meets Yellowman*; *Superstar Yellowman Has Arrived with Toyan*), and three live sound system records (*Live at Aces*; *A Dee-Jay Explosion inna Dance Hall Stylee*; *Junjo Presents a Live Session with Aces International*) for a total of fourteen album releases. In addition, Yellowman released several singles that never made it to LP, or found their way onto compilations, and two concerts from 1982 would be released (*Live at Reggae Sunsplash* [1983b] and *Live at the Rissmiller's* [1982c]).

His wealth of output has led many critics to claim that he flooded the market with too much material, some of it substandard, and that this hurt his popularity. Yellowman told David Rodigan in 1983 that the release schedule of his records was out of his hands because of the way the Jamaican music business worked and that he was unhappy with the amount of his material flooding the market (Yellowman 1983). Still, it did not appear to make a dent in his appeal either at home or abroad, as Yellowman's star continued to rise as dancehall's leading deejay.

The first LP to come out was *Them A Mad over Me* (1982g), released on Hit Bound. Channel One's Jo Jo Hookim was present when Yellowman recorded "Soldier Take Over" for Tanka. Jo Jo was impressed and asked him to come back and record an album at the studio with him as producer. In classic Yellowman style – that is to say, prolific – the deejay ended up voicing enough material for two full-length albums during the sessions at Channel One: *Them A Mad over Me* (1982g) and *One Yellowman* (1982c). *Them A Mad over Me* featured several hits and songs that still show up in Yellowman concerts today, among them "I'm Getting Married", "Mad over Me" and "Gun Man". It also had his Tastee song, "Me Kill Barnie". The slackness is apparent on the album, but nothing compared to what Yellowman was chatting on the mic live in those days. The cover art by Jamaal Pete is a drawing of the deejay as superstar chatting on the mic to a crowd of ecstatic women. It blatantly depicted the image Yellowman was crafting about himself, that of irresistible ladies' man and sex machine.

As with every Yellowman full-length album, there is both slackness and social commentary, both slackness and culture on *Them A Mad over Me*. The title track is Yellowman's lyrical modus operandi most simply put – all the girls want him. His humour on the track is apparent from the beginning when, in a spoken intro indicative of much of his early material, he announces, "Hi, my name is Yellowman, and down in Jamaica they call me Mr Sexy. And you see, I come to make you feel happy." The intro is obviously voiced with an international audience in mind as by this time Yellowman was working hard to break into the UK and US markets knowing that many of his singles were being released overseas. He positions himself as Mr Sexy, as if there is no dispute about it in his home country, and ensures that his audience knows what to expect up front: he is here to entertain. In a later version of the song, released on the album *One in a Million* (1984b), Yellowman expands on his message to his global audience by adding, "Special request to all the girls, in Jamaica and all over the world." But other than announcing again and again how much of a sex symbol he is, this song is quite tame.

YELLOWMAN STORMS TORONTO

The year 1982 saw the first LPs and the first concerts outside of Jamaica for Yellowman. The first stop was the Cayman Islands, where he was backed up by a band from Jamaica called Sagittarius. He would later enlist them as his full-time backing band. In July, Yellowman undertook a small-scale North American tour. One of the cities he stopped in was Toronto. With the city's large Jamaican immigrant population, Yellowman found crowds of fans waiting for him, many of whom had heard him via the live dance cassettes or singles coming out of Jamaica. The live cassettes would be brought or mailed overseas by friends and relatives and Yellowman's records were sold in several Caribbean record stores in Toronto.

A promoter named "Rapper" (Larry Woodcock) booked him to play at the St Lawrence Market on 10 July along with Brigadier Jerry. David Kingston had a radio show called *Reggae Showcase* on CKLN throughout the 1980s and Toronto reggae promoters would routinely encourage their artists to go on the show on Friday afternoons to promote their gigs. Kingston's wife, Beth Lesser, was a photographer and journalist and together the two published a magazine called *Reggae Quarterly*. Lesser has since published several notable books documenting the dancehall artists and sound systems of the 1980s. The couple first met Yellowman when he arrived at the station to promote the St Lawrence Market show: "My husband had a radio show at the time, [Yellowman] would come down to the radio show. Because there were so many rumours of shows, if the artists didn't actually show up on the radio station people didn't think they were really in town. So promoters would make sure their artists were down there every Friday night" (Beth Lesser, interview by author, 21 January 2009). David Kingston remembers that the first Toronto show was oversold and this caused "pure pandemonium". There

were about one thousand people outside without tickets and only two police-
man on horses trying to control the crowd (email to author, 22 January
2009). Yellowman was a star in Jamaica already and his first foray to Canada
suggested the same. Lesser was taken aback by the response when he said,
"Oh my God, it was just masses of people. It was like the Beatles again or
something. There were people screaming for Yellowman."

A review of the show illustrates just how big Yellowman had become
outside of Jamaica and what kind of reaction he inspired in his fan base:

> The Yellowman craze which has been sweeping Jamaica and parts of the United
> States has finally hit Toronto. I have attended all of the major concerts in this
> city and never before has there been any cause for the Metropolitan Police to
> be called in to use their squad cars to seal off a whole area. One officer said the
> crowd at one point grew to 1,500 in the street, while another 1,800 waited inside
> to see the new phenomenon. Trouble started early in the evening when fans got
> tired of waiting as the doors which were scheduled to open at 8:30 p.m. did not
> open until about two hours later, too late for some of the fans who got tired of
> waiting and broke down the doors. ("Yellowman Hit Toronto", *Daily Gleaner*,
> 17 October 1982)

After the crowd stormed the venue, mounted police cleared the remaining
people off the streets. The reviewer notes that at a show in Hamilton the
night before, everything ran smoothly with no riots or police presence.
The *Daily Gleaner* back home also reported on the show with the headline
"Yellowman Storms Toronto", calling Yellowman "one of the hottest reggae
artistes on the international scene at present" ("Yellowman Storms Toronto",
Daily Gleaner, 8 October 1982).

On this first tour Yellowman performed the same way he would have at a
Jamaican sound system show. Instead of being backed by a band, Sunshine
Sound, a local sound system owned by Jamaican musician Leroy Sibbles,
spun riddims while Yellowman deejayed to the excited crowd. Fans used
to dancehall culture saw no problem with this but others, drawn by hype
that suggested Yellowman was the next Bob Marley, expected a stage show
with a live band. "It caused great consternation to many people, as he was
being billed as 'the biggest thing since Bob Marley', so naturally a lot of
mainstream fans later said that [they] felt ripped off because he was 'backed
by records'. The sound system thing hadn't really become understood at that

point" (David Kingston, email to author, 22 January 2009). This confusion had to do somewhat with how reggae is understood in North America, outside Caribbean circles. Marley's crossover appeal meant that white rock fans were drawn into roots reggae via the Wailers' rock-inspired reggae and the successful marketing campaign Island Records' Chris Blackwell concocted to brand Marley as a Rasta rebel, using marketing tools foreign to the reggae industry at the time. These included a focus on albums instead of singles, a band identity instead of an artist with a backing band, and a publicity campaign that sought to shape Marley's identity in the image of tried and true rock and roll youthful rebellion that would help him cross over to a rock demographic. Other roots artists in the 1970s followed the Blackwell/Marley template and so the face of reggae in North America was band-oriented stage shows put on by roots acts like Burning Spear, Peter Tosh, Israel Vibration and Culture. Unlike dancehall fans, who understood the culture of sound systems, deejays and riddims, these Blackwell/Marley-bred reggae fans wanted deejay culture packaged the same way. Yellowman began to understand this and made alterations to his concerts in order to appeal to this international audience. For future tours he decided to enlist the services of a backing band and adopt many of the performance techniques of stadium rock acts. He found the ideal backing band in Sagittarius Band, who he would team up with the following month at Reggae Sunsplash.

REGGAE SUNSPLASH 1982

> You've been here all night long. Stand up for the most popular entertainer in Jamaica. The man blocks the streets; wherever he goes, the man blocks the streets. Look at your clocks, it's twenty minutes after six o'clock. King Yello! King Yello! Yellowman! Yellowman! Yellowman! The sunlight and the moonlight mingling together. King Yello! King Yello! Stand up, you're gonna feel it. Stand up. King Yello!
> —Barry G introducing Yellowman at Reggae Sunsplash 1982

He arrived at Sunsplash as Mister Yellowman and he left as King Yellowman. That is how Reggae Sunsplash 1982 in Montego Bay is remembered in dancehall memory. It is also remembered as the coming of age of the genre thanks to Yellowman, "the man who practically made dancehall with a marathon performance at Reggae Sunsplash" ("Yellowman's Family Second

Only to God", *Sunday Gleaner*, 17 February 2002). The festival, held annually between 1978 and 1996, was at that time reggae's hottest ticket. The *Daily Gleaner's* headline the next day read "Biggest-Ever Crowd Jams Sunsplash: Yellow Man Steals the Show" (7 August 1982), and called him "the Prince of Deejays". It went on to say that "it was the inimitable 'Yellow Man' who walked off with all the glory as he got the audience completely wrapped up in his one-hour performance". A letter to the *Gleaner's* editor from a Virginian reggae fan following the show chided the festival for poor organization but cited Yellowman as the reason she remained on the island – "If he hadn't been billed on the show I would have left Jamaica the second day after my arrival" – and hailed him as "the best of the entire Sunsplash" ("Sunsplash", 27 August 1982).

Yellowman's set that early morning, 5 August, at Jarrett Park, Montego Bay, was literally the crowning moment in his career. He hit the stage around 6:30 a.m., just as the sun rose – Jamaican concerts typically start in the late evening and do not finish until sunrise – and chatted his way into the history books. His one-hour set was welcomed by a record-breaking forty thousand in attendance, the largest Sunsplash audience up until that point. The concert was released as *Live at Reggae Sunsplash* (1983b) and footage of the show, including four songs not released on the LP ("Life Story", "Amen", "This Old Man" – called "Nick Nack Patty Wack" on the VHS sleeve – and "Banana Boat Song"), came out on the video *Best of Reggae Sunsplash, Vol. 2* (1983).

Yellowman kicked off his set with the instantly popular "Jah Made Us for a Purpose", a song about albinism, where Yellowman explains first that even though people cuss him about his colour, everyone, including him, was created by Jah for a reason. After thanking Jah for his yellowness, he then brandishes his typically clever humour that is paradoxically both braggadocio and playfully self-depreciating when he says, "Some a dem judge fe me Yellow colour / But if you want Yellowman yellow colour / Dip yourself inna hot water."

He then breaks into "Herbman Smuggling", a song he still performs today, but foregrounds it with an improvised nod to the festival and reggae culture. First, he chats, "White man line up pon nuff street", implying reggae's growing popularity globally. Then, in "Reggae Sunsplash/Herb Man Special", he makes the point that while the police and government are intimidated by reggae culture, and intimidate reggae fans with their "dog at the gate", in actual fact, reggae fans are peace-loving people simply interested in enjoying good music:

> But watch how de people dem cooperate
> The whole a dem stand up fe de musical rate
> Kaa great is great, great shouldn't underrate
> Remember Yellowman said dem haffi 'preciate

Continuing on the theme he started with "Jah Made Us for a Purpose", Yellowman improvises a lyric listed on the album as "Jamaica Proud of Me" that celebrates his relatively newfound celebrity and his appreciation at overcoming hardship and discrimination to be recognized and loved by the nation of his birth. Yellowman then asks the crowd, "Well you want it in I sexy style?", meaning do they want to hear him chat slackness? The crowd cheers loudly and so Yellowman gives them what they want in the form of "Me Too Sexy". He then runs through several of his most popular songs at the time including "Soldier Take Over", "Gun Man", "Mister Chin", and "I'm Getting Married" before ending with one of his slackest tunes, "Sit under You". Included on the video release is footage of Yellowman moving easily between slackness and culture by incorporating Christian hymns into his set ("Amen", "He's Got the Whole World in His Hands"), announcing to the audience that "I'm in the spirit . . . hallelujah, amen", and telling his fans at the end that "the church is over". The show gives us a glimpse of what a Yellowman set list consisted of at this time. Among fans and media it was a resounding success.

SAGITTARIUS BAND

Whereas the majority of shows Yellowman had played before this were to tracks, Sunsplash had hired Sagittarius as a backing band that all artists could use. By the time they supported Yellowman that morning, they had already played throughout the night for nine hours. Sagittarius was started by Simeon Stewart (keyboards), Derrick Barnett (bass) and Desmond Gaynor (drums) in the late 1970s. Of these three only Stewart and Gaynor remain. They started by initially playing hotels until they landed a gig as the backing band for the Festival Song competition in 1981, touring the island and backing up the contestants. The finals were held in the National Arena in Kingston and were broadcast on television, providing Sagittarius with considerable exposure and recognition.

Yellowman was by now used to doing stage shows with backing bands and had performed with Sagittarius a few times before Sunsplash. The first time Yellowman saw them was the night they backed him up at a multi-artist concert at Ward Theatre. According to Simeon Stewart, there was no interaction between the band and Yellowman outside of the performance itself at that show. This was normal, as backing bands would be required to know all the current riddims that deejays and singers used. As such, there was no need for a rehearsal. The second time he met them was on the tour to the Caymans. Impressed with the band's ability to follow him and keen on developing his international appeal, Yellowman asked Sagittarius to be his steady backing band after the show. Their work with him throughout the remainder of 1982 would be sporadic, but by 1983 they would begin to accompany Yellowman on most of his tours and many of his local shows.

In the history of Jamaican reggae bands there were, by that time, only a few self-contained bands that performed their own material. The Wailers are the prime example, but others, such as Chalice, are extremely rare. There were numerous studio bands and live backing bands throughout the 1960s and 1970s, but very few bands that also had vocals and performed original material exclusively.

Often reggae festivals, especially in Jamaica, feature one backing band that provides the music for a series of singers and deejays. This minimizes costs for artists and promoters and, since most artists record their lyrics over standard riddims, a good backing band has all the material prepared. It is also common for touring artists to play to prerecorded backing tracks, just as they would in the dancehall. By hiring Sagittarius as his near-exclusive backing band, Yellowman bucked this trend. He realized that rock bands were always self-contained units and preferred this model to the Jamaican style of pairing artists with a different band in each city while on tour. On his first few tours abroad, in July and September 1982, he used backing tracks. You can hear this on the bootleg of a show recorded at Rissmiller's Country Club in Reseda, California. A selector ran the riddims, changing them when Yellowman would signal, or restarting them in a traditional "rewind and come again" format.

At times Yellowman has also used local backing bands, such as the Circuit Breakers during a tour of the Virgin Islands in January 1983. But after Sunsplash, Yellowman began taking his own backing band with him as much as possible when he toured outside of Jamaica. Not only would his future tours with Sagittarius help him cross over to global audiences more used to Marley's full-band sound, but by using Sagittarius almost exclusively, Yellowman altered the dancehall business internationally. He felt this would "professionalize" dancehall in the eyes of foreigners. By aligning himself with one band, he was also able to control the quality and consistency of each concert. Stewart says that since venue conditions vary greatly on tour, it is important to have consistency. They may have a bad sound mix or an awkward stage set-up, but knowing that the band is consistent allows Yellowman to turn in quality performances. I've seen Yellowman play to audiences ranging from about fifity people to several thousand and he delivers the same enthusiasm each time.

Having his own band would go a long way to separating Yellowman from other Jamaican artists who toured abroad. It inevitably worked as his international audience has remained diverse and has always included a strong college contingent. Conversely, reggae has suffered in the United States and Canada because promoters have largely stuck to the Jamaican model of backing band and serial artists. This appeals to reggae fans but has hampered the cross-over of reggae artists into mainstream demographics. *Flair Magazine* noted that Yellowman "is the ONLY DJ that tours (not single show trips but over five weeks at a time. He is currently on a 14-week JAMPOP tour of the US) the US EVERY year" ("Yellowman: Jamaica's Best Dance Hall DJ", *Flair Magazine*, 15 October 1990; emphasis in the original). This fact highlights the benefits that Yellowman's adjustments to the industry have afforded him. In addition, the article makes the case that for fans outside Jamaica, Yellowman is reggae royalty, with only Bob Marley above him: "He is second in popularity only to Bob Marley in the US, Europe and Africa" (ibid.). This kind of accolade is a direct result of the way Yellowman has treated deejaying and dancehall in the same way as roots reggae on the international stage.

The collaboration with Sagittarius that started onstage at Sunsplash in 1982 has continued until today. Further to this, since 1991 Simeon Stewart has also taken on the role of managing Yellowman. Yellowman continues to tour regularly with the band and spends four or five months of the year on the road. While the majority of the band is now based out of Miami, Yellowman is still based out of Kingston, where he performs shows around the island at a rate of maybe once or twice a week, and often flies to Central and South America or within the Caribbean for shows throughout the winter. While he continues to tour with Sagittarius abroad, on home turf Yellowman rarely performs with them today. Depending on the show, he might deejay over tracks and is often backed up by a local band when playing for tourists in resort towns.

GONE AMERICA

> Natty gone inna Babylon
> Kaa let me tell you fe go chant down Babylon
> A weh me say
> He left Jamaica and gone America
> —Yellowman, "Youth Man Promotion" (1982a)

In the wake of Sunsplash 1982, the world seemed to open up for Yellowman. A few weeks later, he played to capacity audiences in New York City, Connecticut and Boston. At a show at Harlem World, thousands showed up to the venue that could only hold fifteen hundred people. As in Toronto, fans rioted and broke the gates and the police were called to restore order. The concert went on as scheduled and at one point it was rumoured that Yellowman collapsed due to the heat, but the promoter stated in an interview that this was simply part of the show's drama ("Yellowman a Big Draw", *Daily Gleaner*, 25 August 1982). Another review from this tour recounts Yellowman sharing the bill with Mighty Sparrow, Calypso Rose, Triston Palmer, Marcia Griffiths, Phillip Frazer and others to two sold-out audiences at the Felt Forum in New York on Halloween. Patrons grew impatient for Yellowman and "voiced their disapproval" for having to wait during Sparrow's set. The review makes a point of saying that Yellowman's set was not particularly strong because of a "white American band" who did not have the correct feel to play reggae ("Yellowman in New York", *Daily Gleaner*, 12 November 1982). This is another reason he would soon make sure Sagittarius was with him for these tours.

On 21 November 1982 Yellowman was back in Toronto for his second appearance, this time with Fathead at the Concert Hall. Dressed in his trademark yellow suit and hat, he played two shows to capacity crowds and was backed up by the Band of Faith. A reviewer stated that "it was a magnificent show performance and the fans loved every minute of it" ("Yellowman in Toronto", *Daily Gleaner,* 7 January 1983).

Concert reviews of his shows at home were also glowing, situating him as the new top reggae star and making note of his overwhelming popularity. Writing about the "Battle of the Stars" at the Ranny Williams Entertainment Centre in December 1982, one reviewer said:

> Yellowman is perhaps one of the few Jamaican artistes that can get away with anything on stage. After singing some of his well-known hits with the audience eating out of his hands, he left the stage, but the audience would not have this and demanded through shouts and applause that he should return. Returning he asked what the audience wanted to hear, whether they wanted to hear "culture music", or "nastiness", the audience unanimously settled for the latter and he went into one of his lewdest presentations to date much to the delight of the audience. ("Battle of the Stars: First Class Show", *Daily Gleaner,* 30 December 1982).

KINGSTON'S POLARIZED MEDIA

The new attention in the media was good for his career, but it began to highlight a divide in how Jamaicans thought about Yellowman. Jamaicans had a love-hate relationship with Yellowman. Yellowman was often demonized in the island's newspapers, either in editorials or in letters to the editor. But this was by no means universal – since he was becoming the island's leading reggae artist, he also enjoyed favourable press at the same time.

> On the one hand there would be articles that say "Superstar Yellowman appearing at Sunsplash", and on the next page it would be like "Yellowman and his slackness, they're bringing down the nation and leading the youth astray", that kind of thing. It was a real love/hate relationship they had with Yellowman. They just didn't know what to do with him. On the one hand he's great, he's bringing tourists, he's making reggae international, is he the new Bob Marley? On the other hand, all this gun stuff, all this slackness, this is ruining the image of Jamaica. (Beth Lesser, interview by author, 21 January 2009)

In a letter to the *Daily Gleaner* (20 June 1982), a reader is not just against Yellowman, but all reggae in general, though uses the popular deejay to make a point about the state of the current popular music being rubbish: "We have been forced to swallow Bob Marley and his music but please do not try to push Yellow Man down our throats. We have enough mediocre singers and performers as it is so stop lauding the rubbish that he does and is paid to do." A short article in 1985 uses Yellowman as an example of an artist who is keeping the youth away from church in a story about a Christmas Cantata presented at a church in Benbow. "The minister of the church, the Reverend R.A. Johnson, chided young people for only wanting to sing songs by 'Yellowman, Purpleman and all kinds of men' instead of wanting to come and sing in the church" ("Chided", *Daily Gleaner,* 11 January 1985). Another article from the same period decried slackness but at the same time admitted that the majority of music lovers on the island love it. It quotes Yellowman as saying, "Is slackness de people dem want an a pure slackness me a gi dem" ("Songs of the Times", *Daily Gleaner,* 16 August 1982). In the wake of Yellowman's Sunsplash 1986 show, one journalist wrote a long letter to the *Gleaner* admonishing the media coverage of the event for ignoring Yellowman's "embarrassing slackness". He went on to say:

> One reason that he continues to behave in that way is that he is frequently being showered with praises, like the recent Sunsplash reviews. Yellowman's performance was the epitome of slackness so much so that after the performance one colleague of mine said, "As a man, I was embarrassed." . . . It is not good enough to say "That is what the crowd wants." As a journalist, part of the burden of our mandate is to be responsible and promote standards. . . . I was among the first writers in this country who spotted Yellowman's great talent from the earliest days when he appeared on the Tastee Talent Contest and, if for no other reason, I have a responsibility to tell him in true dancehall style "CEASE" as that was not what I saw and admired in the young man in those days when I used to write about him in a positive way. ("Yellowman at Sunsplash", *Daily Gleaner,* 25 September 1986)

An article from the fall of 1984 carefully weighs Yellowman's appeal and controversy:

> Yellowman is not only a DJ, he is an entertainer and pound for pound for pound will go down as one of the finest, if not the finest this country has produced. He is

able to rap on current affairs, poke fun at his colour and former social background and when demanded to by the crowd can be very obscene, much to their enjoyment. ... Yellow Man is almost always asked to do his dirty act by a crowd that have come to expect this of him. A great majority of us may well turn up our noses at this but one thing is sure, we cannot detract from the fact that this Jamaican is very talented, smart, as he can read his audience like a good politician and finally is the hottest reggae property we have right now. (*Daily Gleaner*, 1 September 1984)

Radio programmers, outside of a few reggae fans like Barrington "Barry G" Gordon, routinely refused to play his material. One song that Yellowman insists was banned was "Mister Chin" (1982d). The song plays on the cultural trope of the ubiquitous Chinese grocer in Jamaica and exemplifies the prejudice against them in society by claiming that "Mister Chin" – a catch-all derogatory term for every Chinese vendor on the island – hides his goods in order to create demand and thereby increase the price. The song enjoyed initial airplay but was removed from radio shortly thereafter. The *Daily Gleaner* Hit Parade lists it as the number one song for the week ending 12 June 1982, so people were buying it even if the radio was not playing it. Incidentally, his "I'm Getting Married" was number ten that week.

Author: Why did they ban "Mister Chin"?

Yellowman: The Chinese, they are the one who got it banned. Because back in the days in Jamaica, the Chinese used to own all the establishments including the wholesale place, the liqueur market, the supermarket. So, I said, "Mister Chin you should sell the right thing" Because back in the day they used to hide the goods because they want the price to hike up. So that they get scared so that the price can hike up.

Of course, the song may also have been banned because of the sexual content in the bridge where Yellowman sings about making love to Mr Chin's daughter, Sandra Lee.

Speaking of radio censorship of dancehall, Beth Lesser, agrees that it was often pretty arbitrary:

They would play for a while and then people started calling up and saying, "you're criticizing Chiney men" or something. And then they would ban them. Or sometimes some deejays would be able to slip them in, maybe Barry G, because he played a little bit more roots things. But a lot of people just heard them from foreign countries. I remember specifically "Mister Chin" being banned because of the Chinese references, and some of his other stuff. He had a bunch – they just banned anything. (Interview by author, 21 Janaury 2009)

When asked in 1984 why Jamaican radio does not play reggae, Yellowman responded, "I don't know. They just try to fight reggae, you know? The only person to play reggae is Barry G" ("Yellowman Takes Over", *Cool Runnings: Reggae Roots Magazine*, 1984, 7). Barry G's support helped him circumvent some of the radio censorship. Considered by some the godfather of Jamaican airwaves, Barry G had a popular show on JBC radio called *Boogie Down* in the late 1970s, and then *Two to Six Supermix* in the 1980s – both shows were immortalized by Yellowman in song. Barry G also worked with Radio Jamaica and Hot 102 and co-founded Power 106. He was one of the few disc jockeys to support dancehall in the 1980s and Yellowman in particular. His regular show, *Two to Six Supermix*, featured many reggae artists, but he also employed a tactic to include more dancehall on radio that was reminiscent of the ska era. Purchasing airtime from the station, Barry G then rented time slots to promoters or producers to "advertise" their new artists. Coxsone Dodd and other 1960s producers had purchased similar advertising time in their day to promote their own songs as well. For Barry G, a typical show might include fifteen minutes for Sugar Minott's Youth Promotion, followed by fifteen minutes for Tuff Gong. "Each producer or record distributor would have his fifteen minutes paid for and that's how they could assure they could get their songs on there", recalls Beth Lesser (interview by author, 21 January 2009).

Barry G's support of Yellowman is seen by some as the seed that produced dancehall's culture of violence and sex today. In the wake of a well-publicized violent clash between dancehall artists Ninjaman and Vybz Kartel at Sting 2004, many blamed the radio host for his role in promoting slackness. One promoter told the *Jamaica Observer* newspaper, "Gordon promoted this and made Yellow Man, a star. Yellow Man brought slackness to the surface, made it popular and accepted." In defence, Barry G argued, "I was blamed by critics for promoting this crudeness, but Yellow Man never fought on stage, nor carried a gun, he was a gentleman" ("Barry G Denies He Promoted Slackness", *Jamaica Observer*, 5 January 2004).

Yellowman was used to being rebuked by society – he spent his early life at its margins. Now he was welcomed by the underclasses but still denounced by the upper class. This was also illustrated in the relationship between Yellowman, an artist from the ghetto playing what was essentially ghetto music, and the class-wide popularity of soca. Yellowman felt that he was snubbed by soca's main Jamaican proponent, Byron Lee. Producer, studio owner, promoter and band leader Byron Lee, once called the "Lawrence Welk of reggae" by Robert Christgau (Chang and Chen 1998, 98), has been disparaged in reggae histories as an uptown musician who smoothed the edges off Jamaican national musical expressions such as ska and reggae, and produced music for the tourism market. Chang and Chen point to Lee's mixed racial heritage, Chinese and African, as one reason for this characterization in an industry where lighter skinned and middle-class record producers often dominated over darker skinned and lower-class artists. Still, Lee's role in popularizing the music beyond the ghetto is formidable. Not only was he Jamaican music's representative to New York's World Expo in 1964, he helped pave the way for acceptance of ska beyond downtown Kingston. "Nobody uptown knew what the music [ska] was about, they couldn't relate to it. It can be said that we were responsible for moving the music from West Kingston into the upper- and middle-classes who could afford to buy records and support the music. Then radio picked up the music and it became the order of the day" (Byron Lee, quoted in Change and Chen 1998, 98).

With this history of animosity between Lee and many reggae artists, it is not hard to imagine two exchanges that Yellowman recounts happening between them. The first occurred in Negril, Jamaica's west coast resort town where musicians hold concerts regularly for tourists. A promoter named Shorty hosted a concert at Kaisers with Byron Lee and Yellowman. Lee was scheduled to go on first, with the more popular Yellowman closing the show, but Bryon Lee played the whole show ignoring calls from the promoter and crowd to exit the stage and let Yellowman perform. A similar thing happened on a live taping of a JBC television programme, where Lee took the entire time allotted for both artists, thereby squeezing Yellowman out. Yellowman interprets these events as examples of the contest between soca and dancehall and the division of race and class on the island.

As the superstar deejay ended 1982, Yellowman was poised for further international success and continued polarizing support at home. First, though, he would have to wage the first battle in the hardest war of his life.

CHAPTER 7

King Yellowman, 1983–1984

Me got de pain in me back
Me got de pain inna me chest
Pain in me ankle straight down to me foot
They treat black people like I and I a crook
A good thing me read the Bible, the holy book
　　—Yellowman, "Pain" (1982c)

1983

Yellowman suffered what seemed to be a minor setback in the spring of 1983, but it would prove ominous for his future health. At twenty-six years of age, he had developed a lump on his neck. He flew to New York on 2 May and was admitted to the Beth Israel Hospital the following day. According to an article that ran in the *Daily Gleaner* ("Lump Removed from Yellowman's Neck in New York Operation", 10 May 1983), it was feared he had "some form of skin cancer" and the doctor said the illness was from "excessive exposure to the sun". A lump was removed from his neck and he was released from the hospital on 9 May, but was never told if it was malignant or benign.

A few weeks later he was in Chicago to receive two awards at Martin's International Second Annual Reggae Music Arts/Awards: Reggae Entertainer of 1982 and Top Recording Artist. Ephraim Martin, president of Martin's International, began the festival and awards in order to promote "reggae as an art form and as a vehicle for the expression of the voiceless people of the world" ("'Yellowman' to Receive Reggae Award", *Daily Gleaner,* 2 March 1983). Yellowman flew to Chicago to accept the awards and was scheduled to play a fifteen-minute set at the ceremony held at the Metro Music Hall on 21 May but Martin remembers that his set extended to forty-five minutes. The event was covered in major papers around the country, back home and even warranted two articles in *Billboard Magazine*. Other artists to win awards that year were Peter Tosh, Rita Marley, Musical Youth and Mutabaruka.

Yellowman returned to Sunsplash in June 1983 – an event the *Daily Gleaner* called "the clash of the DJ giants" – and was noted to have "stayed away from his customary 'slackness' in delivering a remarkable and mannerly performance" (2 July 1983).

In July 1983, Yellowman and Sagittarius landed at Heathrow Airport in London for a one-off show at Edmonton Pickett's Lock. Brought to the city by David Rodigan, then a deejay at independent station Capital Radio, the band was alarmed to find what they thought was a riot in the streets outside their hotel and wrongly assumed that political unrest must be the cause. Instead, crowds had gathered to glimpse the deejay. Rodigan had initially booked Yellowman for one night, but when tickets went on sale at the radio station, the line-up of fans down the street convinced him that he should expand the booking to four nights, each of which sold out (Rodigan 2017). In an on-air interview with Yellowman after the fact, Rodigan put it this way: "My special guest recently took London by storm with four sell-out concerts. Only one man can do that – Yellowman" (Yellowman 1983).

> They just bring me to do one show but because of the massive crowd I have to end up and do four shows at the Pickett's Lock, a big arena. From hotel Scotland Yard escorted me like a prisoner to and from the show for four nights. I did thought it was a riot. I was saying to Rodigan, "What's going on?" And Rodigan said, "No, it's for you they're securing." I said maybe I am Margaret Thatcher.

Yellowman's residency lasted from 7 July until 10 July. The *Times* concert listings pegged the shows as "the reggae event of the year" ("Rock and Jazz", 2 July 1983). Yellowman was getting used to being mobbed by fans back home but did not expect the same treatment across the ocean. He later told a journalist, "I didn't know so much people know of me until I reach these foreign country, I know that a lot of people love me and I love that and I appreciate" (Saunders 1983, 15).

Rodigan (2017) remembers that while Yellowman may have deejayed X-rated lyrics, his behaviour was closer to that of a dedicated family man.

There was no partying, or even smoking and drinking. The entertainer's main concern seemed to be purchasing gifts on this first trip to London for his growing family back home. Simeon Stewart remembers that London tour as one of the best the band had done in over thirty years of playing with Yellowman simply because everybody involved was taken by complete surprise about just how many fans Yellowman had abroad.

Jamaican music had a niche market in England, created by record companies in the 1960s like Island, Trojan and Doctor Bird. England was a main destination of the English Caribbean diaspora – people looking for work who emigrated to the United Kingdom in search of opportunities that were not available in places like Barbados, Jamaica, Trinidad, Guyana and Antigua. With all that good reggae landing in England, British music fans took notice too. By the time Yellowman landed on their soil, he was already a superstar and did not even know it. England had come under his spell, just as Toronto and New York had. Several fan websites list the following quote, attributed to an anonymous reviewer, that gives a sense of how he was received: "Listening to Yellowman sing is like watching Michael Jordan play basketball. He knows he's got it, you know he's got it, and it's a trip just experiencing him perform."

British roots reggae sensation ASWAD opened the shows for Yellowman, demonstrating further that culture and slackness were not dichotomous elements in reggae concerts at the time. Here was one of England's premier roots bands opening up for Jamaica's slackest deejay. The show was a must-see for any reggae fan in London and many of the who's who of the scene showed up to check Yellowman out: Steel Pulse, UB40, Tappa Zukie and Errol Dunkley included.

One reviewer gushed that Yellowman was one of the only reggae artists who could sell out "the sprawling white elephant of a sports complex at Pickett's Lock" and reported that he announced to the audience "Me the first blood claat white man to chat reggae music" ("Yellow Fever: Yellowman, Edmonton Pickett's Lock", *NME*, July 1983).

Jimmy Wynter, who by this time was acting as Yellowman's manager, arranged to have the shows recorded. Following on the heels of *Yellowman: Live at Reggae Sunsplash* (1983b) came *Live in London* (1983a). The record is a snapshot of the deejay wielding the full extent of his powers for the first time in England and the audience reception is thunderous. Some of the set is similar to the Sunsplash show, with Yellowman improvising lyrics and doing medleys of some of his best-known material, though the track listing confusingly either uses alternative names for songs or sometimes misses them altogether, as is the case with "Society Party" (1984e). In "A Me Run de Country" (1983a), the popular deejay jokingly reflects on the state of his fame:

A me run de country
Well hear me mon
Me control Seago, say and Manley
Me control de bank that make de money
Me control Kingston and Mo'Bay city
Me control St Ann's dung a Ochi
Me control Portland and St Mary
Oh Clarendon people encouraging me
Say me put dung de mic and turn a MP

Steve Martin worked as Yellowman's booking agent during this time. I spoke with him in 2014. Originally an agent for Magna Artists, he left to establish the Music Business Agency, where his clients included Loudon Wainwright, Kate and Anna McGarrigle, the Wailers, Toots and the Maytals, Billy Bragg, and Gregory Isaacs. He had booked the Pickett's Lock shows in London and witnessed first-hand the extent of Yellowman's fame both in the United Kingdom and in the United States:

Yellow at the time had two distinct audiences. He had a white college audience and he had a black urban audience. We could bring him up and play a Friday, Saturday in Brooklyn and I'd be the only white guy in the audience. Then Thursday, Friday in the Bronx, then play in Queens, then come back the following weekend and do two nights at the Ritz, which is a white club in downtown New York, and play Queen's College to a white crowd. It was a remarkable thing. He would do like fifteen to eighteen thousand people inside of two weeks in New York City with completely different audiences. (Steve Martin, interview by author, 22 March 2014)

In the wake of two Sunsplash Festivals and successful tours to the United States, Canada and England, Yellowman was on top of the reggae world. Martin booked Yellowman to play two shows at Brixton Academy – with about eight thousand capacity over the two shows – and they both sold out. "He was huge in the UK", he says. The press was scrambling to interview him, but struggling to contact him, as Yellowman had no publicist. In 1983, *Black Echoes*, dubbed "Britain's only soul, funk 'n' reggae newspaper", put Yellowman on the cover of their issue of 16 July. The article portrays Yellowman as camera shy, diplomatic, congenial and a bit uneasy when it comes to answering questions about slackness. Asked about his status as "something of a sex symbol", Yellowman responded, "'No, no.' (After much persuasion, he explained): 'Oh yes, I talk about ladies' clit, right? Ah, just love lyrics'" (Saunders 1983, 15).

By portraying vulgar slackness as "love lyrics", Yellowman was downplaying the controversy slackness was stirring at home. However, he was also insisting that slackness was innocuous in his understanding, nothing to get upset about.

DEM SIGHT THE BOSS

> As they sight de boss dem a mass
> Say that me drive up de BMW and park
> Fathead running by weh them all cork
> Back off, back off mek the breeze cool we off
> —Yellowman, "Dem Sight the Boss" (1983e)

Yellowman's success in Britain was unprecedented for a dancehall artist, and he would eventually turn that success into a major record deal with CBS Records in the United Kingdom and Columbia Records in the United States. In the meantime, he continued to release material throughout 1983, including sound system LPs *Live at Ranny Williams Entertainment Centre* and *Live and Direct (Presenting a Live Session with Aces International Vol 2)*. In what might have been either an honest mistake or an attempt to cash in on Yellowman's fame, Vista Sounds released *Confessions* (Purpleman 1983) with a drawing of Yellowman on the cover. The only problem was that the album had nothing to do with Yellowman and all the vocals were by another deejay with albinism, Purpleman. *Gleaner* reporter Howard McGowan certainly felt it was an underhanded move by France-based Vista Sounds, calling it "one of the most vicious acts of piracy ever in the local recording business" ("Yellowman Gets CBS Contract . . . Pirated on Other Label", *Daily Gleaner*, 22 October 1983).

On 8 September 1983, Yellowman played the Ritz in Manhattan. The *New York Times* ran a short promo article that provided a concise introduction to the deejay for those out of the loop:

Jamaica's current reggae sensation is a character who calls himself Yellowman. He's a 25-year-old albino whose real name is Winston Foster; onstage, he sees the world through lemon-colored glasses, wears one of a rainbow assortment of derby hats, boasts about how popular he is with girls, calls attention to his complexion and spins singsong rhymes – in thick Jamaican patois – that are part doggerel, part lewd innuendo and part pointed pronouncement. Yellowman is one of Jamaica's leading toasters – disk jockeys who became performers when their raps proved more popular than the records they played. Yellowman's ability to drop political messages between punchlines, his husky baritone voice, and the contrast between his odd appearance and his cocksure presentation have made him a star in Jamaica. ("Yellowman: Sensation from Jamaica", *New York Times*, 7 September 1983)

Jon Pareles's review of the show, while wrongly writing that Yellowman used to work as a disc jockey, praised Sagittarius's chops and commented on Yellowman's mixture of X-rated boasts and political commentary. He finishes by saying, "Between Yellowman's chanting and the band's groove, the music was jovial and irresistibly danceable. Rarely has megalomania seemed so endearing" ("Yellowman", *New York Times*, 25 September 1983).

From New York, Yellowman went north to Toronto. The panic had subsided a bit from his first appearance there; one reviewer notes that "there was no riot for Yellowman this time" ("Yellowman after More Than Mere Stardom", *Toronto Star*, 26 September 1983). A promotional article for the show dubbed him the "albino-Jamaican sex symbol" and noted that he "has already been hailed in England as the new king of reggae in the wake of Bob Marley" ("Riff Rap", *Globe and Mail*, 23 September 1983). Two reviews from the show at the Concert Hall reveal that after the initial hype died down, Yellowman's sheer talent started to make an impact on reviewers. Going beyond the hyperbole of earlier reviews, this *Toronto Star* reviewer takes time to consider how reggae has evolved in Yellowman's hands:

What makes Yellowman such an intriguing artist is his ability to bond an obvious literary bent to a populist medium like reggae music. He has, in effect, created a category for himself, one in which he is able to call on popular traditions (he continually works classic pop songs – "Mr Lonely", "I'm Getting Married in the Morning", a dozen others, all incongruously juxtaposed to elicit new meanings, new responses) and work them into a potent, poetic vision of not just his own world (in which Yellowman is always the sexiest, most irresistible man) but of ours too. In "Jamaica Nice", for example, he turns the wealthy, industrialized world into a sordid ghetto, the Third World into paradise – as an illustration of the frailty of our most cherished preconceptions. And he does it to an irresistible dance beat. That's no mean achievement. ("Yellowman after More Than Mere Stardom", *Toronto Star*, 26 September 1983)

In a review for the *Globe and Mail*, Liam Lacey sees Yellowman as an antidote to the over-seriousness of Rasta roots reggae and positions him as a much-needed link with early forms of Caribbean music such as ska. Like ska singers, "Yellowman's delivery and message are endlessly optimistic, sly and inventive."

Last night at The Concert Hall, Yellowman showed himself to be the real item – a bona fide pop-star, comedian, and genuinely weird charismatic figure who is as far from the doom-speaking Biblical visionary Rasta as anyone could imagine. At first impression, Yellowman is something of a throwback – a return to the time when Caribbean musicians specialized in comedy and clever sexual wordplay instead of the abstruse political-religious rhetoric of reggae of the 1970s. The media attention given to the religious ramblings of the Rastafarians and the hype about reggae as "roots music" (as a musical genre, it's younger than acid rock), has deflected legitimate interest from other exciting forms of Jamaican music. Yellowman partly redresses the musical imbalance, and he also reminds everyone how much Caribbean music is a form of play and celebration. ("Yellowman Is Proof Positive That Jamaican Music Thrives", *Globe and Mail*, 26 September 1983)

For Lacey, Yellowman is a boon for Jamaican music at a time when it needed it the most: "A lot of people in the past two years have wondered if Jamaican music could remain vital after the death of Bob Marley; Yellowman reminds us that Jamaican music was around long before Marley, and is continuing to thrive."

ZUNGGUZUNGGUGUZUNGGUZENG

In 1981 or 1982, Yellowman started a four-year relationship with Henry "Junjo" Lawes, who ran a record label and sound system called Volcano. Junjo used to scout out the sound systems for new talent to record, and Barrington Levy introduced him to Yellowman after the Skateland clash with Nicodemus. It is the Lawes material, distributed in the United Kingdom by Greensleeves and in the United States and Canada by Shanachie, that is often considered Yellowman's classic era. He produced *Mister Yellowman, For Your Eyes Only, Super Mix* and *Just Cool* (all in 1982), *Zungguzungguguzungguzeng* and *Nobody Move* (both in 1983), plus various clash albums. Yellowman quickly became Junjo's leading artist and, in lieu of advance monies or maybe even royalties, he gave Yellowman a BMW that he had shipped from New York. Yellowman immediately had the car painted yellow. The car was an anomaly in Jamaica, not only because it was a rare luxury vehicle, but also because it had the North American left-hand drive, instead of the Jamaican right hand. When one of Yellowman's drivers had an accident with the car, he had to ship it to Miami to get repaired since there were no BMW parts or mechanics on the island.

Yellowman's recorded output during this time is not an accurate representation of what he was deejaying on sound systems. Live shows were noticeably slacker, but on record Yellowman toned things down. Yellowman says that this was because of commercial concerns: "Junjo always telling me 'make sure the music airplay', so we always do the airplay songs, the clean songs."

The year 1983 also saw the release of one of his best-known records, *Zungguzungguguzungguzeng* (1983e) which would earn an honourable mention in the list of the year's best albums in British pop magazine *NME*. The songs on *Zungguzungguguzungguzeng* find Yellowman still focusing on his local audience and local reggae culture, themes that by now were ubiquitous in his work, such as how popular he is ("Dem Sight the Boss", "Who Can Make the Dance Ram?"), how sexually desirable he is ("Zungguzungguguzungguzeng", "Rub a Dub Play"), and how sexually experienced he is ("Yellowman Wise"). And, as is normal for him, he mixed these songs with two firmly cultural tracks ("Can't Hide from Jah"and "Jah Jah Are We Guiding Star").

The song "Zungguzungguguzungguzeng" (1983e) continues to be popular among Yellowman fans around the world, most who have no idea what it means. On the one hand, the word is simply a nonsense term that can be used to refer to various things: "Zungguzungguzeng is a slang, you know? It can mean anything. Like, I can say I'm gonna zungguzungguzeng you, which means I gwaan kill you. And I can look on a girl and say, I want to zungguzungguzeng you. It mean I want to 'f' you." On the other hand, Yellowman insists that the song was misunderstood as a political song in support of the PNP because he lifted the melody from a political rally for Michael Manley: "Some guy used to go around with Manley and mic and say, 'you shouldn't trouble Mr Manley, boy'." Yellowman adopted the melody but added *zungguzungguguzungguzeng* to make it:

> Zungguzungguguzungguzeng zungguzungguguzungguzeng
> Jump fe happiness a jump fe joy
> You no fe call Yellowman no bwoy
> Ku Shung Peng, Ku Shu-shu-shung Peng
> But tell you Yellow voice it sound like FM
> The other rest a voice sound like AM
> But tell you Yellowman come fe rock dem again
> You could a live a Kingston, Mo' Bay or May Pen

DUBPLATES

The enduring popularity of "Zungguzungguguzungguzeng" has meant that it is still in demand by fans and has come to be one of the artist's signature songs. Yellowman can often be seen singing it to the camera when fans post candid videos of him to YouTube. I once saw him sing it on a stranger's mobile phone to convince the person on the other line that he was indeed Yellowman. The song also still features in his current live shows. Most tellingly, though, the song is one of his most requested dubplates. Dubplates arose from "dub plates", which were one-off temporary recordings that studio owners would manufacture to test their popularity with audiences at the sound system parties before officially releasing the record. Dubplates evolved from the idea of having an exclusive track; they consist of an artist providing a "custom recording of existing songs that include the name of the sound and sound system selectors" (Chamberlain 2010). Sound systems all around the world purchase dubplates from reggae artists because a library of exclusive dubplates, or "specials", enhances their ability to win sound clashes.

There are small studios all over Kingston that specialize in dubplates. I accompanied Yellowman to several studio sessions to record dubplates in 2009 at tiny studios that typically ran Pro-Tools or Adobe Audition and consisted of little more than a small control room and one or two vocal booths. A typical dubplate destination was Tel's Studio on Old Hope Road. Tel works with over eight hundred sound systems around the world who contact him directly, or through dubplate brokers. A dubplate studio must be stocked with an arsenal of all the popular riddims dating back to the 1960s, which in Tel's case numbered in the thousands. But navigating a genealogy of riddims is not always straightforward; many were versioned by different studios and released under other titles. As such, many riddims are known by several names. More challenging still, some clients request riddims for songs where no instrumental version exists. Tel has had to reconstruct a vintage Studio One riddim using only the mono mix of a vocal version by sampling as much of the instrumental as possible before the vocals come in, and cutting and pasting several sections together to make one seamless chord progression. This, of course, means that his studio might boast the exclusive instrumental version of that riddim.

When I arrived with Yellowman, Tel's basement studio was packed with artists waiting to record dubplates, members of their various entourages, and an international representation of people who come to Jamaica to buy dubplates for sound systems around the world. On this particular day there were brokers from Japan, France and Italy purchasing dubplates for their respective sound systems clients. I watched as Jah Cure, Luciano and Stitchie voiced dubplates of their hits with lyrics altered to praise their client's sound system and selector. At other studios, we ran into Ken Boothe, Ninjaman, Pinchers, Flourgon and Jah Thomas doing the same.

At this particular session, Yellowman was contracted to record five dub-plates all based on "Zungguzungguguzungguzeng", but with some variations in the backing tracks. Some clients requested the riddim used in the Junjo-produced version. This was originally recorded by the Roots Radics' but was a re-lick – a new version – of Studio One's "Mad Mad" riddim. Other clients wanted Yellowman to voice the track over a different version of the riddim best known as "Golden Hen", after the popular Tenor Saw song. At a later session I attended at the same studio, Yellowman recorded twelve dubplates, some based on "Zungguzungguguzungguzeng", others using "Mister Chin",

"Blueberry Hill" and "Soldier Take Over". Some of these dubplates were just to be used as promotional material for sound systems – and one was actually for a clothing store – while others were "Sound Boy Killers", meaning the lyrics would "big up" (promote) the sound that contracted him and describe how they would kill their competition in sound battles.

Dubplates allow artists to continue receiving revenue from their previously popular songs, songs that in many cases received no royalties in the first place due to the way the Jamaican music business worked. An artist gets paid for each dubplate and the amount depends on how much credibility and ammunition that dubplate will provide the sound system in a clash. A current hit-making artist will make thousands of dollars per dubplate whereas a once-popular artist without much current profile might receive US$100 per song. I went to three different dubplate studios with Yellowman and by far his most popular song was "Zungguzungguguzungguzeng", a testament to the enduring popularity of his Junjo-era material.

JOSEY WALES: TWO GIANTS CLASH

As one of the top producers on the island, Junjo Lawes's stable of talent included more than just Yellowman. He brought Josey Wales into the studio after listening to him on Stur-Gav and released two of his classics, *The Outlaw* (1983) and *No Way better Than Yard* (1984). Josey Wales got his start in the industry around the same time as Yellowman but, whereas Yellowman went the slack route, following General Echo in particular, Josey's mentor was cultural deejay royalty Daddy U-Roy. Taking his sobriquet from Clint Eastwood's character in the *Outlaw Josey Wales*, Josey's deejaying persona matched. He became known as the "colonel", the "outlaw" and the "original badman deejay", which in Jamaica provided enough allusions to gangsterism to give Josey all the street credit he needed to impress the youth even before he opened his mouth.

It just so happens, though, that Wales is as tough as his on-screen namesake. He had been in St Ann on 5 February 1997, travelling to see Bob Marley's mausoleum in Nine Miles, when he was robbed. The thief shot him in the back twice and left him for dead. The "original badman deejay" lived up to his name: "There wasn't much ambulance around so I drove to the hospital, cowboy style", he told me outside a little restaurant he was setting up in

Waterhouse. Since he was bleeding and in obvious pain when he arrived at the rural hospital, they had to airlift him to Kingston where he underwent surgery. He spent eight days in the hospital recovering. Josey was so thankful to the medical staff that he bought an ambulance in the United States and had it shipped back to Kingston where he donated it to the hospital that saved him. On the side of the ambulance he had written "Donated to the KPH by the Colonel Josey Wales".

Josey possesses one of dancehall's most loved voices. His gruff delivery is known as the "rockstone" sound, characterized by a deep gravelly voice. Prince Jazzbo and Prince Far I were early rockstone deejays and the tradition continues with some of contemporary dancehall's biggest names, such as Buju Banton and Bounty Killer. "I started playing a little disco, at that time it wasn't sophisticated like we have now – [it had a few] lights on front to make the dance look sexy and good. [Later] I made transition to King Stur-Gav with U-Roy the Teacher" (Josey Wales, interview by author, 25 February 2009).

Josey used to attend King Tubby's Hi-Fi dances where U-Roy was resident deejay in the early 1970s. Josey refers to U-Roy as the "teacher of all deejays" and credits him with not only laying the groundwork of the deejay tradition, but also acting as mentor. Josey's placement on U-Roy's Stur-Gav Hi Fi came at a time when rival sound systems were starting to realize the power Yellowman wielded in the marketplace and were looking for fresh talent to go head to head with him. Stur-Gav had been shut down for a year after it lost both its selector, Jah Screw, and its main deejay, Ranking Joe, in the wake of the 1980 election. When it relaunched with Josey Wales and Charlie Chaplin, it posed a serious threat to Aces International.

With U-Roy's guidance and his Stur-Gav sound system as Josey's main gig, the Outlaw rose in dancehall to become a formidable force by the early 1980s. He and Yellowman would end up sharing producer Henry "Junjo" Lawes and when Lawes decided to put out a clash album featuring the two deejays, the pair hardly knew each other personally, though Josey says he had seen Yellowman perform several times.

> I used to hear him from Aces 'cause I like the voice, 'cause we are rough-voiced deejays. [At this point Josey pretends to deejay like Yellowman and breaks into a solid rendition of "Zungguzungguguzungguzeng"]. We like beat. Not like now, it was timing and precision, you have to ride the riddim. I think it was Sunsplash

1983 [that] I met him, but I see him on some shows before like Skateland. He was the talk of the building when Yellowman was there. He was a phenomenon, this bredren was different. (Interview by author, 25 Feburary 2009)

Their clash album, *Two Giants Clash* (1984e), came out in 1984. But like most clash albums, the two artists never actually had to set foot in the studio at the same time. The album paired the King of Slack with a deejay that came with cultural credibility, thanks to his Stur-Gav pedigree and tracks like "Jah Are We Guiding Star". Yellowman's material on the album, though, was far from slack, in keeping with Junjo's instructions. One of his best tracks is "Society Party" (1984e), where he takes pains to describe to his audience that "when Yellowman chat, nothing slack" which is, no doubt, tongue-in-cheek, but also part of Yellowman's ongoing agenda to convince his critics that he can perform any kind of style. The song is also instructive because it is a good example of one of Yellowman's favourite themes – poking fun at rival deejays in a light-hearted way to prove that he is the deejay king. The song states that there is a conference full of elites in town, such as the prime minister and the American president, and all the deejays on the island are unacceptable except Yellowman. "Peter Metro chat too much Spanish"; "Josey Wales chat too much badness"; "Briggie [Brigadier Jerry] chat too much Christianity"; "Sassa [Sassafrass] come from the ass family." Instead, "they want a deejay would suit everybody" and Yellowman arrives to "chat me culture, roots and reality".

Nobody Move (1983c) would prove to be the last album Yellowman would voice for Junjo during this era, though they would release one more together in 1993, *In Bed with Yellowman* (1993b). Junjo moved to New York and did a stint in prison there, effectively ending his power grip on the Jamaican music industry in the mid-1980s. Yellowman moved to other producers, such as Lloyd Campbell, Kangal and George Phang. Once released from prison, Junjo attempted to regain his foothold in Kingston. Yellowman felt he owed Junjo, since it was Junjo who had given him so many of his early hits, so quickly agreed to do *In Bed with Yellowman*. The album included remakes of three popular Yellowman songs, "Yellowman Getting Married ('93 Lick)", "You'll Lose a Good Thing" and "Zungguzungguguzungguzeng ('93 Lick)". Overall, though, Junjo's comeback attempt largely flopped and his life ended tragically in 1999 when he was shot and killed in England.

1984

On 28 January, a day after he celebrated his twenty-seventh birthday in 1984, Yellowman dominated the Rockers Award Show, hosted by *Rockers Magazine* and held at the National Arena. The Jamaican magazine, dedicated to reggae, started in 1982 and began the awards show in January 1983. Yellowman received an award at the first programme, along with Rita Marley, Third World, Black Uhuru and British radio deejay David Rodigan ("Rockers Magazine Completes 2nd Year", *Daily Gleaner*, 18 January 1983). Such was his popularity by the second show that, according to the *Daily Gleaner*, his "victory was a foregone conclusion" as he picked up the trophy for deejay of the year. The deejay "sent the arena crowd into raptures with his sheer charisma. But characteristically, he received his Smirnoff trophy with sedateness and humility." Yellowman's performance at the show, backed by Lloyd Parks and We the People, had "stolen the show" ("Rockers Award Show: Jones Girls Disappointing", *Daily Gleaner*, 1 February 1984).

In early March, the *Daily Gleaner* called him "one of, if not the most accomplished entertainers this country has produced", who "seems to get better with each performance and has remained at the pinnacle of the DJ world longer than any single performer before him. There seems to be no demise for him in sight" ("Tree House Club Is Where It's All Happening Now", *Daily Gleaner*, 5 March 1984). Later in the month he performed again at the National Arena, this time as part of Sly and Robbie's tenth anniversary concert along with top entertainers like Gregory Isaacs, Black Uhuru, Sugar Minott and Dennis Brown. The pandemonium at the scene was captured by Howard McGowan as thousands of fans attempted to gain entry – "about four times the 8,000 the Arena is reputed to be able to hold comfortably" – to what he calls "the most successful local musical event ever staged – in terms of attendance" ("Sly and Robbie Concert a Broken Rhythm", *Daily Gleaner*, 7 March 1984). The crowd was so thick that police used dogs to clear passages for entry, though reportedly one of them was crushed in the ensuing stampede of concert goers. Musicians even had trouble getting to the stage. Black Uhuru's Michael/Mykal Rose[1] attempted to climb over shoulders and, as Yellowman inched towards the stage, his fans called out, "See Yellowman ya, let him in" (ibid.)

In April, Yellowman left for an American tour with Sagittarius and in

May he would again be honoured in Chicago by the Reggae Music Arts Awards, picking up the award for Best Male Deejay. On 10 April the television show *Black on Black* on England's Channel 4 aired a studio performance of Yellowman and Sagittarius – his first international television exposure. He was in top form and clearly enjoying himself, running through popular hits like "Ram Jam Master", "Body Move", Jamaica Nice" and "Army Life". A few months later, Yellowman would show up on British television again, this time on *Jools Holland in Jamaica*, which aired on 29 June 1984.

By June, newspapers in Jamaica were running ads for "Heat in de Place", billed as "The Greatest Showdown in Jamaica's Musical History". The three nights in July were being touted as "King Yellowman Meets the Mighty Sparrow", a showcase that would travel from Brown's Town to Montego Bay and then Kingston, and from which 50 per cent of the proceeds would go towards sending the Jamaican Olympic team to the Los Angeles games that summer ("D&G Sponsors Calypso Concerts to Aid Olympic Fund-raising", *Daily Gleaner*, 3 May 1984). Yellowman and Sparrow's show on 14 July in St Ann's Bay was reviewed by the *Daily Gleaner*, which said that even though it was billed as a clash between the two artists it was "more of an excellent display of our various types of Caribbean music", though some audience members had hoped to see the two entertainers spar together on stage. Yellowman's performance as usual was the highlight of the show – "the entire audience came alive" – while Sparrow only received a "light response" and "poor applause" for most of his material ("It Wasn't so Hot in de Place", *Daily Gleaner*, 16 July 1984). The last night of the "Heat in de Place" festival took place in Kingston and here Sparrow and Yellowman appeared to be more equally matched according to the published review, though the author reserved the choicest hyperbole for the DJ King:

> [Yellowman's set] had the effect of a hammer as he pounded obscenities right, left and centre, bludgeoning the sensitivities of the elite, winning the affection of the more earthy. Until it was time for him to leave. But the crowds of now sweating DJ fanatics would not be denied. They wanted more of Yellowman and the fever peculiar to him and so he returned to the stage with a dedication to all "church-goers", a dedication which would have given any pastor severe heart failure, but which only met with the roared approval of the masses. ("The Night Was Long and . . . Hot", *Daily Gleaner*, 18 July 1984).

In August 1984, Yellowman performed again in Montego Bay at Sunsplash. His showing at that concert two years previously was dubbed the highlight of the show by the press. In fact, because of Yellowman the fortunes of dancehall were rising; Sunsplash, traditionally a roots reggae festival, was forced to include a dancehall night in 1984. "They started a dancehall night and it premiered at the '84 Sunsplash and that was because there was so much pressure. I mean because of Yellowman's popularity they wanted more dancehall included" (Beth Lesser, interview by author, 21 January 2009).

Also in August, Yellowman "delivered a devastating performance at the Americana Hotel" as the headliner for Summer Jam ("Summer Jam Concert: The Cry Was for More", *Daily Gleaner*, 28 August 1984). Two things are notable about this show. First, the reviewer, Howard McGowan, makes mention that Yellowman's set was "obscenity free". This was his first ballroom show in a posh hotel and McGowan, a loyal fan of Yellowman's, used this as an opportunity to illustrate for his readers that the deejay was "truly a versatile entertainer". He also highlighted the fact that Yellowman had Rolling Stones' guitarist and reggae lover Keith Richards "out of his seat and shouting for more".

LETTER TO ROSIE

> Call a taxi pon de telephone
> Pack up me ting, let me go home
> Me and Rosie and de children alone
> —Yellowman, "Letter to Rosie" (1986b)

While living in Franklin Town, Yellowman often performed at Up Park Camp, the army headquarters in Kingston. It was at one of his shows in Up Park Camp that he met Rosie Smith. Rosie was living with her parents in Rockfort and was still in school at the time. Her father was a Rastafarian drummer who played with Count Ossie's Mystic Revelation of Rastafari. Rosie began to follow Yellowman and meet him at shows and the two started dating, and eventually married. Yellowman eventually moved out of Franklin Town and in with her family before his manager, Jimmy Wynter, bought him a house in Meadowbrook in St Andrew.

Rosie found her way into many of Yellowman's lyrics, either directly in name or simply as the deejay's wife. It may seem incongruous that Yellowman's songs at times praise monogamy and marriage ("Yellowman is a one-woman man" in "Still Be a Lady"), but also brag about serial sexual trysts with casual partners. Like his pendulum swings between slack and culture, these lyrics are meant to demonstrate his versatility even though the latter seem to cancel out the former. Similarly, Yellowman often portrays himself as a Casanova on-stage, but a family man off-stage. This is the image that news articles have focused on since the mid-1990s. He was featured in a full-page article in *Flair Magazine* with the headline "Yellowman: A Happy Family Man" (17 October 1994) and posed with Rosie and two of his children. He was living on the outskirts of the city in Airy Castle, St Andrew at the time. The article seems to be designed, in part, to put a rumour straight that he and Rosie had separated: "Me deh with Rose from me at Eventide Home (Poorhouse), from me no 'ave nothing, so why the hell she a go lef' me when me 'ave something? Me and Rose never lef' yet!" He is presented as a role model father and husband in the story – something quite different from previous articles in the press about him.

Five years later, the *Gleaner* ran a similar article called "At Home with Yellowman: It's a Family Affair" (14 April 2001). The article details his home life with Rosie and their five kids, Katrina, Kareema, Karim, Kamar and Kemo, including trips to Devon House for ice cream and Sundays spent together at home. Yellowman even fashions himself a bit of a stay-at-home dad who does the laundry and washes the dishes. The only hint of anything other than a happy family life is when the article mentions that Yellowman also has a child born outside the marriage. His son Derrick was born to American Gay-Anne Griffiths. Both mother and son live in the United States. His quote that "after God, my family come first" would get picked up in further stories such as "Yellowman's Family Second Only to God" (*Sunday Gleaner*, 17 February 2002). Here, as in the previous articles, Yellowman explains that he is making up for the fact that he never had parents to love him and so is making sure he is there for his children, providing a good education and a loving home.

The projection of a family image is probably because he is known as a slackness deejay and he wants people to understand that slackness is only one element of his repertoire, and not necessarily a reflection on his lifestyle. Lady Saw, a popular slack deejay of the early 2000s, made a very clean separation between the performance she gave in the dancehall as Lady Saw, one of Jamaica's rudest lyricists, and her private life as Marion Hall. For Hall, Lady Saw was a means to an end – in this case fame and fortune.[2] Yellowman does not go as far – he is adamant that "Yellowman" is not a performance persona. The only people I have heard call him Winston, for instance, are his manager and Miss Soares from Maxfield Park Home. However, Yellowman is not the same person whom he sings about in his songs. He calls many of the sexual exploits in his lyrics "drama", as opposed to reality, but is always evasive when it comes to defining what is fact and what is fiction. That Yellowman has had many girlfriends is well-known when you talk to friends and colleagues. And he made sure, for instance, in an interview with a British newspaper in 1983 to mention, "I really have a lot of girl y'know! But the girl at home is the best" (Saunders 1983, 15). As a star deejay, he enjoyed the romantic opportunities available to him and loved to be seen with beautiful women. The cover of *In Bed with Yellowman* (1993b) shows him posing with the Solid Gold Posse, a group of ladies whom Junjo brought to dances. Yet Yellowman's songs about love and sex revolve between lyrics about casual sexual encounters and lyrics about the joys of marriage, family and children. Rosie features prominently in many Yellow-man songs such as "Letter to Rosie" (1986b) and "Mi Believe" (1984a) and what is staged to look like a wedding photo of the two in matching white suits adorns the cover of *Going to the Chapel* (1986a).[3] Rosie is the mother of five of his children and, according to Yellowman, has no problems with his slack material or girlfriends. "Rosie never think any way about slackness. [We] never discussed lyrics or other girlfriends." Even though Yellowman sang about – and by many accounts experienced – a life of multiple sexual partners, he would sing about Rosie, monogamy and family life in many of his songs. Just as he was always mindful of proving to critics that he could perform culture or slack or sing various genres of music, he also ensured that he covered all the bases when it came to love, whether it be romance, marriage, lust, monogamy, polygamy or casual sex.

KING YELLOWMAN

> Yellowman is no stranger to vinyl; avid bin-burrowers can probably track down a score or more of his albums on various Caribbean labels. *King Yellowman* is the albino reggae rapper's first release on a major American label and may represent the first mass-marketing in the US of "toasting" – largely improvised raps spoken or half-sung over a spare, sultry, bass-heavy backing. The result sounds better and more varied than any of Yellowman's early records that I've heard. (Christopher Connelly, "King Yellowman Review", *Rolling Stone*, 21 June 1984)

In the wake of his banner year in 1982, and then his road-blocking tour to England in 1983, Yellowman's fame started growing in the United States. According to Wexler (2001), clubs in New York and Los Angeles began spinning his records. His celebrity in England and credibility in the United States enabled Yellowman to catch the interest of a major record label in the United States – the first for a reggae deejay – and he hoped to emulate his Jamaican and British success there. One of the men behind getting Yellowman a major label deal was Howard Thompson.

In February 1982, while Yellowman was busy making history on the island of Jamaica, Howard Thompson made a lateral career move from the UK office of CBS Records in London to their associate/subsidiary label in New York, Columbia Records. Thompson was the artists and repertoire manager for the US East Coast, responsible for finding and signing new talent to the label. He had proven his instincts were good in London and planned to inject some much-needed swagger into the label's roster of middle of the road romantic rock acts: "Because I'd signed the Psychedelic Furs and Adam and the Ants over there, I was brought in to give Columbia a more modern edge as the label was mired in stiflingly dull, safe, cornball rock (Journey, Loverboy) and much of the 'modern' stuff it was picking up (Tommy Tutone, Scandal, Hooters) wasn't terribly original, or particularly exciting" (Howard Thompson, interview by author, 29 November 2008).

Thompson had a hard time convincing his new American bosses, however, of his hit-making instincts. On his first day at the New York office he tried to sell them on Toni Basil's "Mickey", which "had already been a smash in the UK and it sounded commercial enough to be an American hit to me", but they would not bite. It was later picked up by Chrysalis in the United

States and went to number one. He also introduced Columbia to demos of a new band called R.E.M. The demos sat on a desk for eight weeks and were returned with a note that said "not for us".

Frustrated that he could not get Columbia to sign any of the new artists he brought to them, Thompson started to take successful artists who were already on CBS in the United Kingdom and released their material on Columbia in the United States. Artists signed to CBS in the United Kingdom were signed for "all territories" so had to have their material released on a CBS subsidiary outside of the UK market. This made it easier to convince Columbia to release records that Thompson brought to them by artists like Wham!, Paul Young and others. So if he could get them signed to CBS in London, he could then get Columbia to pick them up for distribution in the United States. He tried this with Fastway, a new band featuring Fast Eddie Clarke from Motörhead, who Thompson had previously signed to UK label Bronze records. This worked, so he decided to try something completely different:

> I told CBS in London about Yellowman and told them if they'd sign him, I'd guarantee a release in the States. He'd started to get a bit of a buzz going here and over there, with releases like "Zungguzungguguzungguzeng", "Operation Radication" and the very excellent "Nobody Move Nobody Get Hurt". An A & R man called Dave Novik there convinced his boss, Muff Winwood, that Yellow was a good call and next we were in business! (Howard Thompson, interview by author, 28 November 2008)

British record labels had been successfully dealing in Jamaican music since the 1960s, with labels like Trojan helping to establish bluebeat, rocksteady and skinhead reggae in communities outside of Caribbean circles such as working class white British youth. Indie labels Island Records and Virgin Records issued several good selling roots reggae acts in the 1970s and Virgin had already tapped the deejay genre with its Front Line subsidiary releasing records by Tappa Zukie, U-Roy, Ranking Trevor and Dr Alimantado. But the United States was still largely a new market for reggae. Johnny Nash, using some songs that Bob Marley wrote for him, had moderate success with his pop reggae crossover material, and Tosh's records sold moderately well after he toured across the country with the Rolling Stones, but even Marley himself was frustrated that he could not break into the US market in the same way he had done in England and Europe. "To get released on Columbia was quite a big deal in those days. Not many major US labels were dealing with reggae. We already had Third World, a pop-reggae band, and they had reached a level of success that must have been very noticeable in Jamaica, so [Yellowman] probably saw that by signing with us, success might follow" (Howard Thompson, interview by author, 28 November 2008).

On 22 October 1983 the *Daily Gleaner* announced that "King DJ Winston 'Yellowman' Foster has just secured a very lucrative contract with CBS Records of the USA". According to the article, the contract was for five albums over six years and had an exclusivity clause, stipulating that no other label could release original Yellowman material during this period. This would prove disastrous for Yellowman in the coming years. With the characteristic unscrupulousness of the Jamaican music business at the time, Jimmy Wynter kept releasing Yellowman material, breaching the exclusivity clause in the contract and ultimately leading to Yellowman being dropped from the deal.

When Yellowman was offered the CBS/Columbia deal he already had the bulk of a new album recorded and produced by Jimmy Wynter. For all these tracks except "Wha Dat", which used a popular riddim called "The Answer" recorded by the Roots Radics, Wynter used Yellowman's live backing band, Sagittarius. It was recorded at Dynamic Sound – the same studio in which Yellowman voiced his first song, "Eventide Fire". But Wynter told the band that these were just demos. Simeon Stewart, the band's keyboardist and later Yellowman's manager, remembers being angry that tracks that were supposed to be demos were sent to a major label as finished songs. Yellowman was unaware of this at the time and only found out later about Wynter's ploy. By telling the band they were demos, he could pay them less than if they thought they were performing for a major label. Regardless, Wynter sent the tapes to New York.

Thompson liked the material but wanted to try and utilize the new buzz around New York's burgeoning rap scene and was interested in seeing if Yellowman's toasting style could mix with it. He chose Material's Bill Laswell to produce new tracks because he "got a big sound in the studio. He was also an innovator and always interested in pushing the sonic envelope." Laswell had a commercial breakthrough with Herbie Hancock's *Future Shock* (1983), on which he played bass, co-wrote songs and produced, and Thompson had him cut two extra tracks, "Strong Me Strong" and "Disco Reggae", for the album in New York with Yellowman. Laswell also provided dub mixes of the tracks for the 12-inch release. The songs were added to the Jamaican tracks and released as *King Yellowman* (1984a), marking the first time a deejay had a major label American release. The US and UK versions differed slightly from each other with the UK version substituting "Wha Dat" for "Bloodstain" and dropping "Keep on Moving" and "Still Be a Lady".

King Yellowman was not a runaway success by any means, but it did get the word out about Yellowman and it is still in print. Yellowman's first foray into major label territory was a financial success on some levels – he is still receiving royalties. In fact, it is one of the few records from that era from which he still receives royalties.

> The single ["Strong Me Strong"] did pretty well in the clubs – Columbia had a great dance promotion department – but nobody else at Columbia really 'got' it, or him, so no promotional effort was put into the album and it was left to its own devices. To this day, though, it stills sells, thanks to Yellow's constant touring and the fact that three of his live staples are on it: "Jamaica Nice (Take Me Home Country Roads)", "Moving On (Keep on Moving)" and "Sea Cruise". (Howard Thompson, interview by author, 28 November 2008)

The songs from the album *King Yellowman* have remained perennial favourites for his fans abroad, possibly because it has consistently been the most accessible album for them to buy. His concerts that I witnessed in the United States and Canada draw heavily from it. The album also demonstrates his diversity, his use of versioning and his attempts at crossing over into new markets. Just as he had on the sound systems, Yellowman includes popular R&B hit songs (Barbara Lynn's "You'll Lose a Good Thing") but also goes further afield with his borrowings. He covers "Sea Cruise", an early New Orleans rock and roll hit by Frankie Ford, Betty Wright's "Can't Do What the Guys Do" and Cliff Richard's "Summer Holiday" in "Mi Believe". And the fact that he offers versions of cover songs made famous by Toots and the Maytals (John Denver's "Country Roads") and Bob Marley (Curtis Mayfield's "Keep on Moving") shows that he is presenting himself as part of the roots reggae genealogy to his new American fans. The diverse tracklisting for this, his hopeful introduction to mainstream markets in the United States, can be read as another tactic to present his breadth of talent.

Yellowman has always wanted to make sure that he is not seen as a one-trick pony and has also set out to show that dancehall as a genre has incredible scope. A few years later, for instance, at Sunsplash 1986, he not only performed his standard deejay material such as "Galong Galong Galong" and "Budget", but also entertained the audience with "Rock around the Clock" and "Blueberry Hill". Apart from the various genres that he draws on, mentioned above, the record also has a track called "Disco Reggae", which, although not disco, still works to present dancehall as a diverse music genre, at least in name. The use of the term disco in reggae music dates to the mid-1970s when 12-inch singles were released with an extended "discomix" that included the dub or deejay version of a song mixed in immediately after the vocal version. While Yellowman's "Disco Reggae" does not follow this format, its title functions to both alert reggae fans of its connection to this tradition and provide a new US urban-dance take on reggae dancehall.

The music for "Disco Reggae", like "Strong Me Strong", was written and produced by Laswell. He built the riddims and had Yellowman come to New York to voice over them. The songs are a departure from the Jamaican riddims that Yellowman had recorded on up until that point and were more representative of contemporary dance-pop crossed with digital dancehall. Yellowman remembers Laswell bringing Herbie Hancock into the studio and thinks that Hancock played on the record, though he is not listed in the credits, which are far more detailed than Jamaican records at the time. As was his habit, Yellowman voiced both songs in one take each, impressing the Americans: "[Laswell and Hancock] said 'amazing'. They say 'how you do that?' I say 'I'm a computer.' One after the other. When I done voice one, I didn't come out of the studio, I stand in the voicing room until they put on the other one. Just one take. Most of my songs is one take."

Even though *King Yellowman* did not amount to the big break both Columbia and Yellowman had hoped for, it further established Yellowman's reputation at home and among reggae lovers around the world. Wyclef Jean, for instance, told *Spin* magazine (2 December 2003) that *King Yellowman* was one of the most influential albums of his life: "Growing up in Haiti, I listened to Yellowman all the time. I was 13 or 14 when this came out. There was something about his style and the clarity of his voice. And the production, the bass lines – when this thing came on in the 'hood, you could hear the bass a mile away. He had this vibe, this charisma. He was King Yellowman, know what I'm sayin'?" Thompson, who thoroughly enjoyed working with

Yellowman, telling me "he is a generous, good man", lays the gradual spread of dancehall in the United States at Yellowman's feet:

> In the end, he showed up in America and created a market for himself. The only reggae to really make much impact here up to that point was Desmond Dekker, Marley, Jimmy Cliff, Burning Spear and Toots and the Maytals, so I'm pretty sure he brought the whole dancehall style here himself. One thing, he's an original and, to me, that counts for a lot. Plus, to succeed under extremely difficult personal circumstances makes him all the more remarkable. (Howard Thompson, interview by author, 28 November 2008)

ROOTS, RAP, REGGAE

> Stomp your feet, clap your hand
> At the microphone is King Yellowman
> In Jamaica, I'm the champion
> This is roots, rap, reggae
> —Run-DMC and Yellowman, "Roots, Rap, Reggae" (Run-DMC 1985)

The *Washington Post* began its review of *King Yellowman* by setting the record straight on the Jamaican origins of rap:

> There's a certain irony in calling Yellowman the "king of Jamaican rappers", because rap music itself developed as an Americanized version of the "toasting" that reggae disc jockeys had been practicing since the late '60s. But toasting remains well out of the mainstream of pop music, while rapping has become as American as mom and break-dancing. So it's no wonder that Yellowman's first major-label album would try to present him as the Kingston equivalent of Kurtis Blow. ("When Yellowman Turns Blue", *Washington Post*, 22 June 1984)

In an article called "The Audience for Rappers Broadens", the *New York Times* further unpacked some of the thematic linkages between the two genres: "The two subjects preferred by the Jamaican artists – protests against racism and pleas for racial solidarity on the one hand, boasting self-delectation on the other – are also the principal subjects on New York rap records" ("The Pop Life: The Audience for Rappers Broadens", *New York Times*, 23 May 1984).

Yellowman's profile in the New York clubs and his connection to Bill Laswell would help him make inroads with rap artists in the city. Laswell introduced Yellowman to New York hip-hop artist Afrika Bambaataa while recording *King Yellowman*. Bambaataa contributed backing vocals to "Disco Reggae" and a few years later Yellowman would return the favour on the track "Zouk Your Body" from *The Light* (1988), a song that also featured members of Parliament-Funkadelic (Bootsy Collins on guitar and vocals, George Clinton on vocals and Bernie Worrell on organ) and Sly and Robbie on drums and bass. Besides working with Bambaataa, Yellowman would also link up with Run-DMC in New York. Darryl McDaniels (DMC of Run-DMC) was one of those people who had been paying attention to Yellowman's rising profile: "Back in the day, Yellowman was respected in the hood like an MC. We grew up worshipping Yellowman, loving him, loving all of his records; he was just cool. The Roxy, Harlem World, Union Square, Latin Quarter, they were all playing hip-hop and they were all playing Yellowman" (Wexler 2001). Run-DMC would get the chance to release a track with Yellowman, marking the first reggae-rap crossover. The song "Roots, Rap, Reggae" (Run-DMC 1985) features the rap band trading lines with Yellowman on top of a lazy digital dancehall riddim. The theme of the song is, typically, its own uniqueness, and Yellowman throws in some of his standard loverman boasts for good measure. The song was released on Run-DMC's platinum selling *King of Rock*, a foundational album whose single "Rock Box" was the first rap video aired on MTV in 1984. While *King of Rock* eclipsed *King Yellowman* in sales and mainstream visibility, it afforded Yellowman further credibility with his existing fans and helped make his name globally.

Yellowman was no stranger to projects that provided him more in the way of exposure than financial gain. *King Yellowman* would mark the first time he made a sizable sum for the recording of a record and he says that he still receives royalties from it. The same cannot be said about many of his other albums. For instance, he received no payment whatsoever for his earlier studio work; singles such as "Eventide Fire" and "Solder Take Over" were recorded purely for exposure. Even after he became successful, Yellowman saw little or no money from studio work, either up front or in the form of royalties. His first manager, Jimmy Wynter, was a novice in the recording industry so was not helpful in securing more lucrative deals. Yellowman remembers that he was paid a J$80 (US$45) advance for his work with Jo Jo Hookim at Channel One, sessions that resulted in the albums *One Yellowman* (1982c), *Them A Mad over Me* (1982g), and *Show-Down Vol. 5* (1984) with Fathead and Purpleman. To this day he insists he has never been paid royalties for these albums, though they are still manufactured and sold through Hookim's Hit Bound record label in New York. When I asked him why he continued to record at Channel One after this, he said it seemed like a good idea at the time because these records were making his name, leading to invites to more prestigious dances, stage shows and tours. Plus, he was acculturated to believe that he was not entitled to royalties: "It was always like that in Jamaica. That's the difference, people would listen to dance cassettes and artists weren't making any royalties off that. But they got all kinds of tours, bookings, other recording contacts or dates" (Beth Lesser, interview by author, 21 January 2009).

Yellowman fared better with Junjo Lawes. Junjo bought Yellowman a BMW in return for his work in the studio, and the record companies Junjo licensed Yellowman's material to abroad – Greensleeves and Shanachie – have continued to honour their contracts with Yellowman: "Junjo was one of the few producers used to be fair with me money-wise and business-wise. I know I never getting what I was supposed to get but Junjo told me what he would get and tell me what he would give me. Junjo say, 'I'm getting x amount for this album and I will give you this amount.'"

Even when he became an international sensation, Yellowman's finances remained problematic. He signed to American reggae label RAS in order to get better international exposure after things fell apart with Columbia. RAS paid an advance for work on albums such as *A Very, Very Yellow Christmas* (1998a), *Freedom of Speech* (1997b), *Dub for Daze Vol. 2* (1997a), *Message to the World* (1995a), *Prayer* (1994b), *Reggae on the Move* (1992), *Party* (1991b), *A Feast Of Yellow Dub* (1990), *Yellowman Rides Again* (1988b), *Yellow like Cheese* (1987c) plus two compilation records: *This Is Crucial Reggae: Yellowman* (2005a) and *Ras Portraits: Yellowman* (1997c), but Yellowman insists he has received very little in royalties from the company. There are also shady business deals surrounding some live records such as *Live at Aces* (1982b), *The Negril Chill Challenge* (1987b) and *Live in Paris* (1994a), all of which Yellowman maintains were bootlegged without his permission.

REGGAE GET THE GRAMMY

While *King Yellowman* would not reach sales expectations, it garnered Yellowman and dancehall reggae one of the industry's highest accolades when it was nominated for the first ever reggae Grammy Award (for records released in 1984 but handed out in 1985). The Best Reggae Recording[4] award was given out that year to Black Uhuru, Jamaica's cutting-edge modern roots band led by Michael/Mykal Rose, Duckie Simpson and Puma Jones. The band was firmly rooted in cultural roots reggae but, with Sly and Robbie pushing the limits of reggae beats and bottom-end bass, they had one foot unequivocally in dancehall as well. That Black Uhuru were nominated, and even won, came as no surprise. In fact, if they had not won, three other certified cultural artists easily deserved it: British roots kings Steel Pulse or Jamaican legends in their own time, Jimmy Cliff and Peter Tosh. But as a shock to roots reggae fans everywhere, Yellowman also made the list. The Grammys were America's seal of approval, pop music's stamp of credibility, and *King Yellowman* had been nominated, and alongside heavyweight roots artists to boot.

Yellowman flew to Los Angeles to attend the awards and memorialized the event soon after in song. His exuberance at reggae's international credibility is palpable in "Reggae Get the Grammy" (1985a) and his appreciation of just being nominated comes across as sincere:

> Every star drive up inna limousine
> As dem come out crowd a people start scream
> Deh sight Stevie Wonder dem a take picture
> Cyndi Lauper and Tina Turner
> Deh sight Lionel Richie as Deh sight Prince
> Everybody shout out "What a ting"
> As Deh sight Yellowman Deh say, "him good looking"
> Reggae get the Grammy, that's why me happy (x 2)
> Me a tell you 'bout the Grammy Award (x 2)
> You know reggae getting big and broad
> Inna Jamaica and also abroad
> Here dis a one you hear it pon de record
> A Grammy for you and Grammy for me (x 2)
> Inna de Grammy Award (x 2)
> Bekaa wah
> There is no business like show business there is no business I know (x 2)
> They nominate five away
> Inna de category

Nominate Steel Pulse, Black Uhuru and me, even Peter Tosh and also Jimmy
I the only deejay inna de category
Reggae get de Grammy and me still feel happy

Yellowman would receive a nod from the Grammys again over a decade later in 1998 for *Freedom of Speech* (1997b) and again he would be the only deejay up against roots artists. This time his fellow nominees were Ziggy Marley and the Melody Makers (who won), Burning Spear, and two British bands, ASWAD and Steel Pulse.

CHAPTER 8

Can't Hide from Jah

Encounters with Religion

Tings me used to do me na go do it no more
The year it changed to '84
    —Yellowman, "Nobody Move" (1983c)

WHEN YELLOWMAN STARTED TOURING OUTSIDE OF JAMAICA AND realized the extent of his fan base, he felt more of a responsibility to them. The power of his position as an entertainer struck him. People listened to his lyrics, his points of view, his ideas. Increasingly, his lyrics added more conscious themes typical in roots reggae and, even when they were blatantly slack, they would often still have a social message. Sometimes this would be instruction in correct morality, as in "Galong Galong Galong" or "Blow Saxophone" (1985a). These are songs that tell his listeners that certain kinds of sex are acceptable – such as casual heterosexual sex, while others are not – such as homosexual and oral sex. Other times it would present itself as ways to purify the body or avoid disease such as "Condom" (1993a). This does not mean that Yellowman ever turned his back on crude lyrics about sex simply to please a crowd. Slackness would always find a place side by side with whatever else he added to his repertoire. But message lyrics, particularly the kind that espoused a limited Rastafarian world view, crept into his lyrics more and more as the 1980s wore on. When I discussed religion with him during this research, I found that Yellowman's encounters with religion over his life helped to provide deeper context to his lyrics, how he promoted himself as an all-rounder, and even his use of slackness.

Religiously speaking, there are three dominant eras in Yellowman's life: his early religious instruction, both Protestant and Catholic, at orphanages in which he lived; his interest in Rastafari that began to develop in the late 1970s; and a period starting in and around 1985 when he underwent a life-change brought on by a brush with death. While he would never use the term "conversion", Yellowman has told me that he moved from considering himself a Christian to calling himself a Rasta during this period.

EARLIEST ENCOUNTERS WITH RELIGION

Though religion did not play a large part in Winston's early life outside of his mandatory attendance at church, he did start to encounter the ideologies of resistance found in Rastafari. It was during his years at Maxfield that Rastafari made its first impression on Winston. Higglers, or street vendors, would come into the compound to sell fruit to the workers and orphans. A Rasta named Windy, who sold oranges, was Winston's favourite. He used to give the children money and, unlike almost everyone Winston had met in his short life, Windy did not discriminate based on colour. "God sent him. I was alone and he gave me love. He was a father figure." This early encounter with a Rasta would have a significant impact on Winston; the powerful mixture of father figure, civility and dreadlocks would remain with him. During his formative years he remained a Rasta sympathizer.

Having attended Methodist church services while at Maxfield, and later receiving Catholic instruction at Alpha Boys', Winston's understanding of God was couched in very Caribbean Christian terms. Rastafarians had a bad reputation in Jamaica at this time, long before Bob Marley and other dread-locked Rasta messengers placated the country's fears that all "blackheart" men, as they were called, were thieves and crooks. Later, when Winston lived at Alpha Boys' School, the nuns there did not allow Rastas on the grounds, and students were forbidden to wear locks.[1] In those days, Yellowman recalls, "Dem would scare children and tell them Rastas would kill them."

His encounter with Windy allowed him on some juvenile level to critique the classist and racist narrative society had constructed around the Rastas, though it is doubtful a boy of his age would have thought of it in these terms at the time. But like them, Winston was an outsider, and he was attracted to them because of this. And like them, his fortunes on the island would soon rise.

FOOLS GO TO CHURCH

By the time we have recordings of Yellowman chatting in the dance in the early 1980s, his lyrics are not only raw and slack, there is often a vehemently anti-Christian strain running through them. One case in point is "Fools Go to Church on Sunday" from *Live at Aces* (1982b). Written at a time when Christians were heavily criticizing Yellowman and dancehall in general, "Fools Go to Church" is a humorous piece of vitriol aimed at getting revenge on Yellowman's most vocal critics by positioning Christian preachers as deceivers.

> The apostle pon the pulpit a tell pure lie
> He dress up inna jacket he dress up inna tie
> A tell you say great God is coming from the sky
> I tell you Yellowman say me know that a lie
> Me tell you de truth nuh tell you no lie

Today he wishes he did not use the word "fools", because he believes that most people who attend church are not fools. Still, it fit his sentiment at the time. The song's main joke is that the preacher keeps the money from the collection plate. Yellowman criticizes the church for deception and theft and presents the listener with an alternative. While he does not name this as Rastafari, it is clear that this is his preference through his use of the term "Jah" for God: "You just pon your knee / praise Jah Almighty."

While the religious ideas in this song are pretty vague, Yellowman would develop them over the next year and release the track on the album *One Yellowman* (1982c). There the Rasta sentiment would be fleshed out and more nuance added to the critique of the Christian church. When Yellowman questions the existence of the Christian heaven, he draws on lyrics by Peter Tosh and Bob Marley in their song "Get Up, Stand Up" (Wailers 1973). This stanza also shows us Yellowman's understanding of himself as a proclaimer of the truth. This idea functions in many of his songs and, as I will show later, draws on the reggae tradition of artist as preacher or teacher.

"Fools Go to Church" also begins to lay the groundwork for a lyrical theme present in several later songs. It is one of several Yellowman songs that include the lyric "can't hide from Jah" and references to being barred from Zion because of wrong-doing.

> You can't go to Zion with your ammunition
> You coulda never hide from Jah
> You coulda never hide from Jah
> You get 'way from man but you no get 'way from Jah
> You get 'way from man but you no get 'way from Jah
> You walking through de jungles of Africa
> You open de Bible and read up a chapter
> Started to chant up de roots and culture
> Tell it to de brothers and me tell it to de sista
> (1982c)

Like most of his Jah lyrics, this one is based on themes and lyrics found in other reggae songs. In this case, the most direct antecedent is the Heptones "Can't Hide from Jah" from 1979. In Yellowman's version quoted here, the deejay is offering a counter reality to the church, which he understands as deceptive. Drawing on Afrocentric imagery and Rastafarian ideology, Yellowman tells us he believes in a higher authority called Jah, insinuates that Africa is a hallowed land, and then presents us with the image of reading the Bible in Africa and preaching roots and culture to the community.

Besides his conspicuous anti-Christian lyrics, Yellowman often repurposed gospel songs and hymns in his sets and albums. Typical examples include "Amen", "And the Lord Said", "Oil in my Lamp" and "Something in my Heart Like a Stream Running Down" (the latter two can be heard in "Give Jah Thanks" from *Super Mix* [1982d]). Often these functioned to promote audience participation among a crowd that would already be familiar with them, and extend the expressive black church musical traditions into the popular music arena, in a method similar to that of artists like James Brown and Bob Marley.

In Yellowman's hands, though, there are two other facets to his appropriation of church music. First, there is the element of parody and satire. Second, by placing a hymn next to a song about oral sex, Yellowman, as always, is showing his audience his diverse musical styles.

REGGAE AND RASTAFARI

As far back as the 1980s' "Eventide Fire", Yellowman had included references to Jah in his lyrics. These references grew, as did the inclusion of more obvious religious themes throughout the 1980s and 1990s. To reiterate, this does not say that he ever turned his back on slack lyrics. Instead, he added religious or cultural lyrics to his repertoire and included them beside his better-known overt slack material. Since slackness and culture are positioned in opposition to each other in much of the way reggae is marketed, Yellowman's liberal use of Rastafari symbols can seem jarring. It would be a fair critique to say that he only adopted Rasta themes because they were popular, not because he had a sincere engagement with them. My interest, though, is not in trying to determine the sincerity of Yellowman's religious world view, but rather exploring the ways he uses religious themes. That being said, the utilization of Rastafari in any reggae music should take into account the way the Afro-Jamaican religion has influenced reggae culture, and how reggae artists have adopted its resources.

It is standard among reggae artists, particularly culture artists, to adopt outward manifestations of Rastafari (dreadlocks, Dreadtalk, dress, proclamations of "Jah Rastafari") whether they identify as Rasta or not, such is the cultural credibility that Rastafari carries in reggae culture. Yellowman's acculturation into the reggae world would have included a basic understanding of Rastafari and its cultural manifestations. To put it another way, he would have absorbed much of Rastafari simply as a reggae fan. Scholars have long pointed to this association: "To feel the reggae beat is to think Rasta" (Murrell 1998, 9) and "reggae is the Rasta hymnal" (Hebdige 1974, 18, 24). Even pre-reggae, Jamaican music included nascent Rastafarian themes and the "internalization of God which marks the Rasta Creed" (24) in the titles of ska tunes such as "Addis Ababa" and "Tribute to Marcus Garvey".

It was not until the late 1960s, after the advent of reggae, that the terms "Rasta" and "reggae" became almost synonymous for many fans of the music. Hebdige calls this the Africanisation or Rastafication of reggae – "taking reggae back to Africa" (26). Jones (1988) and Gilroy (1994) both single out Bob Marley and the Wailers as the ultimate evangelists for Rastafari in the United Kingdom and, indeed, around the world. While the movie *The Harder They Come* (1972) starring Jamaican singer Jimmy Cliff introduced the world to reggae, Marley was the first to capitalize on its success. Jones argues that the "defiance and rebellion" in the Wailers' first two international albums, *Catch a Fire* and *Burnin'*, presented a "compulsive unity of populist, anti-imperialist and Rasta themes" (Jones 1988, 42). Subsequent tours of the United Kingdom by the Wailers popularized both reggae and Rastafari among blacks and whites, and the Wailers' enormous cross-over appeal into white markets would have many later argue that Marley and his version of Rastafari came to represent reggae music for many people globally (Bradley 2001).[2]

The Wailers were part of a growing number of artists to convert to Rastafari as Jamaican music became increasingly politicized. Rastafari presented songwriters with compelling resources for protest songs, and reggae started to be divided into what is variously called on the one hand "dread", "roots and culture", "roots", or "conscious" reggae, and on the other hand "pop", "slack" reggae and "lovers rock" (these latter terms designate non-cultural subgenres of reggae). Roots or conscious reggae is generally defined as reggae that is musically harder or "heavier", usually meaning more prominence is given to the bass and drums over the melody instruments.[3] It is also delineated by lyrical sentiment that sympathizes with the Rastafari movement, often resulting in reality lyrics, and concerned with religion – particularly employing biblical allusions – and promoting equal rights, justice and Ethiopianism.

With the Rastafarian-led cultural awakening of the 1970s, reggae music adopted Rastafarian Nyabinghi drumming and chanting.

> A large portion of the reggae produced during this period, including local covers of North American hit songs, displayed influences from Rasta music. The *nyabinghi* lead drum, the repeater, was now regularly featured on pop records – sometimes even those that made no reference to Rastafarian themes, such as love songs. Studio musicians sometimes transferred *nyabinghi*-derived rhythms, originally played on drums, to other instruments such as organ, piano, and guitar. (Manuel, Bilby and Largey 1995, 166)

This shift towards Rastafarian culture was felt in both roots and deejay reggae. O'Gorman (1988), for instance, argued that the vocalized rhythmic patterns of dancehall deejays in the 1980s are based on the Rastafari repeater drum patterns. And deejay Big Youth, in particular, was instrumental in taking Rastafari mainstream. While reggae acts had been singing the praises to Jah Rastafari on a growing basis since the late 1960s, there were as yet few dreadlocked reggae acts. It was in this climate that Big Youth removed his tam on stage at the Joe Frazier Revue at Carib Theatre one night in 1973 and "first flashed his locks on stage. And it was like everybody's jaw just dropped. People just marveled at what they were seeing" (Frankie Campbell, quoted in Chang and Chen, 1998, 53). Chang and Chen see this as a "defining moment not only in reggae but in Jamaican cultural history" because the island's biggest celebrity at the time rebuked the status quo that marked Rastas as dregs of society and glorified in "the most visible badge of resurgent Rastafarian pride". There were many songs, sure enough, that were not thematically aligned with the religion, but the union of Rastafari and reggae in the 1970s went a long way towards acclimatizing critics to the marriage of reggae and social activism that was at the heart of culture reggae. As Yellowman began to become aware of reggae in the late 1960s and 1970s, these are the ideologies he would be met with.

CLEAN X-RATED SONGS: BOB MARLEY'S INFLUENCE ON YELLOWMAN

In discussions with Yellowman about his usage of Rastafarian lyrics and exposure to the religion, he cites Bob Marley as a key influence. Introduced to the Marley circle by Wailers bassist Aston "Familyman" Barrett, Yellowman came in contact with many practising Rastas at Marley's 56 Hope Road compound, where he sat and listened to reasonings and absorbed the lifestyle of those around him. The house was a gathering space for musicians and Rastas in the community and was a hub of activity in the late 1970s.

Yellowman has stated that he became intrigued by the Rastafari world view and began to make changes to his lifestyle accordingly. It may seem strange to some that Yellowman and Marley not only knew each other, but Yellowman insists he was welcomed at Marley's home and had a good relationship with his family. He remembers playing with the Marley kids often, to the point of wanting to avoid them at times because they always begged him to sing to them.

> Yellowman: I used to go to Bob's studio on Hope Road, play around with Bob. Bob used to say certain thing that I like. He used to run joke and call me a white man, you know.

Author: He didn't have any problems with you being a slack deejay?

Yellowman: No man, no man. Because Bob used to sing song called "push wood" ["Stir It Up"] and "Bend Down Low" and all those things. I am coming around like Bob now, doing clean X-rated songs, you know?

Author: Bob's mother had no problem with slackness?

Yellowman: No, kaa actually she is the one who let Bob know me. She used to love and respect me. Sometime I go to studio but most of the time I go where she at. Even when I go to studio and talking to Bob, when evening time come and school get over, I used to try to leave before Ziggy and Stephen and Cedella come because if they come and see me, they make me sing. They wouldn't let me stop singing, they make me sing on and on. I used to tell Bob, "I going over to your mother, I going to see Miss Booker." So I go and hide from Ziggy and them over there.

By "clean X-rated songs", Yellowman means songs that are about sex but not vulgar. Instead, they might employ double entendre, or words of a less crude nature. Seeing as Bob Marley died in 1981, though, and Yellowman released several explicit X-rated songs after this, any insistence that he cleaned up his lyrics should probably be taken with a grain of salt. What he did do, though, is add more cultural material alongside his continued reliance on slackness. This conversation, though, is instructive for learning how Yellowman uses the Marley connection to position himself as a more cultural artist. He often told me that he was a sort of "second" to Bob Marley, not only in terms of popularity, but as an artist with a message.

Author: Have you reinvented yourself more in image of Marley the last while?

Yellowman: Ya, that type of image that people would look up on you as a normal man that trying to push the message in many different ways. Bob sing love songs, Bob sing liberation songs, roots culture songs, message songs.

Author: Is he your favourite artist?

Yellowman: Ya man, up til now.

Yellowman cites that period of his life as the time when he first was introduced to Rastafari in any great depth. He had friends who were Rastas, but had never really taken the time to listen to the ideological and political reasonings of the dreads. This would be possible at 56 Hope Road with large numbers of Rastafarians hanging out at any given time.

> Yellowman: At that time, I tried to be that religion. I start with [Marley] and a lot more Rasta friends. They always talking about Rasta and you been around them almost any day and you hear that sing in your ears, you know? So it grow on me.
>
> Author: What would they talk about?
>
> Yellowman: They talk about Africa, Ethiopia, Selassie and they talk about things that you not supposed to do like eat certain meat.

Yellowman was influenced by Bob in particular, who lived strictly by the tenets of Rastafari. Yellowman never joined a house such as the Twelve Tribes of Israel, or attended a meeting. He simply learned about the religion through friends like Familyman, Marley, and Joseph Hill of the band Culture, another musician he cites as instrumental in his growing desire to learn more about Rastafari. He decided to make some lifestyle changes immediately; tellingly, slackness would not be one of them. Instead, he cut beef out of his diet, stopped going to strip clubs and changed the language he used to speak about women, being careful not to use words such as "bitch". Later, in "Nobody Move, Nobody Get Hurt" (1983c), he would reflect on his dietary change:

> Natty don't nyam[4] cattle natty don't nyam dirt
> He come from de planet of earth
> He come from de planet of earth
> Granny in the kitchen a cook rice and chicken
> The dread outta door, a cook Ital stew
> No trouble granny granny never trouble you
> Natty cook up him Ital stew[5]

He does not smoke ganja but glorifies it in song and invites the audience to partake in it. He has at times grown his hair in dreads, though more often has braided it. Several of his songs support the Rastafarian interpretation of God as a living black man incarnated in the person of Haile Selassie and speak about repatriation to Africa.

His introduction to Rastafari overlaps with the time when Yellowman was beginning to distance himself from violence. Known for fighting at Eventide Home and even carrying a gun alongside badmen, he perceived Rastafari "livity" as peaceful and tolerant.[6] When I asked him what he gave up when he became a Rasta, his first response was "badness": "Rastas is people who are not violent and we don't discriminate against people or religions." A decade after this change, in 1990, he was asked to play the part of the Rastafarian in the Steven Seagal film *Marked for Death*, but refused as he felt the role wrongly portrayed Rastas as violent and criminal-minded and confused the religion with Obeah.

Yellowman always insists that lyrics about sex are not inconsistent with Rastafarian lifestyle and as such he had no reason to change his lyrics at that time. He would tone down his slackness periodically over the course of his career, but for now, Yellowman began to see the world from a Rastafarian point of view, and that included, for him at least, the use of slackness.

By the time he played London's Pickett's Lock arena in the summer of 1983, he began to think more consciously about cultural lyrics. It was before the second night that Yellowman "composed" what he considers to be his first Rastafarian song.[7]

> Yellowman: I remember I make up a song before the second show and I do it on the second show: "Jah Jah A We Guiding Star".
>
> Author: So you wrote that after the first London show?
>
> Yellowman: Not wrote, I just had it in me head, you know?
>
> Author: And what did you tell the band?
>
> Yellowman: I just tell them to play a riddim. Me just say play something.
>
> Author: But that's going to determine how you perform, right?
>
> Yellowman: Ya, that going determine the key and the melody.

The lyrics went like this:

> Me walk and talk with Jah love inna me heart
> Nuh matter who you is nuh me nuh matter who you are
> Whether white like smoke or you black like tar
> Say Jah Jah a we guiding star

Gradually his clothing would start to exhibit red, gold and green colours, his album covers were often decorated with Rasta-related symbols and his stage shows included call-and-response sections to the audience where Yellowman would utter "Jah" and the audience would reply "Rastafari".[8] He also speaks of feeling compelled to include positive and cultural messages in his music. These connections to Rastafari as a religion on their own are fairly tenuous and not much different from many other reggae musicians. But I will return to this in part 2 to examine how the mobilization of Rastafarian symbols helped Yellowman throw off any insinuation that the dundus is without race by helping him connect his own representation to his African heritage.

STEP IT OUT A BABYLON

My first introduction to Yellowman was via the *One Yellowman* (1982c) album, which I owned as a teenager. It was released in 1982 by the Channel One label, Hit Bound, and featured Yellowman's most cultural material to date, a fact that probably affected my view of him early on as an artist who could easily shift between culture and slack. The album cover was quintessential culture reggae: a painted image of Yellowman's head in front of a red, gold and green image of Africa. The tracks were not all Afrocentric or Rasta-inspired, however. The album starts off with a song about watching sexy girls dancing ("Funky Reggae Party"), followed by "One Yellowman ina de Yard" (1982c), a song advertising his drawing power at sound sessions:

> You want Yellowman fe a ram a session
> Vote fe me name pon de radio station
> Yellowman too important
> Kaa Yellowman will ram your session
> Me just a draw dem attraction
> Now with my yellow complexion

But in "Step It out a Babylon" we find Yellowman deejaying on a pretty standard Rastafarian theme – repatriation to Africa. The riddim is "Truths and Rights", named for Johnny Osbourne's conscious song par excellence, and the title is derived from Marcia Griffiths's "Stepping out of Babylon". Both songs had cultural credibility and Yellowman chose the riddim himself because of its association with Rastafari. Likewise, his slack songs are often produced using riddims that are associated with earlier slack tracks. "Want Vagina", for instance, is voiced on Admiral Bailey's "Punanni" riddim. Yellowman says, "I used to deejay according to how the song, the vocal, play. If the vocal is a reality lyrics, content, if it is a culture song, if it is a Bob Marley song, we sing about culture, you know?"

The lyric of "Step It out a Babylon" (1982c) goes further than the fleeting references to Rastafari that were typical in his earlier material. Drawing on an African American spiritual he starts by mixing the biblical-historical and contemporary Rastafarian symbols: "I looked cross Jordan and what did I see? Selassie and his angel a coming for me?" He then proceeds to portray Jamaica – a land of political turmoil in the form of tribal war – as the Babylon that must be left in order to repatriate to Africa: "How long them a-go keep I dung [down] inna Babylon / We stepping out a Babylon one by one." Further to this, he even proclaims "I love Jah Rastafari", and asks that Jah "send down likkle [little] blessing from above". Taken in context with other reggae songs of the period, these lyrics are not exceptional and, in fact, are quite routine had they been sung by a roots and culture deejay. The fact that the King of Slack is singing them, though, is significant.

As Yellowman's opportunities for touring grew, he found himself on the road with several Rastafarian musicians, notably Black Uhuru, Culture, Mighty Diamonds and the Congos. His time with them would reinforce the positive representations of Rastafari he witnessed at 56 Hope Road and help him to clarify his own religious views, which were becoming a mix of Jamaican Christianity and Rastafari. The fact that he was even on the road with these bands is interesting in itself. In an era when few deejays were popular enough to tour outside of Jamaica, Yellowman could be found on stages throughout the Caribbean, Europe, North and South America, and Africa. International audiences would see him alongside roots reggae bands at festivals and so the divide between dancehall and roots reggae, or slackness and culture, was never as reified among his international fan base as the press has made it out to be.

When asked if people were surprised by his including cultural material, he says that his main audience in the dancehall was unsure about the new direction. "It kinda slow down who I was. 'Cause people know me as talking girl lyrics and X-rated lyrics. That's the reason why I start blending back the girl lyrics with the culture, you know." Sure enough, *Mister Yellowman* (1982d) blended both culture and slackness with "Natty Sat upon the Rock" and "Cocky Did a Hurt Me" on the same album. Over the next few years

Yellowman would release similar material, sometimes culture, sometimes slack – on the same album.

Today, Yellowman's international audience sees him as a carrier of the roots reggae legacy of Bob Marley. This is augmented by the fact that Yellowman has become a symbol of courage for many of his fans because of his ability to overcome the tragic circumstances of his life and rise to the top of the reggae industry. I attended Yellowman concerts in Ontario, Quebec, New York and Ohio, and it was clear by watching fans meet him that his international fans see him as an ambassador for Jamaica, reggae (both roots and dancehall) and even Rastafari. For many of his international fans, he does not represent the end of roots and culture or the end of roots reggae; he is the second Bob Marley. Yellowman says, "Because I change the face of reggae music. You understand? That's why if you look at the album, the Columbia album [*King Yellowman*], you see a likkle paragraph, write up, say I was the man after Bob Marley, you understand?"[9] Reggae pundits have bestowed the title "the next Bob Marley" on a series of promising Jamaican artists. Yellowman was not the first nor the last to enjoy this, but he has taken it to heart in a way few others have. As far back as 1983, he understood that to follow in Marley's footsteps he needed to present his audience with a message. That message, however, would remain largely unshaped and undefined for at least another year. When a journalist asked him in that year whether he felt "the responsibility now as a major artist", he responded, "Yeah, I pick up this responsibility like y'know, now Bob [Marley] gone as what people say, so I just pick up this responsibility, to spread reggae all over the world, as far as I can spread it." The deejay expounds on his message further in the article: "All I have to tell the youth is just have patience and wait until fe dem time come come, and if you have a talent yuh no fe sit 'pon it just go out there and use it" (Yellowman interviewed in Saunders 1983, 15).

I asked him to expand on the connection between him and Marley:

> Yellowman: If I wasn't doing the message my music wouldn't be so popular like Bob Marley. In back of people, mind Bob Marley is first and I am second. But my division is different – reggae, dancehall. We carry the message.
>
> Author: What was the message?
>
> Yellowman: Maybe not in early days, but now: peace and love and unite together and stop tribal thing in Africa, no more way.

Yellowman understands his role as an entertainer to be a carrier of this two-pronged interrelated message. First, he is a reggae ambassador, like Marley, responsible for taking Jamaican culture around the globe. He even has a song called "Reggae Ambassador" (1999). Second, he espouses a message of universal peace, a sentiment he finds rooted in Rastafari and defines as freedom from racial and religious discrimination and freedom from gang warfare, including bipartisan political violence (often referred to as civil war in his songs).

CHAPTER 9

Sufferation, That's All I Know

Cancer, 1985

> Dung in de ghetto that me born and grow
> Say sufferation, that's all I know
> —Yellowman, "Life in the Ghetto" (1982a)

HARDSHIP AND SUFFERING WERE NO STRANGERS TO YELLOWMAN, and the anodynes of fame and fortune were short lived. Just as it seemed Yellowman was on top of the world, in the spring of 1985 he was given dreadful news – that he had cancer of the jawbone and was expected to live no more than a few years. That spring he was scheduled to tour the United Kingdom, but shortly before he left Jamaica with Sagittarius he felt a pain in his face. He assumed it was a tooth ache and did not mention the matter. Yellowman completed the UK tour but suffered increasing pain.

They then went to New York in June to start a northeastern college tour and were scheduled to do four shows over two nights at the famed Lone Star Café on West 13th Street. It was here that Yellowman had to cancel because of the pain. "He complained about an ear ache", remembers Steve Martin, "and we had to cancel the late show – and Winston never cancelled shows. He was really reliable so I knew when he was lying on the couch going, 'My ear hurts', it was for real" (interview by author, 22 March 2014). Yellowman had a slight swelling on the right side of his face. Martin arranged a doctor's appointment the next day and Yellowman was told he had an ear infection. He was given antibiotics and set out to continue the tour. Martin says, "They came back about ten days later and Winston had a growth on the side of his jaw. It was shocking in a week to ten days how much it had grown." He was still complaining about the pain and returned to the doctor but this time the prognosis was grim. "He was diagnosed with cancer of the jawbone that had kinda spread. The doctor at the time said he was hoping to save his life but they would have to perform radical surgery. They said forget singing again, he'd be lucky if he could talk. This was, as you could understand, quite a shock to the guy. To all of us" (ibid.). Yellowman says that doctors gave him two years to live.[1] Sagittarius was sent home and Yellowman checked into the Holiday Inn on 52nd Street. About a week later, he underwent a long surgery that removed part of his jawbone on the left side of his face and muscles in his neck causing a severe deformity. In August, the *Daily Gleaner* reported that Yellowman "is recuperating from a recent operation to his face and will not be able to perform for some time", going on to explain that this was the reason why the performer was not on the bill for Sunsplash '85, held 13–17 August ("Recuperating", *Daily Gleaner*, 12 August 1985). According to the article, Yellowman was to fly back to the island soon and might resume touring that September. In an article published over a year later, Yellowman was said to have undergone a major "20-hour operation last June in New York to remove an abscess from around his left ear. It has left his face slightly twisted" ("Yellowman Back on Concert Trail", *Flair Magazine*, 26 August 1986).[2] Yellowman told the journalist that his doctors had told him the cancer was caused by the sun and that he has to keep out of the sun because it blisters his skin.

After the surgery, Yellowman recuperated. In the *Flair* article, he said that he rested from June to December 1985. After that, "I started to do some light work, like a little 30 minutes on stage. Now I can do more than an hour on stage: I can manage a full show now." Martin, however, remembers things differently: "We stayed in touch for about six to eight weeks and he calls me and says, 'I want to tour.'"[3] Yellowman's voice was weakened considerably by the surgery and his face was disfigured, yet he convinced Michael Whyte, who had taken over managerial duties from Jimmy Wynter by this time, to book a "test" show in Montego Bay. Once they were confident Yellowman could pull off a tour, they flew back to New York to the amazement of both Martin and the doctor who diagnosed the cancer. "The doctor was astonished that he could pull off a show. He came to the first show and wanted to take him to a medical conference because he was like a medical miracle for the doctor – that this guy could get up and do a show within about ten to twelve weeks [of the surgery]" (Steve Martin, interview by author, 22 March 2014). The shows went ahead but were rough on Yellowman. His voice was damaged and it was jarring for many fans to see him. However, Martin says, "He endeared himself to people so much in coming back that they rooted for him. It was a great story and people liked it. They had a great deal of affection for him." By the fall of 1986, he was on the road with Sly and Robbie, sharing the bill with Ini Kamoze and Half Pint. The resulting live album (1986), recorded in Minneapolis on 5 October, shows him in good form. A bit hoarse maybe, but otherwise strong-voiced.

Reconstructive surgery was available to him but he opted not to undergo another surgical procedure. When I have asked him about this, he indicated that the decision was partly due to the high costs involved but mainly because the process of surgery and recovery is extremely draining and painful. He simply does not want to undergo another one unless it is life threatening.

Even though Yellowman's operation was covered in the papers, at times Yellowman even denied or hid the fact that he was sick. The boasting and signifying that deejays regularly practised in the dancehall was designed in part to instill a sense of their invincibility among fans and rivals; to admit to sickness could be misconstrued as weakness. Yellowman had worked hard to overcome the stigma of albinism, which in itself represented a transgression of normative beliefs regarding race and phenotype. As such, it is not hard to see why he initially denied reports that he had cancer. When Shanachie's press release for *Going to the Chapel* (1986a) announced that Yellowman had a cancerous tumour removed from his jaw, Yellowman told one interviewer, "I didn't have any cancer, but I did have an abscess in my jaw" ("Overcomes Affliction: Yellowman Rippin' 'n' Rappin' Again", *Los Angeles Times*, 15 October 1986).

In the wake of the operation, there would be attempts to humiliate him, reminiscent of the days when a rival would cover the mic with a cloth, when some unscrupulous deejays, such as Papa San, took the opportunity to ridicule Yellowman's disfigurement:

> When I damaged the bones in my jaw, some artistes were quick to make a mockery of me. Some artistes go onstage and want their performance to be good, and they call my name and make a joke. . . I talk to (a certain artiste)

several times about doing that on stage show and 'im still do it. So I keep side of him, mi no hate him, but I dislike the things he does. ("Yellowman Has the Midas Touch", *Sunday Gleaner*, 31 August 1997)

Surprisingly, this practice still remains. Deejays still occasionally use Yellowman's disfigurement against him and Kingston comedy duo Twin of Twins made his disfigurement the brunt of one of their jokes on their album *The Resurrection of the Ghetto* (2006).

Another blow came when Yellowman's deal with Columbia disintegrated. One version of this story that Yellowman told me is that Columbia signed him for five albums but graciously let him out of his contract when his illness struck. Other versions of the story are probably more credible – that Columbia severed the relationship either due to the weak sales of the first album or, more likely, that they dropped Yellowman because of breach of contract. This scenario is more probable because reggae artists routinely recorded with any and all producers and record companies available to them – exclusivity was a foreign concept in Yellowman's world. Columbia's exclusive deal restricted Yellowman's recorded output, yet he continued to release product in Jamaica through Jimmy Wynter and Junjo Lawes, which was subsequently released through companies like Shanachie in the United States or Greensleeves in England. The albums that came out during this time, such as *One in a Million* and *Nobody Move,* were recorded previous to the Columbia deal, and were released by other record companies wanting to cash in on the hype in the wake of *King Yellowman's* release. According to Yellowman, he had no control over this. From Columbia's perspective this was an obvious breach of contract but from the perspective of Greensleeves, Shanachie and RAS Records, they were simply releasing material for which they had secured the rights. This would ultimately be to Yellowman's detriment, though, as it meant the loss of a major label deal and would impede his ability to gain the exposure to new markets that major label marketing power and influence can bring. Subsequently, while Yellowman pushed open the door for dancehall on the international stage, it would be artists such as Shabba Ranks – the first deejay to win a Grammy – and Super Cat, with major releases on Columbia and Sony, that would benefit most.

AN INSPIRING LIFE

If Yellowman's career had ended in 1984 he would have accomplished more than any previous deejay had and he would still enjoy a legion of dedicated music fans today. Because of his brush with mortality, however, his celebrity status took on an entirely new dimension. Instead of seeing his cancer as a weakness, fans overwhelmingly began to see a model of inspiration in his ability to overcome extreme hardship. Yellowman's rags-to-riches life story – from a trash can in the ghetto to superstar deejay – was admirable, to be sure, but now his having defeated cancer, and bearing the physical scars to prove it, galvanized his ability to connect with fans on a very personal level and increased their adoration and respect for him. Where he was previously respected for being a resilient ghetto success, overcoming extreme prejudice and being a wildly creative deejay, he now garnered recognition and respect for his resilience and perseverance against a terrible disease. This sentiment was demonstrated with the release of "Blueberry Hill" (1987a), Yellowman's comeback song after his second bout with cancer. Released in 1987, "Blueberry Hill" was the first song that Yellowman sang entirely without any deejaying. It signalled to his audience that not only was he back, but he was still being creative, and he was still as diverse as ever.

POWER HOUSE RECORDS

Despite his health problems, Yellowman's recording and performing schedule hardly suffered. He released three albums in 1985 with George Phang (*Galong Galong Galong, Walking Jewellery Store,* and *Yellowman Meets Charlie Chaplin*) and three more the following year (*Tiger Meets Yellowman, Going to the Chapel* and *Rambo*) with three different producers (Burtland Dixon, Jack Scorpio, and Sly and Robbie respectively). Compared to his output between 1982 and 1984 this was notably slimmer, but considering that most international touring artists would have one release per year at most, Yellowman's work ethic was still extraordinary. In fact, his release schedule remained at the pace of two or three records per year until the mid-1990s, when it tapered off.

Of the 1985 material, the best-known and most widely distributed was recorded with George Phang for his Power House label. Phang, who helped

Yellowman navigate humiliation and discrimination on those early sound system stages, wanted to get into producing in the mid-1980s. Thanks to his relationship with producers/musicians Sly Dunbar and Robbie Shakespeare, and his friendship with top billing artists like Yellowman, he had a successful, though short, run as a producer. The fact that he had no production experience did not really matter. In Jamaica, a record producer does not need specific musical or technical knowledge and rarely has any say in shaping a record. Instead, producers are businessmen (and sometimes women) who either own or book a studio, hire the talent (the engineer, backing band, artist), pay to press the record, and use their connections to market it.

Sly and Robbie at that time were among reggae's most ambitious and successful teams of producers. They had their hands, literally, in much of the music coming out of Kingston, and their reputation would land them gigs as session players and/or producers with some of music's biggest names, such as Bob Dylan, Mark Knopfler, No Doubt and Sinéad O'Connor. When Phang told them he wanted to get into the music industry, they provided him, free of charge, with a tape of freshly recorded backing tracks to use. "Me and Robbie grew up together, you know? From bwoy days, you know. Trench Town is a place that produce a lot of entertainers. That's where I'm from. Like it inna the blood, you know? So from deso [then] it just fulfil" (George Phang, interview by author, 17 February 2009).

This was a tremendous help for the budding producer. Riddims were as important as the vocal talent in ensuring the success of a song and Sly and Robbie's riddims were already legendary. Using Channel One studio, Phang recorded Yellowman, Eek-A-Mouse, then Little John and Michael Palmer.

Phang remembers Yellowman in the studio as a professional, an artist who needed little direction and could accomplish high quality work in a short period of time. The *Galong Galong Galong* album, for instance, was recorded in two days, one day per side.

> Yellow is a man who is a pleasure to work with. Bekaa when Yellow work pon ting you no haffi tell Yellow change a line here. If Yellowman do a tune and him listen back and want to change a line, he would change the line. Him really into what him doing and he know him stuff. You don't have to spend a lot of time with Yellow inna the studio recording a tune. It's a joy to work with him. It's like a more joke inna the studio than work. (George Phang, interview by author, 17 February 2009)

Phang's greatest success would actually come with another artist, Half Pint. Using Sly and Robbie's re-lick of the "Heavenless" riddim, Half Pint's "Greetings" is one of reggae's perennial standards. Phang had seen Half Pint sing the tune over "Heavenless" at a sound system in England and was impressed by the crowd's reaction. Phang said, "The way the crowd react to it I say to [Sly and Robbie], mek that riddim there and do that tune there. And before that tune release, it number one. It go two in national and British chart."

Phang's ear for hits also clued him into the possible success of an unlikely song. While on tour with Yellowman, he first witnessed the deejay sing the first verse to "Blueberry Hill" and "the whole place [went] mad. I say, 'Yellow a hit tune that, you know.' And him go and buy the LP *Fats Domino* and get everyting together and make the man make the riddim. And before that tune release it's like a number one already." But "Blueberry Hill" would not be recorded by Phang. Instead, Yellowman took it to Burtland Dixon to release on his Kangal label. Phang says he had no problem with this as producers worked together back then. Just as Sly and Robbie helped him get into the business, he did the same for Philip "Fatis" Burrell. "It's like the man, Fatis – it a me that bring Fatis inna de ting, give him some riddim. That just how we haffi live. Cause Robbie [Shakespeare] do it for me so me can do it fe somebody too."

CANCER RETURNS

After the lump was removed from his neck in 1983, and the tumour from his jaw in 1985, Yellowman thought he had beaten cancer for good but, in fact, this was just the beginning. He remained cancer-free for nearly a decade until doctors discovered skin cancer in 1994. Then in 1997 Yellowman went to Miami to have another operation to remove a tumour from his chest. In 1999, Yellowman would suffer a double blow; the cancer had returned but this time in the form of a tumour on his vocal cords. The surgery to remove it scratched his vocal cords and his doctor said his voice would be normal in a few months. However, the man with the golden voice would be permanently affected. His voice has become scratchier and harsher in the years since the surgery and he has to be careful of not overusing his voice, or it gets worse. Yellowman had to take a few days off of our interview sessions in 2009 for fear of losing his voice. He delayed studio work as well, in order to keep his voice in good shape for a concert.

These five operations are known to his fans, but a sixth operation took place in 2002 in Jamaica, this time to cut out a tumour that had developed in his head. That makes six operations for tumours, lumps and skin cancer, many of them involving major surgeries. His body is now riddled with surgical scars – he pointed them out to me one day – but that does not deter him from wearing basketball shirts and shorts on stage that reveal them. His face is disfigured by operations, leading one journalist to write that "there's a gaping hole where the left side of Yellowman's ear and jaw should be, but that hasn't dulled his mind or voice" ("Ragamuffin Soldiers", *Flair Magazine*, 7 October 1986). He is as proud of his body today as he was before the scars, a testament to his confidence, self-esteem and dignity.

CHAPTER 10

Message to the World

Prayer and More Slackness

My health coming from the Lord God Almighty, trust me
—Yellowman, "God Alone" (1995a)

IN THIS FINAL CHAPTER OF PART 1, I want to briefly unpack how Yellowman began seeing his role as a messenger of peace and tolerance, following Bob Marley, and began to incorporate a more spiritual outlook into his music. Following his earlier interest in Rastafari, his growing engagement with the religious tradition is outlined to provide context for the arguments in part 2. Yellowman's treatment of Rastafari is instructive specifically for the way he can present himself as religious at the same time as still being the King of Slack.

Yellowman says that being faced with his own mortality caused a shift in how he lived and what he sang about. This was an intense period of spiritual soul-searching. This life change is borne out in his material in the albums he has released since. Increasingly in interviews after this period, Yellowman characterizes this life change as a turn towards God. He was able to overcome cancer, he reasons, because God has a role for him to bring a message of peace and tolerance to the world. In a 1997 interview, Claude Mills frames Yellowman's life this way: he overcame great odds to reach fame and fortune and then defeated cancer, all of which made him "emerge a stronger, more spiritual man". He quotes Yellowman as saying, "I am closer to God now than I ever was" ("Yellowman Has the Midas Touch", *Sunday Gleaner*, 31 August 1997).

His songs are increasingly more conspicuously concerned with ultimate reality. Journalists have understood this as a softening of Yellowman's slackness in his post-cancer material, culminating in his work in the 1990s on albums such as *Prayer* (1994b) and *Message to the World* (1995a). An example of this position can be found in a blog post advertising a 2008 concert in Humboldt County, California: "In recent years, Yellowman's bouts with throat cancer and skin cancer have resulted in a mellower, more serious approach to his music" ("Yellowman", Humcity.com blog, 22 September 2008, https://bit.ly/3knSGLL). Huey (2010) has said that Yellowman's material on 1988's *Don't Burn It Down* – after his second cancer scare – found him "delving more into social consciousness; the title cut was a pro-marijuana protest, while 'Stop Beat Woman' condemned domestic violence, and 'Free Africa' criticized apartheid".

Yellowman's slack material, both pre- and post-cancer, was not oppositional to social and political critique. These journalistic interpretations are oversimplifications because Yellowman wrote socially aware music as far back as "Eventide Fire" in 1980, and started dealing with spiritual matters as early as 1982. In addition, Yellowman not only released his slackest material after this point (such as *The Negril Chill Challenge* [1987b]), he continued his tradition of releasing both slackness and culture throughout his career, usually on the same album. For instance, on *Prayer* (1994b), Yellowman revolves between the spiritual and the carnal – "Girlfriend" is a typical "girls dem" song that brags about his plethora of female companions and "Romance" has Yellowman singing about his penis and the joys of lovemaking. *Message to the World* (1995a), often cited as Yellowman's most cultural release, includes an extremely slack track called "Maximum", a reference to the kind of intercourse his girlfriends must "take" from him. And the Jack Scorpio–produced *Yellowman's Good Sex Guide* (1995b) was released in between *Prayer* (1994b) and *Message to the World* (1995a).

Historians and journalists who portray Yellowman as mellower and less slack during his later career have not engaged with his material adequately. Yellowman has never ceased releasing slackness, though he has increased his output of unabashed spiritual material. Examples include "One God" (1993a), "Deliver Us" (1993a), "Prayer" (1994b) and "God Alone" (1995a). Even though he describes a life change, he also insists that there is an essential Yellowman who never changes and this includes the aspect of slackness. On "One Man" (1995a), he sings "I cannot change, this is the way the Father made me", later chatting that while many deejays opt to "turn Rastaman" because it is economically viable, "Me naw change me image to please anyone."

The metaphor of bowing is used in dancehall to represent submission. It often is associated with oral sex and, therefore, under widely accepted Jamaican sexual ethics, moral deviance. To bow can also imply giving in or acquiescing. When Buju Banton refused to apologize for his anti-gay song "Boom Bye Bye", Saunders (2003, 96) considered his "refusal to bow" an act of defiance against what he perceived as immoral Western values. Banton has since, however, altered his stance on the song. In 2007 he ceased performing it and in 2019 he removed it from digital streaming services.

Yellowman does not want to be seen as bowing or submitting to any agenda other than his own, or a normative homegrown moral agenda. He can include more spiritual material in his music, but does so on his own terms; this means not omitting songs about sex. In songs from the 1980s, Yellowman often tells his audience he is perfectly content putting together slackness and culture. His life change, then, needs to be read in this context. It was not, as many have assumed, a move away from singing slackness.

That being said, Yellowman's religious engagement does indeed change focus at this point. His songs show that before 1984, Rastafarian symbols often functioned to add local colour to his lyrics on one end of the spectrum, but on the other end, they were used as important signifiers to work out issues of race and identity. Cultural songs at that time were also meant to try and confront critics who oversimplified his repertoire and only saw him as a slackness deejay; by singing Rasta songs and Afrocentric songs, Yellowman was able to show the breadth of his material.

RELIGIOUS LYRICS AND OUTLOOK AFTER CANCER

Post-1984, Rastafari is used to assist Yellowman's agenda of moral regulation in songs like "Galong Galong Galong" and "Beat It" (1985a), which I will look at in more depth in part 2. His use of the term "God" increases and becomes interchangeable with "Jah". He began self-identifying as a Rasta, but often did so in very Christian terms, talking about Almighty God, for instance. This is in keeping with what he understands as his multi-religious identity, both Rastafarian and Catholic. Like other Rastas I have spoken to, Yellowman's understanding of God and religion falls under what Prothero calls "religious liberalism". "Chief among the tenets of this faith is the affirmation made famous by Mahatma Gandhi (but articulated much earlier by the theosophists, [Henry Steel] Olcott included, who influenced him) that 'All Religions are True'. A first corollary of this tenet is the mandate for religious tolerance" (Prothero 1996, x). Yellowman, for instance, argued that the Christian God and the Rasta God are the same, but the religions are different: "It's just one God everybody pray to. Some people call God Jah, some say Jehovah, some say Selassie. I think it the same God. Selassie, Jehovah, Jesus Christ." In songs and interviews beginning in the 1990s, Yellowman tends to further blur the lines when it comes to religion. He told one journalist, "I am not a Christian. I believe that there are no Christians left on Earth, only believers in God, and even then, they believe but harbour little doubts. I have no doubts that there is a God and that He lives ("Yellowman Has the Midas Touch", *Sunday Gleaner*, 31 August 1997).

The word "religion" is charged with negative connotations among Rastas. The word is coded to refer to institutional or organized religion, such as the Catholic Church or Christianity in general. Rastafari is non-hierarchical. Edmonds (1998, 349) considers the Rastafari movement reticulate or web-like because it is a loose collection of groups connected by personal networks and "constitutes a cohesive movement with identifiable structures and a shared ideological-symbolic-ritual ethos". Yellowman could be understood as what Pollard (2000, 20) calls an "own-built" Rasta, not belonging to an official community. The move to start calling himself a Rasta was partly predicated on the fact that of the two religions that influenced his thought the most (Christianity and Rastafari), Rastafari never levelled a critique against him, as Christianity did, based on sexual lyrics. In his mind, Rastas, though some may have winced at his rawness, never made his slackness an issue. For this reason, Rastafari appealed to Yellowman more than Christianity, but he is often careful to steer clear of the word religion: "I still consider myself Catholic with the organization, but at the same time I'm a Rasta. But not the kind of Rasta that will be confused by the religion. The only rule for me is the same God, everybody pray to same God." For Yellowman, the feeling of connection to God or Jah is the only necessary aspect of a religious world view. The only rule is to "deal with" God, no matter what name you use: "I deal with the Almighty God. I deal with Jesus, I deal with Selassie 'cause I know it the same God everybody pray to. They only change his name." Belonging to a religious community is also unnecessary: "I don't have to go to a Bobo camp, or a Twelve Tribes meeting or a Catholic Church. I just be myself."

Today, Yellowman sees himself as an entertainer charged with a message of "peace and love, unity". This message came out of a feeling of obligation to God for sparing him; what the cancer scare did was put life into close focus for Yellowman and led to a reordering of priorities.

> Because of the cancer, the sickness, I'm fortunate to be here so I think I'm here for a purpose and I think I should start make people understand about life and what life is, you know. And how life can change because when the doctor say three years I never even think about it. I just say, well if it happen, it happen. But I know it deep in my mind it not going to be three years. It became changed over the years because even this new album that I'm doing right now, 'cause this one I'm going to call *Living Legend*.[1] There's a lot of political view on that album. Issue of the Middle East, immigration, people in general.

In concerts I attended between 2007 and 2013, Yellowman routinely finished his shows with a funny phrase that he sums up as his life philosophy: "If you can't be good, be nice. And if you can't be good and can't be nice, be careful. And if you can't be good and you can't be nice and you can't be careful, you're on your own." Taken in tandem with a general message of peace and unity, and a quasi-religious directive to live good or morally, Yellowman's concerts after the cancer scare see him deepening his commitment to his audience by seeing himself in the role of teacher or preacher. This is a common role for reggae artists, particularly Rasta artists or Rasta-inspired artists, who sense they have a calling to educate the people. In fact, the 1960s and 1970s were chock-full of Rastafarian reggae singers who not only espoused ethics and theology in their lyrics, but even marketed themselves as modern prophets or preachers, even going so far in some cases, such as Peter Tosh, to don robes and carry staffs. Reggae concerts are often imbued with highly religious symbolism – images of Haile Selassie, the African continent and Marcus Garvey for instance. For Yellowman, then, the turn from mere entertainer to entertainer with a social and religious consciousness, shows him following a well-worn pattern laid out by his forebears in roots reggae: "I found that out when I went through all these surgeries that God put me here for a purpose because he make me live through it and I stay strong through it. That's the reason why the people of Jamaica love me and the world love me, 'cause they know what I go through. That's why they call me the King of Dancehall, you understand? All over the world."

During my first interview with Yellowman in 2005 I asked him about whether there was a switch from slackness to culture at this time: "I start out with the sexual lyrics. But growing up now, maturing, having children and responsibility because the people is my responsibility. I found out all over the world people love me so I have to change a little." His desire to be a role model, both to his own children and to his fans, meant that he geared more of his material towards social responsibility. He admits in the quote above that he changed "a little". But this change was not a deep structural altering of his modus operandi, only a surface treatment to make his songs sound cleaner. While he continued to sing about sex after the cancer scare, he often did so using cleaner words, as in the example of the "clean X-rated" material he spoke of earlier. Instead of saying "pussy" or "fuck", he would say "vagina" and "sex". It is interesting how Yellowman understands this transition from what he calls X-rated material to clean X-rated: "I used to more sing about woman and sex but it's now politics and everything." The "everything" here seems to signify everything that is not politics, inclusive of sex and religion.

At other times, however, Yellowman has denied that he has drifted away from slackness, not wanting to be seen as bowing to pressure. In 1986 – three years after his first bout with cancer – he assured one interviewer that he was staying the slackness course: "I got a lot of criticism in my type of music, but it didn't trouble me. I still move in the same track. That's the way I have to stay, no changes" ("Overcomes Affliction: Yellowman Rippin' 'n' Rappin' Again", *Los Angeles Times*, 15 October 1986). He told a crowd at Dance Hall '88 in Kingston that "he was not really into this 'culture' thing" ("Dance Hall '88: A Big Letdown", *Daily Gleaner*, 28 July 1988).

LEGACY: YELLOWMAN AS ELDER STATESMAN OF DANCEHALL

He was named Winston Foster, he called himself Yellowman and the people crowned him King Yellowman.

— "Yellowman's Family Second Only to God", *Sunday Gleaner*, 17 February 2002

Yellowman has enjoyed a long and prolific career since doctors told him he only had a few years to live in 1985. He continues to be a controversial artist because of his slackness, but newer artists have now taken his place as the subjects of local debates on slackness leading the youth astray. Yellowman now enjoys the status of an elder statesman of reggae, at home and abroad.

Yellowman's celebrity remained strong after the period covered in this book and he has continued to make headlines at home and tour around the world. In 1986 alone, he spent two months touring Europe, then six weeks in the United States and Canada. Sandwiched in-between these tours was his perennial Thursday night set at the 1986 Sunsplash held in Montego Bay where he showed the world "that he was still the king of the DJ's" ("Ragamuffin Soldiers", *Flair Magazine*, October 7, 1986). The *Daily Gleaner* did not even have to mention him by name, merely saying that "the stage was set for the entry of the DJ King, the man credited with making Dance Hall night at Sunsplash since 1982 the success it has been" ("Dance Hall Card Rocks 18,000 Sunsplash Crowd", *Daily Gleaner*, 30 August 1986). He would perform the following year to a record-setting forty-five thousand people at the Thursday Dance Hall Night along with Peter Metro, Lovindeer, General Trees and Admiral Bailey, who "gave King Yellowman a run for his crown" ("Sunsplash 10", *Daily Gleaner*, 28 August 1987). At the 1987 Sunsplash, Dance Hall Night would again set records as the crowd "easily tripled anything seen before on Reggae Sunsplash" and were on hand to hear Yellowman, Admiral Bailey, Leroy Smart and Lovindeer. When headliner Yellowman hit the stage just after 7:00 a.m. dressed in a golden crown and yellow cape with the words "King Yellowman" across the back, "photographers and video cameramen jockeyed for position" ("Dee-jays' Power Rocks Sunsplash", *Daily Gleaner*, 21 August 1987). His popularity still at its height, Yellowman's legacy was now being summed up by the journalists who had covered him for half a decade:

> From the moment he arrived the crowd went wild, and in a professional and mature performance, the man who is arguably the best performer this country has produced gave the crowd what they had stood patiently from 9 p.m. the night before. He closed his act with Rosie, his wife, in his arms, gently rocking to the sound of the dee-jay-turned-singer crooning the Fats Domino classic "Blueberry Hill". ("Dee-jays' Power Rocks Sunsplash", *Daily Gleaner*, 21 August 1987)

In a 1988 opinion poll that asked participants who they felt was the most outstanding musician of 1987, Yellowman came in fifth with 5 per cent of the vote. He was beat out by Freddie McGregor, Pinchers, Admiral Bailey and Lieutenant Stitchie, who won with 18 per cent of the vote ("January '88 Stone Poll", *Daily Gleaner,* 8 February 1988). News stories from the period show that while Yellowman's peak fame tapered off by the end of the 1980s to make room for a new generation of dancehall artists, he continued to tour and still played to "jam-packed audiences, especially abroad" in the 1990s ("Yellowman Has the Midas Touch", *Sunday Gleaner,* 31 August 1997). His international stature remained strong and he was nominated for his second Grammy in 1998 for *Freedom of Speech* (1997b). The album, while garnering attention abroad, failed to have any local hits. When asked about this by a reporter, Yellowman opined, "You cannot really follow the charts in Jamaica, it is like a cemetery, in that you have to buy a spot. A song's success is not based on actual sales or popularity, it depends on the weight of the envelope that you pass to certain people within the entertainment community" ("Yellowman Gets Second Grammy Nomination", *Gleaner,* 21 January 1998). A 2005 article made the same point – that Yellowman's presence on Jamaican charts had faded but he continued releasing records abroad and maintained active in markets such as Japan and Israel as well as his mainstays of Europe and America. This is not to say he was not releasing records at home: his clash album with Ninjaman (2005b) attests to this. This local dry spell was temporarily broken with the release of his song "Orphan" (2006), recorded on Dave Kelly's "Eighty Five" rhythm, which received ample radio play back home: "I was a orphan without a home / 100 per cent barefoot ghetto grown."

At the 1998 tenth anniversary of the Heineken Startime concert series, Yellowman again proved that he could still dominate the stage back home. Called the "original dancehall DJ . . . the Grammy nominee gave the audience what they wanted – 'Mister Chin' drove them into a frenzy. Then he added the piece de resistance with his rendition of 'Blueberry Hill'" ("'Startime 10' Show Scores Big", *Gleaner,* 3 June 1998).

Now in his fifth decade in the business, Yellowman is no longer the talk of the town but has settled into a role as a respectable elder statesman of dancehall and reggae generally. Proof of this came when he was one of the first seven artists to be represented on the Reggae Walk of Fame in March 2006. He shared the honour with Culture, Charlie Chaplin, Tony Rebel,

Barrington Levy, Third World and Cynthia Schloss. In July of that year, he received a Lifetime Achievement Award from Red Stripe Reggae Sumfest along with John Holt for their part in "carving out a niche on the world stage and solidifying reggae and dancehall as a separate genre of music" ("Holt, Yellowman to Receive Lifetime Achievement Awards", *Gleaner*, 12 July 2006). Further proof of Yellowman's respectability among factions that once would have scoffed at the controversial deejay is the fact that family-friendly Disney asked him in 2010 to contribute to a record of reggae-fied Disney classics called *The Disney Reggae Club*. Yellowman chatted along with other top reggae artists like Toots Hibbert, Gregory Isaacs, UB40, Ziggy Marley and Burning Spear, contributing the song "Find Yourself" from the film *Cars*.

In a story that partially denigrates Yellowman for his slackness, Oliver Lawson ("'Culture' Lasts, Slackness Is Like Chaff", *Gleaner*, 19 February 1998) also takes a stab at why Yellowman's popularity has continued when many of the deejays from his era were forgotten after a few hit songs. For him, it is Yellowman's non-slack material, like "Blueberry Hill" that continues to be played, the implication being that slackness was fleeting and deejays who did not expand on this one style could not sustain their careers.

Moralizing aside, the diversity that Yellowman has so steadily and care-fully developed throughout his career, has allowed him to enjoy a four-decade (and counting) career in the dancehall business, a business that hardly existed, at least on a global scale, before he entered the fray. Yellowman is an enigma – hard to define, hard to pin down. It would be disingenuous to suggest that Yellowman is any one thing: slack or culture; deejay or singer; Christian, Rasta or neither; family man or playboy. Ask Yellowman today about slackness and he might tell you he's given it up; attend a Yellowman concert tomorrow and you may hear him sing a graphically sexual song. Because of some of his pro-ganja songs like "Herbman Smuggling", many of his fans assume he smokes ganja, yet Yellowman is extremely health conscious and insists that he has never smoked tobacco or ganja nor drunk alcohol. The backstage of reggae shows, in my experience, is generally liberally bathed in ganja smoke (as is the front of stage, to be sure). This is somewhat problematic for Yellowman; he loves to meet fans and peers, yet tries not to stand near second-hand smoke. Once, backstage at Island Village in Ocho Rios, I witnessed as Yellowman stood alone in the hallway instead of entering the Green Room reserved for artists and their entourages. It was the clouds of smoke, he said, that kept him out. Fans would walk up to him dangling a spliff from their lips and he would politely talk to them but noticeably recoiled from the second-hand smoke. In my experience, fans never picked up on this because they assumed, based on the image he projects in his songs and on stage which are supported by reggae stereotypes, that he is a ganja smoker as well.

I have tried to show in this life story that Yellowman is several seemingly contradictory things, usually at the same time. I think there are a few reasons for this: first, Yellowman's entire career has been an ongoing struggle to prove himself. Even when he was at the height of his fame between 1982 and 1986, he often chose to respond to critics of his slackness by demonstrating his culture side, even though that did little to nullify their critiques. In Yellowman's eyes, this was an attempt to prove that he was more than simply slack and he has taken great pains to prove that he is an "all-rounder": he can play all genres, from country to rock and roll to R&B to reggae, and he can sing or deejay all lyrics – romance, sex, religion and politics. He understands that to remain a viable concert draw, he needs to appeal to a broad demographic. He can play the role of consummate entertainer, giving the audience what they want, or he can take on the roles of teacher, preacher and cultural ambassador of Jamaica.

Second, as an entertainer Yellowman has consistently looked at the options open to him in the music business and made decisions that would encourage an internationally sustainable career while still attempting to maintain a level of relevance to current dancehall styles. In the early 1980s, he was not content to do things the way the other local deejays did them – instead he modelled his career on internationally successful artists like Bob Marley when he began touring with Sagittarius and was able to push dancehall reggae into new markets. His recorded output has kept pace with advances in style and technology, whether it be the sound of digital reggae in the "Sleng Teng" era or his ongoing use of contemporary riddims on albums such as *No More War* (2019). Yellowman told a journalist in 1997 that one reason he has been able to sustain a successful career is that he builds relationships with promoters and does not overvalue his services. I have talked to some of the promoters at venues in the United States, who book Yellowman every year, and they can attest to this.

I work for US$4000 a week while other current artistes work for US$5000 a night and still want a limo and to be put up in posh hotels. . . . All I want is a clean bed, a TV and a telephone. Down the line, those artistes can't work next three years because they pressured the promoter, and set up a bad relationship with them. I always remember the little man, and the rainy days. That's why I will always find work. Money is a thing whe corrupt the world, yu must either put it in the bank or spend it. It is not something to covet and look at; I give money freely. To some, money is like a ticket. If yu don't have money, yu don't have a pass. With me, is not that. My main concern is family and life. ("Yellowman Has the Midas Touch", *Sunday Gleaner*, 31 August 1997)

Ephraim Martin of Martin's International says that Yellowman is one of the only reggae artists who can consistently sustain long tours in all parts of the United States. While most artists fly in and do shows in reggae hot spots like Miami, New York and Los Angeles, Yellowman does complete tours of the country and is the only artist who has been able to do this for thirty years, nearly non-stop.

There is also the fact that Yellowman is undeniably talented on the microphone and on stage with clever lyrics, humour and even humility beneath his outrageous boasts. His enthusiasm for performing, whether it be at a small street party in Concrete Jungle (in inner-city Kingston) or at a major international festival, endears him to fans. To most of his fans abroad, the slack vs culture debate is either long over or not even on the radar. Yellowman's legacy now is as one of the foundational reggae artists – a pioneer of the dancehall form – and the king of deejays. His life story, with all its tragedies of abandonment, abuse and multiple triumphs over cancer, has endeared him to his fans, who see him as a self-made man who has not forgotten his roots and as an inspiration. Claude Mills certainly felt this way in an article in 1997 when he spoke of "the courage and vitality of a man who had to first overcome great odds to reach the pinnacle of fame and fortune, and then defeat cancer" ("Yellowman Has the Midas Touch", *Sunday Gleaner*, 31 August 1997).

Another key to Yellowman's lasting success is the fact that many of the trappings of fame and celebrity appear to have left him unaffected. News articles over the last three decades corroborate the several interviews I did with his colleagues, fans, and friends and the impression that I developed of him myself. In my experience, you would be hard-pressed to find someone speaking ill of Yellowman as a person. I have shown in this book that he was and continues to be a polarizing figure because of his slackness, and he has certainly been maligned in the press because of this. But overwhelmingly, when I interviewed people who knew him and worked with him – producers, rival deejays, musicians, drivers – Yellowman was characterized as genuinely good-natured and fun to work with. This is certainly my experience of him in the thirteen years I've known him. For a man who has suffered discrimination in his life and in the music business, he appears to hold very few grudges. Claude Mills says this is the secret to his life's philosophy – live and let live – and suggests that "if Yellowman's skin can be judged to be 'yellow', maybe it's only because he has something that touches every facet of his life – a heart of gold" ("Yellowman Has the Midas Touch", *Sunday Gleaner*, 31 August 1997). Jack Scorpio, who has known Yellowman his entire career, would agree. When I asked him what the secret of Yellowman's appeal was, especially since he was so scorned to begin with, Scorpio replied:

> Yellowman was unusual, and he's a wonderful person. He's a man who entertain you and make you laugh. . . . Modern guys don't understand music hit you in body and feel it, not just sing alone. On stage you must try and make people smile. Yellowman is that kind of character. He will make you laugh. He will come on stage and he will try to bring a smile to you, even if to tell you "you look ugly man". (Interview by author, 19 February 2009)

Yellowman inspired strong opinions among both his fans and detractors, and these opinions are still to be found when talking to older Jamaicans about his legacy. By and large, though, letter writers to the *Gleaner* do not bother with Yellowman today – there are far more tempting targets in dancehall that have amped up the slackness found in Yellowman's heyday. Yellowman's unprecedented successes, first as a person with albinism in Jamaica, and second as a deejay, have garnered him a unique place in reggae history. Howard McGowan ("Yellowman: Jamaica's Best Dancehall DJ", *Flair Magazine*, 15 October 1990), a loyal fan and journalist, covered Yellowman throughout his rise and dominance of dancehall in the 1980s. Early in the following decade he took the time to survey the history of deejay music in Jamaica and chose whom he believed to be the ten best male deejays. Yellowman, predictably, came out on top and the reasons provided demonstrate quite clearly what his legacy within dancehall looks like. Yellowman's list of "firsts" is unprecedented: the first to sign a major record deal, the first to receive a Grammy nomination, and the first to have a song top all the local charts ("Blueberry Hill" recorded after two battles with cancer). Add to this the fact that the first dancehall night at Sunsplash was established because of the popularity of Yellowman (the article says this was 1982, the first year he played there, but other sources say 1984) and at Disco Inferno 1985 he was called back to the stage for eight encores; his popularity as a deejay knew no rivals.

Yellowman's legacy is rich and complex: a potty-mouthed ghetto kid who became the world's first dancehall superstar; an outcast, deemed ugly for his albinism, who told his audiences so often that he was a sex symbol they started to believe it; a bawdy performer known for sexual lyrics and a preacher of moral values. Ultimately, Yellowman's importance not just to Jamaican music, but to global music history itself, is that he almost single-handedly carved a niche for dancehall reggae in markets outside Jamaica and gave a much-needed injection to the art form in the wake of Marley's death – an event many in the foreign press saw as signifying the end of reggae. That he appeared to be the most unlikely person to accomplish this, and that he did so with his characteristic mix of intelligence, humour, machismo on-stage and humility off, makes it easy to see why Yellowman was crowned King of Dancehall and why King of Dancehall he still remains. In part 2, I look at how critics saw Yellowman as the antithesis of Bob Marley because of his dancehall music and his slackness. Yet reggae fans saw things differently. Yellowman became the hottest commodity at home and around the world after Marley passed away in 1981, leading many reggae lovers to dub him Marley's successor. Take, for instance, this article by an Ottawa-based journalist that ran in Jamaica in July 1984 about just how successful Yellowman was abroad:

> Yellowman is ruling the reggae roost nowadays across Canada. His fans and the Canadian press simply cannot get enough of him. Yellowman's horde of fans in this country continue to scream for more of their idol. And the usually fastidious Canadian press entertainment columns and even prime time television newscasts coast to coast have been devoting reams of space and precious minutes to tell Canadians just who this albino livewire sensation is. Yellowman came calling a number of Canadian cities this past week as part of a swing through North America and what he put down really went down well. Concert fans in

such cities as Toronto and here in Ottawa gobbled him up, so to speak. And one night while he was on stage belting out his greatest hits, the Global Television network devoted footage in their main evening newscast to let Canadians know that Yellowman is perhaps the very best thing to come out of Jamaica since the passing of Bob Marley some three years ago. ("'King Yellowman': Marley's Successor?", *Daily Gleaner*, 3 July 1984)

Part 1 has focused on charting Yellowman's early life and rise to global fame. As such, it is concerned mainly with detailing his career up until the 1990s. In part 2, I use Yellowman's life story and songs to theorize his use of slackness as discourses of resistance.

Yellowman at his old playground at Maxfield Park Children's Home, Kingston, 2008. (Author photograph)

Yellowman stands outside the remains of Channel One Studio on Maxfield Avenue, Kingston, 2008. (Author photograph)

Yellowman on stage with Sagittarius at the Opera House, Toronto, 2008.
(Photograph courtesy of Andrew Atkinson)

The author and Yellowman, backstage at B.B. King's Blues Club, New York City,
2008. (Photograph courtesy of Ben Rittenhouse)

Yellowman with his children, backstage at B.B. King's Blues Club, New York City, 2008. (Author photograph)

Yellowman at home in Kingston, 2008. (Author photograph)

Yellowman on stage in Negril, 2009. (Author photograph)

Yellowman deejaying for a local sound system in Concrete Jungle, 2009. (Author photograph)

Yellowman in a vocal booth voicing dubplates at Tel's Studio, 2009.
(Author photograph)

Yellowman backstage at Bourbon Beach, Negril, 2013. (Author photograph)

PART 2.

MEANINGFUL BODIES IN JAMAICAN DANCEHALL CULTURE

THE MAIN PURPOSE OF PART 2 IS TO offer itineraries for theorizing slackness in Yellowman's life and songs and contextualize a misunderstood Caribbean musician by deconstructing the categories of slackness and culture that have functioned as constitutive frames for understanding reggae/dancehall artists and reggae culture by journalists, scholars and fans alike. It provides a sustained analysis of the ways Yellowman's slackness produces meaning by focusing on bodies of music, discursive bodies, and the representation of Yellowman's own body.

The overarching argument is that Yellowman mobilized slackness to contest his racialized and essentialized representation. But slackness also functioned in several other more nuanced ways in his considerably large catalogue of songs. What follows are five trajectories for theorizing slackness in Yellowman's music. First, using slackness Yellowman subverted embedded Jamaican cultural notions of sexuality, gender, race, nationality and beauty by promoting the dundus as sexually appealing, hyper-masculine and part of the imagined black nation (chapter 11). Second, Yellowman's pairing of slackness and culture undermines the neat binary used in reggae journalism and some scholarship that essentialized slackness as apolitical, nonreligious and amoral (chapter 12). Instead, Yellowman's sexual lyrics can be read as an example of Obika Gray's (2004) thesis that slackness was a conscious political project employed by the Jamaican poor to contest the normative values of dominant society (chapter 13). Fourth, Yellowman employed the Jamaican discursive strategy of "tracing" – a Jamaican term for loudly criticizing and vilifying someone – in his slack songs for the purposes of moral regulation, based on conservative Afro-Jamaican sexual mores and his understanding of Rastafarian morality (chapter 14). Finally, the place of sexuality and the body in Yellowman's world view breaches Christian dualism in favour of an Afrocentric body-positive ideology found in African diasporic religions of the Caribbean such as Rastafari (chapter 15).

CHAPTER II

Yellowman, Race, Sex and Masculinity

DANCEHALL AS A GENRE OF MUSIC IS PREOCCUPIED with human bodies. By reading Yellowman's musical career in the context of his own body, which was mapped as deviant in the Jamaican context, we can unpack the ways his slackness served to increase his cultural credibility – and therefore celebrity – by revalorizing the dundus. As a dundus, Yellowman's race, masculinity, virility, African descent, and even Jamaican nationality were questioned. It was through dancehall, and specifically slack dancehall, that Yellowman altered his status in Jamaica to become a major star and sex symbol. Foreign audiences often did not realize the discrimination he overcame at home and therefore were not aware of just how transgressive his sexual lyrics and antics were, or how Yellowman's slackness was far more complex than just entertainment. In his hands, slackness had currency as social power. Chatting slackness would be controversial for any deejay in Jamaican in the late 1970s, but doing so as a dundus was absolutely shocking, causing a moral panic. But as his popularity grew, Yellowman raised the status of albinism in Jamaica. The fact that he did this by remapping his own transgressive body as a site of masculine heterosexual perfection is remarkable.

But why was the dundus body the target of discrimination in the first place? The answer to this question will demonstrate to what extent his very celebrity breached established social and racial codes in Jamaica. Jamaican society was influenced by both African and European discriminatory practices concerning black people with albinism, and Yellowman was subjected to severe stigmatization because of this. This chapter will begin by providing the cultural context that led to social anxiety in Jamaica about albinism. It will then demonstrate that Yellowman's yellow body was a contested site of racial identification that meant that he had no claim to blackness or a place in the imaginary racially homogeneous Jamaican nation, and finally argue that by embracing his yellowness and his albinism, Yellowman was able to steer his representation in the public mind away from that of a social pariah whose sexuality was questioned or nullified, to a sort of super black man with a "modern body" and specialized sexual talents.

AFRICAN AND WESTERN ROOTS OF THE DISCRIMINATION OF THE DUNDUS

The word "dundus" in Jamaica has several meanings. The *Dictionary of Jamaican English* lists "albino, white man", and "European" as possible definitions. Under an entry for the term as denoting "an albino negro", the authors indicate that dundus also refers to "a freak; someone who is not up to the mark of normality" and expand on this with other derogatory uses such as "a freak of nature", "peculiar, inferior, subnormal person" (Cassidy and Le Page 2002, 164).

The meaning of dundus and social constructs around albinism in Jamaica have context in both African and European cultures. The term has a central African etymology derived from the KiKongo word *ndundu*, which means albino (Cassidy and Le Page 2002). *Ndundu* was sometimes used to describe Europeans in the Kongo, people who were thought to be witches from a subterranean world who stole souls (MacGaffey 1968). In some African societies, people with albinism were considered bad luck and, as in Jamaica, were marginalized (Alidou 2005; Diawara 1998). Myths associated with albinism have led to their ostracism in South Africa and Zimbabwe where the condition has been accounted for as the consequence of, variously, a curse, maternal infidelity, or even maternal infidelity with a malevolent spirit (Baker et al. 2010). People with albinism living in sub-Saharan African societies still suffer overt discrimination (Baker and Djatou 2007). In South Africa, the birth of a child with albinism is often interpreted to mean that the family is cursed, the result of some sinful transgression committed by an ancestor (Blankenberg 2000). In Cameroon, a child with albinism can be considered a consequence of transgressing social norms and in other cultures the birth may be thought to be punishment for a mother's adulterous act and the child could be killed (Baker and Djatou 2007). In Tanzania, people with albinism have been hunted for their body parts by witchdoctors who believe them to hold supernatural powers that will make their clients rich (Allen 2008). Celebrated Malian singer Salif Keita, who has established The Salif Keita Global Foundation for the Fair Treatment of Albinos, was sent from his father's house because of his condition, forced to leave school, and lived as an outcast in his village (Diawara 1998). Keita's organization raises awareness of the plight of African children with albinism who can be kidnapped and even killed because they are considered bad omens ("Singer Raises Awareness of Africa Albinos", *Washington Times*, 14 August 2006). Keita has been quoted as saying that in Mali, babies with albinism are sometimes sacrificed and their blood used in rituals (Hilferty 2006; Eyre 2006; "Singer Raises Awareness of Africa Albinos", *Washington Times*, 14 August 2006).

The names used for people with albinism in Africa also tell us about the beliefs surrounding them. For instance, the Bamiléké in Cameroon use the terms *meffeu* (dead), *bwongou* (strange person) and *fogtab gab* (white or chicken). People with albinism among the Bamiléké are not allowed to eat white food; the consumption of chicken, pork and lamb is prohibited because these animals are considered related to people with albinism and such an act would be anthropophagic (Baker and Djatou 2007). People with albinism are often associated with supernatural power. In the Central African Republic, it is believed that they are linked to the aquatic spirit world. The Pahouins from Cameroon use the term *nnanga kon,* or ghost, for people with albinism, as they are seen as being in contact with the ancestral spirit world. J.J. Ndoudoumou, president of the World Association for the Defence of Interests and Solidarity of People with Albinism, says that people with albinism in Africa "are considered mystical beings, ghosts who committed sins in their first life and who, punished by God, return" (67). Other traditions associated with albinism include the belief among the Bakweri that people with albinism turn all food to poison and so one should stop eating and spit food out if they see a person with albinism while eating.

Albinism has also been stigmatized as a contagious disease. Baker et al. (2010) document cases where citizens avoid contact with people with albinism, going so far as refusing to shake their hands and not eating food touched by them. Similar attitudes can be found in Jamaica. Early in Yellowman's career, he shared the stage with other deejays, some of whom would refuse to touch the microphone after him or would wrap it in a handkerchief to avoid touching it. They would make a spectacle of this in front of the audience in order to humiliate Yellowman, thereby targeting and underlining his otherness.

Jamaican attitudes towards albinism are also influenced by Western traditions. In the West, the phenomenon of black albinism has a history of being treated with racist and classist colonial contempt. Black people with albinism were seen as freaks of nature by white Europeans and Americans who were blind to the fact that people with albinism of all racial backgrounds shared the same biological condition. The term albino was coined by seventeenth-century Portuguese Jesuit Balthazar Tellez from the Latin *albus*, meaning "white" to describe white Africans encountered on European excursions to the west coast of Africa (Martin 2002). Black people with albinism, then, were considered wholly other from white people with albinism and, by extension, from white culture (Carnegie 1996).

It bears repeating some of the crude language used to describe black people with albinism by white Westerners to get a sense of the context that helped shape Jamaican attitudes towards people like Yellowman and why, among other things, he would be abandoned at birth because of his skin colour. American president Thomas Jefferson, writing in 1801, described the skin of black people with albinism as "pallid, cadaverous white" (Jefferson 1801, 108). Edward Long's 1774 description is even more contemptuous, especially with the addition of the object pronoun *it* to describe the person with albinism. Long clearly views people with albinism as objects, and of a race and class beneath his own: "The complexion of it was a dead, dull white, resembling that of a corpse; its hair, or rather wool, a light-flaxen colour, strong, coarse, and curling, like that of a Negroe; the features were truly of the Negroe cast." He goes on to offer anecdotal speculation that there is an imagined nation of people with albinism in central Africa called *Dondos* who are "said to be educated in the science of priestcraft, or witchcraft", are "weak and of low stature . . . have scarcely any sight, except by moon or owl-light" and who are at continual war with blacks (Long 1774/1970, 49–50). Cassidy and Le Page (2002) cite this passage as an antecedent to the Jamaican term dundus. Long situates people with albinism as a nation unto themselves and serves the Western ideology that people who look different must be from a different place (Carnegie 1996). In his song "Jah Made Us for a Purpose" (1983b), Yellowman refutes this very idea and tells his detractors that even though he looks different from other blacks, he is still of African descent.

Not only was Yellowman's racial background questioned, his ability to procreate was also doubted. We see this same idea in Long's writing, where he casts doubts on the capability of people with albinism to engage in sexual intercourse and procreation (Long 1774/1970, 49–50). Long's discussion of the alleged impotence of people with albinism also connotes images of mules – animals of mixed parentage that are born infertile. Black people with albinism in Jamaica are often the subject of debates over whether they have mixed (black and white) parentage (Carnegie 1996). This would be in keeping with racist colonial thinking found in terms such as *mulatto*, which comes from the Spanish word for mule; in slave societies it connoted a person of mixed parentage. The dehumanization of people with albinism in the historical literature is also illustrated by the fact that both Jefferson and Long locate their accounts of people with albinism in sections of their manuscripts dealing with the animal kingdom and, therefore, the non-human world (Carnegie 1996).

It is telling that sixteenth- and seventeenth-century white writers did not connect the phenomenon of albinism in Africans to the same in Caucasians, but chose to view it as an African peculiarity (Jordan 1977). Since whites in plantation societies classified humans based on skin colour, with dark skin separating slave from planter, a white African could upset this classificatory system and seriously undermine the colonial logic of Africans as other and Europeans as normal. In order not to threaten the class schema, it became necessary for writers of the period to ensure that black and white people with albinism were not seen to represent the same physiological peculiarity because this would have admitted "a bond and a similarity between the so-called races that was unacceptable in the social order" (Carnegie 1996, 478).

The proliferation of images and attitudes towards "white negroes" reveals that they captivated the European and American imagination because of their inability to fit within strict racial categories (Martin 2002). Black people with albinism and Africans with vitiligo (a skin condition that causes the progressive loss of pigment, leaving light or whitish spots and blotches) were treated as curiosities and spectacles for early colonists and displayed like circus freaks for the gaze of the European elite, who were mesmerized by bodily difference. "Explorers, plantation owners, and medical doctors shipped the transforming bodies of white Negroes back to Europe as a New World wonder; sometimes they commissioned paintings or engravings to circulate as artefacts of the endless variety found in colonial possessions. White Negreos [*sic*] were showcased in the exhibition spaces of seventeenth-century London, before the Royal Philosophical Society, in the salons of eighteenth-century Paris, and later at English fairs" (Martin 2002, 8).

Woodcuts, photographs, lithographs, and etchings of people with albinism with titles like *Primrose, the Celebrated Piebald Boy*, were made for an audience hungry to see "exotic" bodies.[1] At the Bartholomew Fair, souvenir coins bearing the likeness of an "Albino Negress", or copper plates engraved with George Alexander, the "spotted boy", could be purchased. In America, black people with albinism were also the cause of marvel as they or their likenesses were displayed in taverns, national history museums, Barnum's American Museum and philosophical societies. An advertisement for P.T. Barnum's American Museum read, "A Negro Turning White!: He is said to have discovered a weed, the juice of which changes the Colored Skin to White" (Martin 2002, 59). Barnum's spectacles included "Negro Turning White", "Leopard Child" and "Leopard Boy". Both the Ringling Brothers and Barnum and Bailey created sensational histories to promote their exhibits, such as the "Ambassadors from Mars", two dreadlocked brothers with albinism dubbed Eko and Iko (172). In Boston, the Lowell Museum hosted a minstrel show featuring "The Four Snow-White Albino Boys", playing fiddle, tambo, bones and banjo (90). In the United States, these exhibitions were overlaid with pseudo-scientific concerns about "the nature and potential mutability of racial difference, worries over slavery and miscegenation, and yearnings for a national identity" (11). Not only did black people with albinism stymie attempts to fix binary black and white racial categories, there was concern that "black skin could turn white and the African American could become indistinguishable from the European" (2).

These humans, treated as curiosities or freaks because of their skin colour, fit with Yellowman's experience. As a child, he was an unacceptable anomaly, as a teen he was derided for his physical difference, as an entertainer he became a spectacle that drew people as eager to see his body as hear his voice.

THE DUNDUS IN JAMAICAN CULTURAL HISTORY

As with the examples given, people with albinism were treated as abnormal in Jamaica, bordering on social menace because of their difference which, in a country suffering from the vestiges of racial and class stratifications put in place by colonial powers, finds them at the bottom of the social strata, culturally displaced. "The albino's interstitial social positioning is marked by features commonly associated with taboo: anxiety, danger and inhibition" (Carnegie 1996, 480). For Jamaicans, a person with albinism's location in society is assumed to be with the impoverished and disenfranchised; anecdotal cultural knowledge would assume that people with albinism are most often seen fully clothed so as not to expose their body to ridicule, poorly dressed, looking for handouts on the street and assuming a subordinate tone of voice and body language to all passersby (480). People with albinism are not usually entitled to well-paid jobs and positions with influence; Yellowman has stated that before he brought albinism into the spotlight, it was rare to see people with albinism in public and never in professional jobs. Jamaican producer and drummer Sly Dunbar corroborates this and says that Yellowman's success was an anomaly in Jamaica because most Jamaicans at the time assumed people with albinism had no prospects, especially in the music industry (Sly Dunbar, interview by author, 23 February 2009).

Race and ethnicity play a dominant role in the politics of identification for Caribbean peoples, even more so than class (Alleyne 2005). The meanings of phenotypical categories such as hair type and skin colour were socially constructed during the colonial period and this legacy remains in the Caribbean. The slave trade did not create racism, but racial categories emerged in Europe during antiquity and were then transferred to the Caribbean where they became entrenched. Power and political control have historically remained in the hands of European-descended light-skinned minorities on the island, while darker colour and Africanness has been relegated to society's bottom stratum.

Yellowman's position in society is located in a sort of limbo between white and black without being able to legitimately claim either, or even mulatto status. He stands outside the neatly defined and socially enforced colour boundaries. In Jamaican racial terms, he is not white – his African heritage confirms this; neither is he black, his non-black skin colour negates that possibility for a strict reading of race based on this factor. Yet, even though Yellowman's skin is a light colour, the historical meaning of albinism negated any privilege he may have enjoyed because of this, and in effect tossed him to the very bottom of the Jamaican social pyramid.

This effectively means that Yellowman, in the Jamaican context, has no race: "What the dundus lacks is "blackness" in any of its permissible shadings; he is therefore seen either as lacking, as reflecting poorly on, or as letting down 'the race'" (Carnegie 1996, 472). And race is of utmost importance in Jamaican society, where "in the popular imaginary – and rather more ambiguously in official national ideology – blackness has gradually become one of the fundamental attributes of Jamaican nationality" (472). Without visible blackness, the dundus is perceived to stand outside the body politic.

It would have been impossible for Yellowman not to be aware of the racialized meanings of his body, as his representation was essentialized around race or lack thereof. The racial slurs that he was subjected to throughout his life confirm this as they all question his racial heritage by suggesting that his colour is far from black. He was maligned as "buckra", a name connoting a white man, "red bwoy",[2] "red dog" and "yellow dog". At Alpha Boys' School he was usually referred to as "white man". Later, at Eventide Home, that was changed to "yellow man". During this time, a walk down any street in Kingston would cause onlookers to shout out "Hey, yellow man" – a constant reminder to the teenager that blackness was denied to him by society, even though he self-identified as black.

The meanings ascribed to the dundus in Jamaica are historically connected to the colonial project that entrenched, and benefitted from, racialized understandings of human bodies. In a remarkable display of courage, cleverness and subversion, Yellowman successfully contested his racialized and essentialized representation through dancehall's slackness. This is a discussion to which I now turn.

JAH MADE US FOR A PURPOSE: YELLOWMAN AND THE POLITICS OF RACE

Yellowman's slack lyrics have been typically thought of as gimmicks or party lyrics lacking social significance. Yet while they have been enjoyed as party music, his lyrics about sex also contested normative understandings of albinism in Jamaica. He questioned society's accepted racial typology by referring to himself as, variously, yellow, white, black or some combination thereof. He accomplished this through the mobilization of stereotypes of black sexuality and the application of potent symbols of blackness such as ideologies linked with Rastafari, Ethiopianism and pan-Africanism.

Race was used against Yellowman all his life. His identity became essentialized around it and was internalized with the adoption of the sobriquet 'Yellowman'. Adopting a stage name is a normal practice in Caribbean music, but Yellowman's racialized name was unique. Other contemporaneous deejays chose names that offered an association with grandeur. Sometimes this reflected the bravado of Hollywood western heroes (Josey Wales, Clint Eastwood, Lone Ranger), suggested their skill on the microphone (Super Black, Ranking Toyan, Shabba Ranks, Cutty Ranks), or a general exalted social status (Admiral Bailey, Major Worries, Brigadier Jerry, Dr Alimantado, Lieutenant Stitchie). Other deejays chose names that indicated their allegiance to Rastafari (Jah Thomas, Jah Stitch, Jah Rubel, Prince Far I). Each sobriquet in its own way was designed to garner respect. The name Yellowman, however, was just the opposite. The term was mobilized as a tactic of disrespect in an attempt to deny Winston Foster blackness and Jamaicanness. His adoption of it, and the subsequent reversal of its meaning, was a stunning strategy to nullify the discriminatory power of the racist epithet. By employing his detractor's term of derision, Yellowman could radically alter the meaning of the term and of his skin colour. He used racial categories to his advantage by exploiting sexualized racial difference and reinscribed what it meant to be a person with albinism in Jamaica. Shortly after Yellowman's rise to fame, other dundus deejays also found a welcoming audience and they too continued using noms de plume that embraced their albinism (King Mellow Yellow in the 1980s and Prince Yellowman in the 2000s).

Several of Yellowman's songs address the ad hominem attacks he suffered because of his colour. Often the narratives in these songs are constructed as racial warfare with black against yellow, furthering the detailed racially striated categorizes that were created during slavery. Yellowman complains about blacks in various songs, often heightening his counter assault by using the derisive term "nigger":[3] "Why nigger people bad-minded so?" or "Nuh nigger can fight 'gainst I. . . . deh see me pon de road dem a fight 'gainst I / Me go inna de dance dem want see me die" (from "Them A Fight I" [1982f]). In "Why Them A Fight?" (1982a), he makes it clear that the reason for the disharmony is colour: "Why dem a fight I so? / A tru me yellow and dem a negro." This is a theme he returns to often, but instead of presenting himself as a helpless victim, he takes matters into his own hands and offers self-aggrandizing reasons why people would fight against him, usually centred on the fact that other singers are jealous because of his talent and fame. In "Them A Fight I", these include the fact that he has "a good tone of voice" and "when me start chat" the audience is so impressed they "want fe hear me twice"; that he is a star; that he is "sweet like sugar and spice"; and his diversity on the microphone – "him a deal you inna all kind a style". In "King of the Crop" (1984e), he offers a dedication in the introduction "to all of dem man who want to fight against Yellowman", specifically talking about rival deejays who made racially motivated statements against him. The song's lyrics reprobate the racists for not realizing Yellowman's dominance of dancehall: "Nuff dutty nigger want see Yellow drop / They never know Yellow a de king of the crop." The song underlines the paradox of his social positioning: if he had not attempted social advancement his rivals would have taunted him for being lazy.

The racial binary between black and yellow in these songs is quickly dismantled in other lyrics where Yellowman either presents himself as better than black, both black and yellow, or wholly black. In fact, what we see from Yellowman's lyrics is that he plays with racial categories for his own benefit and the entertainment of his audience, sometimes resisting or mocking them and at other times reinforcing or embodying them. He internalized and adopted racial essentialization but radically altered the meaning of his skin colour in doing so. While in many songs he speaks from the position of a black man, in other songs he locates himself as a person with albinism which, in his revalorization, becomes something of a super black man.

In an attempt to stymie nationalistic rhetoric that fences the dundus off from the Jamaican nation because they lack blackness, Yellowman also carefully constructs albinism as a natural part of the Jamaican racial mix. In the song "Jah Made Us for a Purpose" (1983b), for instance, he asks why people always wonder where he gets his colour from. His answer – "it's from the whole a one" – draws on Jamaica's national motto "Out of Many, One People".

> It's one thing Yellowman can't understand
> Weh make de whole a dem a cuss me 'bout me nation?
> A talk 'bout weh me get fe me colour from
> A pity dem don't know it's from de whole a one

The song not only confirms the albino's position in Jamaican nationality (or contests his designation as marginal to the nation) but also uses religion to legitimate his colour, by saying God made him that way for a reason, and presents people with albinism as one integral aspect of the "many" in the motto alongside the "Chiney man"[4] and the "black man" mentioned later in the song.

Under the nationalizing project, this motto in the social imaginary has come to mean that disparate racial strains have been distilled into one black nation (Carnegie 1996). Jamaica is imagined as a racially homogenized nation, a fictional homogeneity that refashions the colour black in the Jamaican flag, originally intended to signify hardships surpassed, for the colour of the majority.[5] Yet the person with albinism, who is often subjected to xenophobic-like taunts of "Russian man" or "German man", is "denied the possibility of Jamaican nationality and placed outside the body politic" (487, 496).[6] Nation and race are conjoined in their "production of normalcy and marginality" and the dundus, lacking both, is marginalized (473). It is not surprising, then, that a child born without nation and without race would also end up parentless. Yellowman humorously rejects this reading in favour of interpreting the motto the way it was originally meant: that the one nation is constructed from diversity and not that the diversity has merged into one.

RASTAFARI AND BLACKNESS

Whereas Yellowman can chat at length about his yellowness, he just as easily uses conspicuous symbols to instantiate his own blackness and, vis-à-vis Carnegie's argument, his legitimate place in the Jamaican nation. In "Step It out a Babylon" (1982c), he situates himself as an African and a Rastaman by invoking the symbols of Haile Selassie as Jah Rastafari and repatriation out of the West back to the African homeland:

> I looked cross Jordan and what did I see
> Selassie and his angel a comin' for me . . .
> We stepping outta Babylon one by one
> Kaa Jah Jah a de magician

In the song, Selassie and his African angels come to Babylon to free the black people and carry them back to Africa/Zion. As shown in chapter 15, Zion in Rastafarian thought is different from Christian theology. The biblical Zion for Rastas is merged with contemporary Africa via an Ethiopianist interpretation, where the term might refer to a heavenly place, Ethiopia (home of Jah Ras Tafari/Haile Selassie), or the African continent as a whole.[7]

Rastafari is a religion born out of the suffering of lower-class black Jamaicans, so by aligning himself with it, especially in conjunction with Africa and an African monarch who himself represented black nationalism and African strength to his widespread supporters in the black diaspora, Yellowman is being conspicuous about claiming blackness. Add to this the fact that in the diaspora blackness has become a "sign of Africanity" and Yellowman's dual deployment of symbols of Africa and blackness confirm for his audience that he is not trading in blackness for yellowness (Appiah 1992, 3). He is, in fact, both. This is also apparent in the song "Stand up for Your Rights" (1982a) where Yellowman explains to his audience that he is still an African, even though his skin is a different colour: "The whole a we come from the African land / Although Yellowman have a different complexion."

In using symbols associated with Rastafari, Yellowman is following a tradition practised by many reggae artists, whether they consider themselves adherents of the religion or not. If you attend a reggae festival anywhere around the world, Rastafarian symbols abound; from the dominating iconography of Haile Selassie, the Lion of Judah and Ethiopian national colours to the dreadlocks, ganja, and ample references to Jah in the music, it appears reggae music is always imbued with religiosity. This, of course, is up for debate. But it is undeniable that even secular reggae musicians often invoke very meaningful religious symbols in their stage wear, performance, and music. Secular and sacred are never far removed in Jamaican music. Yellowman's case is instructive for understanding reggae artists who maintain cultural, musical, lyrical and material links with Rastafari in their songs, however tenuous, fleeting or even self-serving. As Rastafari has taken root around the world, for many adherents their main identification with the movement occurs around more superficial aspects such as reggae, hairstyle, language and clothing (Savishinsky 1994). This has caused concern among some members that "the outward appearances, the paraphernalia and the trappings, become the expression of the faith – rather than the deeper philosophy and discipline" (Burke 1977, 14).

My point here is to acknowledge how intertwined reggae and Rastafari are historically and to show that while there are Rastafarian organizations, music and musicians that stand outside of reggae culture, these two cultures

– Rasta and reggae – are often closely linked and, in the case of Yellowman, paired for compound purposes.

Yellowman's use of Rastafari in his songs is, at times, superficial to be sure. He is first and foremost an entertainer and his lyrics and performances have always been geared towards pleasing a crowd, particularly when, as a social outcast trying to break into the music scene, he was desperate to win their approval. He peppered his lyrics with themes he knew his audience would welcome. And in the interest of appearing as an all-rounder deejay who could broach many topics and styles, not just a slack artist, his lyrics included both "cultural" references to Rastafari and slack references to sex. But like his sexual lyrics, his Rasta lyrics also played an important part in helping him gain acceptance by aiding him in depicting the dundus as an African.

Further to this, Yellowman caused a shift in the look of reggae due to his treatment of blackness. Before his arrival, reggae was racially scripted, privileging and promoting blackness. Reggae helped to mainstream black identity by celebrating the Afro-Caribbean aspects of the music and culture: after Bob Marley, Jamaicans "felt proud to be black as never before" (Manuel, Bilby and Largey 1995, 236). And yet, a few short years later, Yellowman questioned the parameters of this blackness. By expanding them to include albinism, Yellowman may have set the stage for the acceptance of other reggae artists who also did not fit the tightly defined notion of reggae singer in the 1970s and 1980s, such as Purpleman (himself a person with albinism) and UB40, and contemporary artists like Alborosie, Gentleman and Matisyahu.

At the bootlegged 1987 Negril concert that was later sold under the name *Slackness vs Pure Culture* (1987b), Charlie Chaplin defended Yellowman's acceptance into the imagined black nation. In the song "Jah Me Fear", he chats, "The whole of us black although some look clear", an obvious allusion to Yellowman, who was standing on stage beside him at the time, as the word "clear" here refers to light-skinned complexion (Cassidy and Le Page 2002). In the song, Yellowman takes over deejaying using Chaplin's chorus of "Jah Me Fear" and his lyrics continue the portrayal of himself as a black man. He first condemns the South African apartheid and complacency of white South Africans towards it, and then adds, "Government Jamaica act like them care / Treat black people the same everywhere / Oppression we go through you can't compare." The "we" not only counts Yellowman among the black nation, but, in conjunction with his stance against apartheid, allows him to stand in solidarity with Africans worldwide against racism. At the same time, it allows him to separate himself from white culture in case there is any doubt that he might be white, or is "letting down the race" or "playing white" because of his fame and fortune (Alleyne 2005, 238). His many songs about Africa – "Free Africa", "Freedom", "African Drum", "Africa" – also serve to instantiate his own Africanness and allow him to claim an ideological lineage from black nationalism, Garveyism and Rastafari.

His later use of the trope of oppositionality to white culture in the song "Weed Dem" (1997b) also works as a device to make clear the fact that he is (a) not white and (b) a person with yellow complexion who is a full member of the black nation. Christianity is also used here as a racial indicator; it is considered white religion, evident in the song by its connection with the slave trade and colonialism, while Rastafari is black religion.

> Me a tell you black people know about Jesus
> Back dung the slavery days we a know 'bout that
> When white man control everything weh we have
> We used to wear dem clothes we used to feed dem hog
> We used to go a church and praise the white man God . . .
> A me named Yellowman nuh watch me complexion
> You know me a de true Rastaman
> Selassie I me praise and you know me nuh gaze[8]
> Him guide me through twenty-two years
> All of me success all of me glory unto all me fame

The song situates Yellowman as a true Rasta, and a yellow one at that, over and against people who have adopted white Christian traditions and beliefs. Unlike his much earlier "Fools Go to Church" (1982c), however, he is careful to not denigrate Christianity wholesale. He purposely targets slavery-era Christianity, not the religion as a whole, because, as he explained to me, "I don't try to be against Christianity." His later songs have an ecumenical agenda and are careful not to condemn other religions or belief systems. He gradually moves from the "white God" versus "black God" binary to a universalized position where there is only one God with different names. This understanding of God is fully formed by 1993's "One God" from the *A Man You Want* album.

Yellowman's racial ideology follows a similar pattern as his religious thought. While earlier songs find him explicitly adopting blackness and/or yellowness, in later songs he takes on a more universal approach, representing himself as a man for all races and religions. Lyrics such as "Me rock de white and me rock de black / Me rock de baldhead and de dreadlock" ("Coming in from the Cold", *Live at Maritime Hall* [1998b]) are indicative of later material that attempts to not only position himself as a link between white and black, Christian and Rasta, but also is a platform from which to condemn racism. While introducing "Holy Mount Zion" (from *Live at Maritime Hall* [1998b]) in San Francisco in 1998, he told the audience, "Remember, no racism, no discrimination . . . no discrimination of any nation." This platitude has become commonplace at his concerts.

By problematizing racial categories and critiquing their validity, Yellowman has fashioned a privileged position for himself. He can speak from the point of view of a black man and include himself in the black nation, but he can also position himself as an intermediator between white and black.

Read against Rastafarian attitudes of race and nationality, Yellowman's project of "blackening" his representation is even more salient. The Rastas' cognitive model of the universe is a set of binaries: Babylon/Zion, Africa/Europe, black/white. As a black nationalist movement influenced by Marcus Garvey's black pride, Ethiopianism and pan-Africanism and, more recently, America's Black Power movement, blackness is a crucial site of identity negotiation in Rastafari. Rastas trace their cosmological lineage through Haile Selassie, a black Ethiopian emperor understood as Christ incarnate, and their devil/anti-Christ is the Catholic pope, a white European (Yawney 1976). This dichotomous model of black and white leaves no room for albinism, despite black people with albinism considering themselves black. Yawney, who conducted fieldwork among the Rastafari in the early 1970s, provides insight into the attitudes about race and nationalism during the time Yellowman was becoming a teenager. While not speaking about albinism, Yawney does talk about another group in Jamaica who has historically been racially constructed/categorized as "yellow" – the Chinese. According to the Rasta version of African and European history, the whites and Chinese were expelled from Ethiopia/the Garden of Eden/the Kingdom of Zion/Israel (they are one and the same) (247).[9] The Chinese, in particular, cause a problem for the Rasta's dichotomous thinking:

In light of the incommensurability of yellow, in terms of a model of black and white polar opposites, it is interesting to note that the Rastas express difficulty in imaging how the Chinese "sex each other", so they cannot understand how they reproduce. Here the folk belief of the Rastas is of a different order than their daily experiences. The Chinese are not denied sexuality as such but the cognitive paradigm of the Rastas does not permit the Chinese to reproduce. As bearers of the mark of Cain, yellow should be a sterile hybrid in terms of the dichotomous model of black and white. (Yawney 1976, 251)

Bearing in mind the stereotypes surrounding albinism and sexuality outlined above, the Chinese paradigm is helpful for thinking about the cultural context Yellowman grew up in. Yellow skin does not fit the Rastafarian dichotomous model of black and white. If, to Rastas, yellow skin represented an unreconciled contradiction to their world view and was seen as an impediment to reproduction and, therefore, masculinity, Yellowman's discussion of race was not only consequential, it was necessary in order to claim blackness and allegiance to Rastafari. Perhaps this is why one of his first songs to mention Jah is a homily on the need to accept different races into not just the Jamaican national consciousness but also Rastafarian cosmology. In "Jah Made Us for a Purpose" (1983b), he charges, "Some a dem judge me fe me yellow colour" and then begins to explain why race should not come between people:

I want everybody to understand
Jah Jah made us for a purpose
He make de Yellowman for a purpose
He make de Chiney man for a purpose
He make de black man for a purpose

Yellowman does not explicate exactly what the purpose of each race is, but it is enough for him to implicate a divinely predetermined fate. Yellowman has a place in society because Jah gave him a role to play. Further in the song Yellowman makes an important shift. Moving from a position of defending his colour, he begins to celebrate it unabashedly: "Glory, glory, hallelujah / Thank you Jah Jah fe give me this a colour."

Yellowman cleverly uses racial theory to prove his blackness (he is of African descent) while at the same time undermining colonial interpretations of race as based on skin colour (an African does not have to have black skin).

He further problematizes racial theory by telling his audience he is not only both black and yellow, but he was made by Jah for a purpose and intimates that people of all colours are created equally. Taken together, these statements are designed to convince his detractors that he does, in fact, fit into the imagined racialized Jamaican nation and dismantles the dichotomous model of black and white to make room for albinism.

YELLOWMAN WITH THE MODERN BODY

Perhaps Yellowman's most successful tactic to undermine normative Jamaican meanings of albinism is his mobilization of slackness to prove his heterosexual and mature masculine credentials to his audience. Slavery era descriptions of black people with albinism questioned their sexual validity. Jamaican cultural stereotypes mapped albino bodies with images of abnormality and ugliness. Yellowman employed colonial-derived stereotypes of black bodies as hypersexual to adopt a super-sexual persona in his songs, one that allowed him to claim blackness at the same time as carving out a unique characterization of the dundus as super black. By claiming super sexual abilities and endowments, Yellowman was not doing anything unique as far as male performances in dancehall go, but by doing this as a dundus, he was shattering entrenched understandings of albinism.

Dancehall is the predominant source of public discourse on black sexuality in Jamaica, and as such has tremendous power in forming popular opinion around sex and the body, including problematizing racist stereotypes around sexuality. Nowhere is this more apparent than in the work of Yellowman. Long before slack deejays like Shabba Ranks and Lady Saw made headlines, Yellowman disrupted polite society by offsetting racial hierarchies and proliferating hardcore X-rated slackness. He entertained one segment of society by agitating another. Yellowman adopted white society's race-based myths about the sexual endowments and prowess of black men and applied it to himself, even though as a dundus this would be laughable in Jamaican society. His audiences were initially unsure if Yellowman was the joke, was in on the joke, or took himself seriously. His lyrics moved between tongue-in-cheek slackness that suggested he could laugh at himself and confident boasts that left little doubt that he believed his own hype. He satirized embedded mainstream cultural understandings of race and sexuality with the intent of poking holes in their colonial logic and fashioning a place in the social sphere for himself. His sexual content, broadcast to anyone within earshot of a tape deck, sound system or record player, was geared towards upsetting mainstream society as much as it was pleasing ghetto dwellers.

Tropes of black hypersexuality in popular culture are derived from a European culture fascinated with sexualized racial difference that perceived African bodies as abnormal and sexually deviant. These myths were predicated on the notion that whiteness was normal and blackness was exotic which, in turn, facilitated beliefs in white superiority, helping to establish black sexuality as hyper and therefore freakish in the Victorian mindset (Collins 2005).

Yellowman embraced these Western stereotypes and reinvented himself as a sex symbol, the ultimate object of desire for all women. On the one hand, he is desirable because society knows black men are well endowed and sexually insatiable, or so the racial stereotype goes. On the other hand, he positions himself as even more desirable than a black man by espousing the heightened sexual potency of the person with albinism. It is here that the true genius of Yellowman's project is revealed: the lowly dundus is reinvented as the ultimate Casanova. In the process, Yellowman again skews the racialized reading of sexuality by calling his yellow body the "modern body" and telling his audience of his desirable attributes: "I gwaan tell you why de girls dey love de yellow body / When me discharge, me discharge honey / Yellowman with de modern body" ("Sit Under You" [1983b]).

As a victim of Jamaican perceptions of abnormality directed at the black albino body, the state, via its institutions, was in actual control of Yellowman's physical whereabouts for two decades, but racist and classist cultural pressures sought to control his representation as well. We can see just how much Yellowman internalized the lesson that an attack on one's sexuality is an attack on their humanity by looking at some of his lyrics. Society questioned his sexuality as a person with albinism and this put him in a position where he had to fight to maintain control of his body and prove his sexual (and heterosexual) credentials and reproductive viability. Several of Yellowman's lyrics boast about his sexual prowess.

In "Yellowman Wise" (1983e), he calls himself the wisest man who "knows the secret of a ooman" (woman) and that is why he have "nuff ooman" (an abundance of women). In several songs, he playfully puts to rest any rumour that he has no girlfriend. In "100 Sexy Girls" (1991b), he assures his listener that "all of the girls they want a piece of me". In "World of Girls" (1991b), he lists all the countries where his girlfriends live. In "Zungguzungguguzung-guzeng" (1983e), he offers as proof the fact that women he has slept with have children with albinism: "Kaa nuff a dem a talk 'bout me nuh have nuh girlfriend / You a idiot bwoy, me have a hundred and ten / Say all a dem, dem have yellow children." "Girlfriend" (1994b) assures his listeners that he has more girlfriends than "all the man dem".

> Nuff man a talk 'bout dem a don, 'bout dem have nuff woman
> But hear me now, me going to lead dem about a hundred furlong
> Me a go see outta we or all de man dem
> Which one a we have the most girlfriends
> Me have girl over deso, girl over yaso
> Girl up deso and girl down deso
> Say east, west, north and south weh me go
> From Texas to Colorado
> From L.A. to San Diego
> From 'Frisco down to Mexico
> From New York to Toronto
> Not to mention Puerto Rico
> Back to Aruba and Curaçao
> The girls dem love me from me head to me toe

Another set of lyrics also confirms his success with the opposite sex: "Look how she fat a Yellow control that / You look pon me head me hair it plait / There's a hundred and twenty-five girls do that" ("Yellowman A the Lover Boy" [1983c]). Not only does Yellowman exaggerate the number of girls he has, he also makes sure that his critics know that he is in a position of power over them. By putting another in a subordinate position, he exercises his own superiority. The word "control" in the lyric above has a double meaning; besides having power over something, it also implies ownership.

Constant boasting and machismo is nothing new for Jamaican deejays, but I suggest here that Yellowman's sex-centric lyrics can be read as a validation of his virility in light of the fact that society deemed people with albinism sexually questionable. His attempt to validate his sexuality is an attempt to gain back control of his body and representation from society. Yellowman was known as the slackest deejay of his day; he sang more often about sex, and in greater graphic detail, than any other deejay. Perhaps this was because he had more to prove and more at stake. Arguably, Yellowman could not have achieved the level of acceptance in Jamaica that he did without employing slackness. He first had to confront society's discriminatory assumptions about his skin colour and what better way to do that than attacking head-on the myth of the impotent albino?

Inherent in many of the jeers and taunts Yellowman suffered growing up was a denial of manhood. Calling him "bwoy" questioned his masculinity and therefore his ability to be sexually active. In Jamaican culture, men prove their masculinity by how sexually potent they are (Sobo 1993). Dancehall is filled with songs about how long a man can last in bed or how many women he can "service". Yellowman's "Nuff Punany" (1987b) is a good example:

'Tan pon it long, Tan pon it long
Gal a nowadays no want no five second man
Gal nowadays want a five-hour man
Big and strong, like Yellowman.

In "Bubble with Mi Ting" (1985a), he takes up a similar theme, espousing his exhaustive regime in the bedroom: "Make love from one go straight to nine." Yellowman's boasts of virility and endurance are especially important when taking into consideration his need to substantiate masculinity in the face of stereotypes that portrayed people with albinism as impotent and adolescent.

It is not specific to Jamaican popular culture for males to boast about generous pubic endowments but Yellowman takes it to a ridiculous level, just as he humorously over exaggerates the number of sexual partners he has or his stamina in the bedroom beyond any humanly possible level. Again, this can be read as Yellowman going beyond hypersexual stereotypes of black-ness and mapping yellowness with an even greater sexual appetite. It is part of his agenda to represent the yellow body as the super black body or the modern body. A further example from "Bubble with Mi Ting" demonstrates this: "When me roll out me Yellow someting / The gal look pon me say it's a goddamn sin / Your Yellow someting could a never go in." The theme is continued in "Wreck a Pum Pum" (1984d), with a lyric about a large penis:

Me draw down me pants, go down to me knee
She look under me and say "God almighty"

Yellowman you going use that thing pon me?

I said "shut your mouth it's only 10 feet"[10]

Dancehall is not alone in its gendered narratives that at once reflect and reinforce gender roles and stereotypes – whether real or imagined – in Caribbean society. Calypso, like dancehall, is male dominated and its slackness is often manifested as narratives of female sexual conquest, boasts of physical endowment, desirability and coital talent or the creation of machismo at the expense of fellow males or the opposite sex (Warner 1985). And like dancehall, calypso has historically cast the female as a purely sexual object; denigration and degradation of women for the purposes of inflating the male ego are common to both dancehall and calypso. "The calypsonian constantly denigrates the very female partner who allows him to fulfil his sexual ambitions" (120). Calypsonians are sure to gain audience approval for degrading women: "the embarrassment of woman is part of the national ethos" (Hodge 1974, 117).

The female body, along with female sexuality, is a site of male identity negotiation in dancehall – males seek to conquer the punanny and situate themselves in a position of power over women (Hope 2006). This is evident in Yellowman's lyrics about how many women a deejay has, how many children he has produced from different women, and in songs that portray a war between two women over a man. He further uses the female body as a site of identity negotiation to redress the person with albinism's lowly state in society, thereby perpetuating stereotypes of feminine black sexuality, denying women any sort of sexual agency and further instantiating the subordinate status of the female in dancehall and Jamaican society. By employing sexually explicit lyrics and performances, Yellowman could validate his masculinity and flip the stereotype of the adolescent impotent albino.

Yellowman's ideology of race is nothing if not complex. He switches from celebrating his yellowness as an aphrodisiac to privileging his blackness (or both at the same time), but then, in other songs, downplays either colour as the secret to his sexual charms. In "Mad over Me" (1982g), he insists that while many women leave their boyfriends to fall in love with him, it is his self-respect rather than his colour, that they are drawn to: "Dem left dem man and come to Yellowman / Not because my complexion but a true me have ambition."

In several songs Yellowman uses the term "ambition", not in the standard English sense of aspiration but in the Jamaican meaning of "self-respect" (Cassidy and Le Page 2002, 9). This pride of self is his greatest weapon against detractors and is a powerful act of resistance against a society that spent considerable effort to nullify his self-respect. If we look at the meaning of the above songs together, we understand that Yellowman's body is desirable because it is yellow but that racialization is not the only way to account for his sex appeal. Later, in "Them a Mad over Me" (1984b), Yellowman confronts the fact that society considers him ugly but girls are still flocking to him. The very premise of the song is the basis for his entire routine – a humorous narrative of his sexual desirability to the opposite sex despite being an outcast. The audience, however, is never quite sure whether this routine is delivered tongue-in-cheek or authentically serious.[11]

> Dey see me pon de road, and a laugh after me
> Some of dem a talk 'bout me too ugly
> Some of dem a talk 'bout me too boasy
> A man like me shoulda inna cemetery
> The next one a talk 'bout me too facey
> They start ask why de girls dem a rush me
> A sexy me sexy[12]

We can surmise that this is probably based on actual insults Yellowman would have heard on the streets of Kingston. The verse tells us where the albino's place in society should be located. At best, a dundus should be ridiculed, humbled, subordinate and avoid any hint of impudence. At worst, he or she should be killed, a fate suggested by the terms "cemetery" and "duppy" in the original 1981 recording. Instead of responding to these insults with anger, Yellowman's trademark is to laugh at his tormentors by answering the question: "Why do the girls love me?" with the self-explanatory answer: because I am sexy. We could take this to mean that he is sexy because of his albinism or, as in the stanza above, because of his ambition.

There is another layer to why Yellowman sometimes downplays his albinism as the secret to his success with the opposite sex. Even though he was discriminated against based on his colour when he first tried to enter the music industry, after he started to gain fame, some people suggested that he was successful because he looked different – it was the spectacle of a dundus on the microphone that caused crowds to attend his shows. Other deejays, Yellowman remembers, jealous of his success, would chide him: "The deejays used to say it's because of me colour that's why me get famous." Yet by pointing out that he would be desirable with or without yellow skin, Yellowman is inadvertently telling his critics that his fame is not solely based on the spectacle of different skin colour.

Yellowman was born into a society that had inherited both African and European prejudices against black people with albinism. His abandonment by his parents should be understood within this context. Yellowman's colour was singled out by school bullies and later studio thugs as the reason to exclude him and treat him as a marginal member of society. Centuries old ideologies of freakishness, weakness and even sexual impotence or deviance informed the decisions made by the people who marginalized him. Growing up, it would have been a normal everyday occurrence for Winston Foster to walk down a street and hear people he did not know shout things to him such as "dundus" or "yellow man", not politely offering a salutation but underscoring his alterity. To succeed, Yellowman needed to find a way to somehow undermine this powerful cultural stereotype. One of his greatest achievements was to embrace his albino body and ultimately wrestle his representation out of the hands of society and redefine what he, and other people with albinism, are capable of.[13]

By choosing to use society's exclusionary linguistic term "yellow man" as his professional nomenclature, Yellowman accomplished what hip-hop culture would later do by reclaiming the word "nigger" as an empowering epithet, snatching it away from Jim Crow's derisive usage. Like nigger, the use of Yellowman contested culturally embedded views of the albino as subordinate and other and reversed its meaning by revalorizing it in a positive light. Yellowman undermines Jamaica's instantiated moral order through his slack mouth and his stubborn insistence that a person with albinism has as much right to public space (and celebrity status) as any other member of society. By embracing the pejorative term and twisting its meaning, Yellowman throws the slur back at his oppressors and puts himself in control of how the term is understood by society. By attaching beauty and sexual desirability to the term, Yellowman's self-aggrandizing project was outrageous and daring but wildly successful.

CHAPTER 12

Yellowman in Reggae Histories and Scholarship

Dem gwaan like dey slack but me slacker dan dem
Yellowman with the slackness again
   —Yellowman, "Cocky Did a Hurt Me" (1982d)

The decline of radical reggae can be illustrated by reference to the career of
Winston 'Yellowman' Foster, the most popular toaster of the early 1980s.
   —Paul Gilroy 1987, 188–89

YELLOWMAN'S REPRESENTATION AT THE HANDS OF JOURNALISTS AND the scholarly community uncharitably held him up as the cause and exemplar of reggae's demise into a new form of music – dancehall – for which they had little use. Foreign critics made value judgements concerning slackness, musical worth and the digital technologies used to create dancehall based on Eurocentric moral values and Euro-American definitions of musical aesthetics. First, critics were unable to accept that slack music and social critique were not mutually exclusive. Second, they surmised that since dancehall lacked melody, harmony and was often recorded and performed digitally, it was an inferior form of music. Taken together these two arguments, one based on morality and the other on aesthetics, have been used to suggest that Yellowman and dancehall represent a de-evolution of Jamaican popular music.

THE DE-EVOLUTION THESIS

There is a trend among cultural critics ("Dancehall's Betrayal of Reggae", *Gleaner*, 24 February 2008; Burton 1997; Chevannes 1999; Gilroy 1987) to frame Bob Marley's death as instigating a transition from the golden era of reggae to its nadir, offering Yellowman's subsequent rise to popularity as proof. Commentators both inside and outside the reggae community have propagated a thesis that the move to dancehall in the 1980s, with its focus on deejays, male braggadocio, and digital instrumentation, represents the low point of Jamaican music history. Music journalists have equated "reggae with Rasta, and dancehall with decline", according to Stolzoff (2000, xxi). He further says, "Reggae critics, especially foreign-based ones, were nearly unanimous in their condemnation of the dancehall style, because the most popular songs of the new style were not inspired by the 'Rasta consciousness' that so many American and European counterculturalists had come to love and admire" (100). Reggae histories spin a compelling tale that insist factors such as the death of Bob Marley in 1981, the change of government from the socialist party of Michael Manley to the right-wing conservatism of Edward Seaga's JLP, and the surge of narcotics and guns onto the island propelled "an exaggerated, ostentatious selfhood" that manifested itself in a new form of music (Stanley-Niaah 2006, 179). This new music, dancehall, often focused on sex and violence, and these themes aim to dominate representations of the style. Gilroy's version of reggae history, for instance, sees the Marley era as socially engaged, Rasta-centric and revolutionary next to dancehall's flippancy: "The largely Rasta-inspired singers, songwriters and dub poets who had guided the music to its place as a vibrant populist force for change in the society were brushed aside and their place was taken by a legion of DJs or toasters . . . under Seaga, the singers' and songwriters' influence faded and they retreated from the revolution which their Rasta language had demanded. The DJs took centre stage" (Gilroy 1987, 188).

This degeneration thesis is based on two criteria, aesthetics – dancehall is understood as a less complex music form than its predecessors – and morality. It is Yellowman, the King of Slack, who is presented as the key to understanding this shift. Reggae histories that promote the de-evolution thesis position Yellowman as the linchpin between the cultural reign of Rastafari in the 1970s and the spiritual vacuum of 1980s dancehall, and credit slackness with conquering political and religious consciousness. Yet Yellowman's representation in the media as the King of Slack ignores not only his blatant cultural songs, but also offers a one-dimensional understanding of slackness as necessarily devoid of political and social critique and incompatible with spiritual matters. Yellowman's slackness was always motivated by his eagerness to please an audience, but a comprehensive analysis of his slackness reveals that entertainment concerns and poignant social critiques were not mutually exclusive in his career.

Bob Marley called his brand of reggae rebel music, a categorization that has stuck and is liberally applied to all roots-era reggae. But when looking at how roots reggae and dancehall have been constructed in the popular imagination, perhaps it is dancehall that truly deserves the moniker "rebel". Unlike its elder sibling, dancehall has not enjoyed critical acclaim outside of Jamaica in most of the mainstream press. Music reviewers still fall head over heels for Marley reissues and new material from bona fide roots artists such as Burning Spear or Israel Vibration, but dancehall is portrayed as aesthetically disappointing and morally void. Ironically, these roots groups enjoy scant popularity in their home country, yet foreign journalists "lavish ecstatic reviews" on them (Chang and Chen 1998, 61). In fact, controversies surrounding homophobic lyrics in the works of Elephant Man, Sizzla, Capleton and others have portrayed the entire genre of dancehall as an essentially violent and morally corrupt enterprise. This has furthered its representation as inimical to roots reggae. In 2009, a New York group of reggae fans known as the Coalition to Preserve Reggae Music hosted a community forum and panel discussion titled "Could dancehall be the ruination of reggae and by extension, the Jamaica brand?" The discussion stemmed from recent concern over dancehall music, including the Broadcasting Commission of Jamaica's decision to ban slack songs on public airwaves and public transportation, and international pressure to boycott concerts by dancehall artists Buju Banton, Beenie Man, T.O.K., Capleton, Sizzla and Elephant Man because of violent and homophobic lyrics. A co-founder of the Coalition to Preserve Reggae Music, Sharon Gordon, said in a press release for the event, "Instead of music portraying truths, rights, love and respect, we see a popular sound that is demeaning, hateful, destructive and downright vulgar" (TSO Productions 2009).

The segregating of roots reggae and dancehall into exclusive categories sets up an imaginary binary that is not shared by many of the younger fans of dancehall (Cooper 2004). Sound systems, the engine of reggae in the dancehall space, have diverse playlists that may range from contemporary chart-topping deejays to oldies roots reggae and beyond. I have heard soundsystems move through Whitney Houston, Madonna and Kenny Rogers before they get to Ninjaman, Admiral Bailey and any number of contemporary dancehall artists. During my youth in Bermuda it was normal to hear roots reggae next to dancehall at dances, parties, public functions, concerts, bars, and emanating from the ubiquitous ghetto blasters perched on the shoulders of youths. We did not distinguish one from the other in the 1980s – it was all considered reggae – yet many reggae historians have made a clean division that fails "to recognize the continuities across seemingly fixed generic boundaries, routinely emphasizing, instead, absolute differences of tone, tempo and temper" (81).

Yellowman has always been at the centre of the characterization that sets roots reggae against dancehall, since it was Yellowman, more than any other artist, who heralded the start of the dancehall era for the international audience. Online reggae compendium Reggaepedia.com, for instance, has this to say about Yellowman: "Yellowman embodied the shift from roots music to dancehall more than anyone else during the early dancehall era: his method of toasting was highly popular and he also epitomized dancehall's penchant for 'slack' lyrics" (Ghoston 2009).

THE MORAL ARGUMENT

A difference of moralities is at the heart of a moral depravity argument, which, in a nutshell, is that the values of Yellowman [and dancehall] are not conducive to civilized society. Evidence given is the music's preoccupation with guns and violence, suggestive dance routines and slack lyrics. Dancehall is hedonistic, self-centred and destructive for society, so the argument goes.

Nowhere is the morally reprehensible argument more apparent than in discussions of Yellowman, who has been treated as slackness's scapegoat. Critics have singled him out as the artist responsible for ending the era of socially conscious and musically superior roots reggae and initializing a new epoch of populist repetitive dance music whose substance celebrates nothing deeper than carnal pleasures. Yellowman "rubbed many who loved reggae for its uplifting social and spiritual message the wrong way", wrote one journalist ("Overcomes Affliction: Yellowman Rippin' 'n' Rappin' Again", *Los Angeles Times*, 15 October 1986).

One of Yellowman's most prestigious critics, former prime minister (1980–89) Edward Seaga, is no stranger to Jamaica's cultural industries. A Harvard graduate with a degree in social anthropology, Seaga was on the ground floor of Jamaica's indigenous music industry in the 1950s and 1960s, first as a producer and record label owner, and later as a politician. He helped bring mento and ska greater national and international acclaim and as Minister of Development and Welfare in the 1960s he aided in the promotion of ska overseas. He established the Jamaica Festival for literary, performing, plastic and graphics arts, introduced National Heritage Week and created the Cultural Training Centre for all the Arts. He also started *Jamaica Journal*, a quarterly publication dedicated to promoting the arts as well as the social sciences (JLP 2009). Seaga, then, has cultural credentials. He was also in power when Yellowman ascended to the deejay throne and became one of Jamaica's hottest exports. Seaga had a long view of the Jamaican music industry and his opinion was well informed. Yet even Seaga accepted at face value the de-evolution thesis. Later a columnist with the *Gleaner*, he penned this:

> Bob Marley's 'conscious' lyrics overlaid the ideological ferment with a musical, not militaristic, campaign against oppression. After Marley died in 1981 and ideological campaigns became futile because of the new political perspectives of a change of government, the earlier permissiveness did not fade. It hardened in a new direction. Sexual explicitness was an area of wide-open social expression in the culture of folk society, particularly the inner city, but not publicly promoted. It was Yellow Man (Winston Blake)[1] who stepped beyond the threshold of sexual permissiveness in music. 'Slackness' music was born. According to Yellow Man, "is slackness de people want and is slackness I ah give dem". What was thought to be a passing phase became more entrenched and more explicit, growing in the spirit of permissiveness until in the 1990s when the sexual content knew few bounds. Yellow Man popularised the deejay format in his songs. ("The Age of Permissiveness", *Gleaner*, 9 March 2008)

Here Seaga aligns Marley with consciousness, ideological resistance and musical campaigns against oppression, and dancehall with permissiveness, boundary-breaking sexual explicitness, and militarism. This is somewhat ironic given that critics have pointed to Seaga's regime and the "consequent militarization of ghetto life" as integral to the shift towards dancehall (Gilroy 1987, 188; Walker 2005). Seaga, typically, marks the era change with Marley's death, and names Yellowman as the deejay who ushered in the new era. He does accept the earlier existence of sexual permissiveness, but blames Yellowman for not only bringing it into the public sphere, but creating slack music. Seaga is wrong on at least two counts here. Slack music was born long before Yellowman, and Marley's campaigns against oppression can hardly be neutralized as non-militaristic. It was, in fact, considered "militant reggae" by some (Bradley 2001, 490). Marley's music advocated armed struggle to attain world peace, supported revolution in the African context specifically and all colonial contexts generally, and prophesied an apocalyptic war between good and evil. Peace may have been the ultimate goal, but he did not rule out violence as a viable means to that end (Hagerman 2012).

Yellowman is clearly aware of the moral critique used against him and addresses it in several songs where he positions himself as an "all-rounder", or entertainer for everyone. He often notes in his lyrics that he can chat both culture and slackness ("Under Mi Fat Ting" [1985a], "King of the Crop" [1984e]) and has said in interviews with me that this is to prove to his critics that he's not just a slack deejay. He makes this point in his typically humorous fashion in the song "Society Party" (1984e). In the narrative, the Jamaican heads of state are meeting with American president Ronald Reagan and want appropriate entertainment. Being unsatisfied with the other top deejays of the day (because "Peter Metro chat too much Spanish", "Josey Wales chat too much badness", Brigadier Jerry "chat too much Christianity" and Sassafrass "come from the ass family"), they decide on Yellowman because "when Yellowman chat, nothing slack". He can chat cultural lyrics for high society, he tells us in "Society Party" (1984e), so he must be morally upstanding.

> They send a limousine with 10 police
> To escort Yellowman up to Inter Conti
> Me come outta de car police salute me
> Seago and Manley, they come meet me
> We sit around the table, Johnny Walker Whiskey
> Me start chat me culture, roots and reality
> Seago get up with his wife Mitsy
> And start with the style named Water Pumpee[2]

Likewise, in "Strong Me Strong" (1984a), Yellowman tells us that when the queen visits Jamaica, his is the first hand she shakes: "That fe show you say me well important", he chats, enjoying the chance to rewrite his own history and representation as a member of high society. For Yellowman, the fact that he can also chat slackness when it is needed, does not negate his moral or cultural credentials.

In reggae discourse, artists are often defined as either "culture" or "slack"; Yellowman is steadfastly depicted in reggae histories as a slackness deejay. The dichotomy between "culture" and "slack" is apparent in the following entry from the *Official Dancehall Dictionary*: "The cultural DJ deals with livity and up-fullness – he [*sic*] avoids the usage of slackness lyrics and basically sees himself [*sic*] as part of the musical process promoting social consciousness, awareness, and change". Slack deejays, then, are not involved in the process of "promoting social consciousness, awareness, and change" (Francis-Jackson 1995, xiii).

Yet this essentialism breaks down when looking at Yellowman's slackness. For instance, on 21 February 1987, Yellowman performed at the Negril Tree House in the West Jamaican resort town of Negril. Yellowman's set consisted of some of the rudest songs in his catalogue – "Nuff Punany", "Under Gal Frock", "Galong Galong Galong", "Same Way It Taste" and "Don't Drop Your Pants". Beside him stood noted cultural deejay Charlie Chaplin, a man known for chatting Afrocentric, Rasta-inspired and socially conscious lyrics. As often happens in these ludic deejay clashes, the two entertainers took turns trying to win over the crowd, each using their tried and true arsenal, Yellowman with his slackness and Chaplin with his cultural lyrics.

The concert was bootlegged without the knowledge of the performers and later packaged and sold on cassette tapes and vinyl records under the title *Slackness vs Pure Culture* (1987b). It is helpful to realize here that in Jamaican Patwa the meaning of "pure" is extended from standard English to also include "only" or "nothing but" (Cassidy and Le Page 2002, 367). As such, utilizing the binary categories of reggae marketing, the title suggests that slackness and culture are opposites and that each deejay is the antithesis of the other. It plays on the Jamaican cultural trope of musical clashes where two opponents stage a musical battle and the crowd decides who wins. With the *Slackness vs Pure Culture* release, the album's promoters were also playing off the common polarity found in reggae music, suggesting again that each artist represented an orthodox moral position. However, what is instructive about the set is that this is not always so. Yellowman does provide his share of sexually explicit material, but at one point he joins Charlie Chaplin in singing the "Lord's Prayer", only then to turn around and make jokes about oral sex. He contests his representation as a slackness deejay by telling the crowd that he can chat rude lyrics or cultural lyrics: "Me a change the style, haffi change the style . . . kaa nuff people think say Yellowman can't chat culture and all dem ting. Me is a deejay mix everything. When me rude me get rude; and when me don't want get rude me don't get rude, seen?" (Yellowman, banter in between songs, *Slackness vs Pure Culture* [1987b]). He then breaks into "Galong Galong Galong" followed by "Jah Me Fear". Both these songs present Yellowman's view of immorality, including South African apartheid, racism, poverty, prostitution, pornography and homosexuality, and both songs use sexual imagery, and at times sexual maledicta, to make the point.

For anyone familiar with Yellowman, or dancehall in general, the above performance – with its shifting between slackness and culture – is not out of the ordinary. Almost every Yellowman album complicates the notion that he is, in a simplistic or fixed way, the King of Slack, because they almost all contain cultural material and often use sexually explicit lyrics to make a moral point.

The slackness versus culture debate has tremendous stamina in Jamaica and, in conjunction with violence, is at the heart of the moral argument against dancehall. In an attempt, I believe, to combat the de-evolution thesis, even record producers downplay their own culpability in proliferating violence and slackness. Producers George Phang, Black Scorpio and Philip "Fatis" Burrell told me that they do not produce slackness and that when Yellowman recorded for them it was always non-slack material. This is clearly revisionist history. Scorpio produced Yellowman's "Dry Head Adassa" (1988a) about the "girl with the baldhead vagina" and "Want a Virgin (1988a). "Want a Woman" (1987c), produced by Fatis, includes lines like "I just want a girl come rub me down". The George Phang-produced *Galong Galong Galong* (1985a) includes some of Yellowman's slackest tunes, such as "Blow Saxophone". Founder of US reggae label RAS Records Doctor Dread (aka Gary Himmelfarb) even wrote a letter in 2001 to Jamaica's ambassador to Washington claiming that the company has attempted to clean up reggae, using Josey Wales's "Slackness Done" for effect: "It is time to declare that slackness is done! It is time to clean up the dancehall and bring forth a positive message for the youth and grownups alike. We have recruited some positive role models who are soldiers in a new army coming to fight off the lame and crude music that has dominated reggae in the past." Doctor Dread finishes his letter with language reminiscent of an evangelical tent meeting: "The message is clear: join us in this crusade where good shall triumph over evil! It's been far too long that we have allowed ourselves to bathe in the wickedness of music that makes us conspirators to prejudice and hatred. Rise up!!!!!" (Dread 2001).

Doctor Dread insisted in the letter that he had consistently released music with "righteous" lyrics that addressed the "spiritual side of life" and RAS music sent a positive message to uplift people. Conversely, RAS is against music that displays "sexual bravado and rude boy mannerisms", "misogynist" lyrics that are "disrespectful to women", or are "homophobic" or advocate "the power of the gun". While RAS did release very spiritually minded albums by Yellowman, such as *Prayer* (1994b) and *Message to the World* (1995a), they also released typical Yellowman slackness. "I Still Got It" off *Party* (1991b), for instance, begins with Yellowman assuring women that he still has something for them in his pants. And "Romance", from *Prayer* (1994b), has a female groaning as if in the throes of sex, and Yellowman chatting slackness such as "She want Yellowman with the big rusty cock", "The hard and stiff you fe sit down pon it" and "The yellow banana every girl want it". But perhaps "Want a Virgin" (1988b), from *Yellowman Rides Again*, is the slackest example from the RAS catalogue:

> Want, say me want, want want a virgin
> Need, say me need, need need a virgin
> I going make love to Sandra then take a virgin
> Make love to Lorna then take a virgin
> Make love to Sonya then take a virgin
> Make love to Paula then take a virgin
> Make love to Martha then take a virgin
> When I roll out my yellow someting
> The girl look at me say it's a Goddamn sin
> Your yellow someting coulda never go in
> Girl shut your mouth I have a likkle [little] Vasoline
> When I rub it on my curl and it easy fe go in
> She couldn't take the pressure man she couldn't take the agony

> She said Yellowman you know that you hurt me
> Yellow, darling, please take it easy

Doctor Dread, like the other producers mentioned above, no doubt has felt pressure to downplay slackness in certain circles. In doing so, they contribute to the binary categorization of reggae into fictional halves and perpetuate the social construction of slackness as necessarily immoral.

Journalists have been so blinded by the slack versus culture binary that they have even mistaken Yellowman's later culturally minded material for a whole-hearted conversion to the morally upstanding side of reggae. For instance, since his first cancer scare in 1984, Yellowman's songs are increasingly more conspicuously concerned with ultimate reality, leading some commentators to assume that he has left slackness behind. But this argument does not hold up, as he has continued writing new songs with familiar slack themes. "Blow Saxophone", from *Galong Galong Galong* (1985a), refers to oral sex. "Girls Pet", off *Rambo* (1986b), ensures his audience that he can get any woman. *Slackness vs Pure Culture* (1987b) delivers some of the slackest material of his career. *Don't Burn It Down* (1988a) includes the aforementioned "Want a Virgin" and the ode to shorn pubic hair, "Dry Head Adassa". In *Reggae on the Move*'s (1992) "Got the Rammer", he chats about the "yellow rammer" that makes the girls holler. "Hard Core Love", off *In Bed with Yellowman* (1993b), reminds listeners of appropriate locations for sex (the bed and the floor). And Yellowman's *Good Sex Guide* (1995b) includes "Big Dick", "Want You Body" and "Galster".

THE AESTHETIC ARGUMENT

The aesthetic argument against dancehall is simply that dancehall is not real music, or at least a music form inferior to previous Jamaican genres. This same argument was made against hip-hop by rock journalists in the 1970s and 1980s. Both these forms of music – dancehall and hip-hop – employ repetition, privilege rhythm over melody, rapping over singing, display little diversity in chord progressions and arrangements, and are based on the tradition of "versioning" or creating new songs out of existing songs.

Edward Seaga provides, again, a clear example of the aesthetic argument against dancehall. Telling Jamaican reporters that his love for Jamaican music does not include dancehall, he offered these reasons why: "Dancehall music lacks components of classical music, which includes lyrics, melody and rhythms", and "it doesn't have melody, and forget lyrics, but what it does have is rhythm and that has made it hugely popular." Seaga hopes that "somebody comes up with a tune once again" ("Dancehall Music Lacking, Says Seaga", *Jamaica Observer*, 13 October 2009). To be fair, Seaga's comments were in response to the "Gully vs Gaza" conflict that started as a lyrical war between deejays Mavado and Vybz Kartel but spilled out on the streets of Kingston with violent acts being committed by warring factions from garrison communities known as either the Gully or Gaza posse. But Seaga's criticisms are indicative of the aesthetic arguments made against dancehall that construct it as musically inferior to Western music – this is apparent in Seaga's use of classical music as a foil to measure dancehall against. Dancehall, we learn, is all about rhythm and lacks the necessary components of classical music, which is set up as the measuring stick of refined musical taste.

This kind of comparison to classical music, of course, can be found in criticisms of all popular music, including roots reggae. What is more interesting in the reggae world, though, is that dancehall has been routinely stigmatized as aesthetically inferior to roots reggae using clear-cut oppositions in music technology and performance in the late 1970s and early 1980s: singer/deejay, analogue/digital, session musicians/digitally created backing tracks, professionals/amateurs, international reggae culture/local sound system culture. Manuel, Bilby and Largey (1995) locate a major technological change in dancehall as the generative moment when critics sounded the death knell on reggae, saying "with its increasingly violent posturing, its 'lickshots' (simulated gunfire) and sparse rhythm tracks, generated entirely on electronic equipment, the dancehall music of the late 1980s and early 1990s was seen by many reggae fans as a creative low point for Jamaican popular music – a slump from which many feel it has yet to recover" (173).

This started in the mid-1980s when the digital revolution sparked by producers like King Jammy and Black Scorpio changed how reggae was written, recorded and manufactured almost overnight. Rhythms played using only Casio keyboards and a drum machine took the place of bass, drums, organs and guitars in many songs, such as Wayne Smith's "Sleng Teng", the digital song that many finger as ushering in the massive sea change. This meant that professional musicians playing "real" instruments were sidelined in favour of amateur musicians devising simple musical parts using this new technology. This era is often referred to as the digital age of reggae, though this refers to the digital instruments as opposed to the recording technology. Digital production using computers and DAWs was still far off and Jamaican reggae in the 1980s was still recorded to analogue tape.

Professional studio bands had been at the heart of the music's creation through the ska, rocksteady and roots reggae periods, so the shift away from this formula was greeted by many people as a movement from the music's golden age towards an inferior era of music production. Writing in 1988, O'Gorman insisted that dancehall was regarded by some "as a sinister threat to mainstream reggae", and was thought of as a passing fad; "some people", she wrote, "question whether it constitutes music at all" (O'Gorman 1988, 51). Singer Dennis Brown was famously quoted in the *Daily Gleaner* as saying dancehall "won't last forever" ("It Won't Last Forever, Says Dennis Brown", *Daily Gleaner*, 30 August 1987). The new fad put many older roots musicians out of work but others, such as session musicians/producers Sly and Robbie, thrived because they were quick to adapt to the new paradigm, with Sly being the first Jamaican drummer to use an electronic drum kit in the late 1970s. The new style of music, variously called dancehall, deejay, ragga or ragamuffin, became the dominant musical expression of youth in Jamaica from the early 1980s until today and seemed, for critics, to eclipse the Rasta consciousness of reggae produced in the 1970s.

Perhaps British reggae bassist and producer Dennis Bovell summed up this position best: "When computers came in, that's when the amateurs took over." The dancehall era has been maligned for its lack of talent and focus on craft. Bovell called it reggae's "karaoke phase" (Bradley 2001, 501). The focus in dancehall switched from singers and vocal groups – the connotation here is that singers possessed talent, learned a craft, and were rehearsed – to talk-over artists or deejays who are improvisational and did not need, so the argument goes, musical skills such as pitch, tone, technique, melody and harmony. Whereas roots reggae was centred on singers and vocal trios with layers of melody and harmony, dancehall reduced the genre to rhythm – drum and bass. Gone were the horn sections, back-up singers, guitar licks and organ counter melodies and in their place are the mostly male deejay voices. It must be noted, however, that many who criticize dancehall for this very aspect group dub reggae alongside roots reggae. Dub paved the way for the dominance of rhythm over melody, open spaces over full band arrange-ments and bass lines over singers, techniques that dancehall would adopt.

The aesthetic argument is plainly based on the idea that European and Euro-American based music is normal and superior. Foreign critics attrib-uted the popularity of dancehall to bad taste and a diminished capacity for originality and creativity on the part of its creators when compared against reggae of the 1960s and 1970s (Stolzoff 2000). The music that Bob Marley and the Wailers marketed to the West in the 1970s was far from indigenous Jamaican reggae, yet is clearly what critics measure dancehall against most often. Marley's first album for Island Records, *Catch a Fire* (Wailers 1973b), was purposely altered to appeal to a white audience familiar with rock music. American and British rock musicians overdubbed blues and rock guitar solos and keyboard riffs and the tracks were remixed to diminish the role of the bass and highlight the role of the guitar. As well, reggae was a 45s market – albums in Jamaica were normally collections of songs originally released as singles. *Catch a Fire* was the first time a reggae band recorded a full album with the intent of releasing it as a stand-alone LP.[3] A comparison between the original recordings the Wailers did at Harry J's in Jamaica and the sub-sequent Island release conspicuously shows how the Wailers began moving away from a local sound towards a global sound, understandably in order to catch the ears of the global marketplace.[4] As Marley wrote increasingly for his global audience, he used songwriting techniques rarely employed in reggae. His song forms, chord progressions, use of bridges, length of songs and liberal use of guitar solos all share more similarities with black American blues, soul and R&B and white American and British rock and folk songwriting traditions than mento, ska or reggae. Dub poet Linton Kwesi Johnson called this new style of reggae "international reggae", which had "more of a 'toppy' mix, a lighter sound. The emphasis is more on guitar and other fillers" (Davis 1994, 96).

Catch a Fire was a flop in Jamaica where the American and British aesthet-ics of the record went unappreciated. However, it is this pseudo-Jamaican reggae that foreign critics fell in love with and that has since become insti-tutionalized as authentic reggae in the foreign press. It is this faux authentic product that the subgenre of dancehall – a fully local sound – has subsequently been measured against.

The music Marley was producing for Island Records was very different from the music Jamaicans were producing at home in many ways. Almost all Jamaican reggae in the 1970s was recorded using the versioning tradition of creating new songs out of existing songs. Starting in the late 1960s, studios such as Studio One and Treasure Isle began recycling older riddims, or backing tracks, by enlisting singers and deejays to write new melodies and lyrics overtop the old backing tracks. This practice of releasing a new version of an older song is known as "versioning". The original backing tracks were recorded by professional studio musicians and if rival producers wanted to use the same riddim, they would simply hire their studio band to record a new version of it, called a re-lick. So, whereas this music was played by professional musicians, producers would recycle these backing tracks several times. Rupie Edwards was the first producer to use the term "version" to describe the B-side of a 45rpm record in 1969, but the practice of using a previous rhythm goes back to mento (Hurford 2004). Several different song lyrics would be composed on one mento melody (Senior 2003). Versioning is at the heart of all Afro-American and Caribbean genres of music including jazz, blues, rap, R&B, reggae, calypso, soca, salsa, and Afro-Cuban (Hebdige 1987). In fact, versioning is the root of modern remix culture.

With this in mind, roots reggae produced in Jamaica during the 1970s is not that far removed aesthetically from dancehall produced in the early 1980s, which was based on digitally created riddims versioned multiple times. My point is that foreign critics mistakenly assumed that Bob Marley's Island material was the yardstick against which to compare all other reggae, yet Marley's reggae was really a different category of music – a hybrid of Jamaican and Euro-American influences. Dancehall in the 1980s, though sounding different due to its new technologies, was closely based on roots reggae of the 1970s. In the early dancehall era, Yellowman was deejaying over top of the same riddims that roots singers Johnny Osbourne ("Truths and Rights"), the Heptones ("Party Time") and the Mighty Diamonds ("Pass the Kutchie"/"Full Up") sang over. Channel One, the studio Yellowman was aligned with in 1981–82, made its name by rerecording and updating the foundational riddims recorded at Studio One during the 1960s and 1970s. Channel One led the charge towards deejay artists and dancehall music starting in the mid-1970s. The new versions downplayed melody instruments in favour of dominant bass and drums, but the riddims of early dancehall were the same as those played on roots songs. Roots artists employed the same method of recording – they also sang their original songs over top of pre-recorded riddims. These riddims, especially in the case of Studio One, were either part of a producer's existing library of riddims or, as in the case of Channel One, were updated by a studio band hired by the producer.

Yet this fact was lost on many people who wrote about reggae from outside Jamaica. Writing about Yellowman in 1996 for an American newspaper ("Not-so-Mellow Yellowman", *Denver Westword*, 19 September 1996), Joshua Green tried to draw a line between dancehall and roots reggae by way of recording technology: "This practice of rapping, or 'toasting', over the other musical beds made by previous acts contrasted sharply with the roots style of reggae that was prominent in the late 1970s." Green is evidently thinking of the Wailers, and likely did not realize that very few bands apart from the Wailers were stand-alone units that wrote and recorded their own material. Even other major roots acts in the 1970s like Burning Spear, Toots and the Maytals, the Itals, and Culture were vocal groups who sang over riddims created by studio bands. Like any good reggae riddim, it might become versioned several times. This is because since the ska days in the early 1960s, Jamaican music has always been a collaboration between a series of studio bands and performing artists. The studio bands wrote and recorded the riddims, the performing artists then wrote vocal parts that complimented the existing recordings, and other artists were free to create a new song based on these elements.

Even after dancehall shifted towards new digital riddims, producers continued the tradition of versioning older foundational riddims. For instance, George Phang produced Half Pint's massive ragga hit "Greetings"; the song was voiced over Sly and Robbie's heavily electronic update of early Studio One riddim "Heavenless". Riddims with names such as "Ali Baba", "Boops", "Cuss Cuss", "Death in the Arena", "Full Up", "General", "Johnny Dollar", "M16", "Stalag 17", "My Conversation", "Stars", "Bobby Babylon", "Pressure and Slide", "Queen Majesty", "Real Rock", "Revolution", "Satta Massagana", "Shank I Sheck", "Swing Easy", "Vanity" and "Westbound Train" all started life as roots reggae or rocksteady songs and were versioned repeatedly well into the dancehall era. Yellowman himself has recorded on most of these riddims.

The fact that versioning continued into dancehall and was propagated by dancehall is a testament to how Jamaican music – whether ska, reggae, or dancehall – never strays far from its roots. Contrary to the de-evolution thesis that posits dancehall in contradistinction to its antecedents, dancehall remembers its roots and constantly revisits and updates them in the form of riddims and lyrical themes. Yes, dancehall privileged chatting over singing and rhythm over melody, but the dancehall and deejaying of Yellowman and Shabba Ranks in the 1980s, Super Cat and Buju Banton in the 1990s, Sizzla and Sean Paul in the noughts, and Vybz Kartel and Spice in the 2010s has become progressively more complex than the 1970s rub-a-dub of U-Roy, Big Youth, Trinity, Michigan and Smiley, Lone Ranger, and General Echo. Not only have the musicians and producers embarked on a relentless hunt for new sounds and rhythmic textures, but the production values of Super Cat's *The Struggle Continues* or the scope of social commentary and musical diversity on Buju Banton's *'Til Shiloh* rivals the best of what music critics argue is authentic reggae from the 1970s.

Sly and Robbie were foundational in enhancing the role that the bass and drums played in reggae during the early dancehall period. While at Channel One, they recorded new versions of Studio One classic riddims but gave prominence to the bass and drums over the melody instruments. Horn, organ, and guitar melodies would often be absent from the new versions with the bass line and heavy drums taking centre-stage. One of the main aesthetic changes between roots and dancehall was the move away from the sparse "one drop" rhythm of the drums to a heavier rock feel. One drop reggae brought the kick and snare down on the third beat of the bar and left the downbeat – the one – silent. It essentially "dropped" the "one". Most of Marley's Island Records material up until the *Exodus* (1977) album uses variations on the one drop. Beginning in the mid-1970s, drummers such as Sly Dunbar experimented with changing this. While on tour with Peter Tosh in the United States, Sly played at festivals with rock bands. Here he became aware that rock drummers produced loud and powerful beats whereas roots reggae seemed quieter and weak in comparison. It was in response to this that Sly began playing more rock-oriented beats back in Jamaica as a session drummer with several studios, Channel One among them. One of these beats became known as steppers. Steppers is characterized by the kick drum beating out all four quarter notes in a measure. This drastically increased the power of the drums in reggae and was liberally adopted for dancehall. This is how critics of dancehall, such as Seaga, can accurately say that dancehall focuses on rhythm, not melody. But even Marley recognized the need to stay contemporary in his music and keep in touch with his Jamaican fans. When he recorded "Punky Reggae Party" at Lee Perry's Black Ark Studio in 1977, his drummer, Carlton Barrett, refused to veer from the one drop. Marley was forced to bring in Sly Dunbar because he wanted the modern steppers beat that Sly was known for at the time (Sly Dunbar, interview with author, 4 September 2006).

This aesthetic argument – that dancehall has less musical value than roots reggae or Western music – fails to acknowledge that dancehall's musical aesthetics are rooted in African traditions and should not be judged by aesthetic standards derived from European art music. The European tradition was steeped in a mindset of progress and innovation defined by harmonic movement towards resolution – chord progressions moved songs forward and diatonic harmony added complex textures (Hindley 2002). Composers sought to engage with these organizing principles in novel ways so that art music itself continually evolved. We see these aesthetic standards applied to classical, jazz and rock. The Beatles's hallowed place in the rock canon, for instance, is based in large part on their ability to innovate within this idiom. Most African music, though, is organized around rhythmic polyphony (Small 1998). Innovation is found in a musician's adaptability – altering a song or songs to fit new functions – and a tendency for improvisation. It is also different from the European tradition in its participatory nature. Participatory music cultures value repetition, ostinatos and "intensive variation" (Turino 2008).

While both roots reggae and dancehall draw from African musical traditions, dancehall makes fewer concessions to Western musical aesthetics. Dancehall has tended to downplay melody instruments and solos, with keyboards, guitars and even horns adding rhythmic diversity and intensive variation; drum and bass is usually brought forward in the mix; deejays construct deeply rhythmic lyrical lines, but eschew melody; chordal movement is often minimal, repetition is common, and song arrangements simple. All this is to say that dancehall combines musical values from European and African traditions, as do other African diasporic music forms, though critics of dancehall have, by and large, judged it solely based on European standards.

EARLIER NADIRS OF JAMAICAN POPULAR MUSIC

Dancehall was controversial music from its beginning; its lyrics were routinely criticized by authorities for "promoting social disorder and leading the youth astray. Dancehall music was accused of encouraging slackness and the use of guns, glorifying 'badmen' and promoting drug-use" (Lesser 2008, 186). To put this in the context of music history in Jamaica, lewd songs, celebrations of gangsterism and odes to ganja were being sung long before dancehall. Mento, ska, rocksteady and reggae, each in its heyday, were also decried as ghetto music by elite society and were regarded as the music of the lower-class (Barrow and Coote 2004). The upper and middle classes listened to American big band swing music between the 1930s and 1950s and much of the urban population was not interested in mento during this period as it was regarded ambivalently as country people's music. Instead, they looked towards black America for the wildly popular R&B music that began to be played on Jamaica's outdoor sound systems (Chang and Chen 1998). Even the early record producers like Stanley Motta and Ken Khouri – both uptown men who had money to open a business and whose modus operandi was to turn a profit – would have devalued the aesthetic worth of the mento music recorded in their studios as music of the lower-class. These men were interested in the music as a material commodity, not a cultural commodity (Bradley 2001).

Up until independence in 1962, folk culture in Jamaica, and anything considered African in origin, was disparaged. Europe was held up as the zenith of culture and European culture dominated Jamaica's official national identity in terms of value system, art, education, laws and customs (Nettleford 1974). With independence came a new "creole multiracial nationalist project" that saw prominence bestowed on the island's African heritage: "those religious and secular rituals, speech patterns, foods, musical forms, and dances associated with the rural peasantry came to enjoy some measure of legitimacy by the state" (Thomas 2004, 5). As such, mento and rural folk culture enjoyed a level of respectability to which it was previously denied.

Ska, rocksteady, and reggae, while idealized by critics today, fought their own battles in their respective days against a mainstream public who devalued their cultures. Any musician who adopted Rasta ideologies in their lyrics or wore Rastafarian symbols was treated with contempt. Though more and

more of the music fraternity were wearing locks, Rastas still suffered prejudice in society: Duke Reid, owner of Treasure Isle studio, disliked Rastas
and did not allow marijuana; lighting up at Federal Studios would get you
run out the door; and Dynamic studios was owned by uptown entrepreneur
and bandleader Byron Lee – not exactly a welcoming environment for a
musical dread looking to "lick the chalice". In the mid-late 1960s, Coxsone
Dodd's Studio One was the only studio where musicians were allowed to
smoke ganja. Dodd was sympathetic to Rastas and turned a blind eye to
their indulgences. Singer Horace Andy has posited that this is why Studio
One established itself as the island's top studio for so long (Bradley 2001).

When reggae critics claim that dancehall is the nadir of Jamaican music,
they conveniently forget that the genres they are elevating were also once
under fire for much the same reasons. Bob Marley was once the irreverent
dirty upstart playing noisy uncivilized music.

THE DEATH OF MARLEY AND THE RISE OF YELLOWMAN

Yellowman is often singlehandedly blamed for the slackness trend and simultaneously seen as responsible for ending the cultural roots reggae era, the era
that Bob Marley defined so well for so many, at least so many non-Jamaicans.
Cooper calls it "conventional wisdom in Jamaica" that Marley's conscious
reggae is "the peak of culture" (Cooper 2004, 73). Marley not only represents
the epitome of cultural reggae, or even "good" reggae for many, he has also
come to embody authentic reggae for many abroad. His enormous cross-over
appeal into white markets would have many people later argue that Marley
and his reactionary brand of Rastafari came to represent reggae music for
many people globally (Bradley 2001).

The seismic shift in international reggae was, without a doubt, the death
of Bob Marley in May 1981. This date marks the end of the roots era for commentators and the beginning of dancehall's reign. Dave Hill wrote in 1989,
"The consensus is that reggae music has been going through a dry spell.
Within the reggae scene the death of Marley in 1981 is widely held to have
abruptly halted the music's extraordinary development from an indigenous
Jamaican dance form into the profound expression of an international black
consciousness. . . . With Marley's demise, the music, as a coherent cultural
phenomenon seemed to lose momentum" ("Can Reggae Music Bounce Back?",

Daily Gleaner, 8 September 1989). According to commentators like Hill, Marley's death left a void, and deejays like Yellowman stepped in to undo all the hard cultural work that Marley had accomplished:

> In the DJ field, a more delinquent species also emerged from Jamaica, motor mouthed dancehall commentators of whom the most popular and the most infamous was the albino Yellowman. The fact that he was sometimes backed by the jet-set rhythm section of Sly Dunbar and Robbie Shakespeare underlines the box-office appeal of Yellowman. An arch exponent of the "slackness" talk-over style, his habitual third-form prurience exemplified reggae's nadir as a progressive force. (Ibid.)

Other historians have also positioned Yellowman as the fulcrum between the golden age of Marley and the debauched age of dancehall. In an interview, Roger Steffens said, "After Bob died, the biggest star in reggae was this salacious, foulmouthed, homophobic, misogynistic rapper called Yellowman, and it changed the whole tone of the music. . . . The music turned so foul, so debauched, I decided I didn't want to be around it anymore" (interview by Richard Burnett in "Rastaman Vibration", *Hour*, 13 July 2006).[5]

The death of Bob Marley caused an international daze among reggae fans who equated the event as the death knell for reggae ("Can Reggae Music Bounce Back?", *Daily Gleaner*, 8 September 1989). As the daze lifted, the focus for the industry was on finding the next Bob Marley in hopes that they could recreate his success and continue to market reggae into the 1980s. Bradley says that "virtually anyone with an engaging smile, a headful of dreadlocks and a one-drop way with a pop-tinged tune earned such a prefix" and cites Dennis Brown, Freddie McGregor, John Holt and Gregory Isaacs as hopefuls (Bradley 2001, 507).

Many American journalists stopped paying attention to reggae when Marley died. Indeed, many were not listening even when Marley was alive. Legendary *Creem* writer Lester Bangs stated that reggae in the United States was "outright disdained by blacks" in the 1970s (Bangs 2004, 48). As such, it was white music journalists who were the ones representing reggae to other white fans and that was often due to the enormous energies Chris Blackwell spent on marketing Marley to that demographic. Writing in 1976, Bangs, who claims that reggae was "still an acquired taste for the vast majority of US listeners, white or black", was flown to Kingston by Island Records "with a raft of other white journalists and photographers . . . for a sort of Cook's Tour of Jamaican Music and the somewhat obligatory interview with Bob Marley" (47–48). Bangs, and presumably other media personalities, were treated to a week in Jamaica at Island's expense to get the word to American youth about Bob Marley.

The marketing campaign was so successful, however, that it arguably nearly crippled the reggae industry in the United States after Marley died. Reggae remained on the college campuses but was all but dormant in the mainstream. One 1993 article in *Time* magazine claimed that reggae had been in a "slump that lasted for most of the '80s" ("Marley's Ghost", *Time*, 13 September 1993). The same article inaccurately cites dancehall's beginnings as post-Marley, as if Marley's life was so integral to the music that the gap he left needed to be filled with something completely new: "After Marley died of a brain tumour in 1981 at 36, a new generation of Trench Town youths began to forge a harder, denser style of reggae called dancehall. Reflecting the desperate times in Kingston's ghettos, dancehall lyrics were charged with angry diatribes glorifying guns, drugs and sex, and sung often in a fast, talky style called 'toasting'" (ibid.). The mistaken assumption that Trench Town represents every community in Kingston is indicative of how completely Marley-centric Western journalists had become. They were unable to see Jamaican music without looking through the lens of Marley reggae and were blind to the fact that deejaying and dancehall music in Jamaica had gradually been evolving on the island for over a decade.

Western journalists have all too often written hagiographic accounts of Marley, erasing any sexist, violent or incendiary elements that effectively sanitize him for history. Writing in London's *Sunday Times* over a decade after Marley died, Tom Willis portrayed a chastened Bob Marley whose music was centred on lilting love songs over against dancehall (also called ragga in the United Kingdom) which he generalizes as slack, violent, sexist, and homophobic ("From Ragga to Riches", *Sunday Times*, 4 April 1993). Willis's oversimplification of both Marley and dancehall is indicative of the way these genres have been portrayed in the media. Cooper (2004, 74) makes the point that "Willis's generalization engenders a series of clear-cut oppositions: hate ragga versus Bob Marley's love songs; 1980s violence versus 1970s peace (presumably); toasting versus singing; 'lilting' versus 'high speed'; (English) love songs versus patois lyrics – the contrast with English is implied in Willis's pointed reference to 'patois' lyrics; hateful 'misogyny, homophobia, gangsterdom and guns' versus unqualified love, pure and simple."

By 1982, Yellowman was the biggest reggae star in the world. He caused roadblocks in London and Toronto that summer and his popularity both at home and abroad was unparalleled by any reggae artist previous, with the possible exception of Marley. Yellowman could bring downtown Kingston to a standstill in those years simply by stepping out of his yellow BMW at Half Way Tree. Even Marley never achieved that sort of celebrity in his lifetime.

Histories that are careful to compare Yellowman's dancehall slackness to Marley-style roots reggae situate him as Marley's polar opposite – "Yellowman's canon concerns itself with a celebration of the female anatomy [which is] some way from the spirituality and social concern of Bob Marley" ("Reggae's New Breed", *Daily Gleaner*, 13 August 1990). These histories rarely contextualize him in earlier dancehall and rub-a-dub deejay culture, and the tradition of slack entertainment that has been part of Caribbean musics since the slavery era. A few authors, such as David Katz (2012), have recognized that Yellowman's material is diverse, and Salewicz and Boot (2001), at least, recognized this scapegoating in their book *Reggae Explosion*: "Yellowman's alleged 'slack' style was not as one-dimensional as it appeared. In that way typical of Jamaican art, there was always a spiritual underplay, as his general 'rudeness' also contained much irony. Coming immediately after the death of Bob Marley, Yellowman's success appeared to mark a downward slide for Jamaican music, but time shows it was more complex than that" (102). Typical of reggae histories, Salewicz and Boot are vague about what the characteristics of Yellowman's spiritual engagement might be and do not attempt to situate him in anything other than the general gloss of "Jamaican art". While Salewicz and Boot allude to the fact that Yellowman's story is not simply black and white, they never fill in the rest of the shades of the picture.

An earlier article by Salewicz (2004, 138) betrays that he himself was one of those comparing Yellowman to Marley:

> Bob Marley's death in May 1981 stunned the music and stunted its growth. Developments that did occur were tangential, as though no-one had the confidence to make a major move: the rise of the New Wave DJ and DJ double-acts has been the most significant advance of the past two years. Figures like Eek-A-Mouse, Brigadier Jerry, and women toasters like Sister Nancy helped move the music on, or at least prevented it from falling back. A toasting superstar

like Yellowman was an adequate jokey distraction but hardly fulfilled reggae's need for a leader.

Salewicz's almost hagiographic portrayal of Marley's impact on the local Jamaican music industry is overwrought – Bradley (2001) has convincingly shown that Marley's music at the time of his death was far removed from the "advances" in homegrown reggae. This paragraph is indicative of how foreign journalists have written the history of reggae based on their own tastes. The reggae being made in Jamaica was very different than the Wailers' international style, and Marley's influence on the local artists at the time was far below what Salewicz's describes. The music industry was in no way stunted upon his death and it is a ridiculous notion that a genre as diverse and large as reggae needs a leader. The Jamaican music industry routinely released far more records per week than would seem possible for a population of that size. The loss of Marley had an impact on society – his state funeral caused the government to postpone a budget debate and virtually brought Kingston to a stand-still, but the music industry continued apace. It even received an unlikely boost in the form of numerous tributes to Marley.

Travel guides are an accurate barometer to gauge how outsiders who are interested in a country's culture represent it to fellow outsiders. As such, this summary of Yellowman's contribution to reggae is a typical example of the generic caricature you find in popular culture when speaking of Yellowman, and, as expected, uses Marley as an aesthetic and moral foil:

> These days, you're far more likely to be assailed by a clamorous barrage of raw drum and bass and shouty patois lyrics than hear Bob Marley or Burning Spear booming out from Jamaican speaker boxes. Known as dancehall (because that's where it originated and where it is best enjoyed), or ragga (from ragamuffin, meaning a rough-and-ready ghetto dweller), this is the most popular musical form in contemporary Jamaica. The genre first surfaced around 1979 and was cemented in 1981 when a flamboyant albino DJ named Yellowman exploded onto the scene with his massive hits like *Married in the Morning*, *Mr Chin* and *Nobody Move*. Yellowman's lyrical bawdiness and huge popularity signified the departure from roots reggae and cultural toasting (the original term used to describe the Jamaican talking-over-music that inspired US rappers) to the sexually explicit and often violent DJ-ism that took hold in the 1980s. Though none were rawer than Yellow, who added energetic stage performances and self-deprecating humour to the expletives, other DJs – fueled by a positive response

from their Jamaican audience – emulated his lewd approach, and sexually explicit lyrics – or "slackness" – began to proliferate. . . . Essentially, dancehall is a raw, rude, hard-core music designed to titillate and tease its Jamaican audience on home ground and beyond. Whether you like the lyrics or hate them, it's unlikely you'll be able to resist dancehall's compelling rhythm and infectious hype, and while you're in Jamaica, it's futile to try. (Thomas and Vaitlingam 2007, 446)

The writers of this travel guide make evaluative judgements on dancehall by using terms like "clamorous", "barrage", "raw" and "shouty" to describe the genre. Their language connotes cacophony or noise, an attack of bracing, primitive or underdeveloped music that is always loud, amateur and not polished. In its obvious privileging of the Marley/Spear era of reggae, the book represents an ageist and Western view of dancehall. It even assumes that dancehall is only consumed by Jamaicans "on home ground or abroad", therefore is not a music the tourist will be interested in once their Jamaican vacation is over. Is it odd for a guidebook that is supposed to represent the present society and culture of Jamaica to romanticize and be nostalgic about the past, privileging roots reggae over dancehall? Not really. Guidebooks, even ones for travellers not interested in cookie cutter all-inclusive holidays at beach resorts, are designed with tourism in mind, and tourism is inherently orientalist because it seeks to consume a foreign culture through a series of pre-set touristic experiences in a small amount of time. The orientalist goal of the tourist is to get to know the "real" Jamaica through a clutch of stereotypes. The guidebook's claim is that it can reveal the true culture of another country, yet it does so by sampling a relatively small set of activities geared towards Western tastes in the exotic (hotel stays, beaches, festivals, nightclubs, restaurants, sporting activities), and is therefore not based on how the locals view their own culture.

Besides the book's dim view of the genre, it refers to Yellowman as the rawest of all deejays and uses him as the divide between roots reggae and dancehall. It is telling that the piece uses the word flamboyant, which appears to relate to his "energetic stage performances", but if the writers had actually looked at footage of Yellowman in the years they mention, they would realize that he was neither flamboyant nor overly energetic – these attributes were added to his stage show in the 1990s. Instead, the flamboyancy seems to refer to the fact that he has yellow skin and yellow clothes. In the end, the article does spend some positive adjectives on dancehall ("infectious", "compelling") but makes the comment that while you are in Jamaica you should not try to resist it. I might be reading too much into this, but there is latent condescension here – there is no need to enjoy dancehall at home, keep the exotic music at the exotic locale. The subtle racism and classism of the article typifies the moral superiority of the Western guidebook: our music is normal, theirs is exotic.

Jamaica's tourism industry itself was slow to catch on to reggae – while reggae dominated local culture in the 1970s, hotels and coastal resorts still hired calypso and mento bands to entertain foreigners in an attempt to rec-reate the quaint and idealized island paradise planted in their imaginations by travel agents. When the industry did discover reggae, it was largely the Marley variety. Marley's "One Love" and "Smile Jamaica" have both been used on ad campaigns for the island, along with the image of the bathing-suit-clad happy dreadlocked Rasta waiting to serve you drinks or perhaps something more taboo. Dancehall, however, was not used to sell the island. For foreign media and the local tourism industry, dancehall represented "an assault on the image of the placid, harmonious, smiling tropical paradise that Jamaica wished to project" (Lesser 2008, 186).

Other media outlets have produced similar judgements on dancehall and equally inaccurate articles on Yellowman. Chris Coomey of the *Miami Times* (23 February 2006) said that "when Bob Marley died in 1981, a seismic shift in reggae was set into motion . . . the man credited as the pioneer called himself Yellowman". The article inaccurately places Yellowman as a found-ing father of the deejay style – which has roots as far back as the 1950s – and curiously says that "Yellowman became more well-known for his aggressive lifestyle than his penchant for a smooth and utterly revolutionary delivery". I am not sure what the writer means by "aggressive lifestyle" but usually in music journalism that refers to sex, drugs, and violence. What Coomey has probably done is confused Yellowman's lyrics about sexual exploits with his real life and perhaps considers that an "aggressive lifestyle". In fact, Yel-lowman abstains from all alcohol and drugs, including marijuana, and has been quoted as far back as 1984 as saying that he does not smoke or drink ("Yellowman Takes Over", *Cool Runnings: Reggae Roots Magazine*, 1984). There was a period in his later teens when Yellowman carried a gun, but when he started performing in the dancehall, he left that lifestyle behind. He has, in fact, penned several eloquent songs against violence. In "Tourist

Season" (1982a), he and Fathead are concerned that the level of violence on the island will affect tourism and the ability for everyone to have fun. Yellowman furthers the theme in "Stand up for Your Rights" (1982a) where he pleads with gunmen to make peace. A better pastime, he says, is to "nice up" Jamaica and find a lover:

> I beg you throw down your knife and throw down your gun
> Kaa this is our island in the sun
> Just get one girl and go have some fun
> Get one girl and go have some fun
> A me a go nice up Jamdung [Jamaica]

But "Gun Man" (1982g) is Yellowman's most direct impeachment of gun violence. Not only does he reprimand the perpetrators of the violence, he also implicates foreign meddling in the distribution of weaponry – an obvious reference to popular rumours that the CIA provided artillery to the island's gangs to destabilize Manley's party – and presents the social costs of gun violence.

> Gun man, say tell me weh you get yuh gun from
> You must a get it from the foreign land
> You must a check say me a politician
> You don't know say me a musician
> Gunshot a it nuh respect no one
> It kill soldier man, it kill policeman
> It kill policeman, also badman
> It kill badman, also civilian
> It kill civilian, also Christian
> It kill animal, also human
> Gun man, say tell me weh you get yuh gun from
> You must a get it from the foreign land
> You want come shoot dung your own black man

Prahlad also yearns for the moral superiority of the roots era. Calling the Marley years the "golden age of reggae", he argues that they were characterized by "culturally, spiritually, and artistically inspired lyrics and music that may never be duplicated" (Prahlad 2001, xxiii). For Prahlad, this socially aware reggae was international in scope and sound whereas dancehall was a concerted attempt to re-Jamaicanize reggae. But, tellingly, dancehall had little of the cultural value of roots reggae and instead was occupied largely with slackness and violence. Prahlad interprets the lyrics of roots icons Culture and Burning Spear to make his point that dancehall suffers from an inferior moral code, telling us that Culture sees dancehall as unfit for children and Burning Spear wants a return to cultural themes in music. Prahlad's treatment of Marley is typical – not only does Marley represent the apex of real reggae, he marvels that this "genius" has not been given the Nobel Prize for his "contribution to the betterment of human kind" (xxiv). It is this sort of cult of personality that informs much of the writing about Marley and led to a backlash in the foreign press against dancehall because it is constantly compared to a sanctified version of Marley.

Chuck Foster's *Roots, Rock Reggae* is a typical example of how journalists have conceived of the de-evolution thesis. Foster wrote a column in the pioneering reggae and world music magazine the *Beat*. He followed reggae for decades and his insight is valid. It is Foster's view that Yellowman is antithetical to Bob Marley and that dancehall is in binary opposition to roots reggae: "That [Yellowman's] star began to rise just as Bob Marley passed is perhaps no coincidence. Yellow represented a 360-degree spin from the social concerns of the 1970s and helped kick off the 'new' dancehall era with songs replete with sexual braggadocio, misogyny, and violent imagery, pandering to concerns earlier reggae artists might call 'Babylon'" (Foster 1999, 157).

Foster's interpretation of Yellowman's repertoire and impact, while falling well within the normal description music journalists have employed again and again when looking at the deejay, is ahistorical and decontextualized. An unassuming reader would think that "sexual braggadocio, misogyny, and violent imagery" were nowhere to be found in reggae music before Yellowman, which is clearly not the case. Foster pits Yellowman against a morally cleaner, socially concerned and pacifistic Marley. Marley, of course, wrote his share of sexually charged songs ("Stir It Up", "Is This Love", "Guava Jelly") and his extra marital affairs and numerous outside children were well publicized. Cooper (2004) has expertly deflated the "Saint Marley" image in her analysis of Marley's treatment of women. Marley was also not above calling for violence. One poignant example is the line "I feel like bombing a church now that I know the preacher is lying" from "Talkin' Blues".

In *Bass Culture: When Reggae was King*, Bradley (2001) defends dancehall against detractors who seek to disparage it as simplistic and low culture. Yet it is telling that out of 540 pages, only 39 – the last two chapters – are devoted to dancehall, when dancehall accounts for half the period he covers in the book. This privileging of the ska and roots era of Jamaican music over dancehall is rampant among histories of reggae where dancehall is often all but a footnote. Further, Bradley's treatment of Yellowman is typical. To his credit he does give the reader context into the extent that Yellowman dominated reggae at home and abroad in the post-Marley years, but his portrayal of the artist is in strict binary terms, over and against cultural deejays such as Brigadier Jerry, Charlie Chaplin and Josey Wales. Speaking of the 1987 live bootleg release *Slackness vs Pure Culture* (1987b), a clash album with Charlie Chaplin, Bradley calls it a "stylistic marker buoy" that "made palpable what had been happening to reggae music during the last five or six years". It was Yellowman's "thorough routing of the righteous" that Bradley sensed (2001, 508). In other words, Yellow's slackness had all but eclipsed roots and culture so that "previously spiritual deejays" such as Toyan and Ranking Joe started to reinvent themselves as slack artists. Bradley's timeline is off here: Ranking Joe's "Lift Up Yuh Frock" and other slack tunes predate this by seven years. Plus, Bradley does not take into account Yellowman's vast cultural catalogue and his insistence – even on this bootleg – that he is a deejay who can sing both slackness and culture.

Elsewhere, Bradley has offered a more rounded view of Yellowman. In his review of Yellowman's discography on compact disc, he gives the artist credit for making the "break from the previous era's roots deejays and [setting] up the dancehall styles that have dominated since" and is called the "final link between traditional reggae and what happened after 'Sleng Teng'", meaning the dominance of digital dancehall (Bradley 1996, 355). He charges mainstream music critics for denouncing the sexism in Yellowman's lyrics, defending his slackness as inoffensive, tongue in cheek and very funny. And he recognizes that Yellowman routinely issued cultural songs along with slackness songs, calling them "dread" or "righteous". But Bradley also sees slackness and culture as antagonistic to each other, even though Yellowman can do both, and he positions cultural songs as worthier in hindsight. He cites as the best songs on *Mister Yellowman* (1982d) and *Zungguzungguguzung-guzeng* (1983e) cultural tracks such as "Duppy or a Gunman" and "Natty Sat upon the Rock" on the former, and the title track on the latter: "The most remarkable thing about coming back to these albums ten years later is that you remember more of the 'proper' tracks than you do the slackness, even though it was the latter that seemed such a big deal at the time" (356).

Anderson (2004), writing in *Sound Recording Reviews*, offers a musicological history of Jamaican music and rehashes the same obverse relationship between roots and dancehall that plagued other journalists: "Reggae moved away from the smoky, mystical flavors and the religious/political lyrical focus of the roots-and-culture period to become more rhythmically aggressive and, significantly, much more violent and explicitly sexual in nature" (211). Anderson indulges in an orientalism that has served reggae journalists well by describing the roots genre in exotic terms with the far-away timeless imagery of "smoky" and "mystical". For Anderson, the de-evolution was clear cut: "As electronic percussion and synthesizers pushed guitarists, bass players, and wind players from the studio, reggae's rhythms became more minimalist and more robotic; in some cases, entire songs were built on an aggressive and unchanging three-against-two triplet pattern" (211).

Not all media outlets have painted Yellowman with the same brush, nor have they all implicitly supported the de-evolution thesis. Unlike many foreign journalists, many Jamaican writers and international dancehall fans in the black and alternative presses realize that dancehall is a diverse genre with many themes and sounds. The *Daily Gleaner* has routinely oscillated between music writers praising dancehall and columnists and writers of letters to the editor decrying its loose morals and violence. Canada's Beth Lesser and England's Ray Hurford treated dancehall as a valid and important youth and musical movement in their respective magazines, *Reggae Quarterly* and *Small Axe*. Britain's black music magazine *Black Echoes* also covered dancehall next to roots reggae, soul, funk, and jazz without resorting to the de-evolution thesis. And in his history of reggae, the Toronto-based Jamaican-born Klive Walker, speaking of the dominance of dancehall over roots reggae in the early 1980s, points out that dancehall had two main divisions: a secular, X-rated stream lead by Yellowman, and a conscious stream filled with social commentary and Rasta theology led by Brigadier Jerry. Walker does characterize Yellowman as only a secular deejay, but he does not make the implicit value judgement that slackness dancehall is a lesser form of the genre. Instead, he sees it as a form that competed with conscious dancehall (Walker 2005).

By and large, however, Yellowman has been targeted in the mainstream press, both local and foreign, as the progenitor of the slackness style and a stunted form of reggae that strayed from cultural concerns. Walker (2005, 247), who I argued above steers clear of the de-evolution thesis, does share Stolzoff's view that the 1980s saw a lacuna of culture tracks: "there has been a significant shift in thematic approach from the justice and equity sentiments that were dominant in 1970s roots reggae to the language of sex and violence that has characterized dancehall through much of the '90s". Walker locates this shift in the "replacement of Rasta sage as the most influential figure in the ghetto communities of Kingston by the overarching presence of the drug 'don'" (247).

It is necessary to point out that not all reggae in the 1970s was Rasta-centric. There were many pop reggae songs, love songs (called lovers rock) and, of course, slack songs during this period. But "because the Rasta renaissance coincided with the first major break-through of reggae music on the international pop market, many foreign listeners were led to assume that Rastafarian culture and reggae were inseparable" (Manuel, Bilby and Largey 1995, 166).

Jamaican entertainment journalist Trevor "Boots" Harris has argued that because reggae was marketed internationally as Rasta music, international audiences associate Rasta-centric roots reggae with authenticity of the genre. Once this link was established, Lesser (2008, 186) argues, "it was hard to throw an entirely different model into the mix without getting resistance". Lesser quotes Harris: "Reggae music has been marketed as 'Rasta music' by US and European record companies. This brought about an international concept that reggae music was, and should only be played by Rastafarian musicians." This marketing tactic had to do with record companies wanting to reproduce a formula that was already successful. Chris Blackwell felt that he could market Bob Marley initially because Marley was the real-life version of the musical outlaw Rhygin in the film *The Harder They Come* (Salewicz and Boot 2001). As Marley came to also embody a new counterculture hero – the Rasta Revolutionary – record companies scrambled to find more artists who could extend the brand. Manuel, Bilby and Largey (1995) explain, "Jamaican popular music has always been more varied than the one-sided Rasta image that the music industry promoted for many years in its attempts to capitalize on the popularity of outstanding Rasta reggae artists Bob Marley, Peter Tosh, Bunny Wailer, Burning Spear, and others working in the same vein" (166–67). When Canadian journalist Beth Lesser first went to Jamaica in the early 1980s, she had expected "everyone to be Rasta and dreads and Ital, and when we got there they weren't" (interview by author 21 January 2009). Her introduction to reggae in Canada in the 1970s had led her to believe that Rasta and reggae were always linked, but this was not true.

My own experience with this may just prove my own naiveté, but as a reggae fan for nearly thirty years, music journalist, musician in a reggae band, a former resident of Bermuda where reggae dominates the popular youth culture, I too was surprised when I first arrived in Kingston to find very little evidence of what I thought would be the all-pervasive Rastafari-reggae culture. It occurred to me that my own preconceptions about the island were built on an imaginary Jamaica gleaned largely from reggae songs and books. Like Lesser, I had assumed there would be Rastas and roots reggae everywhere, but instead heard mostly dancehall, R&B, rock, and Christian reggae. And to my surprise, dreadlocks were rare. I make this somewhat embarrassing point to illustrate how reggae fans outside of Jamaica perceive the island only through its cultural products. I had the added benefit of reading scholarship on reggae and Rastafari written by Jamaicans, but my preconceptions about reggae and Jamaica remained. I assumed reggae would be everywhere and that manifestations of Rastafari would be blatant. As I became more familiar with Jamaican culture, I found that both these cultural elements were pervasive, though not dominating the landscape.

Even in Jamaica, the ghost of Bob Marley, patron saint of reggae's golden era, hangs over dancehall like a shroud. Buju Banton has complained that the public's fixation on the Marley brand has hurt dancehall's growth because all new artists are compared to Marley ("Bob Marley Is Not the Greatest Musician – Buju", *Jamaica Observer,* 27 April 2009). Banton was heavily criticized in the press by the Marley cult for attacking one of Jamaica's and reggae's sacred cows. But inherent in these critiques were the trappings of the de-evolution thesis. Many writers condemned Banton's music or dancehall as a lesser music form than Marley's. Cooper, in defence of Banton and generations of artists younger than Marley, blames the curators of roots reggae's legacy for their ageist attitudes towards dancehall: "Buju Banton is the voice of a whole generation of not-so-young singers, players of instruments and riders of 'riddims' who are crying out to be taken seriously by elderly gatekeepers who assume the right to determine who is great and who is doomed to mediocrity" ("Buju versus Bob: No Contest", *Gleaner*, 10 May 2009).

In 1987, the *Daily Gleaner*'s "Reports in Sports 'n' Arts" featured interviews with Jamaican authorities that praised Marley and condemned dancehall. Sam McKay, a deputy commissioner, complained that some of dancehall's lyrics promoted drug use and was counterproductive with police actions. Marley's music, "in contrast, portrays hope and morality". Perhaps McKay was forgetting Marley's many songs that advocated smoking ganja, which was then against the law in Jamaica. Assistant commissioner Barry Cross charged dancehall with "using words offensive to decent people", while in Marley's music "there is some moral". And Sergeant D.R. Buchanan, in an attempt to argue for the superiority and authenticity of Marley's music, considered contemporary deejays' music full of "stupidity", in contrast to what Buchanan felt was Marley's music, which was "real, real, real" ("Reports in Sports 'n' Arts", *Daily Gleaner*, 1987).

One of the most vocal proponents of the de-evolution thesis was Jamaican pastor, columnist and radio and television host Ian Boyne. Boyne routinely used his column to denigrate dancehall and those who defend it, especially if they were connected to the University of the West Indies. To be fair, Boyne did not see all dancehall as violent, materialistic and slack: "Of course, there are positive, uplifting, conscious lyrics in the dancehall", he wrote in one article ("Dancehall's Betrayal of Reggae", *Gleaner*, 24 February 2008). However, Boyne selectively historicized roots reggae as something wholly positive, uplifting and serious. It is as if Marley-era reggae could do no wrong:

> Reggae differed from mere pop music which was for entertainment and frivolity. Reggae was serious without being somber. . . . Reggae is message music. The classic reggae artistes were acutely aware that they were not just minstrels. Their songs had us singing along and rocking, most definitely. But there was a message, which represented not just 'brawta'; it was its life force. For it came from the bowels of the working class experience with oppression, injustice, dehumanisation and exclusion. . . . Reggae's appeal is its innate humanism and universalism. For in decrying oppression, colonialism, imperialism and injustice, it was saying, forcefully, that these features are alien to our common heritage as human beings. This was not how humans were supposed to live. We were not supposed to be segregated by class, race, gender, religion and nationality. ("From Bob Marley to Mavado", *Gleaner*, 17 February 2008)

For Boyne, the reggae of the Wailers, Burning Spear and Israel Vibration is authentic reggae because it made powerful social statements and did so without glorifying sex and violence. Dancehall today, he writes, has de-evolved: "What is the message of dancehall today in its most dominant trend? It's about the 'gal dem business', the objectification and commodification of women, the glorification of promiscuity. It is about power over women's bodies" (ibid.). Boyne counterpoises most dancehall against roots reggae as frivolous, materialistic, hedonist and violent. He offers a rosy gloss of roots reggae that ignores its own sexism, objectification of women, glorification of gangs, and odes to the pleasures of the sexual act. By reconstructing roots reggae as fundamentally clashing with the values of dancehall, Boyne selectively chooses how musical and social history should be read and ignores the obvious continuities between dancehall and roots reggae. His insistence that dancehall has no message of substance echoes Seaga and others who fail to look past their own moralities to see that dancehall does indeed provide a social and political message based on the values of the black lower-class. But for Boyne, it is clear that "gal dem business" had no potential for social uplift or political critique but was only a means of male domination and the promotion of promiscuity.

To sum up so far, critics, mostly older and non-Jamaican, have conceived of a de-evolution in the genre from roots reggae in the 1970s to dancehall in the 1980s. The value judgements these journalists made resulted in Yellowman being targeted as the cause of the downfall of reggae and have resulted in a skewed body of knowledge; reggae histories suffer from this bias. Even in Jamaica much of the discourse on dancehall in the media has amounted to "moralizing and sermonizing", decrying its hedonism and negative effect on the country's youth (Hope 2006, 18). The de-evolution thesis is generally based on two criteria: aesthetics and morality. First, dancehall reggae is understood as a less complex music form than its forebears and therefore is demonized as being simplistic, primitive, repetitive, and all sounding the same. Second, dancehall is considered morally reprehensible, morally corrupt, or devoid of ethics, unlike roots reggae which is interpreted as dancehall's conscience-ridden parent; dancehall is treated as the hedonistic progeny.

Having examined the construction of reggae and Yellowman in the popular arena, I now turn to an interrogation of the same in the scholarly literature. As in the examples given of music journalism, Yellowman and dancehall do not fare much better in the hands of the academy, which reproduces both the moral and aesthetic arguments in support of the de-evolution thesis.

NURSERY RHYMES, ANIMAL NOISES AND ANTI-WOMAN JIVE TALK:
YELLOWMAN IN THE SCHOLARLY LITERATURE

Until the early 2000s, the scholarly debates about dancehall were often "demonizing, infantilizing, and romanticizing" (Hope 2006, 19). Most scholars who have mentioned Yellowman have not looked at him in any depth. Like media accounts, he is often the scapegoat for dancehall's sexual trends in the 1980s, but with little time taken to think about him critically. For instance, Chevannes says that Yellowman began the bawdy trend in dancehall that turned away from the conscious lyrics of Bob Marley (Chevannes 1999). Gilroy, for whom Bob Marley is the epitome of cultural reggae, gives Yellowman short shrift by tagging him as the lead proponent of the "decline of radical reggae" (Gilroy 1987, 188). Without bothering to analyse the over fifteen albums Yellowman had released by 1987, Gilroy is convinced that Yellowman only contributed two political songs ("Soldier Take Over" [1981] and "Operation Radication" [1982e]) to reggae and then "opted for the safety of nursery rhymes, animal noises and anti-woman jive talk" (188). It is interesting to note that not only did several cultural Rastafarian singers also use nursery rhyme melodies for their material (for instance, Max Romeo's "Three Blind Mice" and Jacob Miller's "Peace Treaty Special"), but the first time Yellowman did this on record – "Eventide Fire" uses the melody of "London Bridge Is Falling Down" – was in response to a politically motivated fire that killed 153 elderly women. In a country where it was dangerous for artists to offer public political commentary, Yellowman's use of nursery rhymes here can hardly be considered safe. And Gilroy's comment about animal noises – referring to Yellowman's sometime sidekick Fathead, whose trademark was to punctuate Yellowman's lyrics with sounds like "oink", "ribbit", "eh-a" or "right" – not only ignores the well-established tradition in jazz and reggae to use nonsensical words and phrases for scat purposes, but also is indicative of the aesthetic argument against dancehall as somehow a more primitive music by less skilled artists.

According to Gilroy (1987, 188), Yellowman led his contemporary deejays to steer "the dance-hall side of roots culture away from political and historical themes and towards 'slackness': crude and often insulting wordplay pronouncing on sexuality and sexual antagonism". What puzzles me here, though, is that Gilroy singles out artists such as Peter Metro and Brigadier Jerry as deejays who "fought to maintain rhymes with a social content". Besides the fact that Gilroy feels "social content" and slackness are mutually exclusive, he says nothing of the fact that these militants in the war against slackness were not only good friends of Yellowman but they were in fact sparring partners on stage and on record. One of Peter Metro's biggest hits was a duet with Yellowman ("The Girl Is Mine") and Brigadier Jerry (Briggy) was the first major deejay to give Yellowman a break and later often shared a stage with him. The fact that Metro and Briggy did not shun Yellowman should be considered if they, as Gilroy implies, were fighting against slackness. The argument could be made that Metro and Briggy were complicit in the use of slackness in dancehall by performing with Yellowman.

Gilroy's attempts to establish a binary between culture and slack deejays does not reflect reality. There is a fluid continuum between slackness and culture in dancehall; even artists typically described as culture artists accept the place of slackness as a viable aspect of dancehall culture. Josey Wales, who targeted slackness in "Slackness Done" and "Culture A Lick", accepts that dancehall is first and foremost about the freedom to express your mind. As such, he and Yellowman not only released two albums together, but it is his opinion that slackness is as valid an expression as culture:

> Author: You're known as a culture deejay and you have songs against slackness. Yet you and Yellowman did a clash album together: how can a culture deejay and the King of Slack do an album together?

> Josey Wales: There wasn't no barrier there and there is no restriction. Yellow was a warm welcoming person with accommodating spirit. I am that sort of person as well. The job require what you preach – he preach slackness, I preach culture, so we get it together. And Yellow could preach a little culture too.

> Author: And yet you recorded the song "Slackness Done" where you say you want to clean up the dance?

> JW: We didn't take anything personal. It was humorous and speaking your mind at same time. So when I tell Yellow slackness done and we must clean up the dancehall and slackness in the backyard hiding, I'm serious with that. And when Yellow say "Me want a yellow girl pon my yellow hip", him serious.

Author: So, it's just two different philosophies but you're not going to argue over it?

JW: We're not going to argue over it 'cause who am I to dictate? That's my opinion. (Interview by author, 25 February 2009)

Another scholarly depiction of Yellowman can be found among Cooper's writings. Cooper, who elsewhere has taken great pains to revalorize dancehall both as a legitimate cultural expression and as being worthy of scholarly inquiry, harshly takes Yellowman to task for the vulgarity and level of commodification of female bodies he indulges in in his music: "Woman is reduced to a collection of body parts which seem to function independent of her will" (Cooper 1995, 163). Cooper's later work, however, revalorizes Shabba Ranks, a prominent slackness deejay who came after Yellowman, and she finds in his lyrics examples of feminine sexual agency and celebrations of full-figured Afro-Caribbean women who do not fit Eurocentric beauty standards (Cooper 2004). Cooper's (1995) theory that slackness is a metaphorical revolt against mainstream norms and values can easily be applied to Yellowman – indeed that is the theoretical backbone of this book – but in the reductionist treatment she offers of Yellowman I believe she is guilty of not applying her own theory to him.

Thomas, while not mentioning Yellowman specifically, follows the standard binary thinking around dancehall and roots reggae, saying that dancehall distanced itself from the revolutionary politics of the 1970s: "Whereas previous reggae music had emphasized social critique and a belief in redemption, early dancehall music reflected a ghetto glorification of sex, guns, and the drug trade" (Thomas 2004, 80–81). Thomas rightfully points out that the middle class's fear of dancehall was based on their concern for the power it had in shaping behaviour and public perceptions of Jamaicans.

Anthropologist and dancehall historian Stolzoff claims that the 1980s marked a transition in Jamaican popular culture away from the moral leadership of Rastafari to entertainment forms that celebrated consumerism, sexuality and gunplay. He hails pre-dancehall music as simply "reggae" and finds in it a "profound message of antiracism, political protest, and spiritual redemption" whereas post-reggae wallowed in "slackness, a genre preoccupied with themes dedicated to pornography, homophobia, misogyny, and hypermasculinity" (Stolzoff 2000, 100). Stolzoff cites Marley's death in 1981 as the beginning of this decline. In his view, then, Rastafari played a key role in reggae culture in the 1970s and steered the moral compass of lower-class society away from slackness and violence and towards black nationalism, Africa, peace and justice. Stolzoff maps the rise of slackness in dancehall over and against the moral degeneration of Rastafari precepts.

Stolzoff goes further and pits slackness directly in opposition with religious sexual mores, both Christian and Rastafarian. He asserts that the new generation of artists singing about sex were "baldheads" (non-Rastas) and defied and overturned Rasta's "austere version of sexual morality" because they were based on mainstream notions of sexuality (2000, 105). There is truth in this – Rastafarian sexual ethics are derived from a mix of rural Jamaican and colonial Christian morality, but Stolzoff is too quick to see a strict oppositional relationship between Rastafari ethics and dancehall ethics. Nowhere is this more apparent than Stolzoff's section on Yellowman. Like Gilroy, Stolzoff portrays Yellowman as the entertainer who almost single-handedly wrested moral leadership from the Rastafarian reggae community and stamped out culture with slackness. This gloss misses the fact that Yellowman had several Rastafarian-influenced songs dating from as early as 1981, as well as numerous songs of obvious social importance. That Yellowman was able to contest mainstream mores using slackness, and do so by appropriating a Rastafarian world view, demonstrates that Rastafari was still a valid source of moral regulation in the 1980s. It also wrongly assumes that slackness and social critique are mutually exclusive.

Burton (1997, 138) offers the term the "de-Rastafarianization of the youth culture" for the turn from culture to slackness. This de-Rastafarianization goes hand in hand with "the shift in musical styles from reggae to ragga/dance hall, from dreadlocked prophet-singer to the immaculately tonsured, designer-dressed DJ, from ganja to cocaine, and from Ital to McDonald's". For Burton, slackness triumphed over political consciousness in the 1980s: "There are few signs in contemporary ragga of the political, or even the racial, preoccupations that powered the music of the Ethiopians and the Wailers: at first glance it is *punaani*, *glamiti*, and *glibiti*,[6] and not much else."

Burton seems to think that dancehall is all about sex, which it is not. But he also supports the dominant view within the culture/slack discourse that if a song uses sexuality or obscenities it must be politically and racially disengaged. He sees slackness as devoid of political agenda and unable to change the hegemonic structures of mainstream society. Burton's inability to see that symbolic revolt can lead to actual change, and his limited knowledge of both dancehall and its revolutionary accomplishments, blinds him to the fact, for instance, that Yellowman's slackness led to tangible benefits for the albino community. Slackness is what made Yellowman the world's top deejay and Yellowman used slackness to contest dominant racial hierarchies and subvert mainstream notions of sexuality. By doing so, people with albinism in Jamaica have gained social credibility. Yellowman also sang non-slack openly political songs ("Budget", "Operation Radication", "Free Africa") and critiqued mainstream society and government from behind the veil of slackness ("Galong Galong Galong", "Gone a South Africa"). Burton is complicit in the description of dancehall as the de-evolution of roots reggae and uses slackness as the scapegoat to do it.

Finally, Tafari-Ama (2019) follows these scholars in viewing Marley as a fulcrum between the culture and slack eras. Dancehall deejays in the 1970s had positive messages of social uplift and socio-political consciousness, but this focus changed in the 1980s with the passing of Bob Marley and the entrance of Yellowman. For Tafari-Ama, Yellowman changes reggae and pulls it away from cultural consciousness into a realm filled with slackness.

Yellowman has been constructed by the media and scholarly interpretations as the King of Slack whose musical output has most often been interpreted as hedonistic party music lacking any political and social critique or authentic religious sentiment. Tied up in this representation is the evaluative judgement that journalists and scholars have often made where they treat dancehall as antithetical to roots reggae and ignore the possibility that slackness can carry with it social critique. I have shown here that there is an established tradition of moving back and forth between slackness and culture in reggae, and deconstructed the notion that dancehall reggae is a de-evolution of roots reggae, a lesser cultural form not to be taken seriously because of its focus on violence, materialism, sex and pleasure and seeming lack of spiritual or cultural themes.

CHAPTER 13

Yellowman, Slackness and Social Critique

BY 1981 YELLOWMAN WAS THE LEADER OF THE slackness movement, despised by the upper classes and the institutions that enforced traditional morals. He was very adept at shocking society by crossing racial, gender and moral boundaries – as a person with albinism he was not supposed to be in the limelight, nor was he supposed to be sexually virile and boastful. Scandal for Yellowman was a promotional tool. But unlike calypsonians, who spent considerable energies roasting the upper classes with details of intimate exploits every year during the carnival season in the calypso tents, he was the scandal.

Yellowman's popularity among the lower classes was predicated on the fact that he could disturb elite society; he was a voice for the underprivileged and a good comedian too. He disguised social criticism with wit, double entendre, and slackness. Yellowman obviously took pleasure in being the slackest deejay, and saw himself in a leadership role in society with the ability to use his controversial status to put forward an alternative to the mainstream value system.

Whereas the previous chapter surveyed journalists and scholars who positioned slackness in opposition to social or political activism, slackness and social protest need not be separate.[1] Yellowman's slackness can be situated as socially engaged because slackness operated to bring about tangible advances for the underclasses in Jamaica in the late 1970s. For Yellowman's moral critics who refused to allow that licentiousness and social critique can go hand in hand, Gray (2004, 310) offers powerful proof of a conscious plot on the part of the ghetto dwellers in Kingston to invert the sexual norms of society as a protest to a racist and classist system. Gray defines slackness as "indecency, public sexual licence, moral degeneracy and erotic lawlessness among the rebellious black poor" and argues that slackness enabled lower-class blacks to exhibit control over their own value system and openly refuse society's dominant definitions of civility. He further explains, "Slackness is a form of sexual transgression and as such was merely another repertoire employed by the black lumpenproletariat in its ongoing clash with dominant groups. Just as racial identity and class allegiance disrupted social relations in earlier periods, slackness now provoked huge social divisions" (312).

By promoting slackness through dancehall, the lower classes were in effect denying the state the right to define moral norms by rejecting upper-class values in favour of their own. The elites saw the black urban poor as moral failures in need of salvation. They were mapped with racial-sexual stereotypes that attached unbridled ghetto sexuality to blackness and poverty.

Slackness in popular culture in the early 1980s divided the country; it was a symbol of a crumbling value system and civilized society, and of the poor crossing social boundary lines and threatening the moral order of society. Far from being just about the elite's embarrassment at what they perceived was the sexual uninhibitedness of poor blacks, the concern was about political power. In colonial settlements, sex and power were inextricably linked, and the regulation of sexual relations was fundamental to the colonial project. Sexual regulation, like race, was a form of social classification that was at the heart of keeping the rulers apart from their subjects.[2] In Jamaica, the upper classes feared the unbridled sexuality of the lower classes as much as they feared black lower-class violence, leading to the policing of lower-class sexuality as a tool of social management and maintenance of political power, as Gray (2004, 313) elaborates: "In this racially divided and class-stratified society, the more the black poor policed their sexuality and kept their erotic displays out of public view, the better were their chances of social approval and the more likely their inclusion in the community of the respectable people-nation."

Moral regulation by the state was imperative for the ruling classes to remain in power; sexual docility meant political submissiveness. A lower class who internalized the moral regime of respectability of the upper class would not act out, push boundaries or challenge norms. If the lower classes sought respectability in colonial terms, they needed to imitate the behaviour and values of their colonial leaders.

But by the late 1970s, inclusion in the respectable nation had become more and more elusive. Expressions of black nationality a decade before were retooled into expressions of black sexuality in the 1980s; both were politically motivated activism. These expressions of open sexuality were a direct threat to the power structures of society: once the poor exerted agency over their own sexuality, they announced to society that its moral sway over the black lower class was at an end. The poor were no longer controlled by a desire for respectability manufactured by their moral regulators, the church and government.

This experiment was not accidental. Slackness was not the result of moral ignorance or even anti-religious sentiment. Religious knowledge and morality ran high in Jamaica's poor communities and, as Gray (2004, 314) reminds us, "Sexual extremism in the slums did not occur because the ghetto poor did not know better." Instead, slackness was planned and executed with social upheaval in mind and, in the case of Yellowman, this upheaval was accomplished in conjunction with a religiously mediated understanding of correct morality. Slackness was designed to turn the elite's value system upside-down, to intimidate and to threaten.

> "Slackness" and the celebration of it by ghetto youth and popular performers in the 1980s seemed to announce to the society the end of its moral sway over the black lower class. In song, dance and theatre, orthodox sexual morality gave way to uninhibited celebration of all things libidinal. Sexual extremism for its own sake and as a repertoire for challenging social conventions now became the dominant form of expression within an otherwise variegated ghetto culture. (Gray 2004, 313)

Black sexuality was feared and therefore subjected to controlling mechanisms and strategies by the state, which, under a Foucauldian reading, produced a dancehall culture's obsession with slackness. In their attempt to repress sexuality, the state (a) encouraged discourse around sexuality leading to greater public interest in matters of sexuality, and (b) sexualized the black lower class to the point where the lower class adopted and believed this representation of themselves and began to, in effect, refract it back at the bourgeois. Dancehall culture, with its revealing outfits, gyrating dancers, crude lyrics, and popular appeal, confirmed for the elite imagination the racially embedded sexuality among the black lower classes (Gray 2004).

Dancehall did not remain safely ensconced in the ghetto. Its thousand-watt outdoor speakers bathed Kingston with its rumbling bass and slack lyrics. Dancehall was explicit in its attempt to re-colonize urban space by disturbing the peace of the upper echelon of society.

YELLOWMAN'S CRITICAL SLACKNESS

Yellowman harnessed the media attention, and the medium of dancehall he had at his disposal, to highlight the hypocrisy of mainstream sexual values. He ridiculed society's sexual codes and prohibitions while at the same time playing into their fascination and obsession with sex. Yellowman inverted racial and class hierarchies, subverted mainstream notions of black sexuality and espoused a sexual ethic that had more in common with sex-positive African ideologies of the body than with Christian puritans who privileged mind and spirit over flesh. As a slackness deejay, Yellowman was a tremendously successful satirist. He poked fun at the grand narratives of morality such as marriage and sexual propriety as means to gain respect. In many songs, he espouses the benefits of the married life, only to turn around and metaphorically break his marriage vows by singing about sex with hundreds of women. In Yellowman's reworking of respectability, respect is gained through sexual activity not restraint.

When Yellowman celebrates non-marital sex in songs like "Sit Under You" (1983b) or "Blow Saxophone" (1985a) he is undermining the morality of upper-class society and in doing so he is espousing lower-class beliefs and practices surrounding marriage. Marriage rates in Jamaican are among the world's lowest, a holdover from attitudes towards the institution forged under the conditions of slavery. Initially outlawed for enslaved Africans, marriage was later encouraged by missionaries who equated fornication with grave sin. They promoted sexual restraint outside of marriage as the key to moral respectability (LaFont 2001).

Yellowman internalized the respectability of marriage; he has a common-law marriage and several of his songs fashion him as a happy traditional married family man. He often sings about his wife Rosie and explicitly offers her more respect than all other women in his songs, even while he implicitly mocks marriage by desiring other women. This respect is evident, for example, in "Galong Galong Galong" where he chats "Me only trust my wife me no trust no other ooman [woman]." He theatrically re-enacts the role of the good husband – looking after the baby, helping in the kitchen – in "I'm Getting Married" (from *Them A Mad over Me* [1982g]). In the same song, he follows traditional value-norms when announcing that he will marry the woman he has impregnated:

> I'm getting married in the morning
> Ding dong you hear de church bell ring
> She have me yellow baby and I'm gonna mind it
> So take me to the church on time
> You gonna be my lawful wife
> You gonna be my lawful wife
> Say me fry de chicken and you boil de rice

In a later version of the song called "Yellowman Getting Married"(on *Mister Yellowman* [1982d]), he sings about the importance of marriage and his spouse, admitting that while some people criticize marriage, for him it is a natural part of life:

> Say that me wife is a part of me life
> Me wife is a part of me life
> Say some are married and some are divorced
> Some of dem a talk 'bout married life too coarse
> But tell you Yellowman de girls dem love the most
> For when it come to mic Yellowman him can toast

However, Yellowman also turns around and undermines the marriage project in several ways. In the above stanza, he seamlessly goes from speaking of the importance of his wife to bragging about his status as a sex symbol in society. On the original version of "I'm Getting Married" he introduces it by asking "which one a dem a wear de ring?" The insinuation here is that he has several girlfriends and only his wife has legal claim to him. He toys with this notion in a song from the same period called "Which One Will Wear the Ring?" (1982g) but uses the phrase here to lampoon not only marriage but any woman with hopes of marrying him:

> Me go a Haiti find two lady
> A when me come back me babymother hate me
> Man a which one a dem a wear de ring . . .

> Now dat de race is over and ting
> I tell you none a dem did get the gold ring

In the song, his babymother is angry that he has other girlfriends. He likens romance to a race where many women attempt to win a ring from him but their attempts go unrewarded as he prefers to stay single. Not only does this undermine the institution of marriage that was held up as an example of a respectful reciprocal relationship in "Yellowman Getting Married", it also overturns any gender equality espoused in the song.

Yellowman also recorded an answer song to "I'm Getting Married" called "Getting Divorced" (1982a) and the subject matter again subverts much of the positive view of marriage found in the previous song and this time reinforces gender stereotypes more blatantly. The institution of marriage is not so much lampooned here as, somewhat ironically, Yellowman complains in the song that the sanctity of marriage was not upheld by his wife, who is portrayed as a liar who never loved him. "Getting Divorced" then, reinforces popular gender and marriage stereotypes. Yellowman complains to sparring partner Fathead that he is tired of marriage because his wife is ruling his life, a far cry from the previous "me wife is a part of me life" lyric. Significantly though, while Yellowman used his real wife's name in songs like "Letter to Rosie" (1986b), "Mi Believe" (1984a), in "Getting Divorced", he is separating from a woman named Susan. This is in keeping with Yellowman's practice of bracketing his wife from the kind of disrespect he shows other women in song.

In direct contrast to "Yellowman Getting Married", we learn that a woman's place is in the kitchen and her role is to be subservient to her husband and any deviation from that role can result in physical abuse. The double standard of extra-marital relationships is also invoked; Yellowman is heartbroken because his wife, he sings, has three other men. Meanwhile much of his repertoire suggests that it is perfectly fine for a husband to have multiple outside relationships.[3] That the entire song is actually a farce on marriage, though, is made clear in the last stanza as Yellowman relates a story about visiting an Obeahman who tells him that his wife is sleeping with fellow deejay Fathead, after which Fathead and Yellowman join together in a humorous outro for the song.

Similarly, several of his slack songs appear to satirize the sanctity of marriage by celebrating polygyny. For Yellowman, marriage is not a sexually exclusive arrangement. And following from this, marriage is not thought of as a prerequisite to a respectable sexual union, as in the Christian tradition. The role of marriage in Jamaica is different than the one Christian missionaries intended: "It is not that people do not get legally married, but they understand legal marriage not as the legitimizing of sexuality, but as the bestowing of social respectability" (Chevannes 2006, 220). However, Yellowman continually ruptures the idea of the social respectability of marriage by insisting that respect and masculine credibility are better gained by extra-marital sexual relations.

A similar discourse occurs regarding the placement of children in Yellowman's songs. A self-described family man, Yellowman's songs offer two seemingly opposite readings of how society should regard children. Songs such as "Yellowman Getting Married" go against the grain of Caribbean music by espousing a paternal ethic: "She have me yellow baby and I'm gonna mind it." Next to calypsos that treat children like furniture, this demonstrates an enlightened gender politic. Yet in "Getting Divorced" he opts to give his wife financial support for childcare instead of physical assistance. In other songs, he questions paternity claims from former lovers, telling them that if their baby is not yellow, he will not look after it. If they cannot prove he is the father, Yellowman somewhat crudely insists they do not stand to receive any more than a pittance: "Any girl who don't have no baby fe me / When they take Yellowman money, they nuh get no more a dollar fifty" (from "Life Story" [1982b]).

Slackness is one tool in the ghetto activist's toolbox to reject dominant society's rules and regulations pertaining to entry into respectable Jamaican society. Artists such as Yellowman carved out a respectability among the poor that was set apart from high society's definition of what is upstanding. Yellowman and his ilk in the dancehall took every opportunity to announce their values to the island using the latest technology available to them, from the loudspeakers of nightly dancehall lawns to the dubplates and records issuing continually from the island's many studios and labels. He infiltrated public space with underclass values in a way heretofore impossible and helped to mainstream dancehall music around the world. Using Gray's (2004) theoretical framework of slackness, Yellowman's lasciviousness can also be interpreted as the politically attuned project of a social activist.

YELLOWMAN'S AFROCENTRIC SLACKNESS

Yellowman's slackness is also aligned with Afrocentric values. Morality in Jamaica has been historically subject to Eurocentric value judgements that belittle African-derived customs and culture while espousing the superiority of European religion and morality (Nettleford 1974).[4] Yellowman's subversion of Eurocentrism is filtered through his engagement with Rastafari. Since its inception, Rastafari has asked fundamental questions about the relevance of Western values to the Afro-Caribbean identity. By confronting Western values with African-derived values, Rastafarians have debunked the myth that everything African is worthless and everything European is superior.

Yellowman's continual insistence that he sees no difference between slack and culture, that he can chat both, and that slackness to him is culture, are modern manifestations of the struggle to overturn the prevalence of Western values and publicize an African-derived body ethic. Yellowman routinely employs Rastafarian moral rhetoric in his songs in his attempt to subvert Eurocentrism. Rastas were among the first West Indians to establish an alternative system to the Eurocentric myth of superiority. In the early 1980s, Yellowman was among the youth who, according to Nettleford (1974), were in search of values to "legitimize their militancy and protest". They found in Rastafarian doctrine and lifestyle an Afrocentric value system that validated their oppositional politics. Yellowman's two weapons against a racist Eurocentric society were his self-respect and his talent. He used these to fight European values and espoused an Afrocentric value system, not just in his talk of sexual celebration, but in his songs that situate Africa and Haile Selassie as the centre of the sacred cosmos.

YELLOWMAN'S RUDE LANGUAGE

Yellowman's use of rude language is similar to Rastafarian verbal rituals used to contest colonial authority and values. Rastafari uses language, and at times vulgarity, to subvert colonial authority by creating disorder in society with the intent, in some cases, of establishing a new order (Chevannes 2006; Pollard 2000; Slone 2003). Dread talk, the name of Rasta-speech, is "stepped up" Patwa to be able to convey the urgent message of protest (Pollard 2000, 31). Offensive "word weapons" are used to assault the social order, such as expletives that focus on the vagina ("bomboclaat") or anus ("raasclaat").[5] Peter Tosh, for instance, titled a song "Bumbo Klaat" to ridicule mainstream aversion to *maledicta*. Dread talk reflects the speaker's resistance to oppression (historical/colonial and economic) with the intent to destroy the legitimacy of standard English and reclaim the African way of perceiving the world, or, in other words, decolonization (Chevannes 2006; Pollard 2000; Slone 2003). Dread talk and Patwa are used to control the identity of the speaker; the language is more suited to their message and mindset because they have what Alleyne (1988) calls deep structural ties to Africa.

These speech acts are cogent political statements by political activists. In the words of Rastafarian musician Count Ossie, "We were fighting colonialism and oppression but not with gun and bayonet, but wordically, and culturally" (quoted in Pollard 2000, 32). Yellowman, like many reggae musicians who either self-identify as Rasta or are sympathetic to the movement, continues this tradition through the employment of Rastafari symbols and language.[6] He also regularly incorporates Rasta-style *maledicta* into his lyrics. Yellowman's profanity disturbs common notions of decency, particularly in the public sphere.

Yellowman's use of slackness and his insistence that sexual content should be free to be sung in public space is about more than just entertaining a crowd. Yellowman intended to disrupt society and took pleasure in doing so. He promoted an alternative lifestyle, one that society deemed immoral but that he interpreted as clean and upstanding. Further to this, following Rastafarian artists like Peter Tosh and Bob Marley, Yellowman saw himself as a messenger promoting a message of happiness through sexual pleasure and fighting mainstream culture with ghetto culture. For Yellowman, society could be transformed through the breaking down of prudish Victorian attitudes towards sex and marriage.

Yellowman's slackness is an example of how the Jamaican poor black underclasses in the late 1970s contested the moral sway of the elites. Yellowman's sex lyrics contested the colonial-derived Jamaicanness of the upper classes and his foul sexual language can be contextualized in the Rastafarian tradition of employing curses, rude language, and Afrocentric dread talk as political protest to disturb polite society. Ironically, at a time when critics and reggae fans were lamenting the loss of roots and culture, and condemning Yellowman as the lewd foul-mouthed digital dancehall don (equating change in technology with change in content), Yellowman was (a) continuing musical traditions found extensively in roots reggae such as versioning older riddims, updating older lyrics and using the latest available technology, (b) continuing a cultural discourse and maintaining many of the themes, ideologies and body/gender politics espoused by Rastafarian artists in the 1970s, and (c) promoting a discourse on religion and sexuality in the public sphere.

CHAPTER 14

Yellowman as Moral Regulator

Come fe teach the truth the right nuh come fe teach the wrong . . .
Ah some of dem have it in their intention
Turn dem back pon Jah law, upon de Rastaman
And shout out to everyone "I want to be a lesbian" . . .
Put de whole a dem inna old dustpan
And tell the truck driver galong galong galong
　　—Yellowman, "Galong Galong Galong" (1985a)[1]

YELLOWMAN USES SEXUALLY SUGGESTIVE LYRICS TO TRACE MORAL shortcomings for his audience with the purpose of espousing correct sexual behaviour, which in this case is based on creole sexual ethics (LaFont 2001). In songs like "Galong Galong Galong", he frames these as Rastafarian sexual values. The Caribbean discursive apparatus known as tracing is a means for Yellowman to change his representation from that of an outsider by drawing on established cultural moral tropes: the evils of homosexuality, prostitution, pornography and deceptive women. The song, which can be translated as "get lost" or "go away", calls out practitioners of sexual tastes that are abnormal according to creole sexual ethics using biblical imagery. But Yellowman goes further and sets up a superior morality that, according to his songs, is based on Rastafari. He positions himself as a moral teacher espousing correct sexual ethics, from the point of view of Rastafari, which condemns non-heteronormative sexualities and sexual practices. When contextualized with Yellowman's use of Rastafari and the Jamaican practice of tracing, "Galong Galong Galong" presents an example of how he engages in moral regulation through dancehall and further illustrates how slackness functions in Yellowman's material.

"GALONG GALONG GALONG"

"Galong Galong Galong" was first released in 1985 and was a perennial staple of Yellowman's live shows. He omitted the song from British concerts during the late 1980s because of its anti-Thatcher content – he says that he was asked to do this by promoters so as not to draw the attention of the authorities. These days, according to his manager and keyboardist Simeon Stewart, the song only occasionally makes it onto the set list at Yellowman's behest. The lyric is delivered rapidly and in heavy Patwa making it difficult for foreign audiences to catch the words and many, no doubt, have missed the homophobia, masochism, sexism, and violence included in the song. It remains, however, a prime example of Afro-Jamaican sexual ethics packaged in a popular culture art form with the intention of reiterating a strict ethical Jamaican moral code over and against immoral foreign influences.

The song uses tracing about sexual deviancy to police the behaviour of homosexuals, prostitutes, pornographers and the political leaders of the United Kingdom and the United States. The lyric is framed by its introductory statement: "Come fe teach the truth the right, nuh come fe teach the wrong." Yellowman establishes himself as a moral educator who has a claim to truth and knowledge. He continues the chat by stating biblical truths: "David slew Goliath, Sampson was strong." The use of the Bible underscores his claim to religious or revealed truth. That he is speaking on behalf of, or from the position of, Rastafari is made clear a few stanzas later through the invocation of Jah ("Now me give me thanks and praise to Jah the only one / And due to Jah protection me no walk with no weapon"). He is informing the listener that the values of the song are religiously prescribed. He also likens the sexual freedoms of the West to the wickedness of Sodom and Gomorrah, furthering the understanding that Yellowman positions himself on privileged moral ground as he condemns the sexualities of others.

His sense of divine protection and righteousness is bolstered by the power of the spoken word and the Bible: "If I ever approached by a dirty Babylon / All me do me chant Psalms 2, 3 and 21." Here "Babylon" is meant as anyone who contravenes Rastafarian authority; the term at times – and this could be one of them – also refers to the police. When the Bible shows up in Yellowman's writing, it is a symbol for roots and culture:

> Natty trod into the jungles of Africa
> He open the Bible so he read up a chapter
> Started to chant up the roots and culture
> Tell it to the brothers and he tell it to the sister"
> ("Natty Sat upon the Rock" [1982d])

And in this lyric from "This Old Man" (1983d), "Me under me roots and plus me culture / Open the Bible me read up the scripture." Rastafarians engage with the Christian Bible outside of the Christian tradition (Erskine 2005). Likewise, when Yellowman draws on scripture, he is not doing so to invoke Christianity but very often the opposite – to censure it. "Fools Go to Church on Sunday" (1982c), for instance, charges the Christian preacher with greed, theft, materialism, false prophecy and even adultery, yet contrasts this portrayal of Christianity with a more wholesome image of Rastafari based on meditations on the Bible, Zion, Africa, Jah and the community. For Yellowman, then, the use of the Bible gives him moral authority outside of Christianity – derived through his mobilization of Rastafarian symbols – to pronounce judgements via tracing in the song.

In addition to using Biblical authority, he cites "Jah law" without ever detailing what this is. The evildoers in the song have turned their backs on divine law and upon the Rastaman – perhaps meaning Jah or Selassie himself (whose pre-throne title and name was Ras Tafari) – but also the values of Rastafari in general. In the song, he calls upon Jah law to admonish corruption, and clarify what is morally correct and incorrect. It is normal for reggae artists to draw on Rastafari when making moral points, and in this way Yellowman is part of a long-established position. As I will show further, there are added dimensions here that go beyond moral regulation. First, however, I want to situate Yellowman in the dancehall tradition of moral regulation and unpack exactly what kinds of sexual mores Yellow-man's songs either promote or disparage.

CREOLE SEXUAL ETHICS

Jamaican popular culture is intolerant of liberal sexual ethics; a quick listen to any number of the slack lyrics from deejays such as Vybz Kartel, Mavado, Bounty Killer, Spragga Benz or Beenie Man will tell you this much. There is a trend in dancehall reggae for artists to see themselves as morality police and civil educators of proper sexual conduct, condemning any act they feel is immoral as a foreign influence (Saunders 2003). Homosexuality in Jamaica, for instance, is commonly thought of as a sexual proclivity introduced by European contact. Therefore, dancehall artists who release homophobic songs can be understood as moral regulators in a battle against what they see as a sort of cultural imperialism – foreign moralities being unfairly foisted upon them (Cooper 2004; Saunders 2003; Sharpe and Pinto 2006).[2] Far from being a new phenomenon, the practice of moral regulation by Caribbean musicians employing sexual narrative has a long history. Popular culture in the Caribbean is a crucial site where cultural values are policed and maintained.

What are these values exactly? Yellowman's sexual ethics fit well within the parameters laid out by Suzanne LaFont (2001) in her discussion of creole sexuality – an ideology that draws on African and European body politics and treats sex as a natural part of human pleasure but within the confines of respectability. What stands outside of this respectability? The Jamaican usage of "sodomy" sums it up: any anal, oral or same-sex contact.

Contemporary Afro-Jamaican mores have been informed by the agenda of Christian missionaries to instill a dualism that constructed sex as sinful, and a very different non-dualistic sex positive West African world view. For most of Christian history, sex, sin and shame have been linked, since the only "good sex" was that which took place within a heterosexual marriage for the purposes of procreation. In the African approach, lust and sex were not treated as vices to be suppressed or conquered and the body was not vilified. For Africans, sexuality was not deemed immoral, and research suggests that sexual activity in traditional African cultures was viewed as life affirming, positive, natural and pleasurable (LaFont 2001).[3]

It is this difference in European and African sexual mores that led to the development of creole sexuality among Afro-Jamaicans as they adapted to sexual exploitation in the colonies.[4] Afro-Jamaicans, believing Europeans to be morally corrupt, rejected some mores, such as the church's teachings surrounding marriage and monogamy, but they adopted a Victorian sexual ethic that narrowly defined acceptable sexual behaviour. Notably, Victorian attitudes towards same-sex contact stayed intact. So Afro-Jamaicans had no trouble reconciling some non-Christian sexual behaviour with their spiritual beliefs, as Henriques (1964, 156) states, "the [Jamaican] attitude towards sex is hardly that of the ordinary Protestant country. It is essentially ambivalent. . . . The individual may often be extremely religious, yet in his sexual behavior contradict the religious teaching to which he subscribes. There is no apparent conflict within the individual, nor does there appear to be a sense of guilt."

This sense of ambivalence regarding the extremely religious yet sexually promiscuous is apparent throughout Yellowman's material and is shared in much of reggae and dancehall. His sex positive stance is strongly rooted in African ideologies of sex and the body, and dancehall scholarship emphasizes dancehall's reclamation of the positive body image and sexuality of African spirituality (Cooper 2004). It is not hard to see how Yellowman, with his dual deployment of sexuality and spirituality, is conceivably influenced by this African model, and that his treatment of sex as a natural part of human pleasure but within the confines of respectability, is in keeping with creole sexual ethics.

THE ART OF TRACING

Yellowman's slackness is designed to educate his audience on correct sexuality. Moral regulation is found throughout Yellowman's slack repertoire and is often coupled with the Caribbean art of tracing. Tracing implies cursing or speaking abusively and is a common discursive tactic in the English Caribbean among the lower classes (Adams and Adams 1991).[5] Tracing is so called because one party "traces the shortcomings of the other or traces out a personal version of the argument", thereby maligning their opponent (Sobo 1993, 104). Tracing is not unlike signifying or boasting, but has the added dimension of enforcing a shared value system. While an American rap artist might brag about their material possessions, Yellowman will point out some social or moral transgression his opponent committed to bolster his own normative moral position. He often couples tracing with signification in order to reinforce his moral superiority and ensure his status as King of Dancehall. Tracing assumes a communal or shared value system and, by calling into question a member of the community's moral behaviour or ethical judgements, the tracer helps enforce the shared social values, thereby repairing a breach within the moral order (Sobo 1993).[6] Yellowman uses tracing to call out immoral behaviour, humiliate those who engage in it, and offer examples of correct morality.

Yellowman's tracings both validate his normative moral position and gain him recognition in the community as a formidable deejay. As has been established, Yellowman spent his early life as a pariah in society due to his albinism. His use of the speech act of tracing should be seen against this background. As a youth, Yellowman was routinely subjected to public shaming in the form of verbal tracing; he fought back by constructing tracing and curses against his attackers using the power of his performance and position as a popular deejay to silence his critics and win over an audience.

Noise intensity, rudeness and the public character of the argument are important to this discursive tactic.[7] Yellowman's use of coarse language resembles tracing; his "dirty references" to sexual acts, for instance, both entertain the audience and instruct them as to which deeds he believes are deviant. In this way, he acts as a public voice reinforcing the moral order of society. His rudeness can also be read as a tactic to take over public space and dominate an argument. Tracing is a ritual that is dependent on an audience being present; it must take place in the public sphere for it to be effective. Dancehall, with its multi-thousand-watt sound systems, is loud, public, and, to uptown society, nasty. The noise of dancehall is disruptive on its own but combined with Yellowman's unruly mouth it was nearly impossible to contain. Tapes of live dancehall sessions routinely broadcast Yellowman's rudeness out of public buses and taxis for all to hear during the period when he ruled dancehall in the early 1980s. As such, Yellowman uses the volume of the sound system, record player or radio to carry his side of the argument into the public sphere and assumes a normative perspective whereby the songs are constructed as morality plays that pit "us" (local, black, lower-class) against "them" (foreigners or uptown citizens influenced by foreign immorality). Tracing allows Yellowman to be included in the local "us"; he was initially denied blackness but here again he presents himself as a fellow black ghetto dweller. His audience, he assumes, shares his values and so they provide support and validity to the tracing.

Tracing is often accompanied by humour that is employed for the benefit of an audience watching or listening to the dispute. Many of Yellowman's sexual insults and ad hominem attacks use humour to draw an audience in, entertain them, and create solidarity between them and the performer. By tracing his opponents' moral shortcomings in a public space, Yellowman uses this Jamaican discursive tradition to both police morality and establish his own normative place in society. He combats his outsider status by pushing others to the outside and including himself in the general populace. Given the struggles of his youth, this is no small feat.

Tracing used as a counterattack by an outsider has a parallel with another marginalized community in Jamaica. Tracing as "ritualized verbal abuse" is a tactic used by male gay market higglers in Jamaica as a form of protection against a society that demonizes homosexuality. Homosexuals in Jamaica are subject to verbal and physical abuse and widespread public censure because homosexuality is "perceived as a marker of difference from the sexual/culture 'norm'" (Cooper 2004, 162). Likewise, Yellowman used tracing as a counter-attack or even pre-emptive strike against a public who demeaned him as a youth and routinely criticized his sexual lyrics as an adult. Such tracing can be read as a tactic for Yellowman to gain normative status by "othering" those in society who have transgressed the established moral value system he upholds.

COME FE TEACH THE TRUTH: YELLOWMAN AS MORAL REGULATOR

Yellowman's album *Galong Galong Galong* (1985a) includes several occurrences of tracing and goes back and forth between blatant slack songs and songs that express moral concerns, such as proper sexual behaviour, the place of slackness in society and body politics. For instance, "Beat It" (1985a) was written in response to critics who saw in Yellowman's braids a parallel to gender-bending 1980s pop star Boy George. Perceiving this as an attack on his masculinity, Yellowman took aim at two of pop music's effeminate stars, Boy George and Michael Jackson, with the purpose of establishing his own masculinity and condemning cosmetic surgery and transgender fashion statements. Jackson's face, Yellowman chats, is not "normal" and he insinuates that the surgeries have caused Jackson to "favour ooman" (look like a woman). The song ensures us, as if we did not already know from the plethora of Yellowman albums that make the point, that many women think Yellowman is sexy; in this case the reason is that he can dance like Michael Jackson, though does not look like him. The tracing here ensures that Yellowman is presented as the normative masculine role model at the expense of Jackson's and George's questionable gender and sexuality.

"Blow Saxophone" (1985a), another track from the album, is a graphic slack song that depicts oral sex as sinful and traces the immoral behaviour of lovers who engage in it. Yellowman's job, he tells us, is to "get you on the level", or set you straight (pun intended). In true slackness style, in "Blow Saxophone" Yellowman describes for his audience sexual behaviour that is respectable and then enforces societal taboos:

> Me sex pon bed, upon de table
> Me will kiss you pon your lip, and kiss you pon your chin
> Feel up your breast and nuff caress
> But me nuh pass the navel, me nuh pass the navel

Kissing below the navel – referring to cunnilingus – is not part of his bedroom repertoire, and he is instructing his audience to follow suit. In the song, Yellowman links sexual deviancy with transgressing religious law. When you bend down to give oral sex, you are "giving your prayers all to the devil". Using the analogy of a two- or three-legged table for men and women, he tells us "You no fe eat under two-foot table / When you under de table you deal with devil", and reiterates "Yellowman going get you pon de level". "Level" here could be read to insinuate "straight", as in respectable heterosexual behaviour, and also "horizontal", referring to one of the standard heterosexual coital positions.

Yellowman sees himself as modelling acceptable sexual behaviour to his audience and condemns perceived deviant behaviour as oppositional to the teachings of Rastafari – this is made clear in "Galong Galong Galong". Like in the earlier example of using Rastafarian symbols and slackness to revalorize the dundus and portray Yellowman as black, masculine and sexually viable, this use of tracing functions to reinforce Yellowman's place within normal society and overcome his previously ostracized status. In other words, by calling into question some aspect of an opponent's sexual practices in "Galong Galong Galong", Yellowman is able to substantiate his own claim to normative sexual behaviour.

What we see in Yellowman's tracing in "Galong Galong Galong" is the deejay calling out sexual deviance from the point of view of Rastafari: this is apparent when he says "some of them have it in their intention [to] turn them back pon Jah law, upon the Rastaman". Yellowman is appropriating Rastafari once again here, this time to speak from a moral position aligned with the religion. Thinking back to my early discussion about the construction of reggae histories, this is significant as it is a departure from how Rastafarian sexual ethics have been depicted. Most scholars who have looked at Rastafarian sexual ethics have focused on the group's similarities with Christianity: patriarchal, conservative and misogynous with slackness seen as opposite to an austere Rastafarian sexual ethic (Austin-Broos 1997; Chevannes 1994; Cooper 2004; Lake 1998; Rowe 1998). It is Stolzoff's view that slack lyrics were performed by non-Rasta artists and defied both Protestant and Rastafarian mores. Slack artists, he writes, "eschewed their roles as social reformers, preferring instead to give the people what they want" (Stolzoff 2000, 104). In Yellowman's case, however, we see this neat binary collapsed. He positions himself as a Rasta singing slackness. In fact, whether he is a Rasta or not does not really matter – the point here is that once again he is presenting evidence counter to the way reggae history has been constructed. He uses Rastafari in tandem with slackness, showing that there is space within a Rastafarian world view, in his view at least, for slackness and a sex-positive philosophy. Stolzoff's understanding of the social influence of Rastafari and the trajectory of slackness in the early 1980s is representative of the dominant view found in reggae histories and scholarship. But whereas he argues that Rastafarian reggae music functioned as a sort of moral conscience of society in the 1970s and the religion's influence waned in the music in the 1980s, being replaced by slackness, violence and material concerns, I find in artists like Yellowman enough evidence to contest this cut-and-dried binary. Several artists who chatted slackness in the late 1970s and early 1980s were also aligned with Rastafari, in so far as they also chatted cultural and Rasta-centric lyrics. In addition, Yellowman's use of slackness for the purposes of moral regulation undermine Stolzoff's too tightly defined rubric of slackness. Not only does he insist that slackness is a populist agenda designed only to pander to an uncritical public, he asserts that slackness deejays do not see themselves as moral regulators, and instead are either morally neutral or amoral:

Slackness artists, most of whom are DJs, disavow being moral role models. They claim a stance of moral neutrality or a mischievous amorality, asserting that music is only entertainment, not a medium that should carry the burden of education and social reform . . . furthermore slackness artists do not claim the ethical high ground by talking about spiritual values. Rather, they are fully committed to the hedonistic path of individualism, sexual desire, and material consumption. (Stolzoff 2000, 163)

Far from this, slack artists routinely participate in social reform through the constant espousal of Afro-Jamaican sexual ethics in the face of foreign liberal sexualities that they see threatening the social fibre of the island. This is hardly a morally neutral stance. Yellowman is blatant about being an educator; dancehall for him is the perfect arena for education on correct sexual values, body politics and morality.

Reggae histories tend to deny that sexual desire and spiritual values can go hand in hand, at least as far as slackness goes. Yellowman's use of overt sexual narratives side by side with praises to Jah Rastafari was the initial entry point for me into this topic. Knowing something of the oppositional relationship in Western society between sex and religion, I wondered how Yellowman could so easily put them together. In Yellowman's view, singing about sex with a hundred women is perfectly in keeping with his religious morals. My point is that slackness does not always represent a critique of Rastafarian sexual ethics, but can be informed by those very sexual ethics. When weighed against Marley, it is almost preposterous to think that Yellowman had any sort of social agenda, much less a spiritual one predicated on upholding a moral order. But Yellowman often couches his slackness in a Rastafarian world view. In other words, by singing graphically about sex and demeaning sexual practices that stand outside the narrowly confined definition of Afro-Caribbean respectability, Yellowman articulates responsible Rastafarian sexual ethics. He links creole sexuality with Rastafarian sexual ethics through the crucial deployment of Rastafarian symbols and language. Slackness for the purposes of moral regulation are neatly laid out in "Galong Galong Galong", where certain sexual preferences are immoral because they transgress the divine order set in place by Selassie, or God, himself. "Galong Galong Galong", then, is not only a condemnation of sexual deviance using the device of tracing, it is a sermon on what is acceptable under "Jah law". And perhaps only in dancehall reggae could a sermon be X-rated.

So, just what kind of sexual deviance does the song trace? "Galong Galong Galong" contains three main acts of tracing chastising female sexual agency, homosexuals and the dangers of liberal Western sexual ethics framed in lyrics about foreign superpowers. The second tracing, against "sodomites" or lesbianism, illustrates how Yellowman has used the device of tracing the moral shortcomings of others in order to bolster his own superiority.

In the song, Yellowman is offended when women "shout out to everyone 'I want to be a lesbian'". The lyric tells us that this invites divine retribution, alluding to the biblical Sodom, whose destruction is often interpreted as punishment for homosexual behaviour (Jude 1:7). This was not the first time Yellowman voiced an anti-gay opinion. Part 1 detailed a clash with Nicodemus where the two deejays traded verbal barbs. Nicodemus tried to diminish Yellowman in the audience's eyes by calling him a dundus, meant to position him as an outsider. Yellowman responded by insinuating his rival was gay because he came from the tourist town of Ocho Rios. This was enough for Yellowman to win over the audience because, through homosexuality, Yellowman found the transgression that aggravated society even more than albinism. Both the dundus and the homosexual are freaks of nature, according to Jamaican constructions of the body and sexuality as heteronormative; the dundus because their phenotype appears to breach racialized understandings of body aesthetics and the homosexual because of their proclivity for non-procreative sexual behaviour. The severe homophobia in Jamaica made tracing against homosexuality a safe bet for any deejay intent on disparaging an opponent.

The insinuation that Nicodemus associated with homosexuals was enough for Yellowman to defeat him in the crowd's eyes and it importantly strengthened Yellowman's own masculinity and heterosexual credentials. By tracing Nicodemus for an alleged social transgression, Yellowman participated in representing the sexual mores of the masses and provided evidence that he was one of them. This functioned to both include the outcast albino in the body politic, as well as to regulate moral behaviour for the audience present; after the roasting Nicodemus suffered, it is doubtful any audience member would want to be seen as gay or even tolerate a publicly gay acquaintance.

The homophobic lyric in "Galong Galong Galong", like the clash with Nicodemus, allowed Yellowman to draw on the importance of sexuality as an identity marker. To question or challenge a group's sexuality reinforces one's own superiority; if one can establish that an opponent's sexual behaviour is improper then one can also suggest that person is inferior.

As a youth, Yellowman learned what correct sexual behaviour entailed through this sort of public tracing. He was introduced as a child to tracing as a discursive tactic to enforce moral regulations and learned what sorts of sexual behaviour are tolerated and how to use sexual deviancy to minimize a threatening contender. He remembers listening to coarse jokes and public arguments as a boy where a contender might chide an opponent by questioning their sexual respectability in order to turn the crowd in his favour: "In Jamaica, when you hear a argument occurring, the seriousness come in when you tell the guy about his mother, like 'suck your mother' or 'you is a batty man', or 'you suck pussy'."[8] According to Yellowman's example above, even more so than statements about an opponent's mother, statements concerning sexual deviancy (including incest) are the most harmful in an argument or tracing. By insinuating that Nicodemus was gay, Yellowman employed the most serious discursive means of social control available.

This sort of tracing is found in arguments, jokes, songs and even graffiti. If a deejay's set is not going particularly well, a sure-fire way to rally the crowd is to garner solidarity around an anti-gay lyric. I witnessed this at a 2007 Buju Banton concert in London, Ontario, when a deejay spinning records to a restless crowd in advance of Banton's set peppered the gaps in the music with interjections asking for all those present who loved their mothers to raise their hands, knowing perfectly well that no one could abstain from such a request. He followed this by asking all those present who hated "batty men" to raise their hands, to which most in the crowd enthusiastically obeyed. The action is an attempt to solidify solidarity among a fickle crowd and win support for an entertainer by playing into the crowd's moral code – everyone loves their mother and everyone is supposed to hate gays according to creole sexual ethics.

This tactic for social cohesion is common in dancehall. In Yellowman's song "Care Your Body" (1989), he invites his audience to share his opinion that skin bleaching is unnatural and therefore undesirable. Singing about the popular bleaching cream Ambi, he seeks to garner public support by chatting "Kick out your foot if you nuh use Ambi / And jump around you nuh use Ambi / Shout it out you have a healthy body." In 2008, several examples of anti-gay graffiti caught my eye in Kingston, particularly near the

Papine area. Graffiti sprayed onto grey concrete walls and at bus stops read "Don't bow / don't suck / hormone" and "Hormone imbalance cause cancer / gay-ism". This type of public art is the sort of impromptu educational tool that instructs society in proper sexual conduct and, again, employs sexual misdeeds to ostracize and police deviants. The directive against bowing or sucking refers to oral sex.

Yellowman internalized the lessons of his youth and absorbed the moral tenor of his culture to become, like many reggae artists, the moral conscience of society, teaching right from wrong through tracing and sexual insults. A further example of this occurred in the early 1990s in California. Some of Yellowman's anti-gay jokes sparked a controversy that ended in at least one of his shows being picketed by gay rights protestors. The incident was generated by a column called "One World Beat", in San Francisco's *BAM* (*Bay Area Music*) magazine by Jonathan E., aka DJ Jack Daw. Daw was responding to homophobic comments Yellowman made at a show he attended and called on promoters and concert goers to boycott Yellowman in the future. He wrote about the incident in a blog post on the now-defunct Charliegillett site:

> So, Yellowman came to town and for some reason I went to see him. . . . I had no great regard for him to start with, although a couple of his 12" singles had appealed to me over the years. I forget which venue it was at, but it was a fairly large one, and there was a reasonably diverse audience. Someway into his set, which was otherwise fairly unremarkable, he launched into a vicious toast against lesbians and gays, which went pretty much like this: "If you see a lesbian in the street, fuck her. If you see a faggot, kill him." I was completely and utterly stunned and so were many, but not all, in the audience. This was San Francisco in the early 1990s and it was not acceptable to incite street violence against gays or rape of lesbians – and still isn't, no way no how nowhere. However, it must be said that there was a certain amount of homophobic sentiment in the Jamaican and reggae community. ("My Yellowman Story", 24 February 2008)

Daw goes on in his blog to say that the next time Yellowman toured the American west coast he did not get booked in San Francisco. The closest show was in Santa Cruz, about seventy miles south of the Bay Area, "and famous for being even more radically activist in a hippyish way than San Francisco". Here is his account of this show:

About a week before the gig, I got a call from someone down there telling me that, because of my column, they were going to organize a boycott and have a picket line. I hadn't often felt that good about the results of anything I'd written. After the show, I called my contact and was told that the show had been poorly attended, but the somewhat amazing thing to me was that Yellowman had invited the protesters backstage and had apparently been completely bewildered by the whole thing. He'd claimed that he had meant no offence and that what he said was just intended as "entertainment"! (Ibid.)

There were other incidents of activism against Yellowman for homophobia. In a comment in response to Daw's blog post on 2 August 2008, Papa M recalled a concert in England where Yellowman repeated the incendiary anti-gay comments: "I DJ'd at a Yillo-mahn [*sic*] concert at The Zap Club in Brighton (gay capital of UK). He sang the same lyrics here and the lighting engineer (gay) slammed the power off and refused to put it back on. The show was abandoned. It was hilarious."

Daw later makes a point several commentators share, that it is odd that Yellowman would direct incendiary comments at one minority group when he, as a visible minority, has suffered greatly at the hands of mainstream Jamaican racial prejudice. Under the rubric of tracing, however, this is not a paradox. Yellowman was the victim of curses and tracing because of his colour and he fought back using tracing against moral transgressions he deemed far more serious, such as homosexuality. Yellowman would not liken homosexual prejudice to the racial prejudice he suffered because of the parameters of "respectable" morality – he feels that he never breached these boundaries whereas gays have. While he may admit that people with albinism and homosexuals both share or shared public estrangement in Jamaica, that is where the similarities end, as his moral respectability trumps anything that would separate him from the Jamaican majority. By continually referencing respectable creole sexual mores in his songs and performances, Yellowman firmly establishes himself as part of the majority, wiping away his former minority status. Thus, the discrimination he suffered was unwarranted, but the tracing he delivers about gays is, in his view, deserved.

Unlike many contemporary dancehall artists, Yellowman has largely avoided controversy over homophobic lyrics, probably because he has toned down most homophobic sentiments since the early 1990s. He espouses a "live and let live" philosophy in interviews and in concert and based on reading online YouTube and blog posts, and talking to and observing members of his audience, I believe that this is something many fans have come to see as exemplifying his total world view. Going along with this, he makes public displays of embracing multiculturalism, often saying that all religions are equal, and everyone worships the same God with different names. Most of his concerts that I witnessed ended with a homily comprised of what Stephen Prothero (1996) might call "religious liberalism": "Let me hear you say freedom, freedom, freedom. And remember, no racism, no discrimination. One love, one heart, one destiny, Jah Rastafari. And remember, I want you to love each other and be good to each other and be nice to each other. And if you can't be good, you can't be nice, you can't be careful, you on your own."

Many of his songs, both old and new, espouse this general tolerant agenda and offer further proof of a religious liberal world view. I am thinking here of "God Alone", "One God" and "Prayer" specifically. For Yellowman, this sentiment can be seen in a slight change of lyric, beginning around 1983, where he moves from speaking exclusively of Jah, the Rastafarian word for God, to describing the divine as simply God. It is also characterized by a coming to terms with his Catholic upbringing and so, even though he is a non-practising Catholic, he still feels an affiliation to the Catholic faith. In fact, he told me he considers himself a "Catholic Rasta".

Yellowman told a journalist in 1997 that it is this "live and let live" philosophy that allows him to forgive people who have caused him hardship, but also is a source of tolerance. He played gay bars, he said, even though at the time he did not condone homosexuality because "mi nah be prejudice 'gainst dem 'cause is just tolerance mi a deal wid, everybody has rights" ("Yellowman Has the Midas Touch", *Sunday Gleaner*, 31 August 1997).

Aware that he now has an international following that includes many gay fans, Yellowman has also taken the unorthodox step (for a dancehall artist, at least) to publicly condemn homophobic lyrics, welcome the support of his gay fans, and denounce discrimination against the LGBTQ+ community. I do not point this out to downplay, minimize, or offer an apology for his earlier displays of homophobia, or even to present Yellowman as a changed man. On the contrary, gay jokes are still part of his conversation.[9]

By using the art of tracing as a theoretical frame, we can better understand the nuances of Yellowman's position on homosexuality. Tracing is not dependent on a truthful or even logical argument. The winner of the argument is the person who stands up for moral correctness. As such, in "Galong Galong Galong", as in the example of statements made from the stage in San Francisco, Yellowman used anti-gay statements for the purposes of moral regulation and entertainment but did not necessarily direct them at or see them connected to actual persons. Such tracing allows Yellowman to defend a strict sexually conservative ethic – and garner support from his home base – but, in his mind at least, may have no implications for actual gay people. Yellowman instructs his manager, for instance, to respond in kind to email from gay fans and enjoys the fact that he has gay fans but this does not mean that he has permanently shelved songs like "Galong Galong Galong". Anti-gay tracing, like tracing against oral sex, is more about the perception of moral superiority than any moral truth. This is how Yellowman can espouse a live-and-let-live religious liberalism while tracing the wrongdoings of others at the same time.

For Yellowman, tracing is more about establishing for himself normative social status – meaning heterosexual, masculine, black – and claiming a superior moral consciousness in a society that routinely demeaned him for his lack of sexuality, race and masculinity and portrayed him as public enemy number one for his antisocial slackness. Due to the value Western societies place on sexuality as an identity marker, he can get away with changing his representation by simply focusing on his sexuality in his songs.

Yellowman was consciously concerned with putting into the public sphere an understanding of sexual ethics drawn from creole sexual mores for the purposes of regulating correct sexual behaviour in society and establishing for himself normative social status. The song "Galong Galong Galong" demonstrates how slackness was employed to condemn sexual behaviour deemed unrespectable by Afro-Jamaican standards. The song also draws on Yellowman's mobilization of a Rastafarian religious world view by aligning respectable sexual behaviour with religiously prescribed values, or "Jah law", whereas sexual deviancy is ascribed to satanic influence.

Slackness and sexuality often function in Yellowman's songs as an insult to, or attack on, his critics and rivals. By using the Caribbean rhetorical technique known as tracing, Yellowman outlined the moral failings of subjects he deemed immoral while at the same time strengthening the validity of his own sex-positive world view. Tracing at once ostracizes the beliefs of the opponent and substantiates Yellowman's claim to normative sexual behaviour. By espousing the sexual ethics of his peers, Yellowman also was able to validate his normative status in society. In other words, as an outsider due to his albinism, Yellowman was more at risk of appearing "other" than his fellow deejays, and any hint of behaviour or beliefs outside the accepted norm could be used against him by his opponents tracing him. As such, by adopting and maintaining stances on homosexuality, polygyny, prostitution and oral sex that were in keeping with the norm-value system of the Jamaican lower class, Yellowman portrayed himself as an insider in the community, helping to nullify his "other" status.

CHAPTER 15

Yellowman, Sex and Religion

You can't go to Zion with a carnal mind
Say dem de dirty mind you haffi left them behind
You can't go to Zion with your M16
Your hands and your heart to have be pure and clean
Clear off with the tin and butterbean
I tell you beg you pass me the Ital green
Come on now Natty chant up the roots and culture
Come and get it to the brothers and sister
Kaa natty sat upon the rock and watch de wicked dem drop
Sat upon the rock and watch de wicked dem drop
    —Yellowman, "Natty Sat upon the Rock" (1982d)

FAR FROM JUST BEING A SLACKNESS DEEJAY, AS his dominant representation by reggae historians suggests, Yellowman's sex-centric lyrics are at times paired with lyrics citing Rastafari, if not in the same song then on the same album. His concerts can shift between pious religious ceremony and hedonistic carnality. He regularly uses the microphone as a phallus onstage in conjunction with slack lyrics, but most concerts also include elements not far removed from the Pentecostal or Revival worship experience: the call-and-response of "Jah / Rastafari", group singing and religious instruction. Earlier chapters touched on this. I now explore this connection in greater depth.

This kind of juxtaposition – sex and religion – would be unthinkable for, say, a Christian rock band, and creates tension when it routinely shows up in pop music, whether in Yellowman's era of the 1980s (think Madonna's

"Like a Prayer" video) or Lady Gaga's provocative 2010 video for "Alejandro". Katy Perry, who, given her own repertoire up until that point, clearly did not mind a little sex in pop music, took the characteristic socially conservative Christian point of view that "Alejandro" was blasphemous and told *Rolling Stone* magazine, "I think when you put sex and spirituality in the same bottle and shake it up, bad things happen. Yes, I said I kissed a girl. But I didn't say I kissed a girl while f-ing a crucifix" ("Sex, God and Katy Perry", *Rolling Stone*, 19 August 2010).

Yellowman is in no way mocking religion by combining sex and religion. For him, there is no dichotomy represented by the two. Like his Afro-Caribbean and African forebears, he is tapping into a non-dualistic unity of experience to celebrate the sanctity of human sexuality. As I have already shown, the mixing of the sexual and spiritual is not out of place in Afro-Caribbean culture, and the criticisms lobbied against Yellowman's slackness were informed by the same conservative values as those against Madonna and Lady Gaga. Just as his slackness was an example of creole sexual ethics, Yellowman's use of religious ideas is more than just entertainment. Instead, his pairing of sexuality with spirituality is in keeping with an Afrocentric body-positive ideology found in African diasporic religions of the Caribbean such as Rastafari.

What I find fascinating in reading slackness and religion against this background is the way Yellowman reiterates Rastafarian dualism in songs that clearly dismiss Christian dualism. Rastafarians have a dualistic world view that is shaped by, but different from, Christianity. Unlike the dominant Christian understanding of sexuality that pits the spiritual against the physical, Yellowman draws on an Afrocentric understanding of the body and sexuality that allows him to keep a dualistic framework of spiritual/ material but without the sinful body theology found in Christianity. Whereas Christian thinkers through the ages – such as Augustine, Aquinas, Luther and Calvin – often considered sexuality an evil to be conquered through the repression of desire, and privileged virginity and chastity as higher ideals, Rastafari has shifted this dualistic focus to a Babylon/Zion binary and displays little of the negative view of the body and sex found in Christianity. Further, the very notion of secularity has no place in traditional African cultures, problematizing "dualistic splits between the soul and body, heaven and earth, divine and flesh" (Douglas 1999, 132).

By focusing on Yellowman's mobilization of the word *carnal* in songs such as "Natty Sat upon the Rock" (1982d) and "Can't Hide from Jah" (1983e), we can see how he upholds a Christian-derived dualistic world view but has moved from the typical Christian oppositional relationship of body/ spirit to a Rastafarian theology where the body, as long as it is pure, can be included in the spiritual realm. I am not speaking of the body in the context of embodied spirituality, but rather unbridled sexual passion that, in Yellowman's interpretation, is perfectly in keeping with a Zion mindset. The significance of this is as a further example of the way slackness functions in Yellowman's music, overturning earlier assumptions that slack music lacked worth beyond its role as entertainment.

YOU CAN'T GO TO ZION WITH A CARNAL MIND

In several songs (such as "Can't Hide from Jah" (1983e), "Fools Go to Church" (1982c), "Youthman Promotion" (1982a), and "Natty Sat upon the Rock" (1982d)) Yellowman repeats a lyric that lays out criteria for entering Zion. His central idea is that carnal-minded people are banned from Zion. His popular refrain "You can't go to Zion with your carnal mind" holds a key to understanding how Yellowman balances the carnal and the spiritual, and by extension offers a way to understand how he incorporates Rastafarian attitudes towards the body.

Modern usage of the word carnal relates to the body and sexuality. Etymologically it is derived from the Latin *carnalis* meaning "of the flesh". Early Christian writers used it to mean "fleshly", which had a negative connotation because it was oppositional to the spirit following Paul in Galatians 5:17: "What the flesh desires is opposed to the Spirit, and what the Spirit desires is opposed to the flesh." Augustine follows this usage in *Confessions* when he states "So my two wills, one old, the other new, one carnal, the other spiritual, were in conflict with one another" (2008, 140) and further connects the flesh with sexuality in phrases such as "I intend to remind myself of my past foulness and carnal corruptions" (2008, 22). Aquinas's (2006) usage of the term is in keeping with Augustine's, using it to refer to sinful sensual pleasure and vices.

The *Oxford English Dictionary* provides several meanings of the adjective, some of which are derived from its connection to the body and sexuality:

"of or pertaining to the flesh or body; bodily, corporeal"; "pertaining to the body as the seat of passions or appetites; fleshly, sensual"; and, simply, "sexual". Other definitions offered focus on carnal as material and temporal. The prhase "carnal things", for instance, refers to temporal or worldly goods.

Yellowman's songs that use the phrase "You can't go to Zion with a carnal mind" can be read in several ways. This phrase could be a ludic tongue-in-cheek reference to himself. As the King of Slack, Yellowman surely had the most carnal mind of all, yet here he was preaching about the road to Zion. The song can certainly be interpreted this way – a clever jab at a society preoccupied with Judeo-Christian sexual constraint. Under this reading Yellowman is saying one thing to mean another; in effect telling us that he is bound for Zion even though society would deny him this because of his slack lyrics and actions. He lampoons Christianity's abhorrence of the sexual – the dualism of the body and spirit – to point out that the taboo is a mere social construction that he does not share. Indeed, within the context of his entire oeuvre, this is a natural way to read this song. Yellowman continually champions the carnal by boasting about his own body, desiring the female body, and lauding sex drive, physical pleasure and even materialism such as in the song "Walking Jewellery Store" (1985b). He often does this alongside material that praises variously God, Jah and Haile Selassie, and in general his juxtaposition of the carnal and religious is closely aligned with standard Rastafarian principles. Yellowman's entire project is nothing less than a dismantling of the centuries-old Christian dualism that pits the pleasures of the body and the physical world against the greater pursuits of the mind and spirit and as such is a cunning plot to undermine colonial Christian mores.

My research, based on how Yellowman understands his own lyrics, suggests a more nuanced interpretation of these songs. In fact, Yellowman did not use the word in a sexual sense at all. His mobilization of the term is closer to corporeal, worldly, secular, material, and temporal.[1] His own definition of the word is "bad-minded" which can be read as "unrighteous"; he offers the following example: "if somebody [was] jealous of you they would be carnal-minded". The song, then, becomes a judgement on people who put material needs and evil deeds ahead of spiritual concerns. Yellowman offers examples of the carnal mind: "You can't go to Zion inna limousine / You can't go to Zion with your M16" (From "Youthman Promotion" [1982a]), or "You can't go to Zion with your ammunition" (from "Can't Hide from Jah" [1983e] and "Fools Go to Church" [1982c]). If you follow the various trajectories of Yellowman's songs, however, you can get to Zion even if you sing graphically sexual songs about your coital talents ("Bedroom Mazuka" [1983c], "Bubble with Mi Ting" [1985a], "Morning Ride" [1982d], "Nuff Punany" [1987b]), brag about your one hundred sexual partners ("Zungguzungguguzungguzeng" [1983e], "Yellowman A the Lover Boy" [1983c], "100 Sexy Girls" [1991b]) and pine for a virgin ("Want a Virgin" [1988b]).

Yellowman borrowed the carnal mind phrase from similar songs of the early 1970s by Yabby You ("Carnal Mind"), Ras Michael and the Sons of Negus ("Carnal Mind") and Brother Joe and the Rightful Brothers ("Go to Zion").[2] These songs are closely based on an old Jamaican hymn but were reworked as reverential Rastafarian songs (Grass 2009, 181). Yabby You's version, for instance, uses the following lyrics from the Melodians' "Rivers of Babylon" (1970) (themselves taken from Psalm 19): "So let the words of our mouth / And the meditation of our hearts / Be accepted in thy sight, oh Far-I." Ras Michael's version insists that "Rastafari no want no carnal mind".

Just as Yellowman employed the Jamaican artistic tradition of borrowing and updating lyrics from other artists, his own lyrics have been subject to reinvention at the hands of his contemporaries and followers in a somewhat interlocutory fashion. His carnal mind lyrics were adopted by Damian Marley and Chew Stick in their song "Carnal Mind" (1995) and the sentiment in the updated version remains much as Yellowman had intended it two decades before.[3] This version announces, "Me say dash your badness, and your bad mind / The carnal mind, have to stay behind", confirming Yellowman's own linking of the word carnal to badness. For Damian Marley, badness in the song is demonstrated in much the same way as Yellowman: according to Marley you cannot go to Zion with material goods ("chain and ring", "portable phone") or implements of violence ("big rusty nine", "big .45").

Yellowman's carnal mind lyrics are an opportunity to examine how he can dismantle Christian dualism and replace it with a "West African model of wholeness" (Cooper 1995, 148).[4] More than this, however, Yellowman's carnal mind lyrics are indicative of another sort of duality found uniquely in Rastafari. Here the categories of Babylon and Zion function as powerful modes used to order Rastafarian truth and reality. Notably though, this binary, while still maintaining a material/spiritual split, remains body-positive.

FORWARD INNA ZION, BACKWARD INNA BABYLON: RASTAFARIAN DUALISM

Yellowman intended the word carnal to express negativity and explicated it in song by showing examples that are close to the meaning of the word as worldly, anti-spiritual and materialistic. References to guns and ammunition – and their associations with death and destruction – reiterate that carnal, for Yellowman, is the opposite of spiritual. This is more apparent when read against Rastafarian understandings of Africa, Zion, Babylon, repatriation, and death. Rastafari eschews anything to do with death, even to the point that words like "dedicated", with its homophonic link with the word "dead", are altered to "livicated" in order to emphasize the Rastafarian preoccupation with life over death. Rastafarians believe that they will enter Zion in this life, without going through death first.

The dualistic relationship between the concepts of Zion and Babylon – which represent the forces of good and evil in Rastafari – is a major organizing principle for the movement. All aspects of life are envisaged through the Babylon/Zion binary, including categories such as health and disease, sacred and profane, purity and contamination. People are also grouped using this dichotomy as a rubric. Bad-minded people represent or are inclined towards Babylon whereas spiritually minded people are inclined towards Zion (Yawney 1976). In Yabby You and the Prophet's "Carnal Mind" (1975), for instance, Zion represents purity: "Holy Mount Zion is a holy place / No sins cannot enter there." Likewise, whole categories of people – whites, Catholics, politicians or law enforcement officers for instance – can be categorized as Babylonians. Yawney (1976) suggests that this dichotomy was constructed by Rastafarians as a model to understand their situation of oppression at the hands of colonial and neo-colonial society, as well as to envisage solutions for their plight.

The Zion and Babylon symbols are multivalent. Zion is a sort of real-time heaven, part physical part spiritual, and is situated in Ethiopia and/or Africa, though its geographic locale is overlaid with Biblical terrain. As such, Jordan River might be said to flow through Zion. It is the domain of Haile Selassie, the living God. Africa, for Rastafarians, is the Promised Land, a both mythical and tangible Zion situated in Ethiopia. Rastas view Zion in much the same way as another Afro-Jamaican religion, Revival Zion. For Revival Zionists, Zion is both "geographic and existential, where Africans were ensured freedom, dignity, the conditions for authentic self-reposses-sion, and the eradication of European colonial authority" (Stewart 2005, 134). Drawing from this understanding of Zion, the Rastafarian interpre-tation utilized Ethiopianism, an already established hermeneutic among black Christians in America and the Caribbean and widely disseminated by people such as Marcus Garvey, Henry McNeal, Martin R. Delany and Robert Athyli Rogers. Ethiopianism approached the Christian Bible and the white Christian tradition with suspicion and reinterpreted biblical stories through the eyes of Africa. Common characteristics were positive presentations of Africa, a reverential self-identification of diasporic Africans with the African continent and its history, and a race-centric theology that understood God, Jesus and the biblical population to be black Africans (Gebrekidan 2001).

The importance of Ethiopia to Rastafari was augmented by its role in anti-colonial campaigns in the early twentieth century. The only African power to resist European colonialism, Ethiopia stood alone on the continent as a free African country with a black head of state (Stewart 2005). Indeed it was Selassie's well-publicized 1930 coronation as emperor that scholars credit as the catalytic event that sparked the establishment of the religion (Edmonds 2003).

It was this Ethiopian pan-Africanism that informed how the Rastas under-stood Zion and was influenced, to be sure, by the theology of black destiny taught by Garvey and others at the time. Garvey, the de facto generative prophet of Rastafari, preached an African Zionism that involved separating the races, establishing a black religion, liberating Africa from white control, black nationalism on a global scale, and the ultimate redemption of the black race. For the early Rastas, who were beginning to preach Selassie's divinity, Zion became a utopian concept that offered solutions to both their physical predicament (solved through repatriation) and their mental imprisonment (solved through an identification of Zion with spiritual freedom, heaven and black destiny). Zion, then, is a catch-all concept that encompassed heaven and Africa and everything these two terms connote for African diasporic populations: a spiritual homeland that offered a connection between the biblical myth-world and the historical Africa.

Alternatively, Jamaica, along with the Western world with its legacy of colonialism and slavery, is understood as Babylon. This too is a broad concept that includes all oppressive and corrupt systems of the world and injustice in any form (Edmonds 1998). Yawney has defined it in conjunction with the Babylon/Zion binary as "non-Rasta society" and notes that many Rastas separate themselves from Babylon by living, for example, in autonomous camps (Yawney 1976, 232). With the African continent able to represent Zion, the natal land of Jah and Rastafarians, Babylon therefore becomes its opposite: geographic areas as well as political, social and religious entities that are non-African. And while Selassie reigns over Zion, and his subjects are largely black, Babylon is the jurisdiction of the Pope – whom many Rastas have historically branded the Anti-Christ, Satan, even the head of the Mafia, and his subjects are understood as mostly white (Yawney 1976). The Babylon/ Zion binary mirrors the colonial project's own categorical distinctions but reverses the colonial hierarchies: Africa/Europe, black/white, non-Christian/ Christian, civilized/savage, life everlasting/damnation.

The prime objective in Rastafari is to get to Zion. But whereas enslaved Africans believed that in death they would return to Africa, Rastafarians claim that repatriation is something that will happen in life. Christianity taught the enslaved Africans to be obedient and subservient and wait to achieve their reward in the afterlife. Rastafarians – who not only identify as descendants of enslaved Africans but also see themselves in a similar scenario of "sufferation" at the hands of neo-colonialists – saw this Christian doctrine as a ploy to deceive blacks. Instead, they preach that Rastas do not die to see God, they live to see God (Owens 1982). Rastas downplay the Christian idea that sin is an earthly state followed by a sinless heavenly transcendence; transcendence for them occurs on earth (Austin-Broos 1997). This is realized in Yellowman's songs as the celebration, not the denial of, the flesh; not only are humans inherently sin-free, their sexual desires are not some devilish strategy to impede their spiritual transcendence.

Rastafarians, following the Afrocentric philosophy of Marcus Garvey, self-identify as African. Yawney's fieldwork in the early 1970s found that Rastas regard themselves as citizens of Ethiopia and, on this basis, refuse to partake in the Jamaican census (Yawney 1976). Yellowman includes himself in this; even though his skin colour is not black, songs like "Jah Made Us for a Purpose" make it clear that he still comes from the African land. Rastafarians have a religio-political allegiance to Africa. Leonard Howell, a prominent early Rastafarian leader, taught his followers that they were not under the authority of the Jamaican government or the

British Crown, but instead were subjects of their God-king, Ethiopia's Haile Selassie (Lee 2003).

As such, repatriation to Africa has been one of the main goals of Rastafari since the movement's inception, but by the early 1980s, repatriation was reinterpreted as either voluntary migration to Africa, returning to Africa culturally and symbolically, or rejecting Western values and preserving African roots and black pride (Murrell 1998). This has become realized as a common sense of identity/solidarity within the group that is predicated upon a movement-wide embracing of the African past, recognition of the historical suffering of slavery, a shared sense of pain living in poverty in Jamaica, and the common struggle for liberation from Babylon.

As a key influential Rastafarian thinker, Bob Marley plainly laid out the scope of the Babylon/Africa dualism with Africa as the geographic and spiritual centre of Rastafarian cosmology.[5] In several of his songs, such as "War" and much of the material on the album *Survival* (1979), Marley speaks of a final apocalyptic battle of good over evil in which Selassie will defeat the forces of Babylon and Rastas will be repatriated to Africa. In this eschatological vision, Selassie reigns supreme over creation (often referred to by Rastas as "Earth's Rightful Ruler") and Africa appears as a physical and metaphysical holy land/homeland. As the natural home of Rastafarians, Africa functions as the religious-political geographic centre of the religion while Babylon is characterized as the hinterland of captivity and diaspora.

A Rastafarian dualism between Babylon and Zion pervades Yellowman's lyrics thoroughly: Babylon is affiliated with death, violence, negativity, uncleanliness, unrighteousness and materialism and Zion with life, peace, positivity, purity, righteousness and the spiritual. In examples above, guns and ammunition represent death whereas Africa represents life. Yellowman sums up the Rasta ideology around this binary succinctly in "Youthman Promotion" (1982a) when he chats "Forward inna Zion and backward inna Babylon." Forward not only implies a direction (as in onward to Zion), it also is the chant used by a dancehall audience to praise a particularly pleasing song. Backward is an indictment of the unstable world of Babylon and suggests that Africans cannot succeed in Babylon.

PURE AND CLEAN

These songs, then, portray carnal as the material realm as well as a bad-minded urge or action over and against Zion as the spiritual realm that is only entered if one is "pure and clean". It is here we can see the beginnings of how Yellowman and Rastafari can include aspects of the temporal world (the body) within the spiritual realm. Unlike in Christianity, the body can enter Zion – seen both in the doctrine that Rastas do not die to enter Zion, and in Yellowman's continued pairing of the sexual and spiritual. The proviso is that it is not just any body – it must be one that is "pure and clean". Rastas reject the notion of a heaven-dwelling God in the sky that transcends humanity in favour of a God-man who is fully human and fully divine; a man rules over Zion. Likewise, Rastas believe that each African is a manifestation of the divinity; all blacks are divine incarnations (Stewart 2005). The allowance for divinity in the flesh ruptures dualism to a far greater extent than the Christology of the son of God because it is not simply the divine that can choose to adopt the flesh temporarily to visit the temporal world. Rather all Africans possess humanity and divinity all the time, whether in Babylon or in Zion. Repatriation to Africa does not change this (as death would in Christianity) and this world is not simply temporal, as transcendence occurs in this life and in this body.

While the body is not anathema to Zion, Rastafari does have strict codes around its cleanliness and purity to ensure an inclination towards Zion. Purity involves not only physical cleanliness but also spiritual cleanliness (Yawney 1976). Rastas have developed a physical hygiene rubric to keep the body pure that involves dietary restrictions, taboos concerning the preparation of food, elaborate rules concerning the preparation of and consumption of or smoking ganja and prohibitions against sodomy and surrounding menstruation (Saunders 2003; Sobo 1993; Yawney 1976). Spiritual purity entails living naturally and being inclined towards Zion and Jah or what Rastas refer to as "livity" or righteous living. "In Rastology, naturalness and purity are essential for conforming to the livity" (Stewart 2005, 123). Livity can be maintained through rituals such as reasoning, meditation and chalice smoking. "The smoking of herbs in a communal setting provides the rite of passage wherein one temporarily enters a sacred realm and partakes of Zion despite one's Babylonian attachments" (238).

"Natty Sat upon the Rock" (1982d) offers further ideas on how to conform to the livity: the "Ital green" that takes the place of guns in the song could refer to marijuana or the *ites* (red), gold and green – the Ethiopian-cum-Rastafari flag. Either would certainly qualify as necessary for clean living under the terms of Rasta livity. The use of *Ital*, especially in conjunction with the lyric "Natty don't nyam [eat] cow" found in "Youthman Promotion" (1982a), also connotes the near-vegetarian Rastafarian diet, again, a means to purify the body. In short, Ital refers to livity.

The song's subject, simply dubbed "Natty", an obvious reference to a Rastafarian, exemplifies clean living by going to Africa seeking spiritual enlightenment (the use of the Bible in the song signifies this) and begins to "chant up the roots and culture" or adopt and promote Rastafari as a life choice:

Natty gone inna Babylon
Kaa let me tell you fe go chant down Babylon
He left Jamaica and gone America
He left America and gone inna Africa
He open the Bible read up a chapter
He started to chant up de roots and culture
(Yellowman, "Youthman Promotion" [1982a])

The Babylon/Zion dualism is further demonstrated in "Natty Sat upon the Rock" when the same subject builds a house in Africa:

Natty trod into the jungles of Africa
Open the Bible so he read up a chapter
Started to chant up the roots and culture
Tell it to the brothers how he tell it to the sista . . .
You come a with your hammer so you come a with your saw
You build a lickle house inna Africa
(Yellowman, "Natty Sat upon the Rock" [1982d])

Africa here is conceived as a safe haven, a home or a homeland, whereas in Babylon there is nothing but death and destruction: "Inna Babylon a pure manslaughter / Me can't get no fun, neither laughter." His use of "pure" here could refer to an Ital person (observant, Zion-inclined) or pure in the Jamaican usage of "nothing but" or "only" (Cassidy and Le Page 2002, 367).

Other songs also go further in outlining purity, such as "Care Your Body" (1989) mentioned earlier, and "Beat It" (1985a), which is critical of practices that unnaturally alter the body. Yellowman's denunciation of body modification centres on purity and health. The *Gleaner* reported in 1999 that health officials became alarmed at the detrimental effects of some of these products when many people reported damaged skin after usage (*Gleaner,* 16 July 1999). He counteracts the unnatural practice by telling his audience about his own fitness regime, including early rising, jogging and push-ups in order to reiterate a focus on bodily health. Physical health, including sexual health, are part and parcel of the livity in Yellowman's philosophy of Zion.

The song also makes an important critique about how European beauty standards have infiltrated black culture to the extent that even black society thinks lighter skin is more beautiful. Charles sees this phenomenon as an example of low self-esteem among blacks due to the internalization of the hatred of black skin bestowed on enslaved Africans by their colonizers: "Skin bleaching is the contemporary evidence of the deep-rooted and lingering psychological scars of slavery in particular and colonization in general" (Charles 2003, 712). Yellowman's promotion of a natural body is in keeping with Rastafari's Afrocentric agenda and its confrontation of the white supremacist Afrophobic legacy. A natural or Ital lifestyle includes the avoidance of processed foods and beauty products, particularly if they can be associated with white supremacy (such as hair straighteners and skin lighteners) (Stewart 2005, 123).

Purity of mind and body are prerequisites for entering Zion. But in Yellowman's usage of the word carnal, it seems as though the fleshly or sexual connotation is omitted. He was surprised when I presented him with my interpretation of "Natty Sat Upon the Rock" – that it was a sarcastic and facetious salvo at critics of slackness that uses self-deprecation to make a larger point about the ridiculousness of the body/spiritual dichotomy. Obviously used to outsider's interpretations of his songs, he was comfortable with my reading, but insisted that he did not mean the word in the sexual sense.[7] In support of his own interpretation, there is no hint anywhere in his music that sexuality is antithetical to spirituality.

Yellowman's use of the word carnal, understood against the background of Rasta history and theology, functions to rupture the standard Western and Christian body/spirit duality. He upholds the dichotomous thinking –

the carnal is still evil – but the carnal is redefined and thereby Yellowman twists the Western usage according to a Rastafarian-influenced outlook. By insisting that "your hands and your heart have to be pure and clean" before you enter Zion, he perforates a truly dualistic understanding of carnal which would separate hands (of the body) from heart (of the spirit). But Yellowman includes the body here, just as Rastafarians include the body in their repatriation to Zion. And since for him this is not a tongue-in-cheek song, we can safely assume that Yellowman sees no problem with entering Zion as an adulterer, a sex symbol and a slackness deejay. We can see the connection of the idea of purity in Yellowman's slack songs with sexual respectability as found in creole sexual ethics (LaFont 2001). Indeed, in my interviews with him, he would often frame discussions of religion and sexuality by pointing out that sex cannot be sinful as sex is a gift from Jah, and only through the holy act of procreation do we all exist. This sentiment is also demonstrated through another theme found in many Yellowman songs where he insists that you cannot hide from Jah ("Fools Go to Church" [1982c], "Can't Hide from Jah" [1983e], "Step It out a Babylon" [1982c] and "Morning Ride" [1982d]). Yellowman makes no attempt to hide or obscure his sexual lyrics, which would seem to be an open acknowledgment that there is no need to hide sex from Jah.

Part of this has to do with how Yellowman defines slackness. Whereas in Jamaican society the word "slackness" carries a connotation of impropriety or transgression of the moral order, for Yellowman, slackness is just sex, reality and entertainment. Like other deejays, he often revolves between the term slackness and "reality" to describe his music. Reality songs depict everyday ghetto life – guns, sexual encounters, social struggles, and so on. By defining sex as reality, Yellowman is able to categorize it as natural or Ital, a part of the livity and in no way a transgression of the moral order. Slackness, like sex, is not impure so is not anathema to Zion. Another of Yellowman's defences of slackness is that we all come from sex. Sex is a divinely granted gift from Jah so to sing about it and celebrate it cannot be immoral or sinful.

JAMAICANIZING CHRISTIAN DUALISM

The carnal mind lyric is salient because it subtly twists a traditional Christian world view and refashions it as Afro-Jamaican. In a 1784 missionary tract, a

Christian missionary admonishes a Jamaican slave for having sexual relations with multiple women outside of matrimony and reminds the slave that "no fornicator shall enter the Kingdom of heaven."[7] Directives like this one regarding entering the kingdom of heaven are found throughout the New Testament which, no doubt, is where the carnal mind lyrics of Yellowman and his musical forebears ultimately originate. In their rubrics for entering heaven, the New Testament authors were concerned with materialism ("It is easier for a camel to go through a needle's eye, than for a rich man to enter into the Kingdom of God" [Matthew 19:24]) and general wickedness ("Know ye not that the unrighteous shall not inherit the kingdom of God?" [1 Corinthians 6:9]). The Pauline epistles in particular are interested in controlling sexual desire and immorality.[8] For instance, the King James Version of 1 Corinthians 6:9 bars not only fornicators and adulterers but also the effeminate. The New International Version translates this same passage as "neither the sexually immoral nor idolaters nor adulterers nor male prostitutes nor homosexual offenders" shall enter the kingdom of heaven. Similar rubrics for entering heaven can be found in Ephesians 5:5.

Presumably Yellowman is riffing on this kind of translation of the biblical verse but in his version fornication and adultery are perfectly acceptable in Zion, as his usage of carnal removes the taint of sin from the body. Body purity must be observed, of course, and this includes sexual propriety. For Yellowman, proper sexual conduct must follow creole sexual respectability. As such, fornication is fine, prostitution and homosexuality are not. But, unlike in Christianity, these sinful acts are not rooted in the body but rather in the inclination towards Babylon. In Christianity, the body is *a priori* profane and contaminates the sacred. The same distinction is not made in Rastafari. Babylon itself is profane but the body, as long as it conforms to the livity, is sacred.

As a slack reggae artist who employs Rastafarian ideologies in his songs, Yellowman's usage of the perforated dualism is significant to the discourse on Jamaican popular music which has largely portrayed slackness in opposition to culture, or songs that include religious, political and socially conscious themes. Yellowman's songs demonstrate that the slackness/culture binary is actually a continuum that closely mirrors Rastafarian notions of a sacred and profane continuum characterized by the multivalent symbols Babylon and Zion. As such, Yellowman's sex-positive or slack lyrics can be read using

Rastafarian dualistic ideas concerning the spiritual and material realms. Yellowman, in effect, puts slackness and culture together by including the carnal in the religious.

YELLOWMAN'S MARLEYIAN DISCOURSE ON RASTAFARI

Yellowman first became seriously interested in Rastafari when he spent time at Marley's 56 Hope Road residence in the late 1970s and cites Marley as a spiritual mentor. As a friend of Marley's bassist, Aston "Familyman" Barrett, Yellowman was able to hang around Marley's inner circle, largely made up of dreads. The close proximity to Marley had a significant impact on Yellowman and the Marley connection is an important one for contextualizing Yellowman's Babylon/Zion dualism. Marley was most certainly an ad hoc spiritual mentor for Yellowman; Yellowman finds spiritual sustenance in Marley's songs and life example, but it is his combined religious and musical legacy that has affected Yellowman most. Marley is the king of reggae and the world's most famous Rastafarian, the man who globalized the religion virtually singlehandedly. Within reggae royalty, Yellowman has come to see himself as a second Bob Marley, a title that others have bestowed on him for his contribution to globalizing dancehall. In "Poco Jump" (1998b), Yellowman situates himself next to Marley, the two reggae musicians who have been crowned: "Me no see no deejay fe take my crown. . . . They never take Bob Marley crown." Bolstered by the fact that he was called the king of deejays or the king of dancehall as early as 1982, Yellowman takes seriously his role in the Jamaican musical pantheon next to Marley.

But what is especially interesting for this study is how Yellowman's world view and message dovetails with Marley's, and particularly how Yellowman has come to frame his own music as part of a Marleyian discourse on Rastafari, purity and Zion. Both artists seamlessly dealt with the overtly sexual and blatantly spiritual in their music and both were heavily criticized in their heyday by polite society for contesting value-norms. Like Yellowman's, Marley's music not only critiqued mainstream society, it also offered solutions for the sufferahs living within that constrictive society. Marley's solutions were multiple: the end goal was to overthrow Babylon, a feat accomplished through faith in Selassie as the living God. Involved in this was activism in the form of standing up for your rights and chanting down Babylon – in short, staying proud and strong in the face of oppression and maintaining the livity. And what does Marley prescribe to do in the meantime, to alleviate the pain of systemic racism, poverty and inequality? According to Dawes (2002), Marley's invocations to play music and dance (in "Them Belly Full (but We Hungry)" [1974] and "One Drop" [1979] respectively) are far more revolutionary than they first appear. Dance for Marley is not a secular act, particularly when he tells his audience to dance to "Jah music" in "Them Belly Full": "the dancer is worshipping Jah as he or she faces the hardships of life in the ghetto" (Dawes 2002, 125–26). Dancing here is not escapism, but rather a ritual activity that invokes the power of the black God to solve problems. Similarly, reggae music for Marley is a transformative force, able to beat down Babylon, awaken those lost to mental slavery and take the message of Rastafari around the world.

For Yellowman, the solution was similar but decidedly slacker. Fighting oppression and chanting down Babylon certainly play a role in Yellowman's music, as does faith in Jah and promotion of Afro-Jamaican culture and pan-Africanism. But at the root of his world view we find an aphorism that contains the pithy truth, the kernel of his prescription for a troubled society. For Yellowman, in "Stand up for Your Rights" (1982a), the answer is sex.

> I beg you throw down your knife and throw down your gun
> Kaa dis is our island in the sun
> Just get one girl and go have some fun
> Get one girl and go have some fun
> And me a go nice up Jamdung[9]

Physical pleasure, exemplified here through the hetero-male-centric instruction to "get one girl", is on one level the release that can calm society but, on another level, a celebratory act of the enjoyment of life, fashioned as the defiance of a tyrannical system that keeps the poor ghettoized. Contextualized with his other songs, sexuality as a weapon against Babylon is a pseudo-spiritual solution. Sexuality comes from Jah and it is through sexuality that we reproduce – two of Yellowman's most ardent defences of slackness. Sexual pleasure is therefore natural, wholesome, divinely gifted and community-enhancing. Its opposite – celibacy, abstinence, barrenness – is decidedly antisocial in the Jamaican context. For Yellowman, sex as solution to transcend everyday oppression and hardship is parallel to

Marley's spiritual-rituals of dancing and playing music. They are examples of spiritual embodiment in what Dawes has called the "pseudo-spiritual world of the dancehall" (124) and are consistent with the Rastafarian Babylon/Zion dichotomy that does not degrade the flesh.

SLACKNESS/CULTURE: A PERFORATED DUALISM

Zion represents purity, a realm without sin or contamination. In Yellowman's world view, slackness and sexuality are neither sinful nor contaminating. The sexual body is still a pure body. The slack/culture dichotomy found in reggae mirrors this relationship. The dominant view is that slackness is antithetical to culture just as sexuality is in opposition to spirituality. But Yellowman continually perforates this dualism, just as he collapses Christian dualism.

As the first scholar to write about the slackness/culture paradigm, Cooper (1995, 148) draws on the Abrahamic creation myth to show the difference between Afro-Jamaican and Christian approaches to sexuality and the body. Whereas "the official Christian morality of the Garden of Eden" institutionalized the suppression of sexuality when a naked Adam and Eve hid from God, the celebration of the body in dancehall can be read as a "continuity of West African ideological traditions in the diaspora". For Cooper, a "West African model of wholeness" is a non-dualistic world view. This world view can be glimpsed in one of Yellowman's favourite lyrics, repeated in several songs, which suggests either the futility of the Eden paradigm or refutes its application: "You coulda never hide from Jah / You get away from man but you no get away from Jah" ("Can't Hide from Jah" [1983e]). Jah is ever-present so it is futile to try to hide. Similarly, slackness could never hide from culture even if it tried. Further to this, there is no need to hide sex from Jah; a believer who is Zion-inclined has nothing to fear. Yellowman, obviously believing that he is conforming to the livity, is guided by Jah in all he does and sings, including slackness:

> You coulda never hide from Jah
> You know why?
> Kaa I love Jah Rastafari
> Kaa everywhere me go a Jah a guide I
> No matter weh you do me say no matter weh you try

No matter weh you do a me no matter weh you try
A Jah Jah a guide I
A Jah Jah a keep me
Jah Jah over me him a rule over me
Jah Jah over me him a rule over me
    (Yellowman, "Can't Hide from Jah" [1983e])

The "can't hide from Jah" lyric is also found in "Step It out a Babylon" (1982c) and "Morning Ride" (1982d). In the former, Yellowman waits for impending salvation from Babylon by the hand of Jah. He has a vision of Selassie "and his angels" traversing the River Jordan, bringing love and freedom to "me black brother and sister" and abolishing war. Based on the spiritual "Swing Low Sweet Chariot", "Step It out a Babylon" furthers the binary of Babylon/ Zion where Babylon is the land of captivity and violence and Zion is the realm of peace, freedom, love and Selassie.

But perhaps it is in "Morning Ride" that this lyric best demonstrates Yellowman's view that sexuality does not need to be cordoned off from spirituality. The pairing is a shrewd but subtle commentary on the Garden of Eden incident. Yellowman recorded two versions of "Morning Ride", a song that duplicitously uses the title of a popular morning radio programme that was hosted by Fae Ellington as double entendre. His earlier version, recorded for Junjo Lawes at Channel One and released on *Mister Yellowman* (1982d), includes blatant slackness that details the sexual positions Yellowman would like to perform with Ellington. In the song, the radio host asks Yellowman to sing her a love song, to which he responds by covering Brooke Benton's 1959 hit "Endlessly". He then offers an account of a graphic lovemaking scene, presumably one he would like to re-enact with her: "You dweet on the bed you dweet on the tile / You give me sideway and you give me front way." Yellowman insists that the song became the radio show's theme song, despite its slack verse.

The second version (1984b), recorded by Lloyd Campbell at Aquarius Recording Studio, is Yellowman's attempt at cleaning up the song for his critics. He removed the lovemaking scene, but the song is arguably more offensive because it maintains its sexual connotation and adds several elements of "pure culture". Originally recorded over the "Rougher Yet" riddim (also known as "Love Bump" after Lone Ranger's pseudo-slackness song), the second version employed the far more culturally credible "Black Disciples" riddim, named for Burning Spear's song of the same name. Spear is unmistakably roots-credible and the use of one of his riddims is by no means accidental. Yellowman was obviously sending a message to critics and fans with this. Yellowman wanted to display his cultural credentials on this track so he added the following lyrics to version 2 of "Morning Ride" (1984b):

I say you coulda never hide from Jah
Cho man you coulda never hide from Jah
Is only Jah is my meditator
Is only Jah give I strength and power
Is only Jah Earth rightful ruler
Is only Jah give I strength and power

This version represented the clean version yet still was overwhelmingly about sex. The ride in the title was a blatant allusion to intercourse and anyone who had heard the previous version would be aware that the song was a "sweetly smutty ode to JBC Radio broadcaster Fay Ellington" (Stelfox 2010). When I asked Yellowman what the title means, he said, "Some people make love long in the morning. It is the nicest time, 'cause everything fresh in the morning." The inclusion of the religious verse in this context demonstrates Yellowman's belief that culture and slackness are not mutually exclusive. Taken together, the "carnal mind" and "can't hide" lyrics present us with a moral position that does not dichotomize sex and religion or the physical and spiritual. The Babylon/Zion binary divides the world into two realms but does not relegate the body or sexuality to a place of hiding from culture.

Notably, while society took offence at Yellowman's slackness, there is little evidence that the same can be said for Rastafarians. Some Rastas did frown on Yellowman's open slackness – Peter Tosh famously derided Yellowman's song "Shorties" as demeaning against women – but Yellowman's slackness shares the same life affirming and sex-positive morality as the Afro-Caribbean religion. His slackness was and is always in keeping with creole sexuality. Dancehall journalist and photographer Beth Lesser has made the point that Yellowman's slackness is not outside cultural norms:

By being slack, it sounds like he [Yellowman] is outside of some cultural norm but in fact he isn't because all of his slackness is within the culturally accepted norms. He's not advocating anything shocking; he's simply talking about adult sexuality. Yes, Jamaica is a very conservative culture but if you go back into mento and all the folk music and the African roots where sexuality is much more accepted and looked upon as life affirming and a positive thing, the censorship, it's very family-oriented heterosexual sexuality. It's not anything kinky or weird really. (Interview by author, 21 January 2009)

Rather than Rastafarian morality giving way to a hedonistic slackness in the 1980s, as reggae histories have claimed, slackness was in part derived from Rastafarian ideologies of sexuality. As such, slackness does not always offer a critique of Rastafarian sexual ethics, but often is informed by those very sexual ethics.[10]

Charting the terrain of the slackness/culture discourse is confusing because artists like Yellowman often shift what they mean when they speak of slackness, just as the term culture will connote different meanings to different readers. Slackness is short-hand for sex lyrics, but as used in society also implies general impropriety and vulgarity. But for Yellowman, slackness might also include poor government, poverty, and disenfranchisement. As such, Yellowman might say variously that (a) sex lyrics are not slack – because he does not believe sex to be an inappropriate topic of conversation, (b) sex lyrics are slack – when he adopts the discursive device of society to speak of sexuality, or (c) that what is really slack are lyrics and actions that fall outside the tightly defined rubric of creole sexuality (that is, sodomy) and activities that he deems are deconstructive to society, such as government corruption: "[Slackness is] government not doing what they supposed to do, like help education, help the youths, help the children, the woman, the unwanted pregnancy, the street people. Fix the road. They do nothing, that is slackness."

The ongoing "battle" between slackness and culture that is a common theme of reggae songs, albums, concerts and even artist typologies is really not a battle at all, though sources often depict it that way. The *Official Dancehall Dictionary,* in its attempt to delineate the difference between culture and slackness, says that the slackness deejay "sees himself as a social commentator. On the other hand, the cultural DJ operates as a social activist – a vehicle for change" (Francis-Jackson 1995, 191). Despite Francis-Jackson's attempt to maintain a duality, Yellowman and deejays who follow him and who mix the slackness and cultural tropes cannot be contained within these stringent barriers. Yellowman sees himself as a social commentator and a social activist.

Hope's (2006) typology of deejays is helpful for looking at the thematic array of songs in dancehall but still is based on a slack/culture dichotomy. Yellowman fits two categories here, according to Hope, the "girls dem deejay" and the "slackness deejay". Yet Yellowman has attempted throughout his career to break down these categories. That he can deejay either slackness or culture is the subject of several recurring lyrics. Here he is concerned with showing his critics that he is more than a slackness deejay and, in the manner of an astute businessman, is trying to widen this popular appeal to increase his market share. But in doing so, he always demonstrates what I see as his implicit agenda to perforate the culture/slackness antinomy, and the fleshly/spiritual binary. Several songs deal with this agenda:

Ah true man, me a change the style,
Ya mon, haffi change the style, Lord have mercy
Well, right now we gone South Africa right now
Kaa nuff people think say Yellowman can't chat culture and all them ting de deh
Me is a deejay mix everyting
When me rude me get rude
And when me don't want get rude, I don't get rude, seen?
(Yellowman, introduction to "Galong/Gone a South Africa/Jah Me Fear" [1987b])

When me take up de mic me started to chat
Me chat de culture me nuh go chat no slack
(Yellowman, "King of the Crop" [1984e])

Favourite colour man it yellow and black
Sometime me culture sometime me slack
Know 'bout me Bible know me scripture
Know 'bout me roots also me culture
Deejay fe baldhead and Rasta
(Yellowman, "Under Mi Fat Ting" [1985a])

The drive to define reggae as either slack or culture comes directly out of the European Christian derived dualistic mindset. The splitting of the sexual and spiritual, the body and mind, is an artificial construct in Jamaica adopted by the upper classes and many Christians, but actively and dynamically contested regularly in dancehall. Yellowman's constant collapsing of slack and culture is an example of his denial of Christian dualism. In Jamaican culture, the sacred and profane are not poles separated by a great distance. There is a continuum, to be sure, and each artist negotiates their comfort level along that continuum. For Yellowman, this collapsing is manifested in (a) his definition of sexuality as "reality" instead of sin, (b) his insistence that sex is a gift from Jah, and that we exist only through the holy act of procreation, (c) his insistence that sex should not be hidden from Jah, (d) his utilization of an Afrocentric model of wholeness that refutes Christian duality, and (e) his mobilization of the Rastafarian Babylon/Zion binary and its allowance for the purified body in Zion.

Conclusion

Yellowman's Slackness as Resistance

AS AN ARTIST WHO CHATS SLACKNESS, YELLOWMAN HAS been pigeon-holed as a one-dimensional potty-mouthed entertainer by those who are oblivious to the rich web of dramatic, humorous, discursive, allegorical, religious and salacious traditions of Afro-Jamaican dancehall culture. Like dancehall itself, Yellowman has tended to be misunderstood outside the country by commentators who are unable to see the complexity of his art form, often constructing it in opposition to roots reggae and writing it off as disposable noise.

What I have hoped to accomplish in this book is to illuminate multiple ways to think about slackness in Yellowman's music and, in doing so, present a counterargument to those who failed to see worth in his slackness or in dancehall. I have been aided in this by Yellowman himself, whose voice is integral to this text as an artist who works in this idiom and is cognizant of the discrepancy between how local and international audiences interpret dancehall.

Yellowman takes his role as an entertainer very seriously and loves to please an audience. This, no doubt, stems from his youth spent ostracized, relegated to the fringes of society. There are also financial considerations – slackness sells and allowed Yellowman to become the world's top dancehall deejay. But like all bodies of popular music, the meanings of lyrics, cultures and performances are negotiable, varied and changing. In Yellowman's life and music, there are nuances to his slackness that are generally overlooked, even, perhaps, by Yellowman himself. There are several discourses of resistance to be found in Yellowman's slackness. By looking at Yellowman through this lens, I have been able to explore meanings around sexuality, gender, race, class, religion, subjectivity, and representation in dancehall.

Yellowman's image has been constructed and maintained in the media and the scholarly literature as the King of Slack, a caricature that ignores the deeper critical discourses at work in his material. Slackness allowed

Yellowman to wrest his representation as an albino pariah away from dominant society and to revalorize the dundus as an object of sexual desire. Yellowman was subjected to racist and classist social biases that denied the dundus African and Jamaican nationhood. Slackness became a methodology that Yellowman employed to adopt stereotypical depictions of black hypersexuality and masculinity for the purposes of including himself in the black nation. Using slackness, Yellowman subverted normative notions of sexuality, gender, race, and beauty by promoting the albino as sexually appealing and hypermasculine, as having blackness yet at times trumping blackness in favour of yellowness (thereby both playing on and problematizing the socially constructed links between race and skin colour).

Yellowman's sexual lyrics were the most popular at a time when the underclasses in Jamaica were contesting the normative values that the dominant society had laid claim to in their definition of proper Jamaicanness. Yellowman's slackness, then, was more than simply crowd-pleasing antics: it functioned as an activist platform to contest the moral sway of the upper-classes.

Another function of Yellowman's slackness was for the purposes of moral regulation whereby he espoused a correct morality using, at times, extremely lascivious lyrics to demean dominant Christian attitudes towards sexuality such as monogamy, sex as sinful behaviour and the impurity of the body. He also contested liberal "non-Jamaican" sexualities (such as homosexuality) and practices (like oral sex). Yellowman instead espoused conservative Afro-Jamaican sexual mores. He used the Jamaican discursive device of tracing to critique his opponents' moral transgressions, bolster his own normative representation in the public's eyes, and model upstanding moral sexual behaviour based on a rubric of creole sexual ethics. According to many reggae historians, dancehall in the 1980s saw the loss of moral sway on the part of Rastafarians. But Rastafari does not share Christianity's austere sexual morality, and Yellowman's example suggests that, instead, his slack dancehall did not necessarily negate Rastafari. He presented positive expressions of the body and sexuality and espoused mores that were in keeping with Rastafarian ethics. Further, he mobilized Rastafarian symbols to chat culture side by side with slackness. According to Yellowman, and the lyrics of his songs, he speaks from the point of view of a Rasta in order to maintain a moral agenda through slackness.

It follows that Yellowman's music perforates the traditional Western Christian body – spirit dualism in favour of non-dualistic African-derived ideologies of the body and religion. By putting sex and religion, or slackness and culture, side by side, Yellowman undermines colonial binary categories in favour of an Afrocentric model of wholeness. The Rastafarian oppositional relationship of Babylon/Zion demonstrates how the body and sex in Yellowman's music are not anathema to Zion or the spiritual realm. Yellowman consecrates slackness, exults sexuality and extols embodied spirituality implicitly by continually mingling the slack and culture themes in his music. In doing so, he perforates the sacred/profane binary and the slackness/culture dichotomy.

This book began backstage at a Yellowman concert in Negril, where Yellowman stood alongside Bunny Wailer and Toots Hibbert, who, in my eyes, are the three essential building blocks of Jamaican popular music from the 1960s to the 1980s. Yellowman's success took him and dancehall reggae around the world, making him the biggest Jamaican celebrity for a period in the mid-1980s. I never cease to be amazed at his success, though, when I think of all he had to endure and overcome. He did not just start out in the ghetto, he started out in the gutter with all odds against a tiny orphan with albinism. Dancehall was his ladder up and out of this life of alienation and poverty and it is through the cultural space of dancehall that he has made his mark on the world.

Beyond the arguments about discourses of resistance in this book, Yellowman stands as a compelling story of human fortitude and one of the great entertainers of our time. I feel fortunate that I had a front row seat for a little while to watch him ply his trade, and each time I have experienced him perform, his exuberance ignites the crowd. In fact, if I had to pick a favourite Yellowman performance, I think it would be one where his sheer joy at his recognition and achievements is palpable, a performance where, instead of bitterly decrying the crushing inequity that he surely must have felt into his teenage years, he revealed the traits that endeared him to thousands of fans: wit, style, skill, and authenticity. That performance? "Jamaica Proud of Me" (1983b) at 1982's Reggae Sunsplash, where, after deejaying an uplifting lyric about his hard-won acceptance in his own country, in true Yellowman style he lets the audience decide his next move. "You want it in I sexy style?" Of course they do, and so he starts to chat "Me Too Sexy".

Appendix 1

"Galong Galong Galong" (1995a)

Come fe teach the truth the right nuh come fe teach the wrong

Know me as a MC me no come fe sing no song

David sling Goliath me say Sampson was strong

Him did fool no hell, him was trick by a ooman

Now me give me thanks and praise to Jah de only one

And due to Jah protection me no walk with no weapon

But if I ever approached by a dirty Babylon

All me do me chant Psalms 2, 3 and 21

Got to scare the hell outta all Babylon

Now me give me thanks and praise to Jah the only one

Now me age a 22 me age no 21

Me ongle trust my wife me no trust no other woman

Some woman love to tell me lie and some just love to con

They say "a you me love" that time they love six other man

Some fly go a Germany go make nuff grand

Outta the nasty business they call prostitution

Suck dead penis til it whole cock stand

Don't remove them mouth until ejaculation

Drink it down nice like a soup outta can

All because they want a car and house and lan'

Some a them spread their legs from yaso to Japan

Play with them clitoris in front of cameraman

Dem de kind of ooman don't have ambition

They pray for a cash more than their reputation

Well still I'm goin change up me conversation

Whether at me yard, at the microphone stand

Tell you Yellowman come fe tell everyone

So if I sound slack I don't care a damn

A some of them have it in their intention

Turn them back pon Jah law, upon the Rastaman

A shout out to everyone "I want to be a lesbian"

Feel up one another with them fingers pon them hand

Suck down below for ten minutes long

What the hell when the bitch them mouth get jam

The biblical days it did a gwaan a Sodom

But tell you Yellowman him know that wrong

Me no want me children living in no confusion

Call pon Jah law, you know corruption

You know Yellowman come fe tell everyone

Still again me a go change up me conversation

The biggest threat to man is the nuclear bomb

And who rule: Russia, America, a England?

If me have the chance me kill them one by one

Betwixt one a dem¹ crotch me a woulda plant atom bomb

Blow two seed from yaso to Taiwan

Me go shoot the next one² titty nipple with a M1

Full her crotch's hole fill it a radiation

Pon top abuse with a pump action

Put de whole a dem inna old dustpan

And tell the truck driver

Galong galong galong . . .

Appendix 2

Selected Album Covers

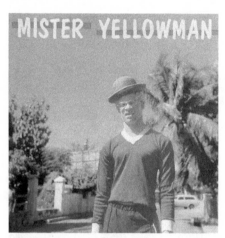

Mister Yellowman, 1982

One Yellowman, 1982

Superstar Yellowman Has Arrived with Toyan, 1982

Just Cool (feat. Fathead), 1982

Live at Reggae Sunsplash, 1982

Them A Mad over Me, 1982

Yellowman and Fathead Live at Aces, 1982

Yellowman and Fathead: Bad Boy Skanking, 1982

Junjo Presents a Live Session with Aces International, 1982

The Yellow, the Purple and the Nancy, 1982

King Yellowman, 1984

Yellowman/Purpleman: Show-Down
Vol. 5, 1984

Galong Galong Galong, 1985

Walking Jewellery Store, 1985

Girls Them Pet, 1986

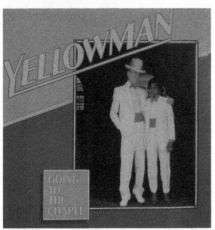

Going to the Chapel, 1986

Rambo, 1986

Negril Chill Challenge (with Charlie Chaplin),
1987

A Reggae Calypso Encounter (with General
Trees), 1987

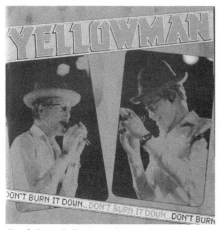

Don't Burn It Down, 1988

In Bed with Yellowman, 1993

Prayer, 1994

Message to the World, 1995

Just Cool, 2004

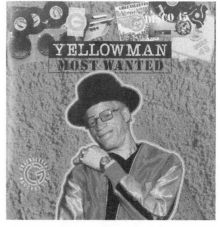

Most Wanted, 2007

Notes

INTRODUCTION

1. *Dundus* is a Jamaican term that in this context, and on the surface, refers to a black person with albinism. It is a pejorative term that, similar to the word "freak", signifies abnormality and inferiority (Cassidy and LePage 2002). For a full treatment of this term and concept, see chapter 11.
2. While today hip-hop is considered a music genre, the term originally referred to a group of cultural practices that included the music genre rap.
3. As Cooper (2004) has reminded us, non-Jamaican commentators tend to critique the role of slackness in Jamaica without regard for local epistemologies.

CHAPTER 1

1. Squidly Ranks and Welton Irie are deejays and were contemporaries of Yellowman during this period.
2. Don't bother loving me just because I am rich.
3. "Blueberry Hill" was the ninth most popular song of 1987 in Jamaica (Chang and Chen 1998, 228).
4. Hope outlines this helpful deejay typology and situates Yellowman in both the "girls dem deejay" and the "slackness deejay" categories (Hope 2006, 31–32). It is accurate that this is how Yellowman is perceived by most people but he has continually attempted to broaden this representation.
5. For more on the social stigma of albinism, in Jamaica see Carnegie (1996).
6. Alpha Boys' School records say he was born on 25 February 1957. There are other discrepancies with the school records, as I will show later.
7. Many of Yellowman's songs decry violence ("Gun Man", "Duppy or Gunman", "Tourist Season") or use violence in a joking manner ("Herbman Smuggling"). But a few songs, such as "Galong Galong Galong", actually incite violence against groups such as politicians and homosexuals. I look at this song in depth in chapter 14.

8. *Backra* or *buckra* is derived from an Ibo word meaning "white man" (Cassidy and LePage 2002, 18). *Weh*, in this usage, is Patwa for "what" or "where" (466).

9. Alpha records state that Yellowman began attending Alpha in 1967 and moved to live there in 1969 from Maxfield Park orphanage. This timeline leaves no room for his tenure at Swift-Purcell. Yellowman himself remembers that he was at Swift-Purcell from 1967 until 1971, at which time he came back to Kingston to live at Alpha.

CHAPTER 2

1. He also recorded the song as "Yellowman Getting Married" (1982d).

2. When I asked Sister Bernadette Little about this, she felt that Sister Ignatius's concern may have been misunderstood. "I do not think that Sister Ignatius disliked Rastas. She was very careful not to have their weed [marijuana] available to the boys who were under her care" (email to author, 28 July 2009).

CHAPTER 3

1. As will be described in the following pages, Winston adopted the nom de plume Yellowman early in his career.

2. For a good history of sound systems and dubplates, see Chamberlain (2010).

3. Wexler (2001) lists the sound as Black Mafia and says that Yellowman was thirteen, which would make this 1970. Yellowman insists the sound was called Little Mafia and it occurred in 1977.

4. The freedom bell was introduced as a party symbol by Edward Seaga in 1961.

5. A youth who helped set up and tear down the speakers. Willa was a box man when he met Yellowman and soon became his driver.

6. Apprentice.

7. McDaniel (1998) points out that titles such as King and Lord among calypso singers are colonial hierarchical names and that younger calypso singers avoid them.

CHAPTER 4

1. Many online biographies suggest he won this competition. Yellowman remembers coming second, the Tastee website says he came third, and a later *Daily Gleaner* ("'Stylistic' Ivor Wows 'em", 6 December 1989) article says fourth.

2. *Dulcimina* was a popular radio serial written, produced and directed by Elaine Perkins that ran from 1967 to 1980. According to the *Gleaner* ("Pieces of Our

Past", 8 July 2012), the show was so popular on the island that when one of the actresses died, her funeral caused road-blocks in downtown Kingston for hours. In the show, Dulcimina was a girl who moved from the country into Kingston but her name was often used to refer to the kind of suitcase she carried – "one of those very old travelling cases, usually made of a brown, cardboard-type material, commonly referred to as a 'grip' in Jamaica" and also has the connotation of something being "countrified" (Donna P. Hope, email to author, 27 November 2009).

3. The chain of events is unclear here as Johnson believes he may have hired Yellowman before Tastee's.

4. According to Yellowman, he had already been wearing yellow suits. I also interviewed a friend of Yellowman's from Franklin Town that said her mother made Yellowman his first yellow suit.

5. *Ray ray*: "and so on and so forth" (Williams 2008, 95).

6. All figures in Jamaican dollars. The exchange rate at the time was approximately J$2 to US$1.

7. Whether this was his first recording is uncertain. According to a 1979 news story, his win at the Tastee Talent Contest enabled him to record "Barnabus Killing" for Ruddy Thomas ("Music Round-a-Bout", *Daily Gleaner*, 8 September 1979). Yellowman recorded "Me Kill Barnie" at Channel One for the record *Them A Mad over Me* (1982g) but the only listing for a Ruddy Thomas–produced version of the song is "Death of Barnabus", which was not released until 1982.

8. I am going by Yellowman's recollection here. The Roots Knotty Roots online database lists its release as 1981, though the site acknowledges release dates may be off by a year. It also lists 1980 releases of "Eventide Home" by Trinity and "Eventide Fire a Distaster" by Barrington Levy and General Echo, both of which bear similarities to Yellowman's version.

9. According to Yellowman. I have not not been able to confirm that this song was released.

CHAPTER 5

1. "Soldier Take Over" was released as a single, but never on a Yellowman LP. It was, however, released on *Crucial Reggae Driven by Sly and Robbie* (Island, 1982) and was later rerecorded for the film soundtrack *Club Paradise* in 1986.

2. Yellowman was already deejaying a song called "Operation Radication" in the dance that was critical of the way the authorities dealt with gang violence.

3. Wexler (2001) quotes Yellowman saying that he had a run in with soldiers in 1979 during a curfew and they made him walk on his knees. This probably

occurred in 1980 or 1981, though, since that is when it was recorded. During outbreaks of political violence, the authorities would instigate curfews on the citizenry to help curb violence.

4. Up Park Camp is the military camp and barracks of the Jamaica Defence Force in Kingston.

5. By vocals, she means singers.

6. This album is attributed to General Echo's other sobriquet, Ranking Slackness.

7. Senior (2003) points out that this description of mento would be laughable to Jamaicans today, especially next to the eroticism of dancehall.

8. "Etheopia" is misspelled on the record label. The track was issued by Kalypso and attributed to the Jamaica Calypsonians with vocals by Lord Lebby (Garnice 2011).

9. "Etheopia", according to Garnice (2011), is considered the earliest recording of a back-to-Africa song, and Barrow and Dalton (2004, 7) list it as "one of the first expressions of Rastafarian consciousness on record".

10. Yellowman sang these lyrics in the song "Nuff Punany" (1987b) at a concert in Carson, California, in 1988 and they are also in "Want Vagina" (2016).

11. This is basically a song about sex with a large woman, with "bubble" referring to the gyrating motion of intercourse and "rock inna dat" referring to vaginal penetration.

12. For a detailed analysis of this, see Cooper's chapter "Slackness Personified: Representations of Female Sexuality in the Lyrics of Bob Marley and Shabba Ranks" (2004).

13. The article this information is based on was published on wayne&wax.com in 2007, but is continually updated, hence the data from 2019.

14. To jab or poke (Cassidy and Le Page 2002, 253).

CHAPTER 6

1. Don't forget about Sister Nancy.

2. While *One Yellowman, For Your Eyes Only, Just Cool* and *Super Mix* are billed as Yellowman and Fathead, I have not listed them as combination records since Fathead does not perform any songs on his own.

CHAPTER 7

1. Michael Rose changed the spelling of his name to Mykal.

2. Lady Saw has since given up slackness and now performs gospel under her birth name, Marion Hall.

3.   While Yellowman has said he and Rosie were married in 1984, other sources suggest they are common-law.

4.   Its name was changed to Best Reggae Album in 1991.

CHAPTER 8

1.   According to Yellowman. Sister Bernadette from Alpha Boys' School is unsure about this.

2.   Marley was a member of the Twelve Tribes of Israel, a moderate Rastafarian "house" with membership drawn from the lower and middle classes.

3.   This was especially true as the rhythm section of Sly (Dunbar) and Robbie (Shakespeare) started to control the evolution of reggae in the mid-1970s from Channel One studio. In an effort to make the music more "militant" and heavy, they started to produce records with mixes that accentuated bass and drums over everything else (Sly Dunbar, interview with author, 4 September 2006).

4.   *Nyam* means to eat in this context, and can also refer to food (Cassidy and Le Page, 2002).

5.   Many Rastas are vegetarian; therefore, Ital stew is vegetarian stew.

6.   *Livity*: nature living, living according to Rastafari precepts.

7.   By my estimation, he was already singing some Rasta lyrics by this time. Of the at least fifteen albums he recorded in 1982, many contain Rastafarian references. Even though Yellowman was singing Rastafarian-themed songs, he pin-points this as his first musical expression of his Rastafarian faith.

8.   This call-and-response is characteristic of many reggae shows, regardless of whether the artist self-identifies as Rasta.

9.   The liner notes of *King Yellowman* (1984a) did not mention Bob Marley. However, the liner notes to *Life in the Ghetto*, a 1990 rerelease of *Jack Sprat* (1982a) say, "This time, the ghetto is where Yellowman's coming from." "Life in the Ghetto ain't easy", he reminds. Echoing Bob Marley, he urges, "Stand up for your rights." As always, Yellowman encourages his followers to love one another. "Why Them A Fight?" he asks. And how many other tough boss deejays would be tellin' you to "honour your mother and father, respect your brothers and sisters!"

CHAPTER 9

1.   Elsewhere Yellowman has said the doctors gave him three years.

2.   A much later article listed the duration as twenty-six hours ("Yellowman Has the Midas Touch", *Sunday Gleaner*, 31 August 1997).

3. When I asked Yellowman about the discrepancy between these two timelines he indicated that if Steve Martin remembered it as six to eight weeks, he was probably correct.

CHAPTER 10

1. *Living Legend* was released in 2008

CHAPTER 11

1. "Piebald" refers to skin marked by vitiligo or patches of white.
2. In folk use the colour "red", as in "red man", includes orange and yellow (Cassidy and Le Page 2002, 377). The use of *bwoy or bwai* [boy] calls into question the subject's age and level of maturation (Carnegie 1996).
3. The *Dictionary of Jamaican English* has this to say about *nigger* or *nayga*: "the term is avoided by whites, and resented among negroes if used of them by whites. As used among negroes it is a term more or less derogatory, commonly implying extra blackness, backwardness, laziness, stupidity, etc." (Cassidy and Le Page 2002, 317). Yellowman's use of the term suggests to his detractors that he (a) must be black because only a black person is socially sanctioned to use the term in the off-handed way he does, and (b) that there are levels of blackness and he situates himself above his critics.
4. *Chiney* is a common term to describe members of the Chinese Jamaican population in Jamaica.
5. This association of black with hardship was officially annulled in 1997 when the House of Representatives offered a new definition for the colour: "strength and creativity" (Senior 2003, 349).
6. According to the World Bank, 97.4 per cent of the Jamaican population is of African descent, and Stanley-Niaah (2010, 1) points out that "those who are not reflected in this statistic feel excluded" by Jamaica's motto.
7. Ethiopianism interchanges the terms Africa and Ethiopia.
8. Meaning to not turn your head or gaze upon something other than Selassie.
9. In this version of history, the white race is created by a union between Eve, a black woman, and the snake, a white man. The ensuing daughter and her half-brother Cain create the Chinese race. Eve's mixed race daughter is referred to by Yawney as a "buffer pickney": "the product of the overlapping of black and white, not the merging of black and white. The buffer pickney represents the unresolved presence of opposites. Here black and white continue to exist in unreconciled form, in contradiction" (Yawney 1976, 244, 247).

10. This version is taken from Yellowman's performance at the 1984 Rockers Awards and differs from the studio recording.

11. To further complicate matters, Yellowman appears to always be in on the joke that he, as a person with albinism, could be sexy. In "Yellowman Wise" (1983e), he states that he has girlfriends in Kingston, Negril, Portland and London and that "when me done chat they goin' give me romance / But this is something me haffi laugh with everyone."

12. This is taken from the *One in a Million* (1984b) version of the song. The version from *Them A Mad over Me* (1982g) uses the term "favour duppy" instead of "too ugly." *Duppy* is Patwa for ghost (Cassidy and Le Page 2002, 164) and is an insulting term since it connotes death, while *favour* means to resemble (174). *Boasy* and *facey* mean "boastful" and "impertinent" respectively (57, 172). Yellowman could also be using the Patwa term *fasi* here which refers to sores or abrasions on the skin (173).

13. This is not to say that people with albinism do not still suffer discrimination in Jamaica. See Carnegie (1996, 482) for details of his experiences there in 1993.

CHAPTER 12

1. Seaga gets Yellowman's birth name wrong here. It is Winston Foster.

2. Yellowman pronounces Edward Seaga's name See-a-go; Inter Conti refers to the Intercontinental Hotel; Water Pumpee is the name of a dance.

3. Some argue that they first did this on the Leslie Kong–produced *Best of the Wailers*, released a year earlier.

4. The 2001 re-release of *Catch a Fire, Deluxe Edition* (Island Records) includes the original Jamaican versions.

5. This quote is not fully representative of Steffens's current point of view. In August 2008, I sat in on an interview he conducted with Yellowman at the Midwest Reggae Festival in Nelson, Ohio. The interview had none of the sentiment found in the above quote. In addition, Steffens has been supportive and helpful with this research.

6. These are all euphemisms for vagina.

CHAPTER 13

1. Critical theories of dancehall (Hope 2006; Cooper 1995, 2004) remap dancehall as a locus of feminine empowerment and slackness as a post-colonial critique of dominant Eurocentric values. Cooper (2004, 81) reminds us of the history

of merging political critique and erotic lyrics in reggae, showing common ground between Marley's confrontational social justice and Shabba Ranks's X-rated celebrations of carnality because they both sought to "destabilize the social space of the respectable middle class".

2.   For more on how sexual regulation was central to the management of colonial societies and hierarchies of race, gender and class, see Stoler (2002).

3.   Here we find another similarity with calypso: for calypsonians the male role is to be an unfaithful husband and absent father while expecting loyalty from his wife (Warner 1985).

4.   Nettleford, writing the same year Winston Foster finished high school, details the extent of Eurocentrism in West Indian society.

5.   *Bombo* is of Central African origin and means vagina; *ras* or *raas* is Patwa for anus; and *claat* or *klaat* means cloth (Chevannes 2006, 98). Therefore, *bomboclaat* refers to a sanitary napkin. The word is often translated as the incendiary "motherfucker" (Slone 2003, 32).

6.   In fact, Pollard (2000, 32) argues that reggae "has employed, almost exclusively, the language of Rastafari".

CHAPTER 14

1.   For full lyrics, see appendix.

2.   The idea that heteronormal sexuality is prerequisite to inclusion in the nation is taken up in Alexander's (1997) study of the heteropatriarchal discourse of the nation-state in the Bahamas. Homosexuality is seen as originating outside of the Caribbean and its presence there now is constructed as a contaminating influence. Discussing this ideology, Sharpe and Pinto (2006, 16) write that "for queer-identified Caribbean people, [this] is a logic that creates a split between their sexual and their national/regional identities".

3.   We cannot know for sure what the sexual ethics of the enslaved Africans were, but Alleyne (1988) argues that it makes no sense to think that Africans were stripped of their culture.

4.   Austin-Broos (1997), Chevannes (2006, 2001), LaFont (2001) and Stewart (2005) further unpack how Christian attitudes towards sex were integrated with an African world view in the Jamaican context.

5.   Patrick has speculated that the term *tracing* may be derived from the leather traces used to whip horses and mules and defines the word as "curse"; to trace is to "insult or argue with someone using rough language, including obscenities" (Patrick 1995, 257). Tracing became standardized into a dramatic and aggressive Caribbean poetic genre in the twentieth century practised by

poets such as Louise Bennett, calypsonians and dancehall deejays (Simpson 2004).

6. This can be found in Trinidadian calypso where songs are used to draw attention to lascivious scandals to publicly humiliate sexual misdemeanours. By parodying shameful acts, calypsonians control social behaviour (McDaniel 1998).

7. *Tracing* is "a loud, nasty, public quarrel between two or more persons . . . in which dirty references and words are freely exchanged" (Allsopp 2003, 564).

8. Hodge corroborates this and says that due to Caribbean males' tremendous respect for their mothers, the worst insult is to curse a man's mother (Hodge 1974, 117).

9. While onstage at B.B. King's Blues Club in New York in 2009, for instance, Yellowman made a joke alluding to San Francisco being more open to homosexuality than New York. On the surface this might not seem offensive, but he still uses homosexuality as a something that is the brunt of a joke.

CHAPTER 15

1. While Yellowman insists that he did not intend carnal to infer sex, the term does have an established connotation to sex in Jamaica. For instance, in the Jamaican legal code, "carnal abuse" refers to sexual assault. This leaves open the possibility that Yellowman used the term knowing its double meaning.

2. Several other reggae songs take up this theme as well, among them "Can't Enter Zion With Your Big Checkbook" by Niney and the Observers and "Enter the Kingdom of Zion" by Barry Brown.

3. "Carnal Mind" was released as a UK-only bonus track on *Welcome to Jamrock* (2005).

4. Cooper (1995) suggests that slackness should be read as a West African–derived model of wholeness in society where the body and spirit are not separated in binary opposites as in European Christianity.

5. Marley was a member of the Twelve Tribes of Israel and is commonly cited as the person responsible for the dissemination of Rastafari on a global scale (Bradley 2001; Gilroy 1994; Jones 1988).

6. His exact words here were as follows: "You could say that, even though it not meant to mean sexual." And, of course, reading the song apart from the author's intended meaning can be instructional for making discoveries about latent or implicit meanings in the material that might not be apparent even to the creator.

7. Found in LaFont 2001, n1. Unknown author.

8. Knust has written of Paul's "anxious response to sexual desire" in his epistles, and characterizes him as determined to "instill sexual self-mastery" among new Christians (Knust 2011, 81, 85).

9. Jamaica.

10. I have situated Yellowman's sexual ethics in Rastafarian attitudes towards sexuality but not in Rastafarian sexual ethics directly. This is because there is currently no in-depth research into Rastafarian sexual ethics to tell us exactly what they are, their range or scope, the diversity of beliefs among Rastas, and how they differ from Christianity, Afro-Christianity, and creole sexual mores. Scholars have either uncritically collapsed Rastafarian sexual ethics with Afro-Christian mores (Stolzoff 2000) or, more typically, generalized an African sexual-positive world view without providing much evidence of this. I have based my research on how slackness and Rastafari have been negotiated in reggae culture, Yellowman's own ideas of what it means to be a Rastafarian, interviews with other reggae artists about Rastafari and slackness, and the scant literature available on this topic. As such, I make no assumption that Yellowman's sexual ethics are the same as the broader Rastafarian community.

APPENDIX

1. The *Live in Paris* (1994a) version of the song has "Reagan" or "Bush" here.

2. The *Live in Paris* (1994a) version has "shoot Margaret Thatcher titty with a M1" here.

References

Adams, L. Emilie, and Llewelyn Adams. 1991. *Understanding Jamaican Patois: An Introduction to Afro-Jamaican Grammar*. Kingston: Kingston Publishers.

Alexander, M. Jacqui. 1997. "Erotic Autonomy as a Politics of Decolonization: An Anatomy of Feminist and State Practice in the Bahamas Tourist Economy". In *Feminist Genealogies, Colonial Legacies, Democratic Futures*, edited by Jacqui M. Alexander and Chandra Talpade Mohanty, 63–100. London: Routledge.

Alidou, Ousseina. 2005. *Engaging Modernity: Muslim Women and the Politics of Agency in Postcolonial Niger*. Madison: University of Wisconsin Press.

Allen, Karen. 2008. "Living in Fear: Tanzania's Albinos". *BBC News*, 21 July. http://news.bbc.co.uk/2/hi/africa/7518049.stm.

Alleyne, Mervyn C. 1988. *Roots of Jamaican Culture*. London: Pluto.

———. 2005. *Construction and Representation of Race and Ethnicity in the Caribbean and the World*. Kingston: University of the West Indies Press.

Allsopp, Richard. 2003. *Dictionary of Caribbean English Usage*. Kingston: University of West Indies Press.

Anderson, Rick. 2004. "Reggae Music: A History and Selective Discography". *Sound Recording Reviews* 61 no. 1: 206–14.

Appiah, Anthony. 1992. *In My Father's House: Africa in the Philosophy of Culture*. New York: Oxford University Press.

Aquinas, Thomas. 2006. *Summa Theologiae*. Cambridge: Cambridge University Press.

Asad, Talal. 1993. *Genealogies of Religion: Discipline and Reasons of Power in Christianity and Islam*. Baltimore: Johns Hopkins University Press.

Augustine, of Hippo, Saint. 2008. *Confessions*. Oxford: Oxford University Press.

Austin-Broos, Diane J. 1997. *Jamaica Genesis: Religion and the Politics of Moral Orders*. Chicago: University of Chicago Press.

Baker, Charlotte, and Medard Djatou. 2007. "Enduring Negativity: Literary and Anthropological Perspectives on the Black African Albino". In *Crossing Places: New Research in African Studies*, edited by Charlotte Baker, and Zoe Norridge, 63–76. Newcastle: Cambridge Scholars.

Baker, Charlotte, Patricia Lund, Richard Nyathi and Julie Taylor. 2010. "The Myths Surrounding People with Albinism in South Africa and Zimbabwe". *Journal of African Cultural Studies* 22, no. 2: 169–81.

Bangs, Lester. 2004. "Innocents of Babylon: A Search for Jamaica Featuring Bob Marley and a Cast of Thousands". In *Everything Little Thing Gonna Be Alright: The Bob Marley Reader*, edited by Hank Bordowitz, 46–88. Cambridge: Da Capo.

Barrow, Stephen, and Paul Coote. 2004. Liner notes to *Mento Madness*. New York: V2 Records.

Barrow, Stephen, and Peter Dalton. 2004. *The Rough Guide to Reggae*. 3rd ed. London: Rough Guides.

Blankenberg, Ngaire. 2000. "That Rare and Random Tribe: Albino Identity in South Africa". *Critical Arts* 14, no. 2: 6–48.

Bradley, Lloyd. 1996. *Reggae on CD: The Essential Guide*. London: Kyle Cathie.

———. 2001. *This Is Reggae Music: The Story of Jamaica's Music*. New York: Grove Press.

Brathwaite, Edward Kamau. 1984. *History of the Voice: The Development of Nation Language in Anglophone Caribbean Poetry*. London: New Beacon Books.

Brown, Karen McCarthy. 2001. *Mama Lola: A Vodou Priestess in Brooklyn*. Berkeley: University of California Press.

Burke, Shirley M. 1977. "Interview with Cedric Brooks". *Jamaica Journal* 11, nos. 1–2: 14–17.

Burton, Richard D.E. 1997. *Afro-Creole: Power, Opposition, and Play in the Caribbean*. Ithaca: Cornell University Press.

Carnegie, Charles V. 1996. "The Dundus and the Nation". *Cultural Anthropology* 11, no. 4: 470–509.

Cassidy, F.G., and R.B. Le Page. 2002. *Dictionary of Jamaican English*. Kingston: University of the West Indies Press.

Chamberlain, Joshua. 2010. "So Special, So Special, So Special: The Evolution of the Jamaican 'Dubplate'". *Jamaica Journal* 33, nos. 1–2: 20–28.

Chang, Kevin O'Brien, and Wayne Chen. 1998. *Reggae Routes: The Story of Jamaican Music*. Philadelphia: Temple University Press.

Charles, Christopher A.D. 2003. "Skin Bleaching, Self-Hate, and Black Identity in Jamaica". *Journal of Black Studies* 33, no. 6: 711–28.

Chevannes, Barry. 1994. *Rastafari: Roots and Ideology*. Syracuse: Syracuse University Press.

———. 1999. "Between the Living and the Dead: The Apotheosis of Rastafari Heroes". In *Religion, Diaspora, and Cultural Identity*, edited by John W. Pulis, 337–56. New York: Gordon and Breach.

———. 2001. *Learning to Be a Man: Culture, Socialization, and Gender Identity in Five Caribbean Communities*. Kingston: University of the West Indies Press.

———. 2006. *Betwixt and Between: Explorations in an African-Caribbean Mindscape*. Kingston: Ian Randle.

Collins, Patricia Hill. 2005. *Black Sexual Politics: African Americans, Gender, and the New Racism*. New York: Routledge.

Cooper, Carolyn. 1995. *Noises in the Blood: Orality, Gender, and the "Vulgar" Body of Jamaican Popular Culture*. Durham: Duke University Press.

———. 2004. *Sound Clash: Jamaican Dancehall Culture at Large*. New York: Palgrave Macmillan.

Davis, Stephen, and Peter Simon, eds. 1982. *Reggae International*. New York: Rogner and Bernhard.

Davis, Stephen. 1994. *Bob Marley: Conquering Lion of Reggae*. London: Plexus.

Dawes, Kwame. 2002. *Bob Marley: Lyrical Genius*. London: Sanctuary.

Diawara, Manthia. 1998. *In Search of Africa*. Cambridge: Harvard University Press.

Dread, Doctor. 2001. "Slackness Done: I and I Come to Clean up Dancehall". Press release. RAS Records. https://bit.ly/3eUJE81

Douglas, Kelly Brown. 1999. *Sexuality and the Black Church: A Womanist Perspective*. Maryknoll: Orbis Books.

Dunkley, Daive A. 2011. "Eventide". Dis 'n Dat. Jamaica National Heritage Trust. http://www.jnht.com/disndat_eventide.php.

Edmonds, Ennis Barrington. 1998. "The Structure and Ethos of Rastafari". In *Chanting down Babylon: The Rastafari Reader*, edited by Nathaniel Samuel Murrell, William David Spencer and Adrian Anthony McFarlane, 349–60. Philadelphia: Temple University Press.

———. 2003. *Rastafari: From Outcasts to Culture Bearers*. Oxford: Oxford University Press.

Eldridge, Michael S. 2005. "Bop Girl Goes Calypso: Containing Race and Youth Culture in Cold War America". *Anthurium: A Caribbean Studies Journal* 3, no. 2: 35.

Erskine, Noel Leo. 2005. *From Garvey to Marley: Rastafari Theology*. Gainesville: University Press of Florida.

Eyre, Banning. 2006. "Salif Keita: 2006". *Afropop Worldwide: Music and Stories from the African Planet*. https://bit.ly/2H2vpBA.

Figueroa, Mark. 1994. "Garrison Communities in Jamaica, 1962–1993: Their Growth and Impact on Political Culture". Paper presented at the symposium Democracy and Democratization in Jamaica: Fifty Years of Adult Suffrage, Kingston, December.

Figueroa, Mark, and Amanda Sives. 2003. "Garrison Politics and Criminality in Jamaica: Does the 1997 Election Represent a Turning Point?" In *Understanding Crime in Jamaica: New Challenges for Public Policy*, edited by Anthony Harriott, 63–88. Kingston: University of the West Indies Press.

Forgie, Andell 1993. Liner notes to *Soldering: The Starlights Featuring Stanley Beckford*. Heartbeat Records.

Foster, Chuck. 1999. *Roots, Rock, Reggae: An Oral History of Reggae Music from Ska to Dancehall*. New York: Billboard.

Francis-Jackson, Chester. 1995. *The Official Dancehall Dictionary: A Guide to Jamaican Dialect and Dancehall Slang*. Kingston: Kingston Publishers.

Garnice, Michael. 2011. "Lord Lebby". Mento Music. http://www.mentomusic .com/LordLebby.htm.

Gebrekidan, Fikru N. 2001. *Bond without Blood: A Study of Ethiopian-Caribbean ties, 1935–1991*. Dissertation Abstracts International, vol. 62–08A.

Ghoston, Stephanie. 2009. "Yellowman". *Reggaepedia*. http://reggaelicious.pbworks .com/Yellowman?SearchFor= yellowman&sp=1.

Gilroy, Paul. 1987. *"There Ain't no Black in the Union Jack": The Cultural Politics of Race and Nation*. Chicago: University of Chicago Press.

———. 1993. *The Black Atlantic: Modernity and Double Consciousness*. Cambridge: Harvard University Press.

———. 1994. "Police and Thieves". In *The Empire Strikes Back: Race and Racism in 70s Britain*, edited by Centre for Contemporary Cultural Studies, 143–82. New York: Routledge.

Goulet, Jean-Guy. 1998. *Ways of Knowing: Experience, Knowledge, and Power Among the Dene Tha*. Lincoln: University of Nebraska Press.

Grass, Randall. 2009. *Great Spirits: Portraits of Life-Changing World Music Artists*. Jackson: University Press of Mississippi.

Gray, Obika. 2004. *Demeaned but Empowered: The Social Power of the Urban Poor in Jamaica*. Kingston: University of the West Indies Press.

Hagerman, Brent. 2012. "Everywhere Is War: Peace and Violence in the Life and Work of Bob Marley". *Journal of Religion and Popular Culture* 24, no. 3 (Fall): n.p.

Hall, Stuart. 1997. *Race: The Floating Signifier*. Directed by Sut Jhally. Northampton, Massachusetts: The Media Education Foundation.

Harriott, Anthony. 2000. *Police and Crime in Jamaica*. Kingston: University of West Indies Press.

Hebdige, Dick. 1974. *Reggae, Rastas and Rudies: Style and the Subversion of Form*. Birmingham: Centre for Contemporary Cultural Studies, University of Birmingham.

———. 1987. *Cut 'n' Mix: Culture, Identity and Caribbean Music*. London: Comedia.

Henriques, Fernando. 1964. *Jamaica: Land of Wood and Water*. New York: London House and Maxwell.

Hilferty, Robert. 2006. "Albino Afropop Star Salif Keita Talks about Mali, Magic, Murder". *Bloomberg News*, 18 July. http://www.salifkeita.us/press/.

Hill, Errol. 1974. "The Calypso". In *Caribbean Rhythms: The Emerging English Literature of the West Indies*, edited by James T. Livingston, 286–97. New York: Washington Square Press.

Hindley, Geoffrey. 2002. "Keyboards, Crankshafts and Communications: The Musical Mindset of Western Technology". In *Music and Technology in the Twentieth Century*, edited by Hans-Joachim Braun, 33–42. Baltimore: Johns Hopkins University Press.

Hodge, Merle. 1974. "The Shadow of the Whip: A Comment on Male-Female Relationships in the Caribbean". In *Is Massa Day Dead? Black Moods in the Caribbean*, edited by Orde Coombs, 111–18. Garden City, NJ: Anchor.

Hope, Donna P. 2006. *Inna di Dancehall: Popular Culture and the Politics of Identity in Jamaica*. Kingston: University of the West Indies Press.

Huey, Steve. 2010. "Yellowman: Biography". *All-Music Guide*. https://www.allmusic .com/artist/yellowman-mn0000681340/biography.

Hurford, Ray. 2004. "History of Version". *Small Axe People*, July. www.smallaxepeople .com/HistoryOfVersion.htm.

Hutton, Clinton. 2007a. "Forging Identity and Community through Aestheticism and Entertainment: The Sound System and the Rise of the DJ". *Caribbean Quarterly* 53 no. 4 (December): 16–31.

———. 2007b. "The Social and Aesthetic Roots and Identity of Ska: Interview with Garth White. *Caribbean Quarterly* 53, no. 4 (December): 81–95.

Hyatt, Cottrell. 2011. "History of Alpha Boys' School". Alpha Old Boys Association. https://bit.ly/3eWCMXz.

Jahn, Brian, and Tom Weber. 1998. *Reggae Island: Jamaican Music in the Digital Age*. New York: Da Capo.

JLP (Jamaica Labour Party). 2009. "Hon. Edward Seaga". https://www.jamaicalabour party.com/content/hon-edward-seaga.

Jefferson, Thomas. 1801. *Notes on the State of Virginia*. Newark, NJ: Pennington and Gould.

Jones, Simon. 1988. *Black Culture, White Youth: The Reggae Tradition from JA to UK*. Basingstoke: Macmillan Education.

Jordan, Winthrop D. 1977. *White over Black: American Attitudes toward the Negro, 1550–1812*. New York: Norton.

Katz, David. 2012. *Solid Foundation: An Oral History of Reggae*. London: Jawbone.

Kiernan, Pauline. 2007. *Filthy Shakespeare: Shakespeare's Most Outrageous Sexual Puns*. London: Gotham.

Kinsey, Alfred C., Wardell B. Pomeroy and Clyde E. Martin.1948. *Sexual Behavior in the Human Male*. Philadelphia: W.B. Saunders.

Kinsey, Alfred C., Wardell B. Pomeroy, Clyde E. Martin and Paul H. Gebhard. 1953. *Sexual Behavior in the Human Female*. Philadelphia: W.B. Saunders.

Knust, Jennifer Wright. 2011. *Unprotected Texts: The Bible's Surprising Contradictions about Sex and Desire*. New York: Harperone.

LaFont, Suzanne. 2001. "Very Straight Sex: The Development of Sexual Mores in Jamaica". *Journal of Colonialism and Colonial History* 2, no. 3: n.p.

Lake, Obiagele. 1998. *RastafarI Women: Subordination in the Midst of Liberation Theology*. Durham: Carolina Academic Press.

Lee, Hélène. 2003. *The First Rasta: Leonard Howell and the Rise of Rastafarianism*. Translated by Lily Davis. Chicago: Lawrence Hill.

Lesser, Beth. 2008. *Dancehall: The Rise of Jamaican Dancehall Culture*. London: Soul Jazz.

Long, Edward. 1774/1970. *The History of Jamaica; or, General Survey of the Ancient and Modern State of That Island: With Reflections on Its Situations, Settlements, Inhabitants, Climate, Products, Commerce, Laws, and Government*. London: Frank Cass.

MacGaffey, Wyatt. 1968. "Kongo and the King of the Americans". *Journal of Modern African Studies* 6, no. 2: 171–81.

Manley, Michael. 1982. *Jamaica: Struggle in the Periphery*. London: Third World Media.

Manuel, Peter Lamarche, Kenneth M. Bilby and Michael D. Largey. 1995. *Caribbean Currents: Caribbean Music from Rumba to Reggae*. Philadelphia: Temple University Press.

Martin, Charles D. 2002. *White African American Body: A Cultural and Literary Exploration*. New Brunswick, NJ: Rutgers University Press.

McDaniel, Lorna. 1998. "Trinidad and Tobago". In *Garland Encyclopedia of World Music*. Volume 2: *South America, Mexico, Central America, and the Caribbean*, edited by Dale A. Olsen and Daniel E. Sheehy, 972–87. New York: Garland.

Murrell, Nathaniel Samuel. 1998. "Introduction: The Rastafari Phenomenon". In *Chanting down Babylon: The Rastafari Reader*, edited by Nathaniel Samuel Murrell, William David Spencer and Adrian Anthony McFarlane, 1–19. Philadelphia: Temple University Press.

Nettleford, Rex. 1974. "Caribbean Perspectives: The Creative Potential and the Quality of Life". In *Caribbean Rhythms: The Emerging English Literature of the West Indies*, edited by James T. Livingston, 298–318. New York: Washington Square Press.

———. 1994. "Dance-Hall: Part of the Jamaican Heritage?" *Gleaner*, 22 July, 7

Nye, Stephen. 2007. Liner notes to *Trojan Slack Reggae Box Set*. Kingston: Trojan Records.

O'Gorman, Pamela. 1988. "Gleaner Top Ten". *Jamaica Journal* 21, no. 4: 50–54.

Owens, Joseph. 1982. *Dread: The Rastafarians of Jamaica*. London: Heinemann Educational.

Paglia, Camille. 1992. *Sex, Art, and American Culture: Essays*. New York: Vintage.

Patrick, Peter. 1995. "Recent Jamaican Words in Sociolinguistic Context". *American Speech: A Quarterly of Linguistic Usage* 70, no. 3: 227–64.

Pollard, Velma. 2000. *Dread Talk: The Language of Rastafari*. Kingston: Canoe Press.

Prahlad, Sw Anand. 2001. *Reggae Wisdom: Proverbs in Jamaican Music*. Jackson: University Press of Mississippi.

Prothero, Stephen R. 1996. *The White Buddhist: The Asian Odyssey of Henry Steel Olcott*. Bloomington: Indiana University Press.

Rodigan, David. 2017. *My Life in Reggae*. London: Constable.

Rohlehr, Gordon. 1970. "Sparrow and the Language of Calypso". *Savacou: A Journal of the Caribbean Artists Movement* 2:87–99.

———. 1990. *Calypso and Society in Pre-independence Trinidad*. Port of Spain: G. Rohlehr.

Rowe, Maureen. 1998. "Gender and Family Relations in Rastafari: A Personal Perspective". In *Chanting down Babylon: The Rastafari Reader*, edited by Nathaniel Samuel Murrell, William David Spencer and Adrian Anthony McFarlane, 72–88. Philadelphia: Temple University Press.

Ryman, Cheryl. 1980. "The Jamaica Heritage in Dance: Developing a Traditional Typology". *Jamaica Journal* 44:3–14.

Salewicz, Chris. 2004. "The Chapel of Love: Bob Marley's Last Resting Place". In *Every Little Thing Gonna Be Alright: The Bob Marley Reader*, edited by Hank Bordowitz, 137–43. Cambridge: Da Capo.

Salewicz, Chris, and Adrian Boot. 2001. *Reggae Explosion: The Story of Jamaican Music*. New York: Harry N. Abrams.

Saunders, Cyril. 1983. "Mellow Yellow". *Black Echoes*, 16 July.

Saunders, Patricia J. 2003. "Is Not Everything Good to Eat, Good to Talk: Sexual Economy and Dancehall Music In the Global Marketplace". *Small Axe* 7, no. 1: 95–115.

Savishinsky, Neil J. 1994. "Rastafari in the Promised Land: The Spread of a Jamaican Socioreligious Movement among the Youth of Africa". *African Studies Review* 37, no. 3: 19–50.

Senior, Olive. 2003. *Encyclopedia of Jamaican Heritage*. St Andrew, Jamaica: Twin Guinep.

Sharpe, Jenny, and Samantha Pinto. 2006. "The Sweetest Taboo: Studies of Caribbean Sexualities – A Review Essay". *Signs: Journal of Woman in Culture and Society* 32, no. 1: 247–74.

Simpson, Hyacinth M. 2004. "'Voicing the Text': The Making of an Oral Poetics in Olive Senior's Short Fiction". *Callaloo* 27, no. 3: 829–43.

Slone, Thomas H. 2003. *Rasta Is Cuss*. Oakland, CA: Masalai.

Small, Christopher. 1998. *Music of the Common Tongue: Survival and Celebration in African American Music*. Middletown, MA: Wesleyan University Press.

Sobo, Elisa Janine. 1993. *One Blood: The Jamaican Body*. Albany: State University of New York Press.

Stanley-Niaah, Sonjah. 2006. "'Slackness Personified', Historicized and Delegitimized". *Small Axe*, no. 21: 174–85.

———. 2010. *Dancehall: From Slave Ship to Ghetto*. Ottawa: University of Ottawa Press.

Stelfox, Dave. 2010. *The eMusic Dozen: Greensleeves*. Emusic.com Inc. https://bit.ly/3lqEhQv.

Stewart, Dianne M. 2005. *Three Eyes for the Journey: African Dimensions of the Jamaican Religious Experience*. Oxford: Oxford University Press.

Stoler, Ann Laura. 2002. *Carnal Knowledge and Imperial Power: Race and the Intimate in Colonial Rule*. Berkeley: University of California Press.

Stolzoff, Norman C. 2000. *Wake the Town and Tell the People: Dancehall Culture in Jamaica*. Durham, NC: Duke University Press.

Tafari-Ama, Imani. 2019. *Blood, Bullets and Bodies: Sexual Politics below Jamaica's Poverty Line*. Burscough, UK: Beaten Track.

Thomas, Deborah A. 2004. *Modern Blackness: Nationalism, Globalization, and the Politics of Culture in Jamaica*. Durham, NC: Duke University Press.

Thomas, Polly, and Adam Vaitlingam. 2007. *The Rough Guide to Jamaica*. New York: Rough Guides.

TSO Productions. 2009. "Community Forum Sparks Lively Debate". Press release, TSO Productions, Brooklyn, NY.

Turino, Thomas. 2008. *Music as Social Life: The Politics of Participation*. Chicago: University of Chicago Press.

Wald, Elijah. 2004. *Escaping the Delta: Robert Johnson and the Invention of the Blues*. New York: Amistad.

Walker, Klive. 2005. *Dubwise: Reasoning from the Reggae Underground*. Toronto: Insomniac.

Warner, Keith Q. 1985. *Kaiso! The Trinidad Calypso: A Study of the Calypso as Oral Literature*. Washington, DC: Three Continents.

Wexler, Paul L. 2001. Liner notes to *Reggae Anthology: Yellowman: Look How Me Sexy*. New York: VP Records.

White, Gareth. 1982. "Voices Crying in the Wilderness". In *Reggae International*, edited by Stephen Davis and Peter Simon, 25–33. New York: Rogner and Bernhard.

Williams, Joan. 2008. *Original Dancehall Dictionary*. Kingston: Yard Publications.

Yawney, Carol D. 1976. "Remnants of All Nations: Rastafarian Attitudes to Race and Nationality". In *Ethnicity in the Americas*, edited by Frances Henry, 231–62. The Hague: Mouton.

Yellowman. 1982. "One in a Million: Yellowman". Interview by Beth Lesser. *Reggae Quarterly* 1, no. 2.

———. 1983. Interview by David Rodigan, Capital Radio, July. https://youtu.be /rPz8EG9Eaa8.

DISCOGRAPHY

Baldhead Growler. 1967. "The Sausage". Jump Up.

The Jamaican Calypsonians. 1955. "Dr Kinsey Report". Kalypso.

Lord Kitchener. 1967. *Lord Kitchener's Greatest Calypso Hits*. RCA Victor.

———. 1977. *Melody of the 21st Century*. Charlie's Records.

Lovindeer, Lloyd. 1982. "Yellow Fellow (Straight to Yellowman)". TSOJ.

Marley, Bob, and the Wailers. 1974. *Natty Dread*. Island Records.

———. 1977. *Exodus*. Island Records.

———. 1979. *Survival*. Island Records.

Marley, Damian. 1995. *Welcome to Jamrock*. Tuff Gong.

The Melodians. 1970. "Rivers of Babylon". Beverley's Records.

Mighty Sparrow. 1964a. "Congo Man." National Record Company.

———. 1964b. "Village Ram". Jump Up.

———. 1965. *Tattooed Lady*. National Record Company.

———. 1969. "Sell the Pussy". RA.

———. 1976. "Salt Fish". Tysott.

———. 1996. *Renaissance*. BLS Records.

Prince Buster. 1969. "Wreck a Pum Pum". Prince Buster.

The Prophets. 1975. *Conquering Lion*. Micron Music Limited.

Purpleman [this album was mistakenly attributed to Yellowman]. 1983. *Confessions*. Vista Sounds.

Run-DMC. 1985. *King of Rock*. Profile Records.

Sly and Robbie [Featuring Ini Kamoze, Half Pint and Yellowman]. 1986. *Taxi Gang Live 86*. Taxi.

The Starlites. 1975. "Soldering". GG Records.

Tony Johnson and His Carousel Band. n.d. "Give Her Banana". Melodisc. Trinity. 1975. "Three Piece Suit". Belmont.

The 2 Live Crew. 1989. *As Nasty as They Wanna Be*. Skyywalker Records.

The Wailers. 1973a. *Burnin'*. Island Records.

———. 1973b. *Catch a Fire*. Island Records.

The Wrigglers. 2010. *Jamaica: Mento 1951–1958*. Frémeaux & Associés.

Yellowman. 1980. "Eventide Fire". Thrillseekers.

———. 1981. "Soldier Take Over". Tanka.

———. 1982a. *Jack Sprat*. GG's Records. [Released by Jam Rock in 1982 as *Hotter Reggae* and Tassa Records in 1990 as *Life in the Ghetto*.]

———[featuring Fathead]. 1982b. *Just Cool*. Jah Guidance.

———. 1982c. *Live at the Rissmiller's, Reseda, Ca.* KPFK-FM Broadcast. [Released by Klondike Records in 2016.]

———. 1982d. *Mister Yellowman*. Shanachie. [Released by Jah Guidance and VP Records in 1982 as *Duppy or Gunman*.]

——— [featuring Fathead]. 1982e. "Operation Radication". Jah Guidance.

———. 1982f. *Superstar Yellowman Has Arrived with Toyan*. Joe Gibbs.

———. 1982g. *Them A Mad over Me*. Hit Bound.

———. 1983a. *Live in London*. Thunder Bolt.

———. 1983b. *Live at Reggae Sunsplash*. Sunsplash Records.

———. 1983c. *Nobody Move*. Volcano. [Released by Greensleeves in 1983 as *Nobody Move Nobody Get Hurt*.]

———. 1983d. "This Old Man." Gussie 80's.

———. 1983e. *Zungguzungguguzungguzeng*. Arrival.

———. 1984a. *King Yellowman*. Columbia.

———. 1984b. *One in a Million*. Joe Gibbs Music. [Originally released by Pama Records as *Operation Radication*, c.1982.]

———. 1984c. "Ram Jam Master". Jah Guidance. [Released by Greensleeves in 1984 as "Wreck a Pum Pum".]

———. 1984d. "Wreck a Pum Pum". Rockers Award Show Live Broadcast, National Arena, Kingston, Jamaica, 28 January. Reggae and Dancehall Vault, https://youtu.be/HkZN9f7xS14.

———. 1984e. *Yellowman versus Josey Wales: Two Giants Clash*. Jah Guidance.

———. 1985a. *Galong Galong Galong*. Greensleeves.

———. 1985b. *Walking Jewellery Store*. Power House.

———. 1986a. *Going to the Chapel*. Black Scorpio.

———. 1986b. *Rambo*. Moving Target. [Released by Taxi as *Girls Them Pet* and by M.I.L. Multimedia as *Love and Classic Tracks*.]

———. 1986c. *Tiger Meets Yellowman*. Kangal.

———. 1987a. "Blueberry Hill". Greensleeves.

———. 1987b. *The Negril Chill Challenge*. RIOR. [Released by Ayeola Records in 1987 as *Live in Concert: Slackness vs Pure Culture*.]

———. 1987c. *Yellow Like Cheese*. RAS.

———. 1988a. *Don't Burn It Down*. Black Scorpio.

———. 1988b. *Yellowman Rides Again*. RAS.

———. 1989. *Strikes Again*. Mixing Lab. [Released by Nyam Up in 1995 as *Yellowman Strikes Again*, and by Mixing Lab in 1989 as *Thief*. Their 2016 release of *Thief* shares some tracks.]

———. 1990. *A Feast of Yellow Dub*. RAS.

———. 1991a. *Mi Hot*. Black Scorpio.

———. 1991b. *Party*. RAS.

———. 1992. *Reggae on the Move*. RAS.

———. 1993a. *A Man You Want*. Shanachie.

———. 1993b. *In Bed with Yellowman*. Volcano. [Released by VP Records in 1993 as *Mello Yellow*.]

———. 1993c. *Reggae on Top*. Pow Wow Records.

———. 1994a. *Live in Paris*. Déclic Communication.

———. 1994b. *Prayer*. RAS.

———. 1995a. *Message to the World*. RAS.

———. 1995b. *Yellowman's Good Sex Guide*. Greensleeves.

———. 1997a. *Dub for Daze Vol. 2*. RAS.

———. 1997b. *Freedom of Speech*. RAS.

———. 1997c. *Ras Portraits*: Yellowman. RAS

———. 1998a. *A Very, Very Yellow Christmas*. RAS.

———. 1998b. *Live at Maritime Hall*. 2B1 Records. [Also released by 2B1 Records as *Live in San Francisco*.]

———. 1999. *Yellow Fever*. AO! Records.

———. 2001. *Look How Me Sexy*. VP Records.

———. 2003. *New York*. RAS.

———. 2005a. *This Is Crucial Reggae*: Yellowman. Sanctuary Records.

———. 2005b. *Yellowman vs. Ninjaman: Round 1*. RCR.

———. 2006. "Orphan". Maverick.

———. 2008. *Living Legend*. Road Dog Productions

———. 2016. *Thief*. The Mixing Lab.

———. 2019. *No More War*. Yellow Baby Records.

Yellowman and Fathead. 1982a. *For Your Eyes Only*. Arrival. [Released by Burning Sounds in 1983 as *Divorced! (For Your Eyes Only)*.]

———. 1982b. *Live at Aces*. Jah Guidance.

———. 1982c. *One Yellowman*. Hit Bound.

———. 1982d. *Super Mix*. Volcano. [Released by Greensleeves and Shanachie in 1982 as *Bad Boy Skanking*.]

———. 1984. *Show-Down Vol. 5 with Purpleman*. Channel One.

Yellowman and General Trees. 1987. *A Reggae Calypso Encounter*. Rohit Record.

Index

CPSIA information can be obtained
at www.ICGtesting.com
Printed in the USA
JSHW021458190822
29483JS00001B/10